The Pattern Library

TPL

Volume One • A - H

Little Acorn Books™

The Pattern Library A-H

• instruments • tools • pets • wild, exotic & domestic animals • maps • transportation • food • containers • vegetables • inventions •
• appliances • household objects • architecture • dinosaurs • plants • insects • sea creatures • and more. •

by Marilynn G. Barr

The Pattern Library

TPL

Volume One • A - H

LAB201411P
THE PATTERN LIBRARY • VOLUME ONE • A - H

black and white, large illustrations in printable pattern format for:
• instruments • tools • pets • wild, exotic & domestic animals • maps • transportation • food • containers • vegetables •
• inventions • appliances • household objects • architecture • dinosaurs • plants • insects • sea creatures • and more. •

by Marilynn G. Barr

Published by: Little Acorn Books™
Originally published by: Monday Morning Books, Inc.

Entire contents copyright © 2014 Little Acorn Books™

Little Acorn Books
PO Box 8787
Greensboro, NC 27419-0787

Promoting Early Skills for a Lifetime™

Little Acorn Books™
is an imprint of Little Acorn Associates, Inc.

http://www.littleacornbooks.com

Permission is hereby granted to reproduce student materials in this book for non-commercial individual or classroom use. *School-wide or system-wide use is expressly prohibited.

ISBN 978-1-937257-62-0

Printed in the United States of America

The Pattern Library

Volume One • A - H

Table of Contents

A
aardvark	8
abacus	9
acorn	10
acrobat	11
Africa	12
airplane	13
Alabama, USA	14
alarm clock	15
Alaska, USA	16
Alberta, Canada	17
alligator (animated)	18
alphabet	19
ambulance	20
anchor	21
angel (add a photo format)	22
angel	23
ankylosaurus	24
Antarctica	25
ant	26
anteater (animated)	27
anteater (stylized)	28
antler	29
antlers	30
anvil (outline)	31
apartment building	32
apron	33
aquarium	34
Arizona, USA	35
Arkansas, USA	36
armadillo	37
armchair	38
arrow	39
arrowhead	40
arrows	41
Asia	42
asparagus	43
astronaut	44
Australia	45
avocado	46
award	47
axe	48

B
baby (crawling)	49
baby (frontal view)	50
bacon (slice)	51
badge	52
badger	53
bag (paper)	54
bag (shopping)	55
bagpipes	56
ball (beach)	57
ballerina	58
balloon	59
bamboo	60
banana	61
banjo	62
barbell	63
barbells	64
barn	65
barrel	66
baseball	67
baseball and bat	68
baseball glove	69
basket (basketball)	70
basket (berry)	71
basket (bushel)	72
basket (hand)	73
basket (outline)	74
basket (peck)	75
basketball	76
bass (instrument)	77
bat (animated)	78
bat (stylized)	79
bathrobe	80
bathtub	81
bean	82
beans	83
bear (black)	84
bear (polar)	85
bear (sloth)	86
bear (standing)	87
bear (stuffed, outline)	88
bear (teddy, with overalls)	89
bear (with top hat)	90
beard (pointed)	91
beard (rounded)	92
beaver (with bowtie)	93
beaver (walking)	94
beaver (upright)	95
beaver (stylized)	96
bed (frontal view)	97
bed (side view)	98
bee (animated)	99
bee hive	100
bees (animated)	101
beetle	102
bell (jingle)	103
bell (large)	104
bell (hand)	105
bib	106
bicycle	107
billiard balls	108
birdbath	109
birdhouse	110
bird of paradise	111
bird (in flight)	112
birds	113
bird (stylized)	114
black (crayon)	115
blanket	116
blender	117
blimp	118
block	119
blouse	120
blue (crayon)	121
blueberries	122
boar	123
boat	124
bone	125
bongos	126

The Pattern Library

TPL

Volume One • A - H

Table of Contents

bonnet...........................127	brick (top)......................167	can (tuna)......................206
book (closed)................128	bride.............................168	Canada..........................207
book (open)...................129	bridge (suspension).......169	Canada (boundaries)......208
bookcase......................130	bridge (walking).............170	candle (pillar)................209
boomerang....................131	British Columbia, Canada......171	candle (thumb candle holder)210
boot (rain-left)................132	broccoli.........................172	candles.........................211
boot (rain-right).............133	brontosaurus..................173	candy cane...................212
boot (Western-left).........134	broom (push).................174	candy (cherry cordial)....213
boot (Western-right).......135	broom (swish)................175	candy corn....................214
boot (work-left)..............136	broom (whisk)................176	candy hearts.................215
boot (work-right)............137	brown (crayon)...............177	candy (peppermint).......216
boot (child-left)..............138	brush (grooming)............178	cane.............................217
boot (child-right)............139	brush (hair)....................179	canoe...........................218
boot (ladies-left)............140	brush (scrub).................180	cap (plain)....................219
boot (ladies-right)..........141	bubbles.........................181	cap (with stiches)..........220
boot (ski-left).................142	bucket (wire handle)......182	cap...............................221
boot (ski-right)...............143	bucket (rustic)...............183	Capital Building (Washington, DC, USA)...222
bottle (juice).................144	buckle...........................184	car 223
bottle (milk)...................145	buffalo..........................185	car (Model-T)................224
bottle (pop)...................146	bun (hotdog).................186	carafe...........................225
bow (archer's)...............147	bunny...........................187	card (playing)................226
bow (knot)....................148	bunny (outline)..............188	carousel.......................227
bow (pompom)..............149	bus (city)......................189	carrots..........................228
bowl.............................150	bus (school).................190	castañet.......................229
bowling ball..................151	butter............................191	castle...........................230
bowling pin...................152	butter churn..................192	cat (laying)...................231
bowling pins.................153	butterfly (animated).......193	cat (outline)..................232
bowtie..........................154	butterfly (full view).........194	caterpillar.....................233
box..............................155	butterfly (side view).......195	cattail...........................234
boxers..........................156	butterfly (outline)...........196	cello.............................235
boy..............................157	**C**	cereal (in bowl)............236
boy..............................158	cactus..........................197	chain (links).................237
boy..............................159	cage (bird)...................198	chair.............................238
boy..............................160	cage (circus train).........199	chameleon...................239
Braille alphabet chart....161	cage (hamster).............200	cheese (Swiss)............240
brain............................162	cake.............................201	cherries........................241
branch.........................163	California, USA............202	chick............................242
bread (loaf)..................164	camel (dromedary).......203	chicken (outline)..........243
bread (slice)................165	camera........................204	chicken (nesting).........244
brick (side view)...........166	can (coffee).................205	

The Pattern Library

Volume One • A - H

Table of Contents

chicken (standing) ...245	crown (short)...285	dress...324
chimney...246	crown (tall)...286	dresser...325
chimpanzee...247	cube...287	dreidel...326
chipmunk (animated)...248	cucumber...288	drill (power)...327
chisel...249	cup...289	drum...328
chocolate kiss...250	cupcake...290	duck (animated)...329
Christmas stocking...251	cups...291	duck...330
church...252	cylinder...292	dugong...331
circle...253	cymbal...293	**E**
clipboard...254	**D**	eagle (in flight)...332
clock...255	dart...294	earmuffs...333
clothespin (spring)...256	deer (buck)...295	ears (bear & fox)...334
clothespin...257	deer (doe)...296	ears (elephant)...335
cloud...258	Delaware, USA...297	ears (human)...336
clown...259	diamond (baseball)...298	ears (wolf)...337
club (symbol)...260	diamond (jewel)...299	easel...338
coat...261	diamond (shape)...300	echidna...339
collar (pointed)...262	diaper...301	eel...340
collar (rounded)...263	dice...302	egg...341
Colorado, USA...264	die...303	egg cup...342
comb...265	dimes...304	egg (Easter)...343
computer...266	dingo...305	eggplant...344
cone...267	dinosaur (animated)...306	elasmasaurus...345
Connecticutt, USA...268	dog (Basset)...307	elephant (animated)...346
cookie jar...269	dog (outline)...308	elephant (African)...347
cookies...270	dog (Scotty)...309	elephant (Indian)...348
corn...271	doghouse...310	elephant (outline)...349
cornucopia...272	doll...311	elf...350
couch...273	dollar (20th c.)...312	elk...351
cow (frontal view)...274	dollar (play)...313	envelope (closed)...352
cow (side view)...275	dollars (Susan B. Anthony)...314	envelope (open)...353
cowbell...276	dolphin...315	envelope (pattern)...354
cowboy...277	donkey...316	Europe...355
cowgirl...278	door...317	eye...356
crab...279	doorknob...318	eyes (two pair)...357
cracker...280	doughnut...319	eyes (animated)...358
cradle...281	dove...320	**F**
crate (wood)...282	dragon (animated)...321	face (outline)...359
crayons...283	dragon (Komodo)...322	fairy...360
crayon box...284	dragonfly (animated)...323	feather (broad)...361

The Pattern Library

TPL

Volume One • A - H

Table of Contents

feather (pointed) 362	gingerbread girl..............401	hat (pillbox) 440
feathers..........................363	giraffe............................402	hat (straw).....................441
fire hydrant (outline)........364	girl 403	hat (top hat) 442
fire safety (poster)..........365	girl 404	hat (top hat) 443
fire truck........................366	girl 405	Hawaii, USA...................444
fire truck........................367	girl 406	heart (shape).................445
fire truck........................368	glass (drinking) 407	helicopter.......................446
fireplace........................369	glasses 408	helmet (football-3D).......447
fish bowl (empty) 370	glove (left).....................409	helmet (football-side view).....448
fish bowl (with water).....371	glove (right)...................410	helmet (race car) 449
fish (animated 1)...........372	glue (bottle)...................411	hemisphere (Eastern)...........450
fish (animated 2)...........373	goat (frontal view) 412	hemisphere (Western)..........451
fish (Oscar)...................374	goat (nanny) 413	hen (animated) 452
flag................................375	goat (mountain) 414	hen (stylized) 453
flashlight 376	gold (crayon).................415	hermit crab....................454
Florida, USA 377	golf club and ball...........416	hexagon.........................455
flower pot......................378	goose............................417	hippopotamus................456
flower (multi-petal).........379	gorilla (frontal view) 418	hippopotamus (animated)......457
flower (tulip outline) 380	gorilla (side view)...........419	hippopotamus (outline)..........458
fly 381	grapes...........................420	holly (with veins) 459
football..........................382	grasshopper..................421	holly (plain) 460
fork................................383	gray (crayon) 422	horse (animated) 461
fox (animated, sitting) ...384	green (crayon) 423	horse (stylized) 462
fox (animated, standing)........385	Guinea pig 424	horseshoe.....................463
fox (stylized) 386	guitar.............................425	hot air balloon................464
fraction pie (eighths) 387	**H**	hourglass.......................465
French fries...................388	half-dollars 426	house............................466
frigate............................389	ham................................427	hummingbird..................467
frisbee...........................390	hamburger 428	hummingbirds................468
frog (animated, sitting)...........391	hammer 429	
frog (leaping) 392	hamster..........................430	
frog (stylized) 393	hands (outline)...............431	
funnel............................394	hanger 432	
G	hat (cone) 433	
gecko............................395	hat (cowboy).................434	
Georgia, USA................396	hat (derby) 435	
ghost.............................397	hat (fedora) 436	More patterns for letters I through Z are featured in *The Pattern Library™ • Volume Two*, LAB201412P.
ghost (outline)...............398	hat (firefighter's) 437	
giant panda...................399	hat (lady's) 438	
gingerbread boy............400	hat (mountie's)...............439	

The Pattern Library

Volume One • A - H

***The Pattern Libary*™**—is a two-volume treasury of large, black line illustrations in printable, pattern formats. This, **Volume One** contains over 400 patterns for letters **A** through **H**. It's a rich collection of illustrations from our image libraries and an invaluable resource for children, parents, teachers, crafters and anyone who requires blackline images for an infinite number or projects. Illustrations are labeled and easy-to-find as they appear alphabetically in the table of contents (pp. 3-6). Multiple versions of a given object or animal are also labeled accordingly in the table of contents.

Note: In most instances, patterns are listed by category or species names first with details, if any, in parenthesis:

bird (in flight) - Volume 1, A-H
bell (jingle) - Volume 1, A-H
car (Model-T) - Volume 1, A-H
elephant (African) - Volume 1, A-H
elephant (outline) - Volume 1, A-H

Patterns include a wide selection of items found around the house, around town, in recreational environments, domestic, wild, and exotic animals, musical instruments, tools, dwellings, containers, the vintage and the unique.

Decorate workstations, display and bulletin boards, take-home communications, work folders, book reports, book covers, scrapbooks, picture albums, stationary, desks, doors, windows, flags, paper bag lanterns, and daisy chains or embelish presentations.

Create activity sheets, picture word walls, flash cards, picture dictionaries, index fact cards, collages, matching card games, door knob hangers, signs, tags, labels, picture blocks, bag puppets, stick puppets, mobiles, flannel boards, and anything else you can imagine.

aardvark

abacus

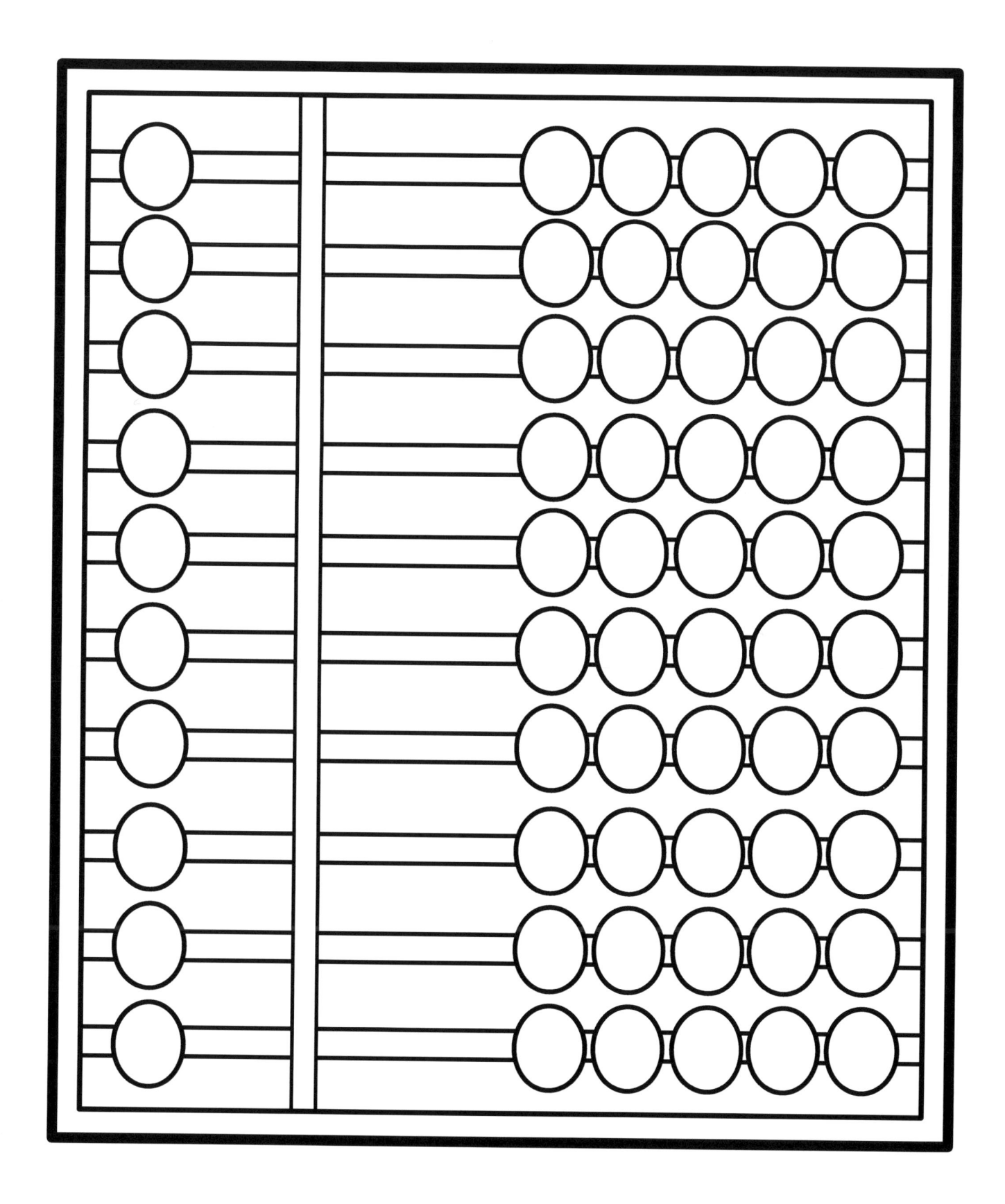

acorn

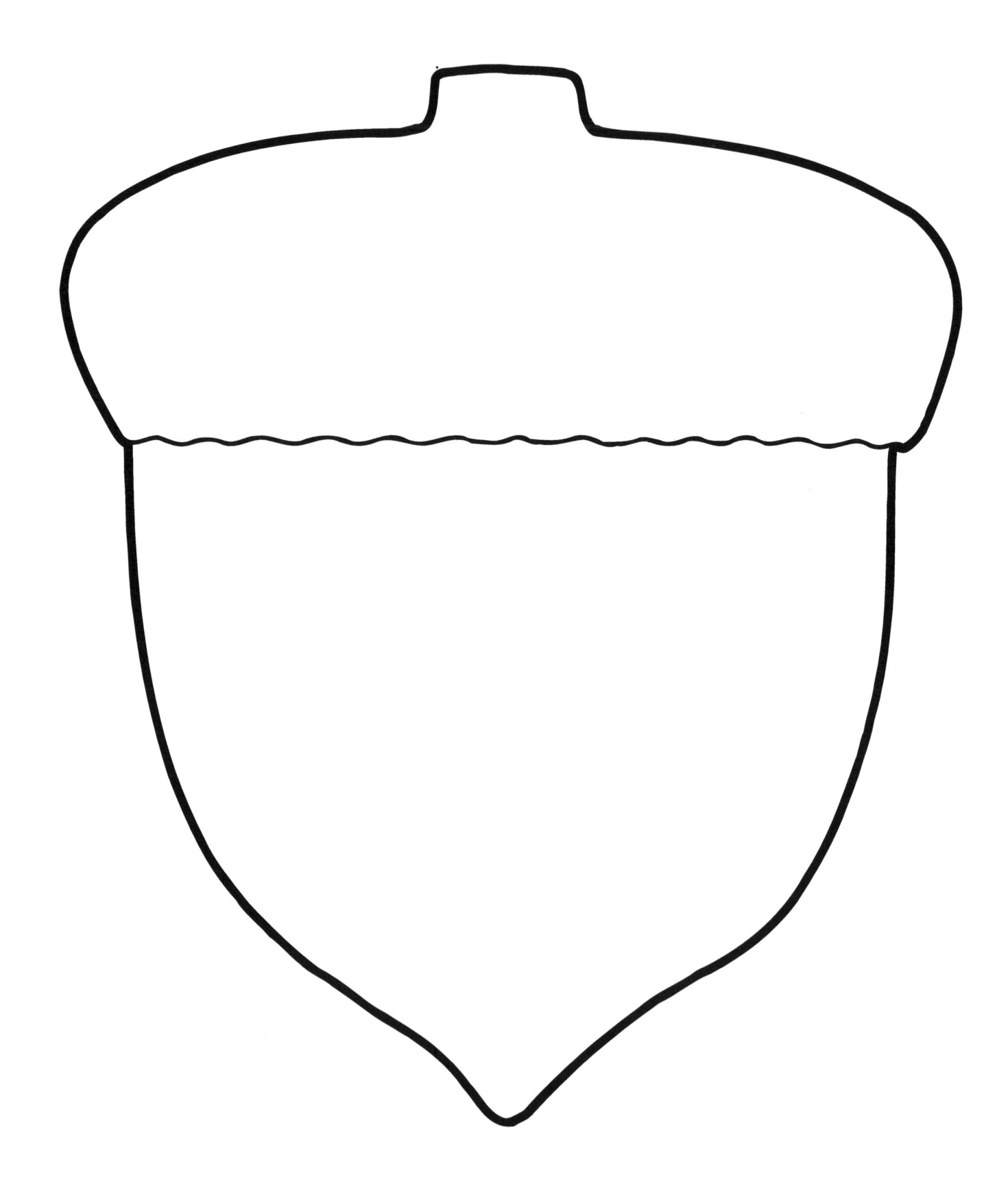

acrobat

Africa

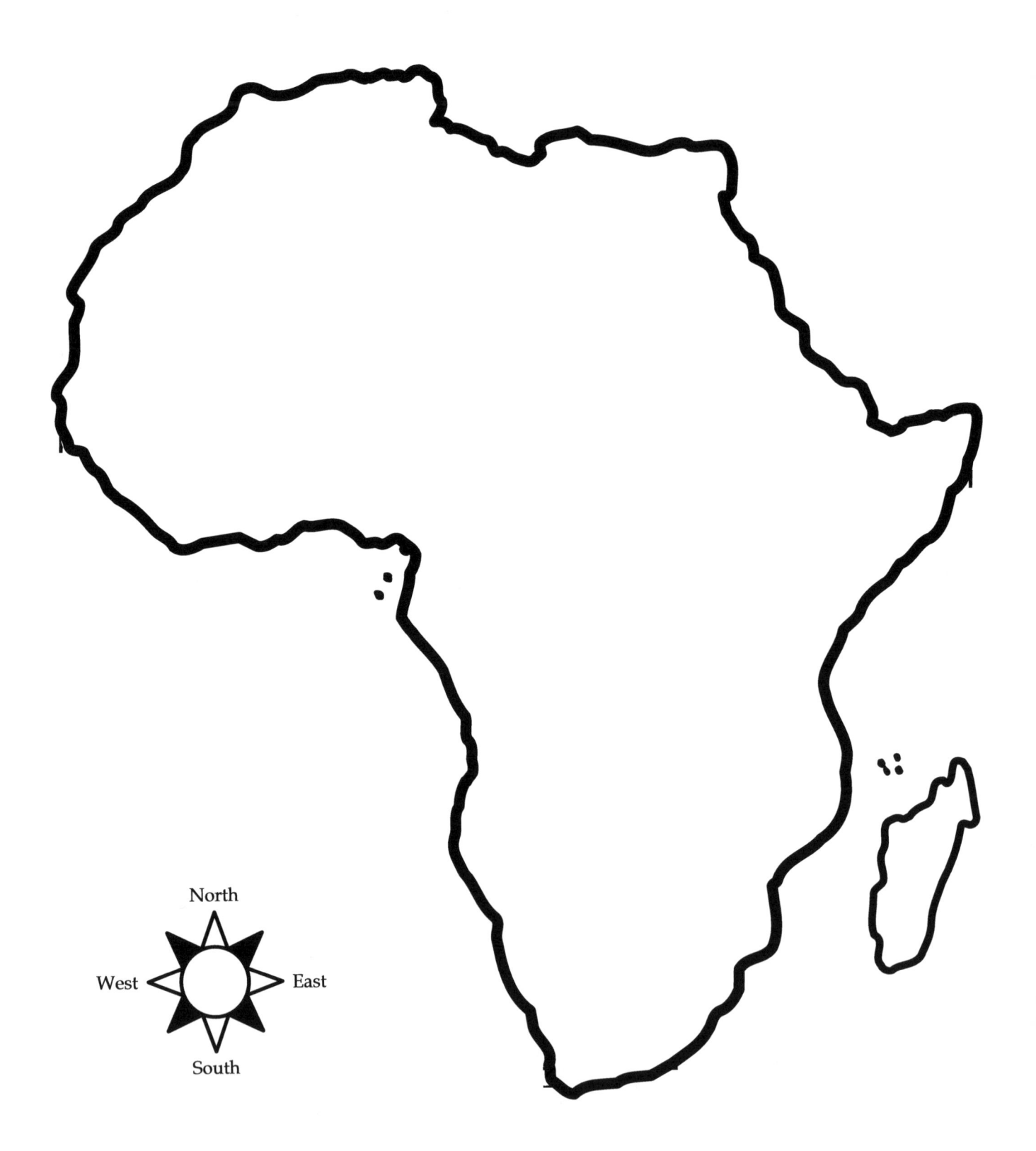

Maps are representations and boundaries are not exact.

airplane

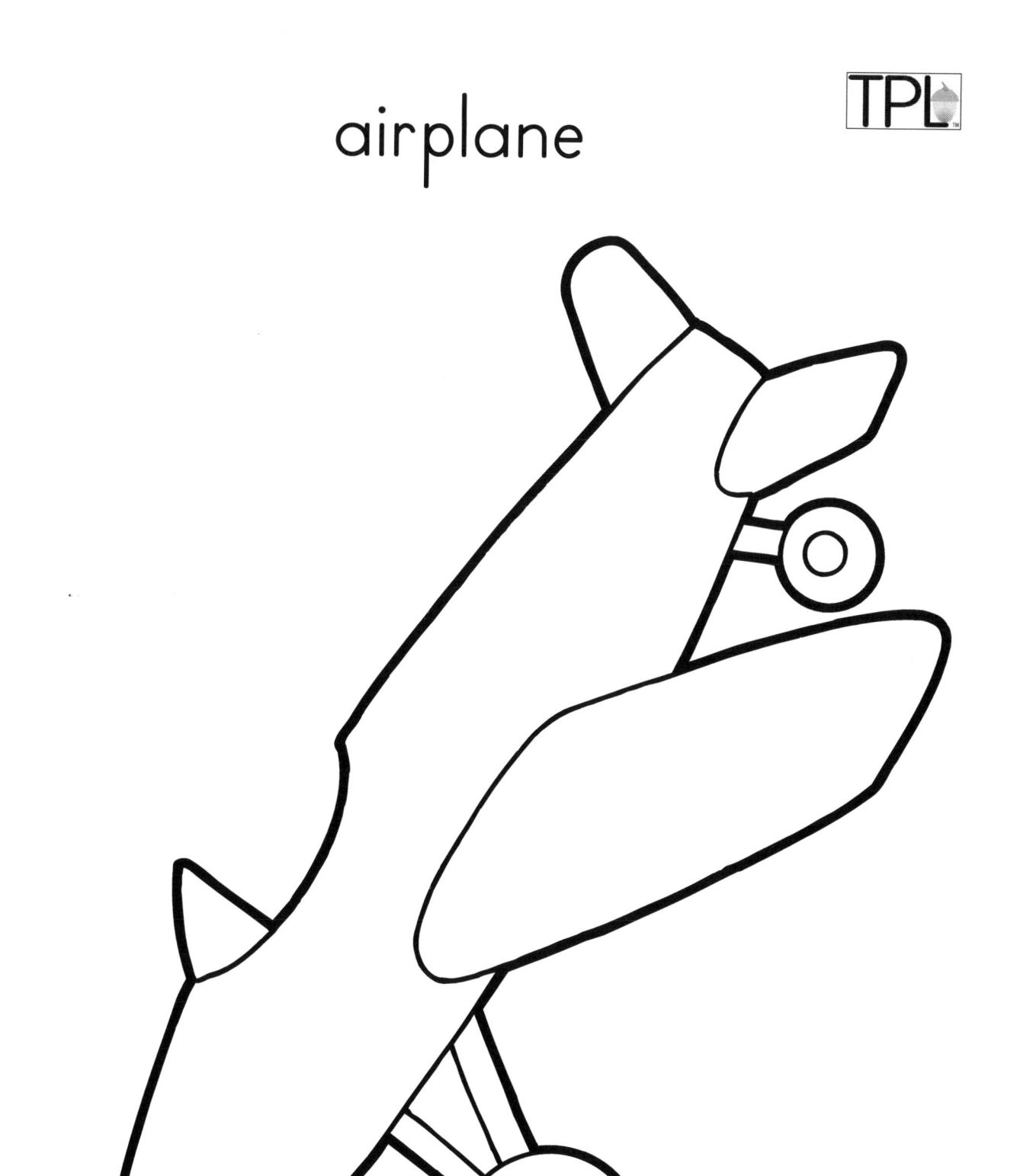

Alabama, USA

Maps are representations and boundaries are not exact.

LAB201411P • THE PATTERN LIBRARY • VOLUME ONE • A-H • 978-1-937257-62-0 • © 2014 Little Acorn Books™

alarm clock

Alaska, USA

Maps are representations and boundaries are not exact.

Alberta, Canada

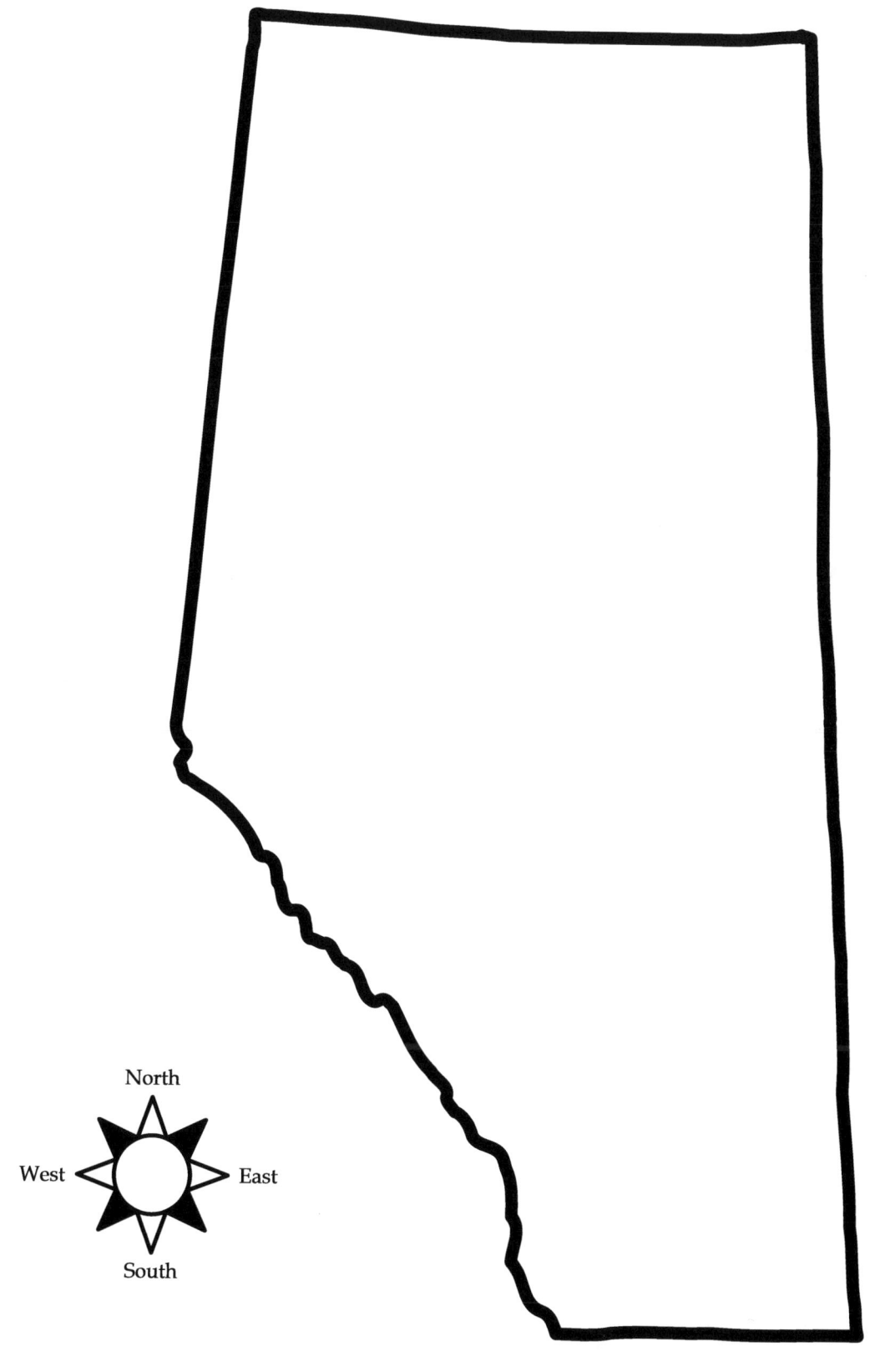

North
West East
South

Maps are representations and boundaries are not exact.

alligator (animated)

alphabet

Aa Bb Cc Dd Ee

Ff Gg Hh Ii Jj Kk

Ll Mm Nn Oo Pp

Qq Rr Ss Tt Uu

Vv Ww Xx Yy Zz

ambulance

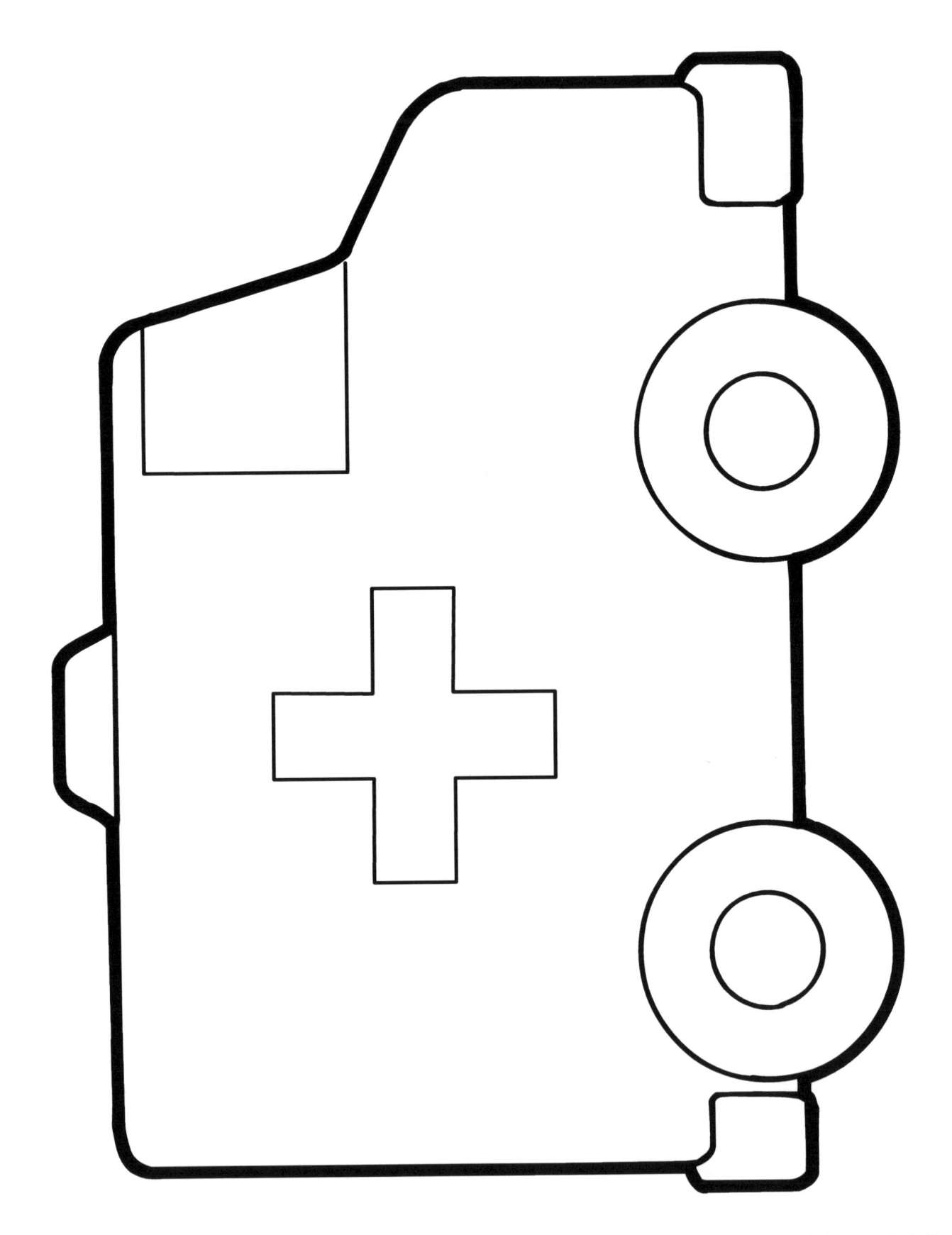

anchor

angel (add a photo format)

angel

… ankylosaurus

Antarctica

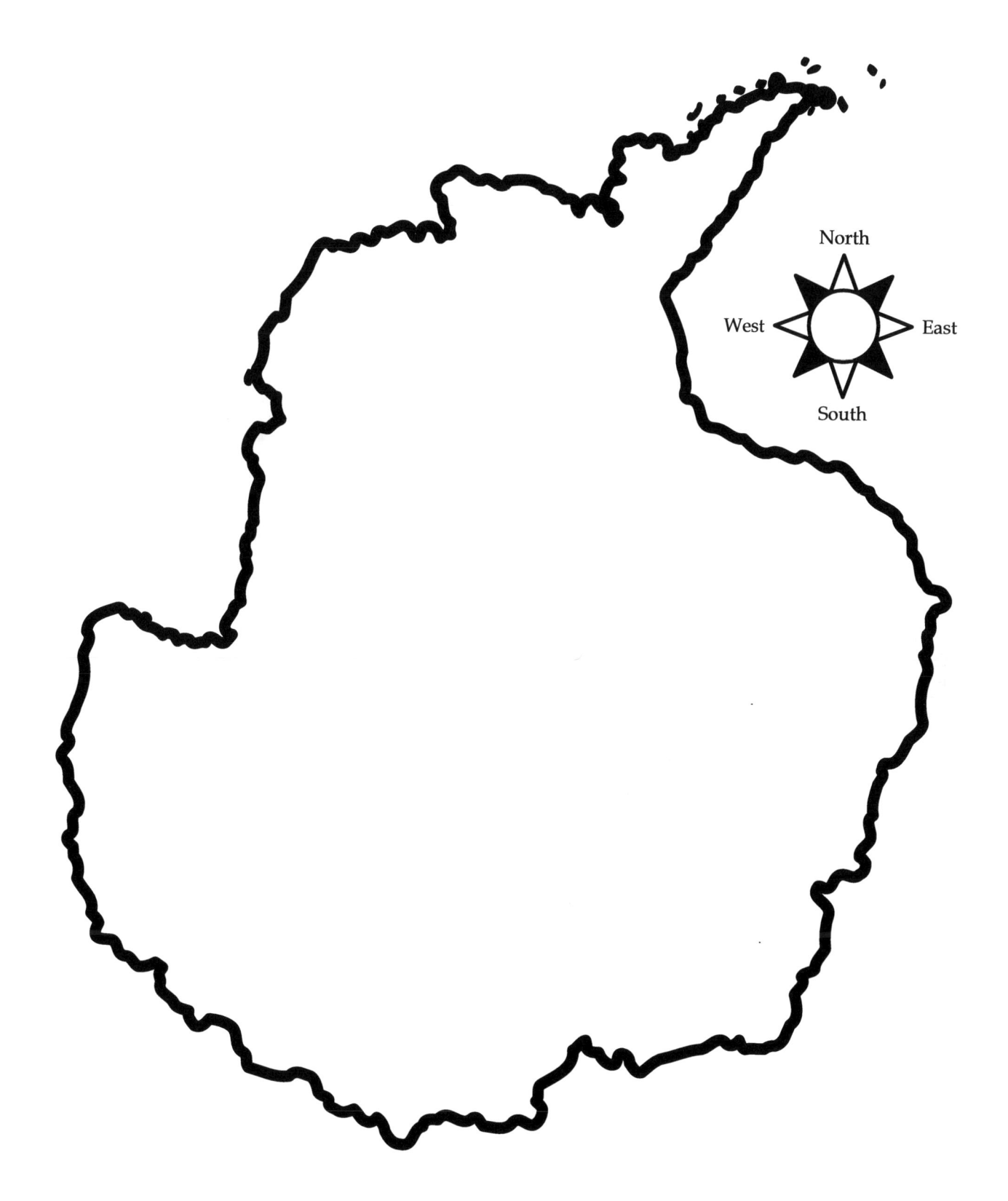

West · North · East · South

Maps are representations and boundaries are not exact.
LAB201411P • THE PATTERN LIBRARY • VOLUME ONE • A-H • 978-1-937257-62-0 • © 2014 Little Acorn Books™

ant

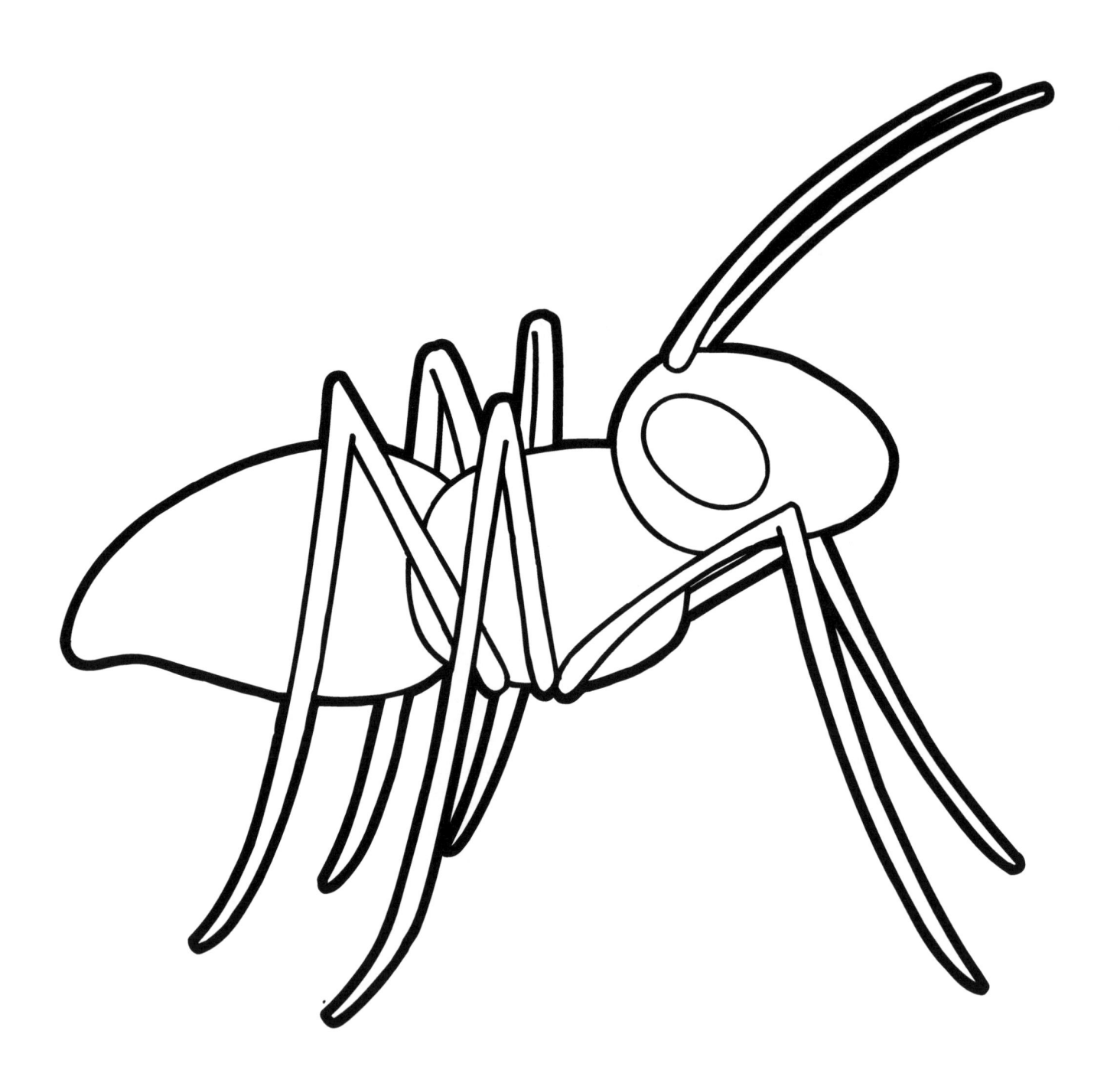

anteater (animated)

anteater (stylized)

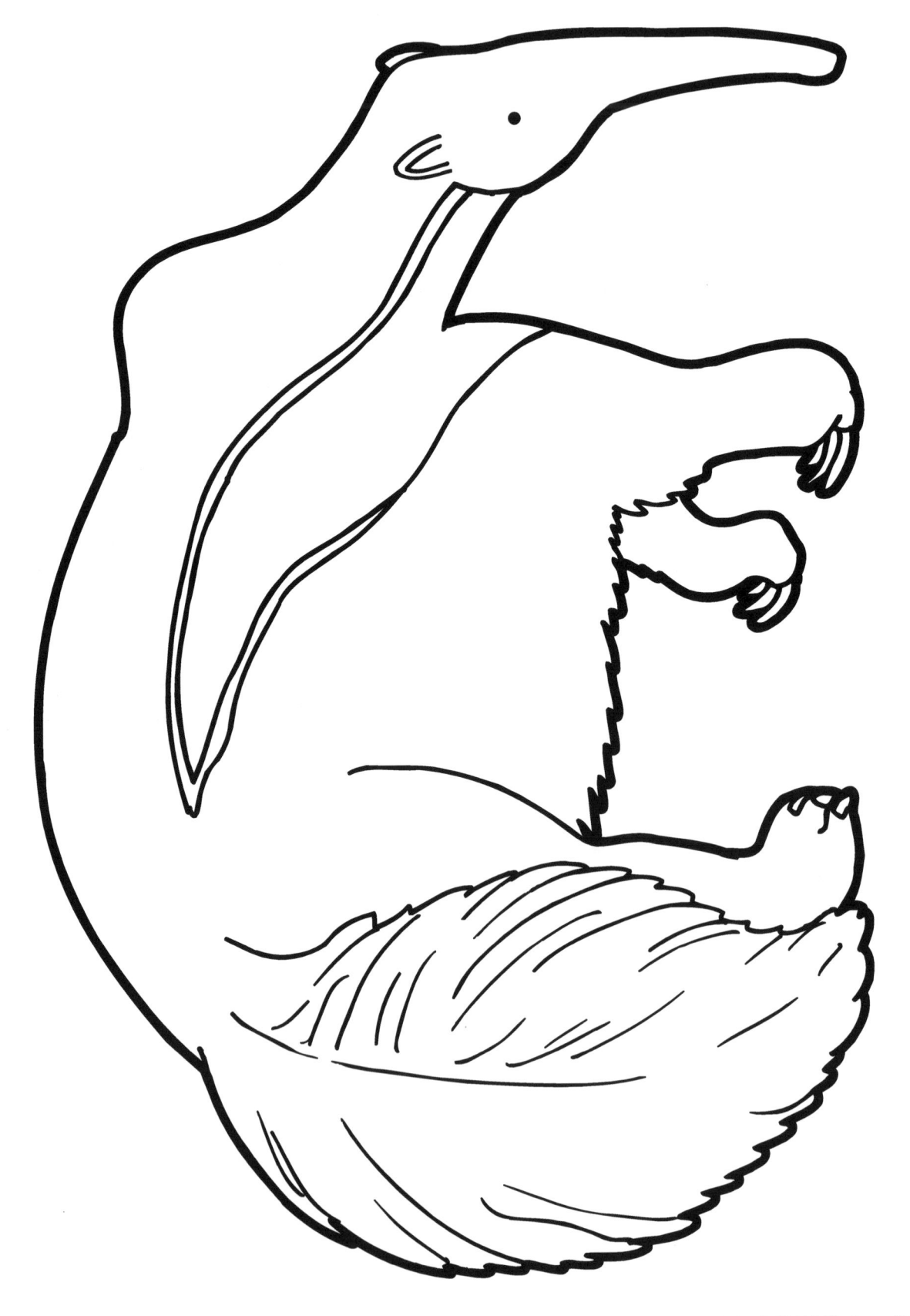

antler

antlers

anvil (outline)

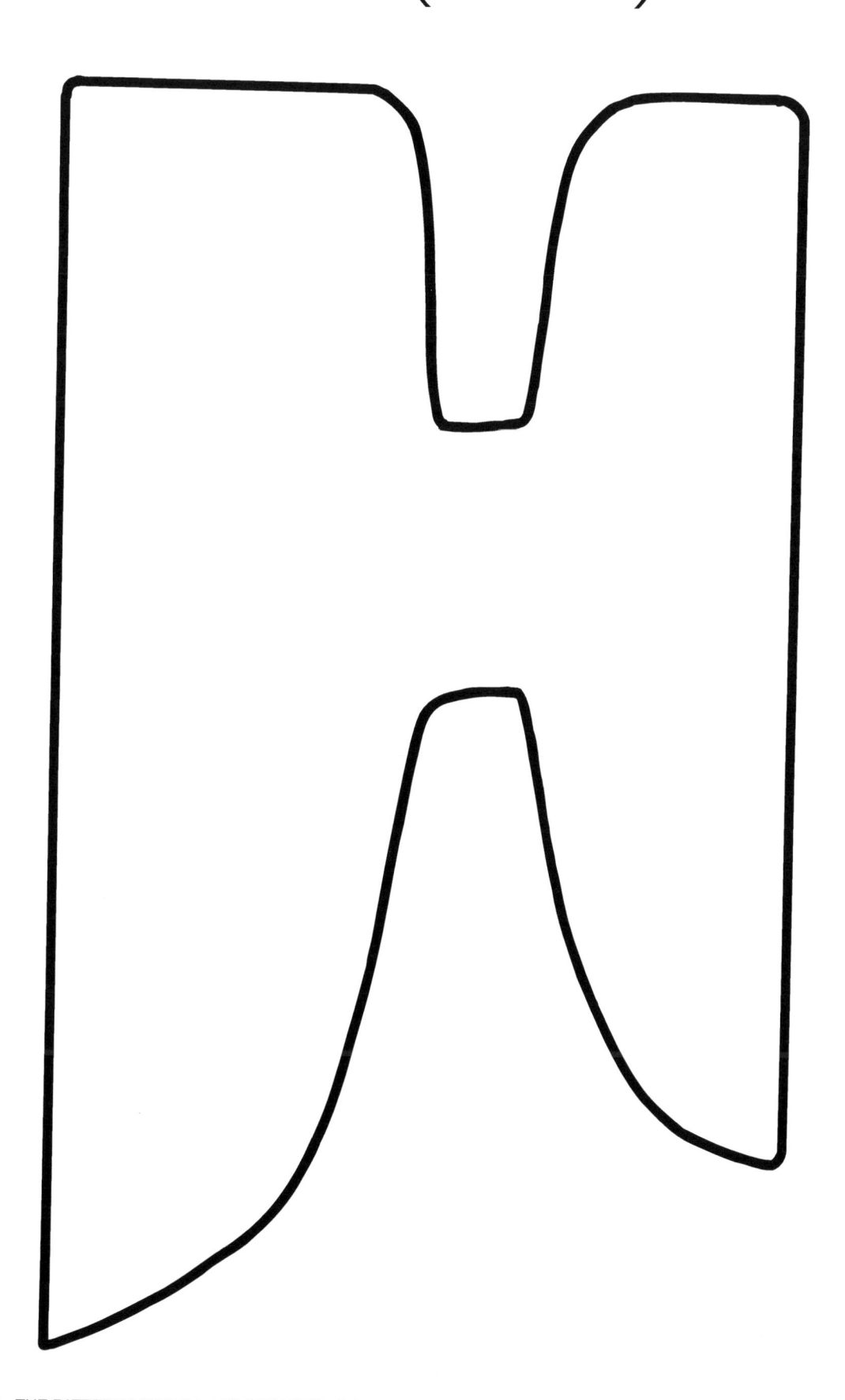

apartment building

apron

aquarium

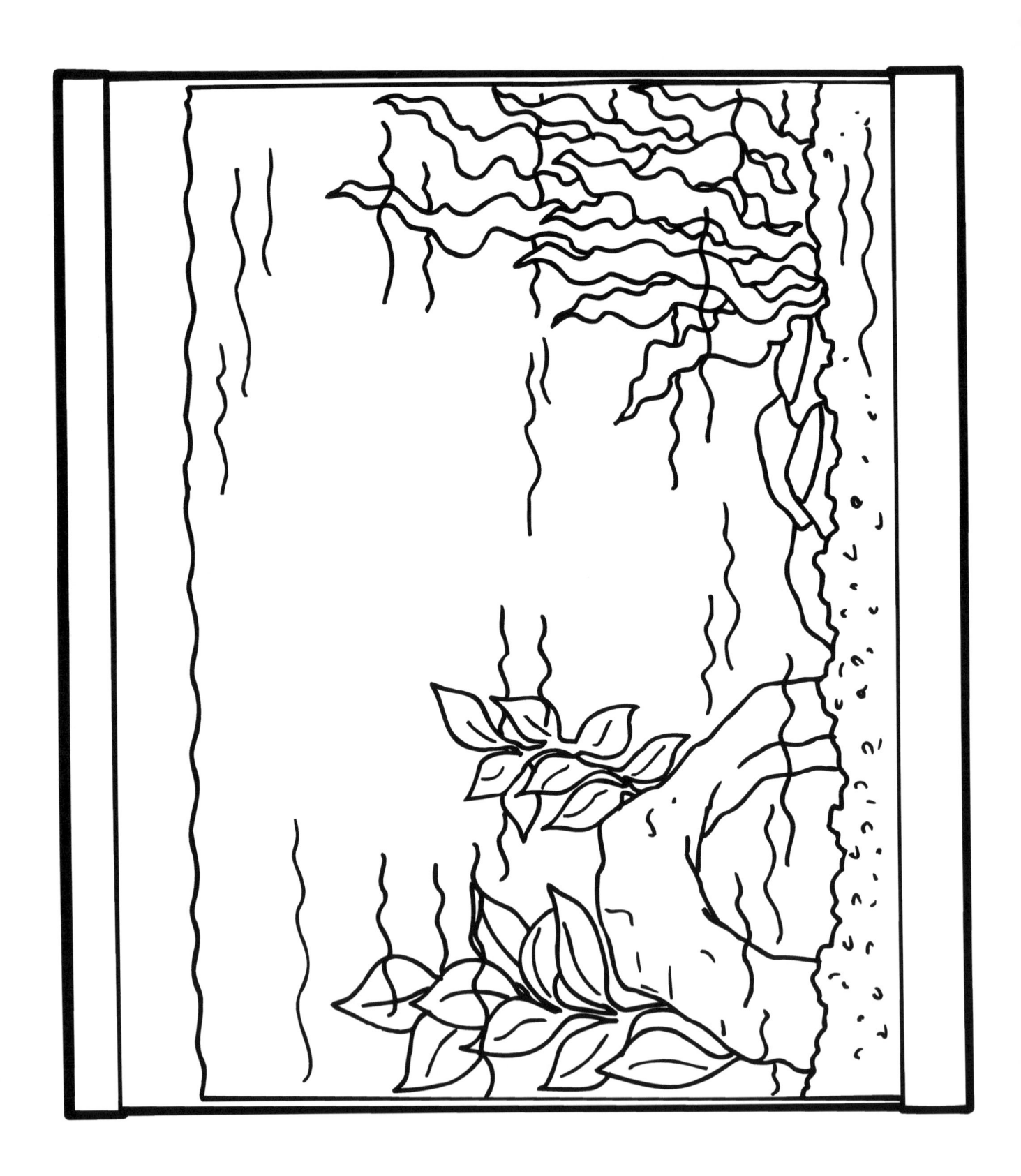

Arizona, USA

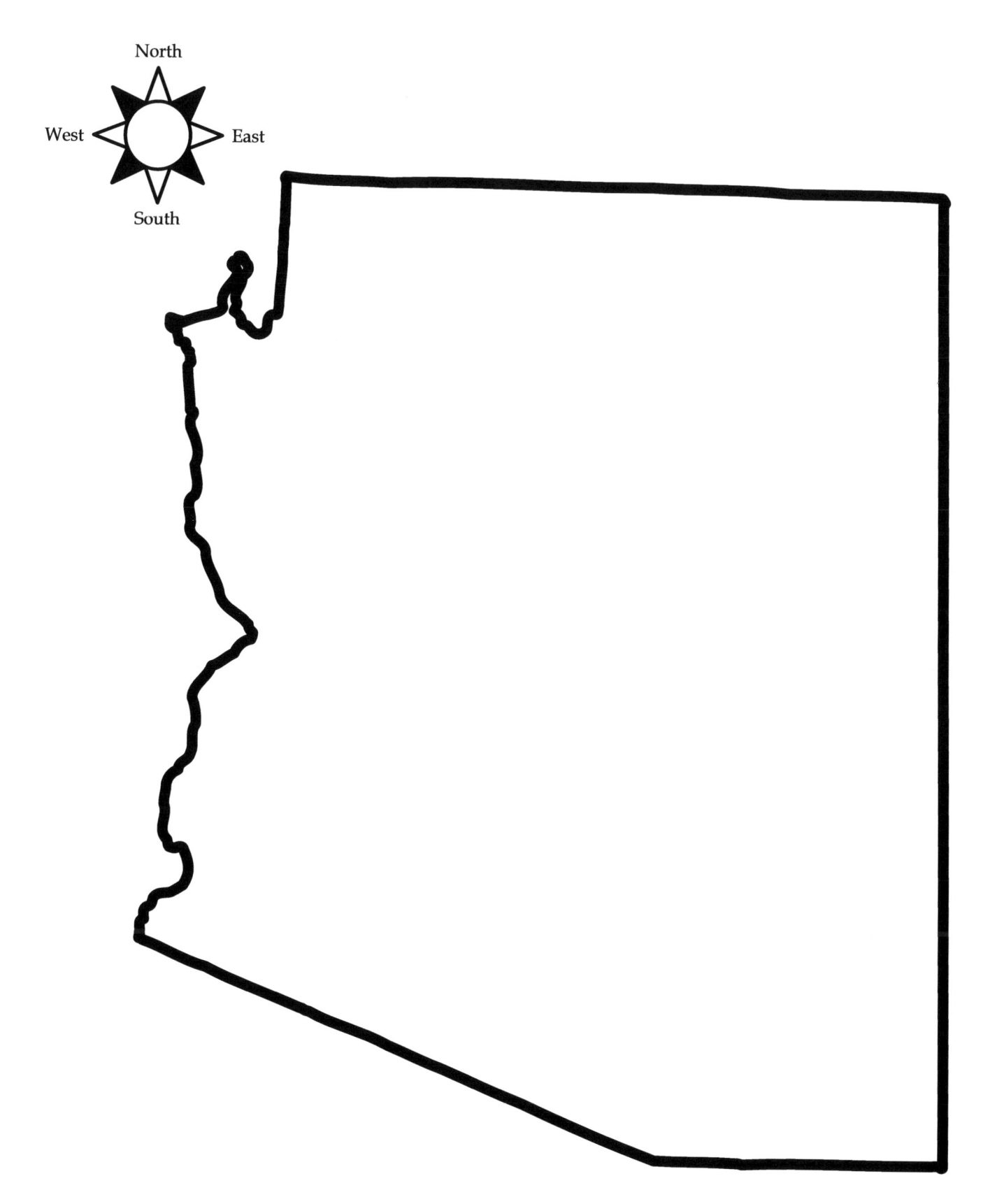

North
West East
South

Maps are representations and boundaries are not exact.

Arkansas, USA

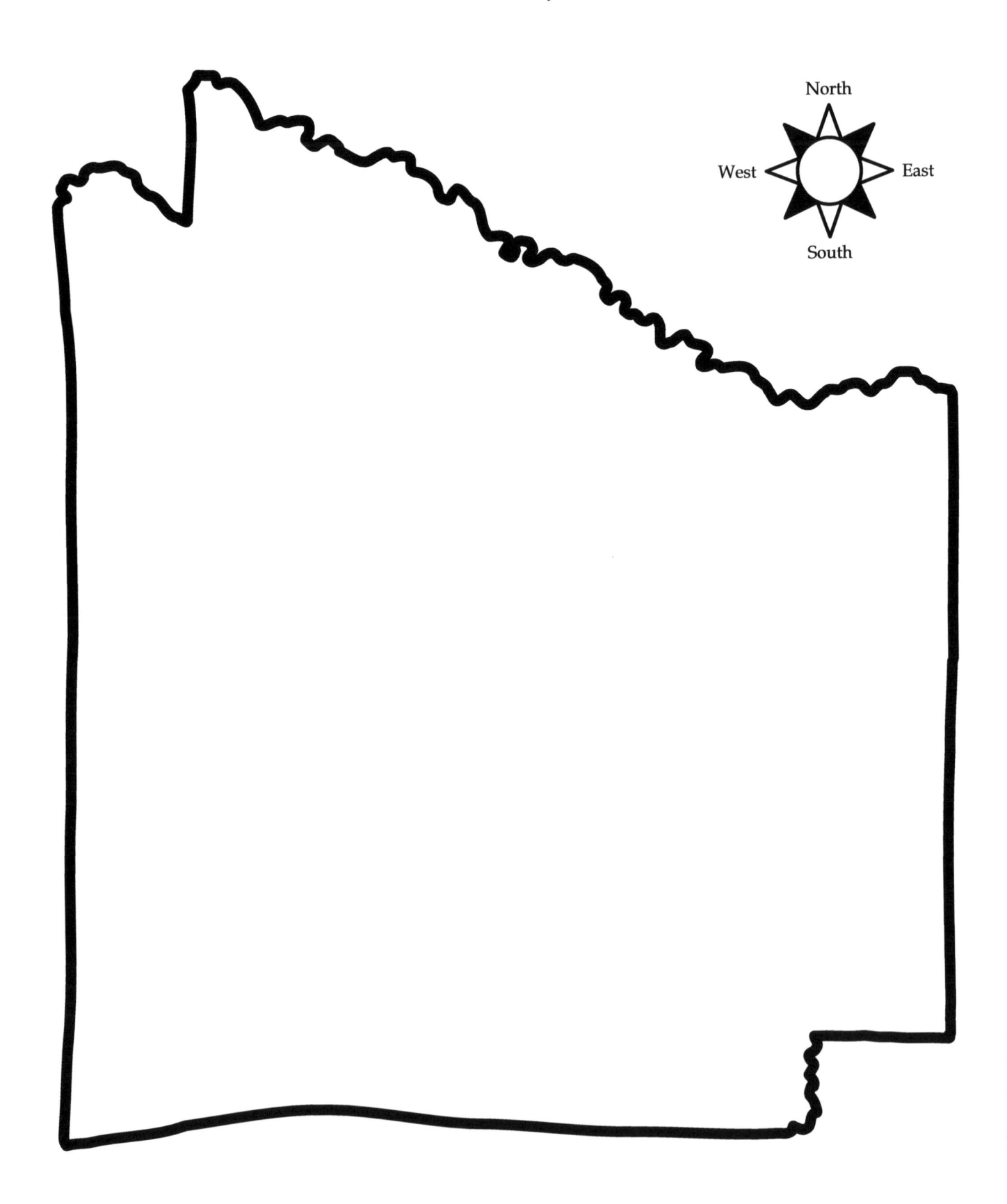

North
West East
South

Maps are representations and boundaries are not exact.

armadillo

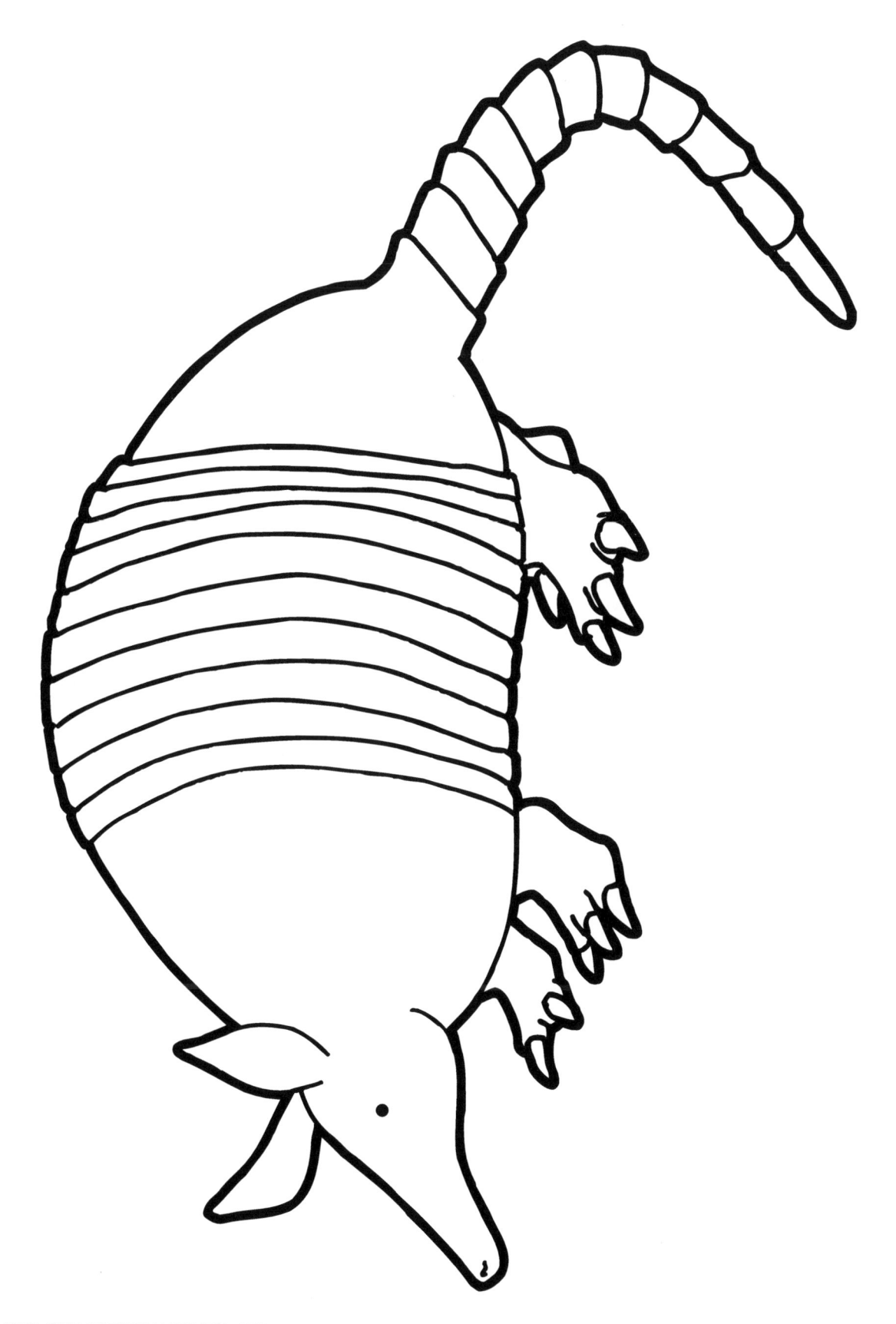

armchair

arrow

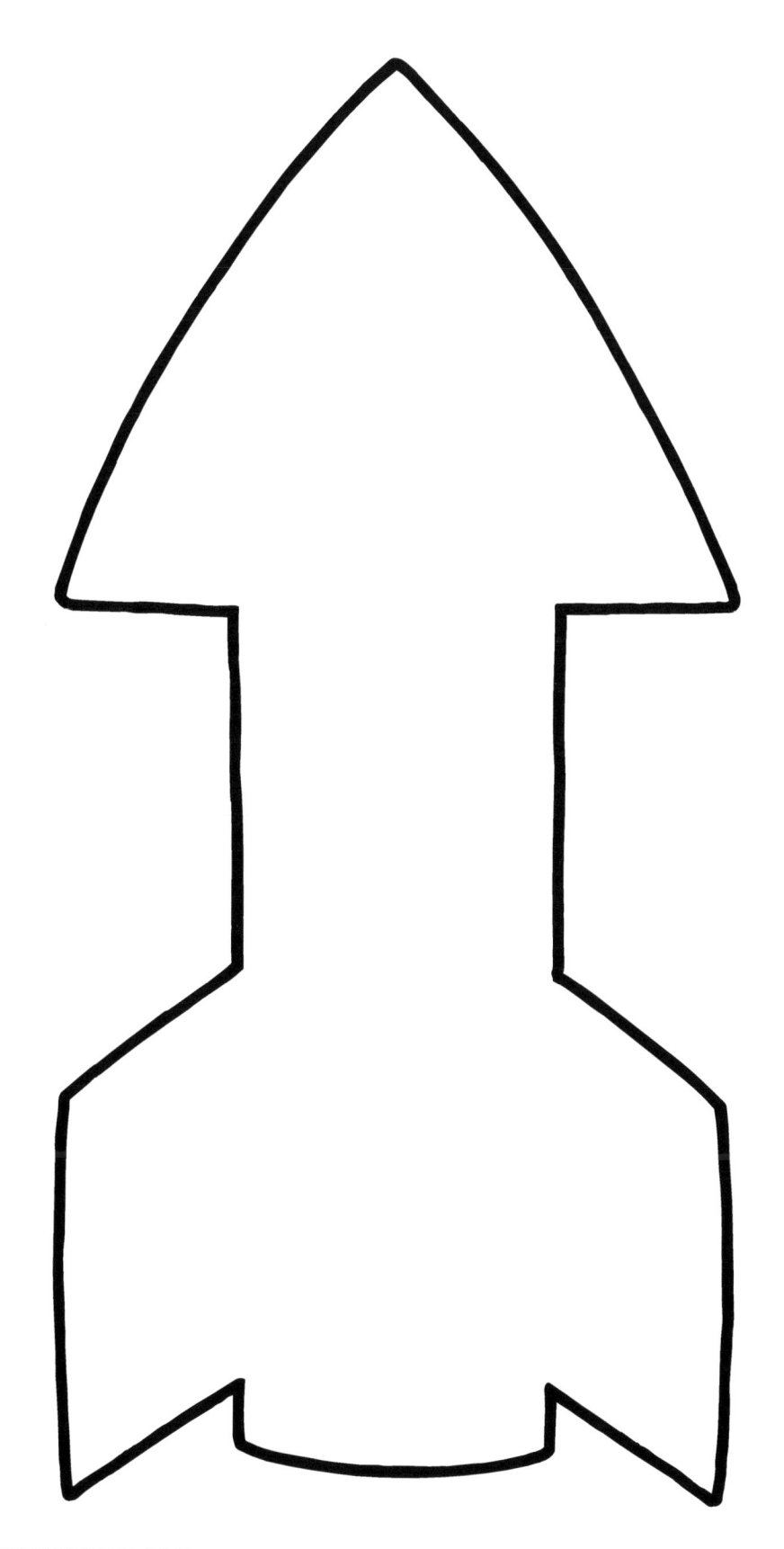

arrowhead

arrows

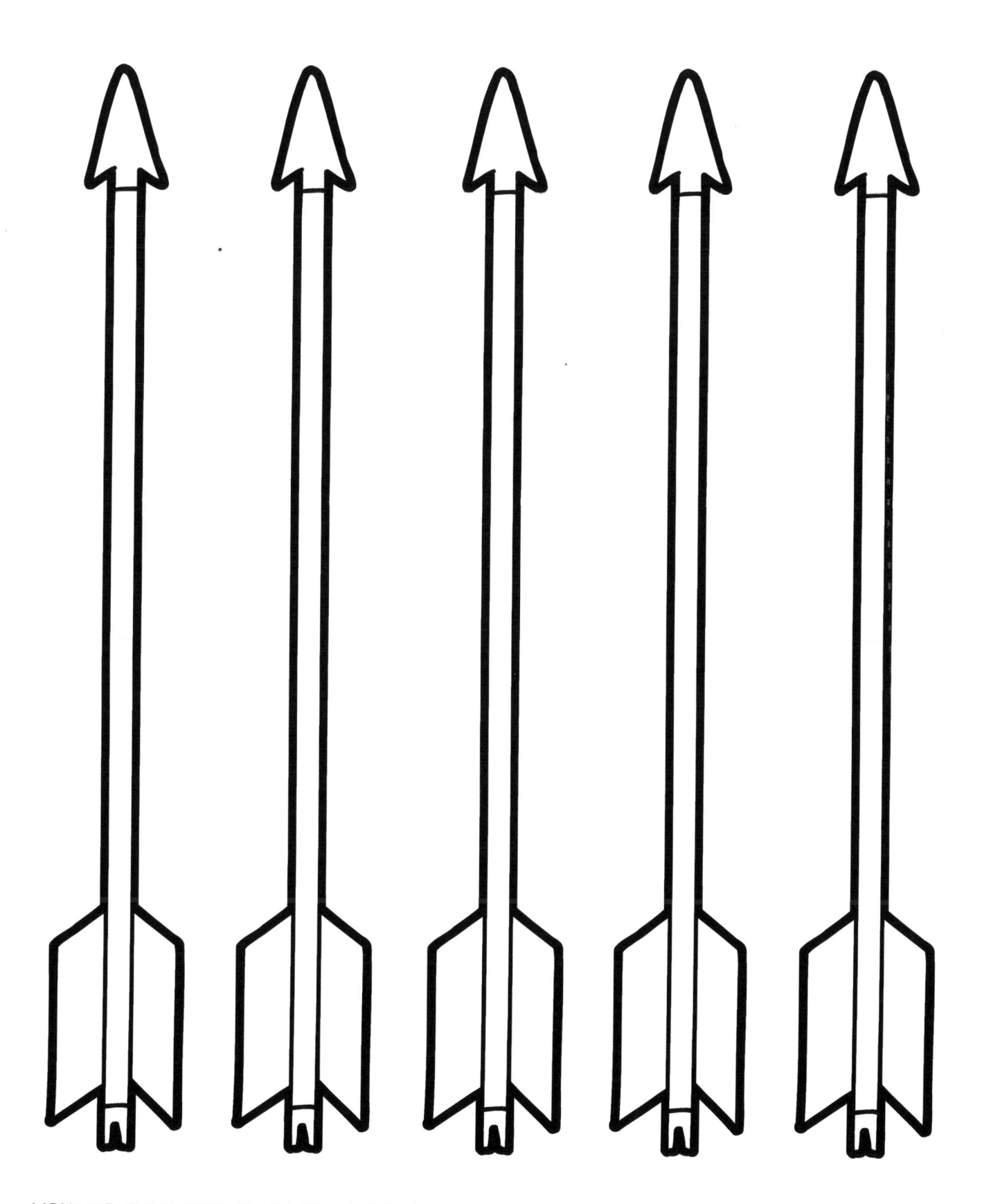

Asia

North East South West

Maps are representations and boundaries are not exact.

42 LAB201411P • THE PATTERN LIBRARY • VOLUME ONE • A-H • 978-1-937257-62-0 • © 2014 Little Acorn Books™

asparagus

astronaut

Australia

Maps are representations and boundaries are not exact.

LAB201411P • THE PATTERN LIBRARY • VOLUME ONE • A-H • 978-1-937257-62-0 • © 2014 Little Acorn Books™   45

avocado

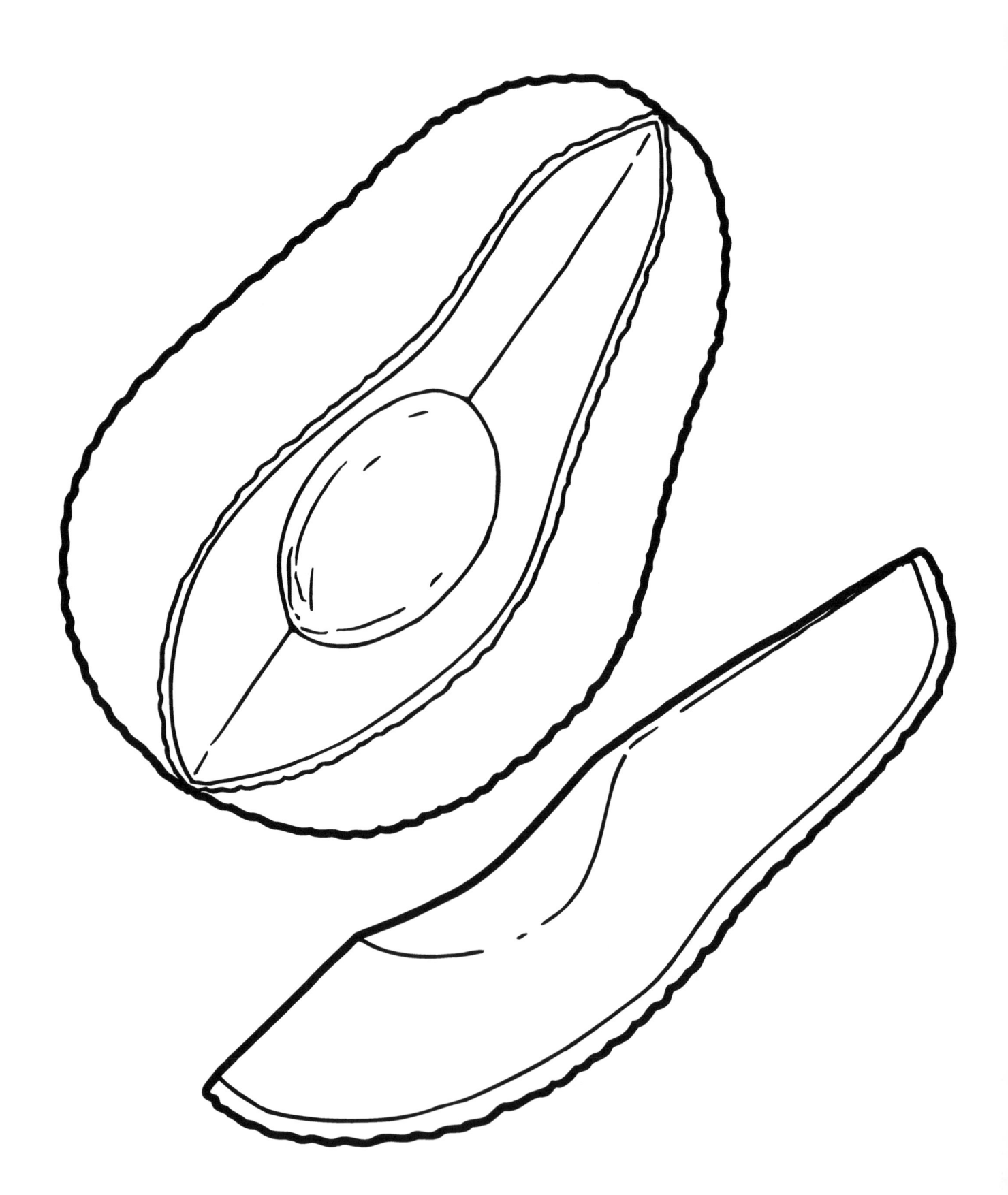

award

axe

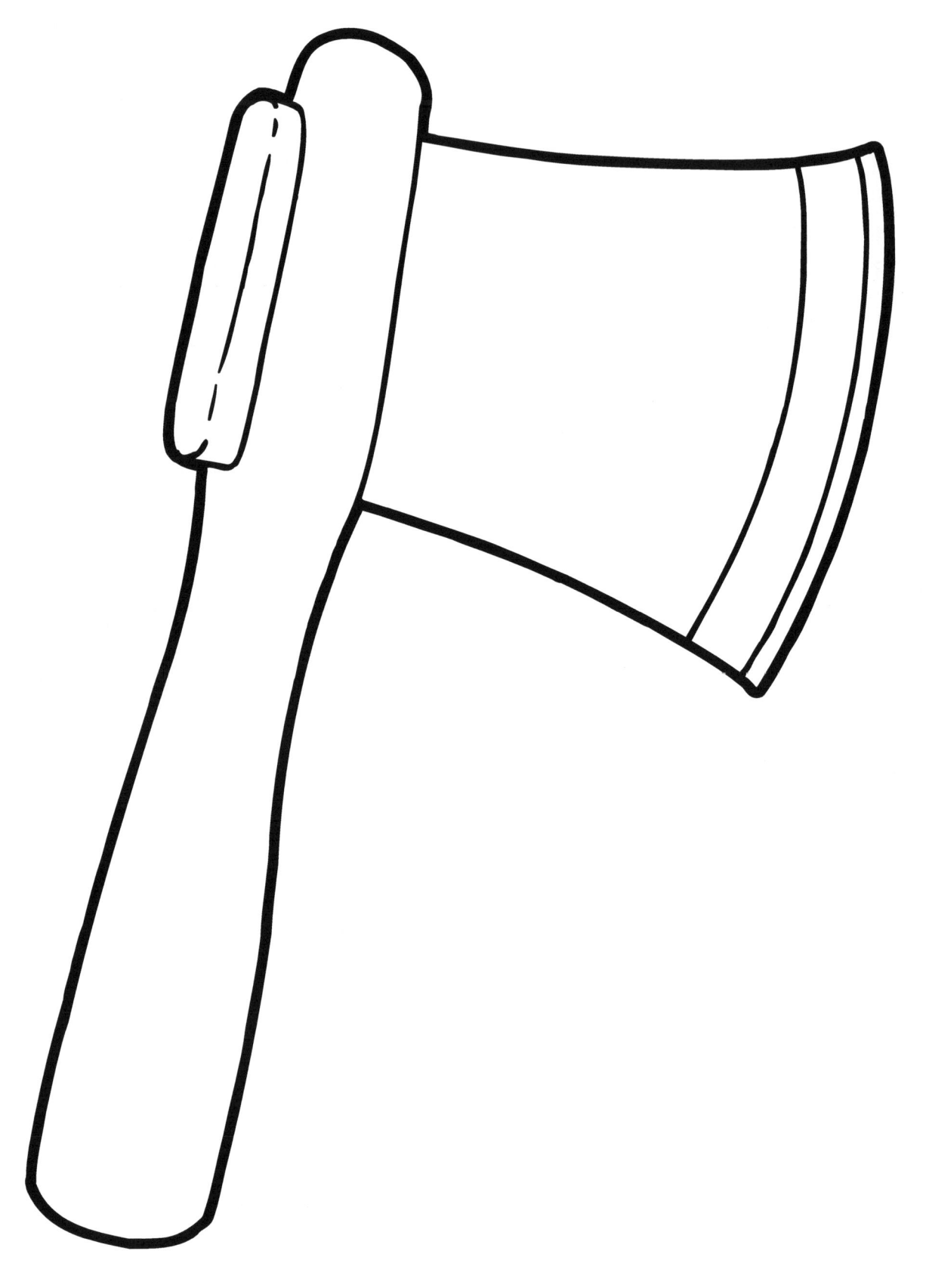

baby (crawling)

baby (frontal view)

bacon (slice)

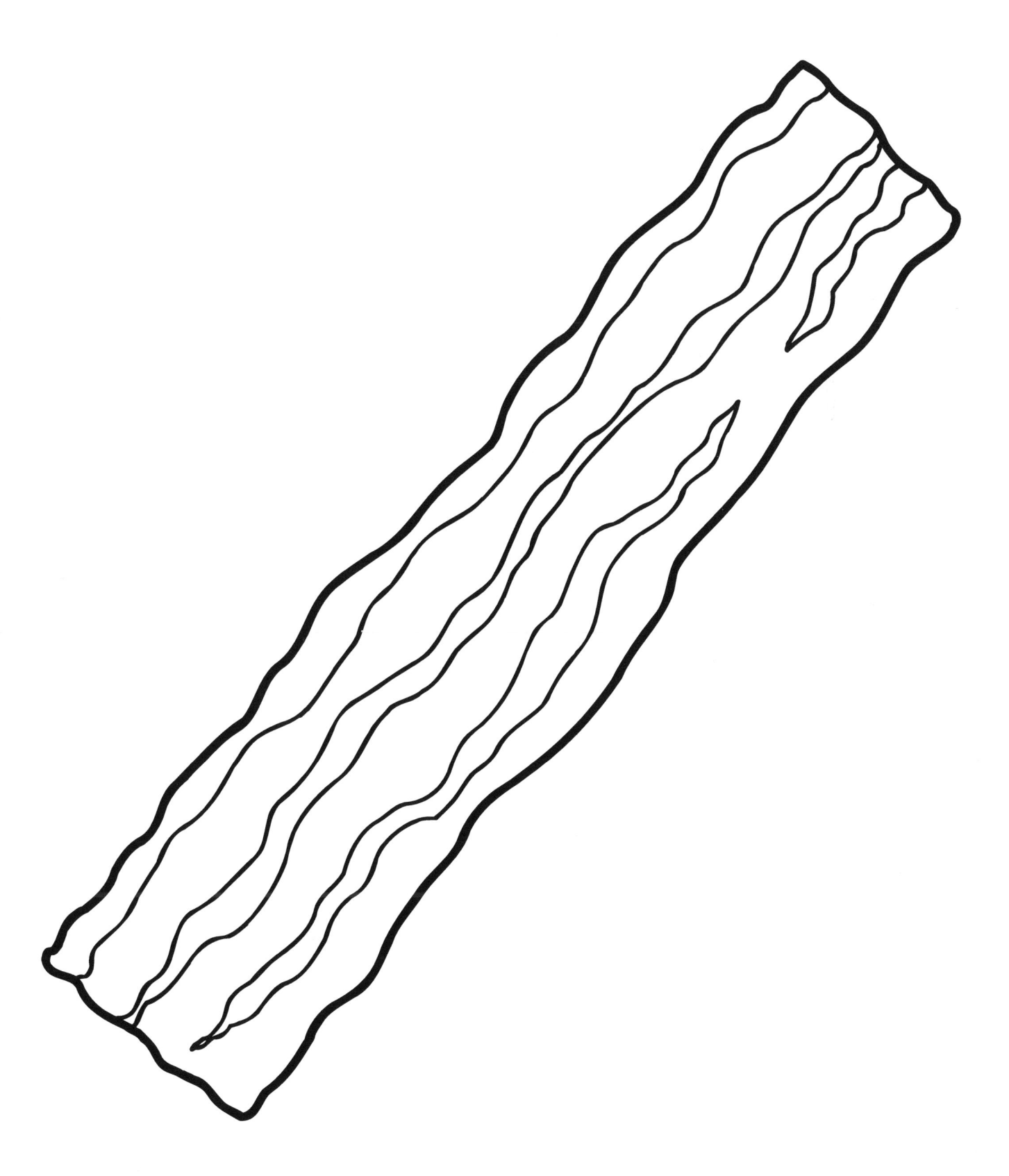

badge

badger

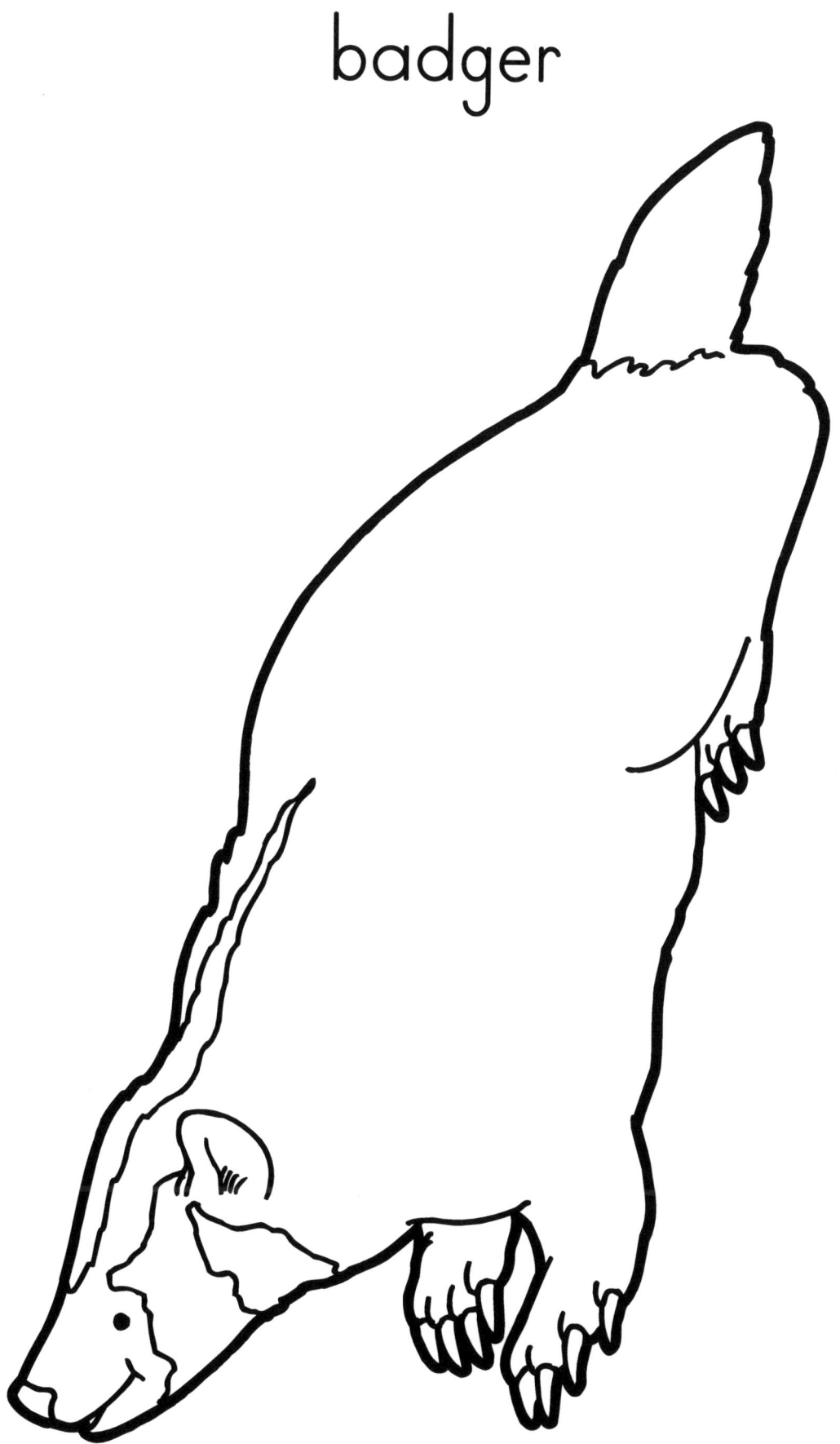

bag (paper)

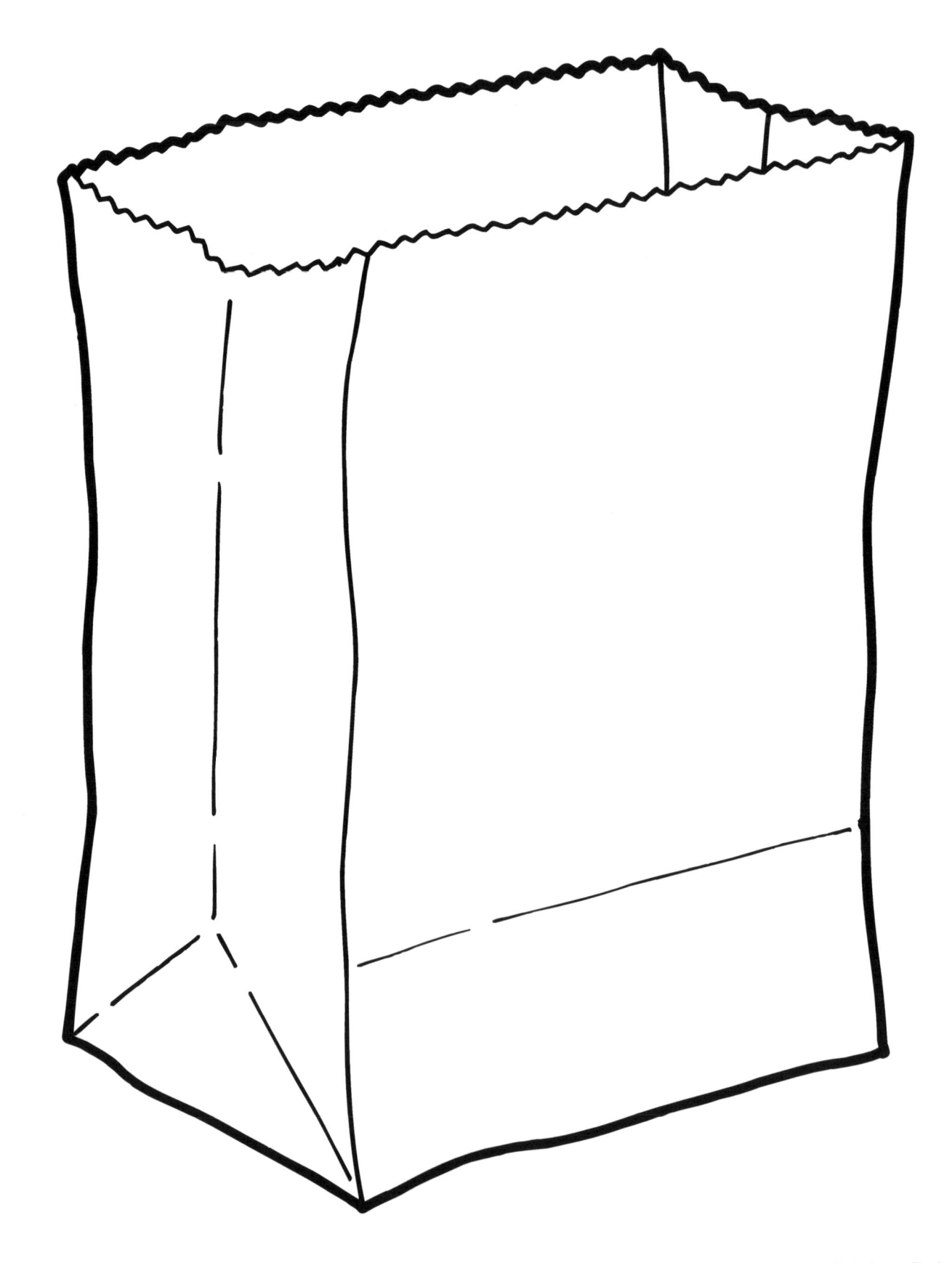

bag (shopping)

bagpipes

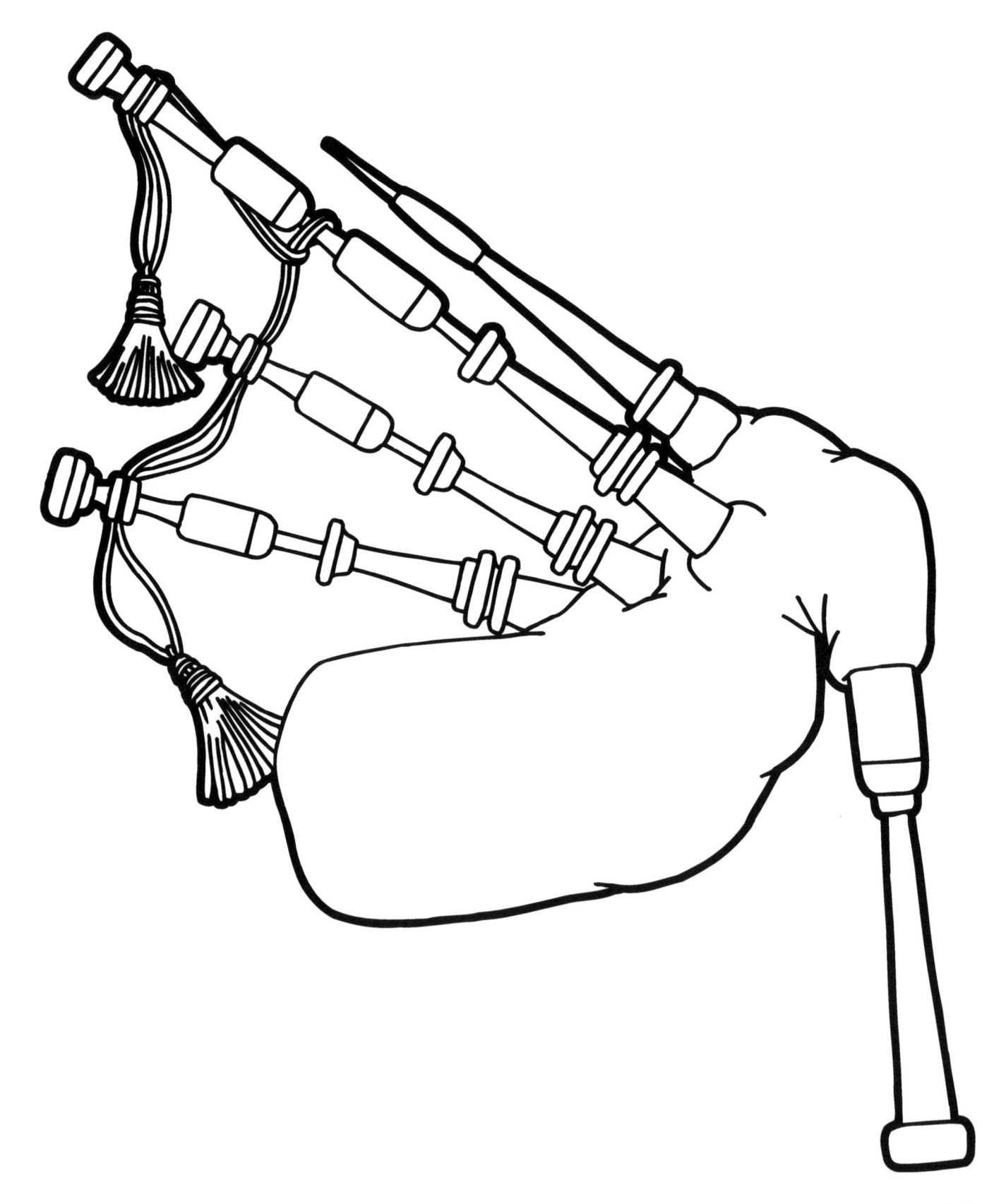

ball (beach)

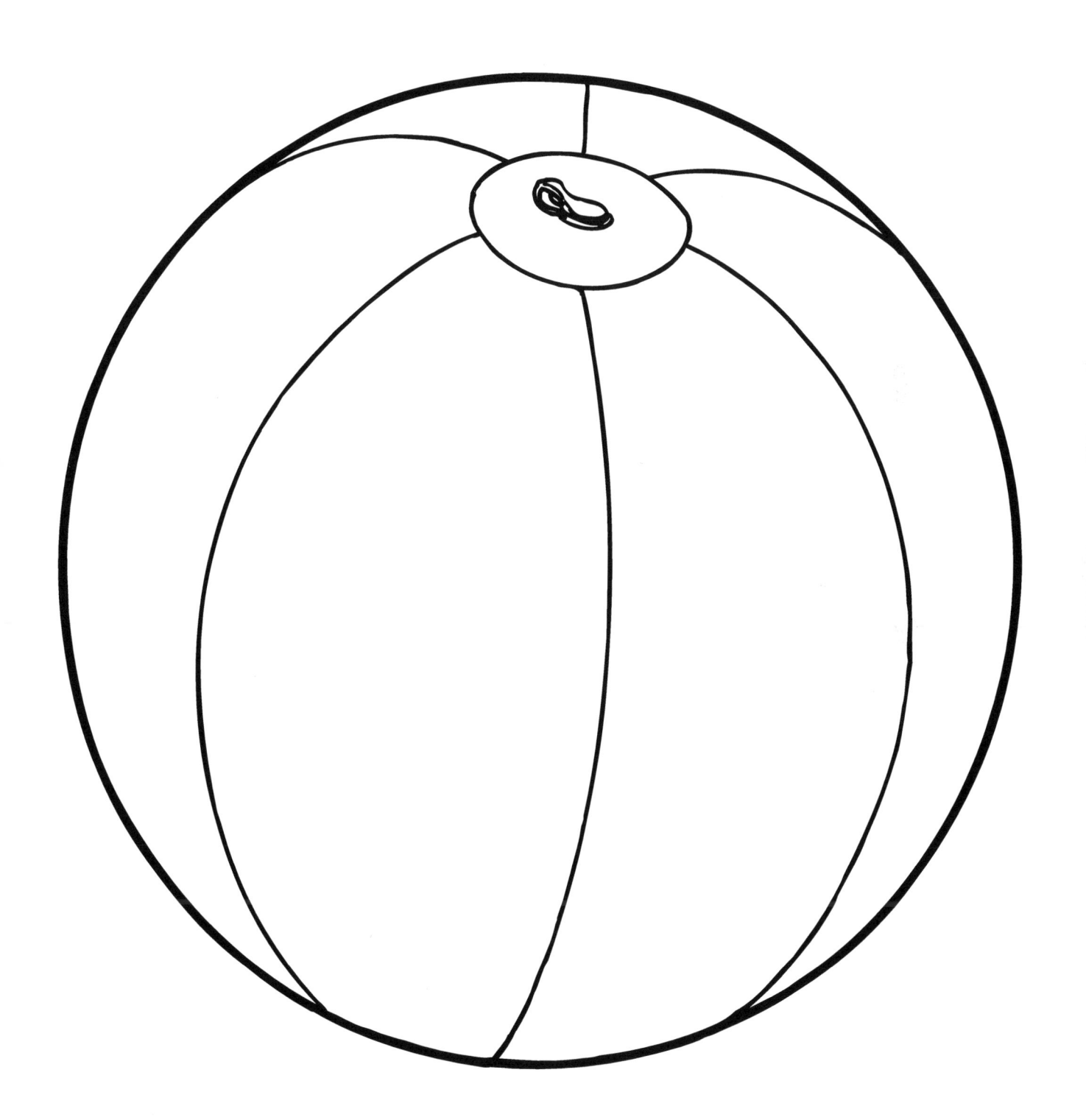

ballerina

balloon

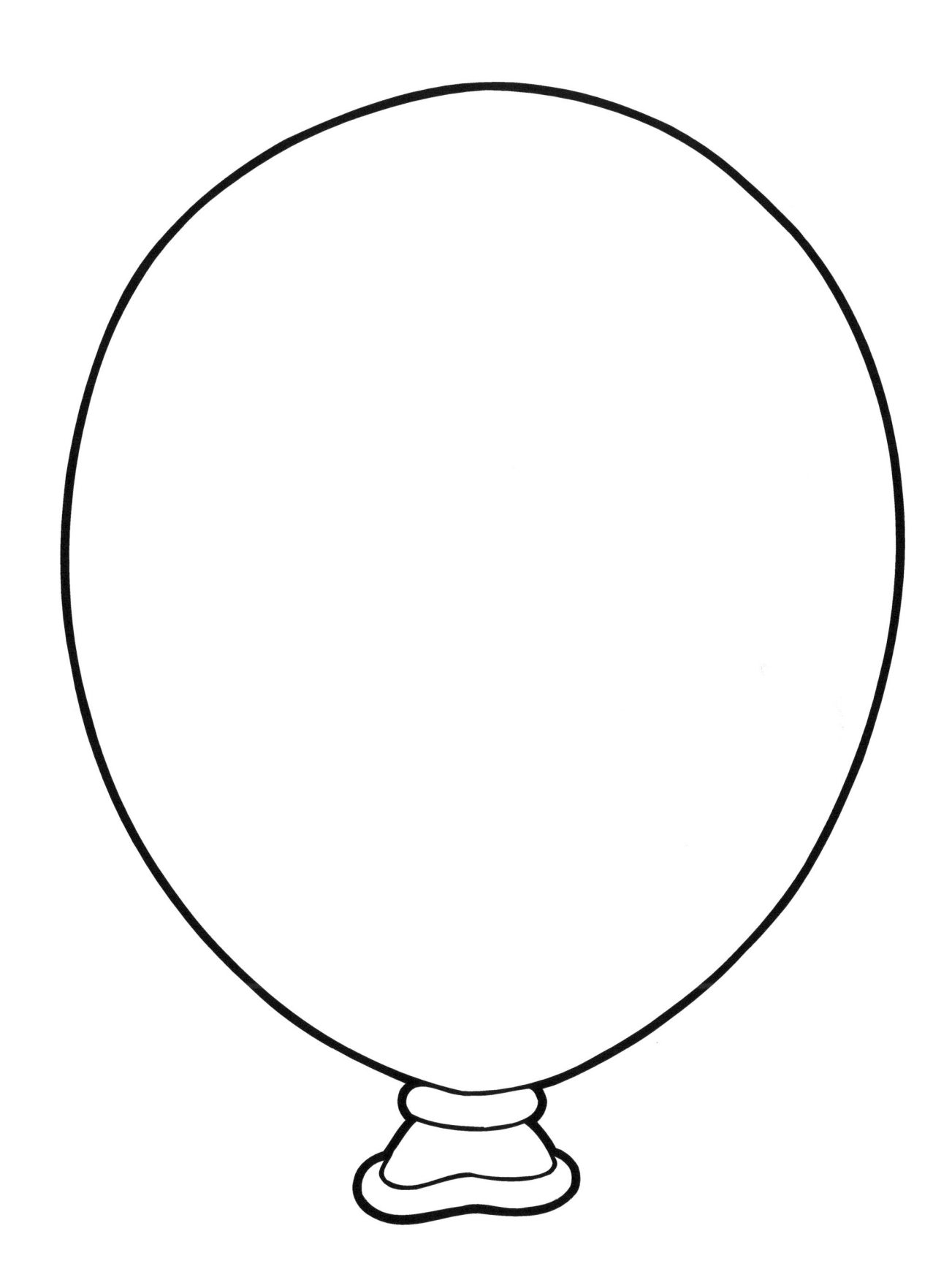

bamboo

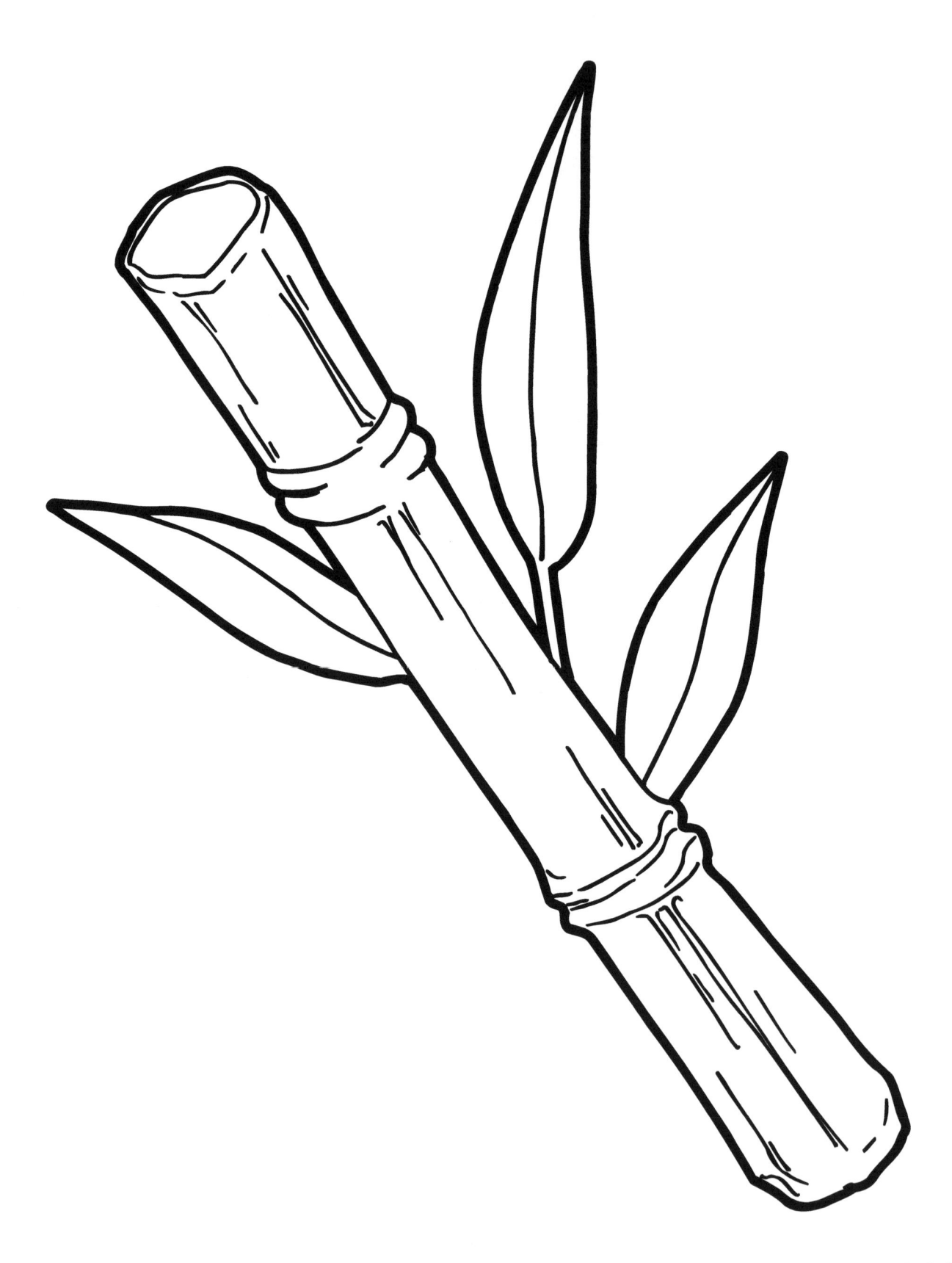

banana

banjo

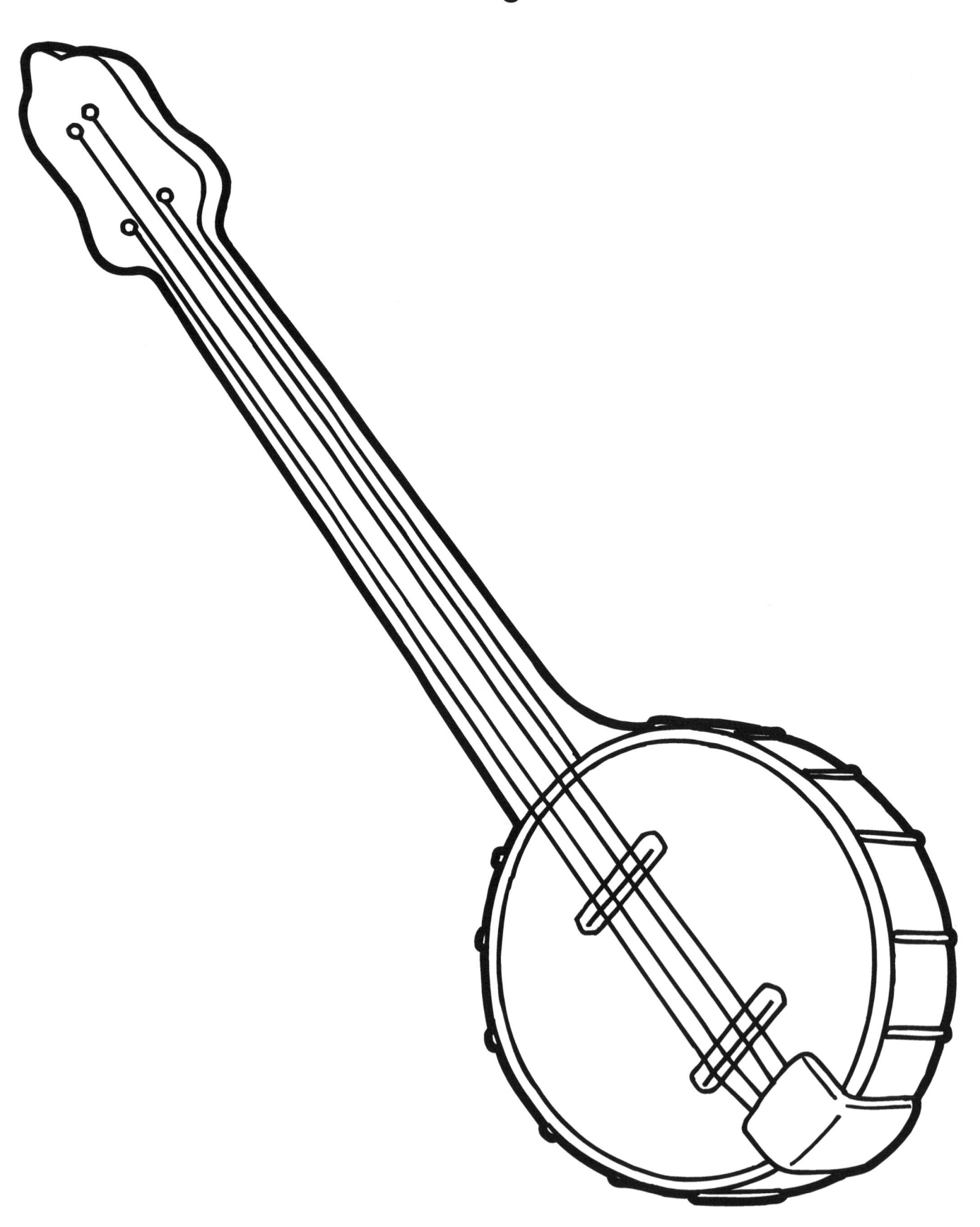

barbell

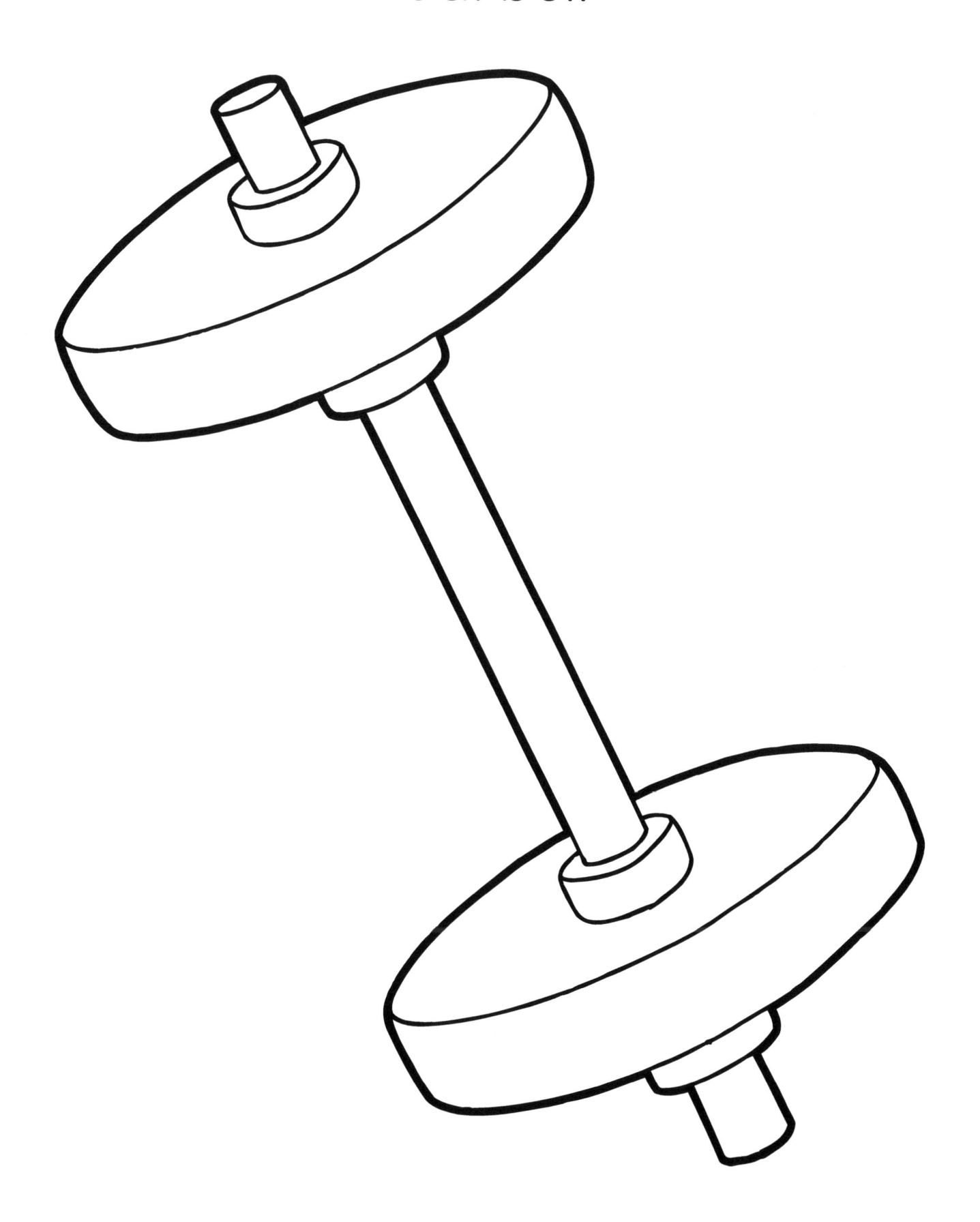

barbells

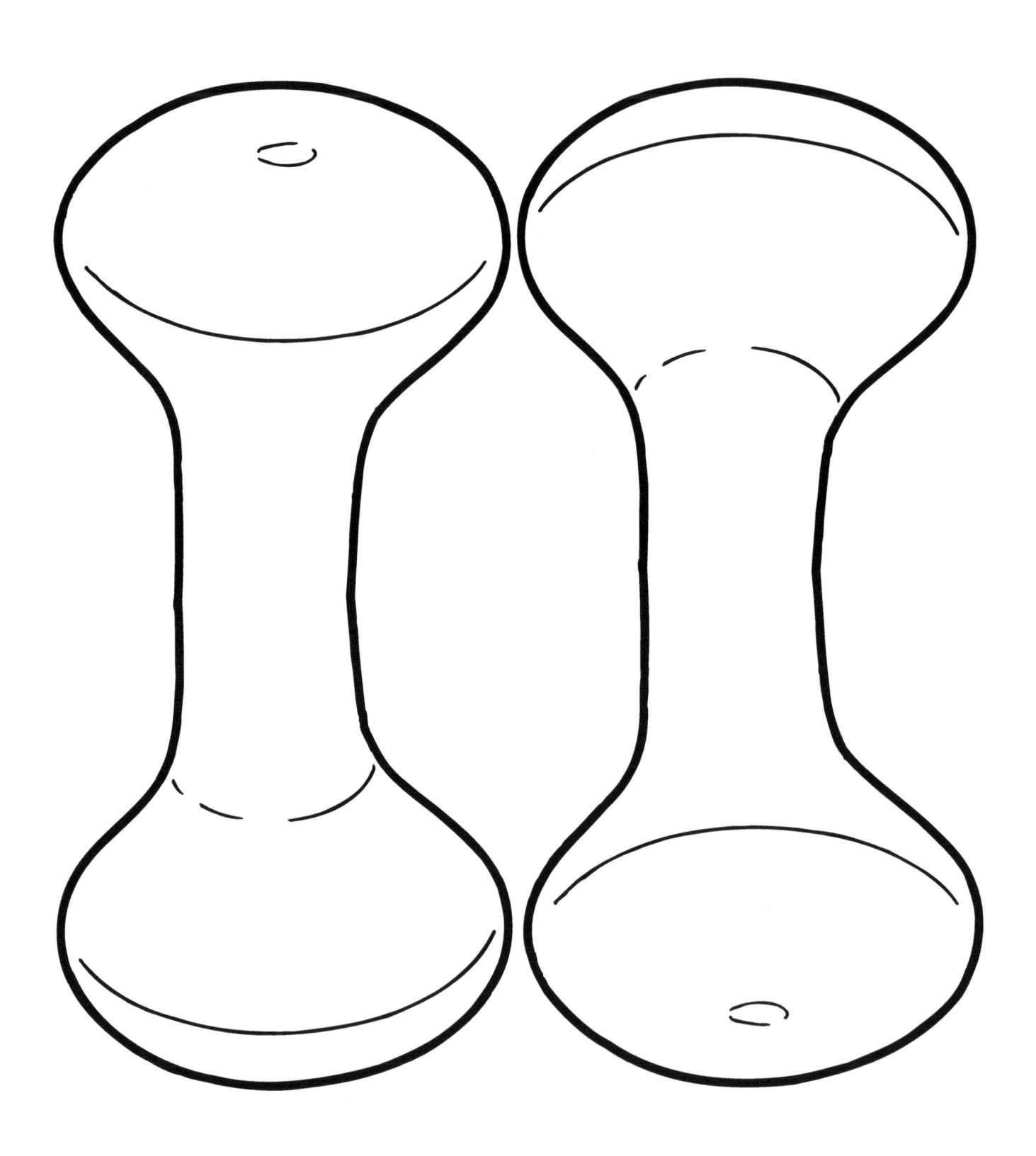

barn

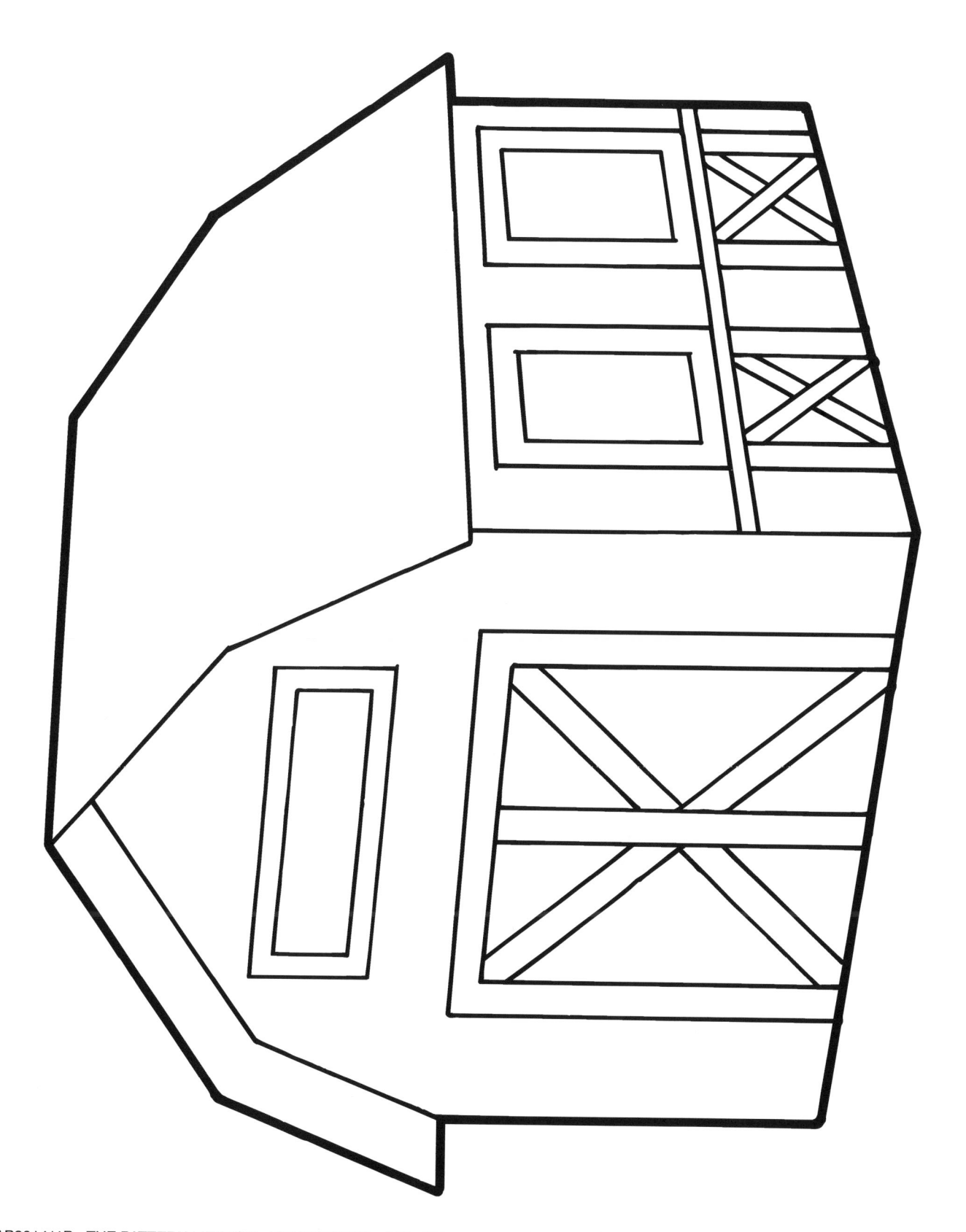

barrel

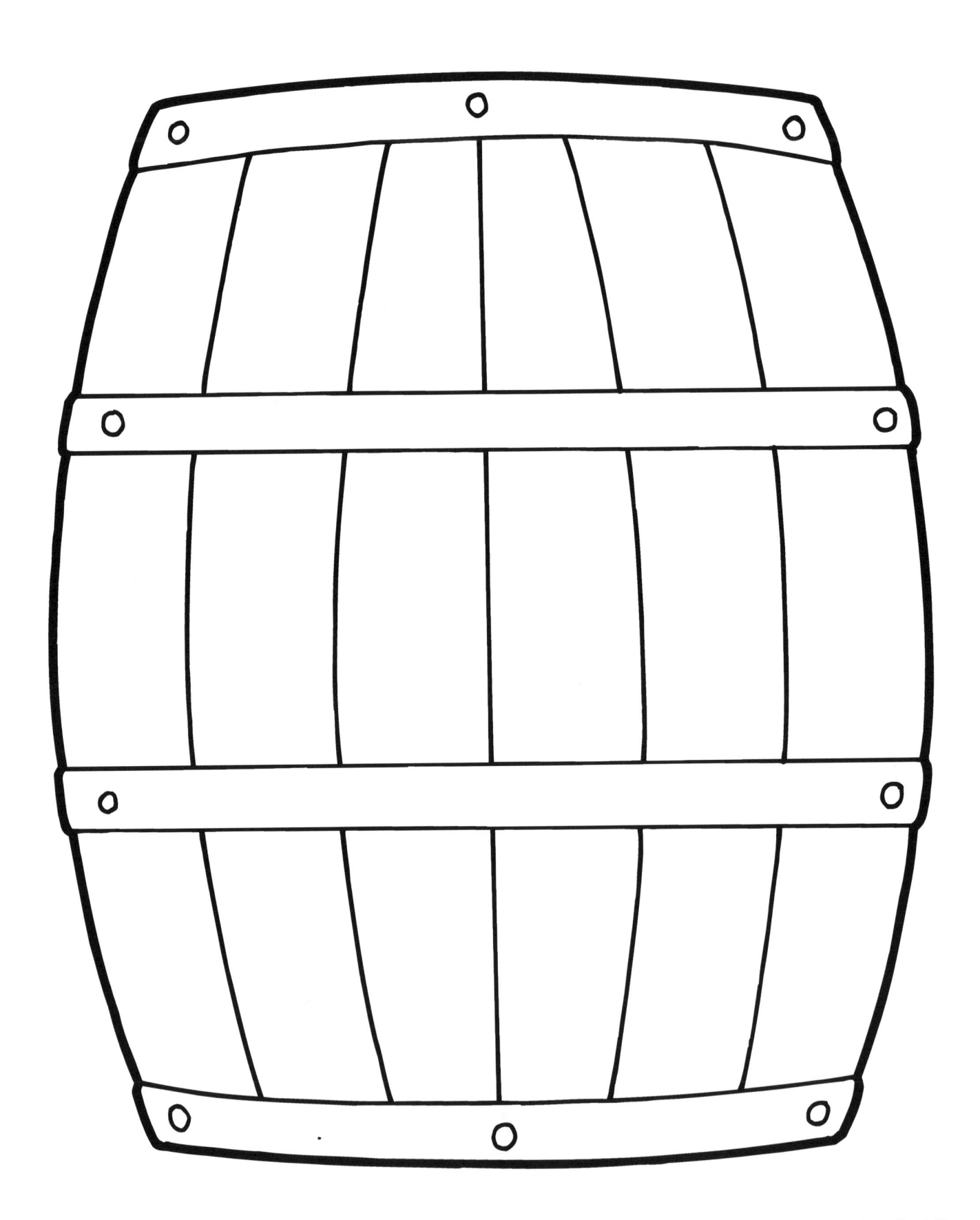

baseball

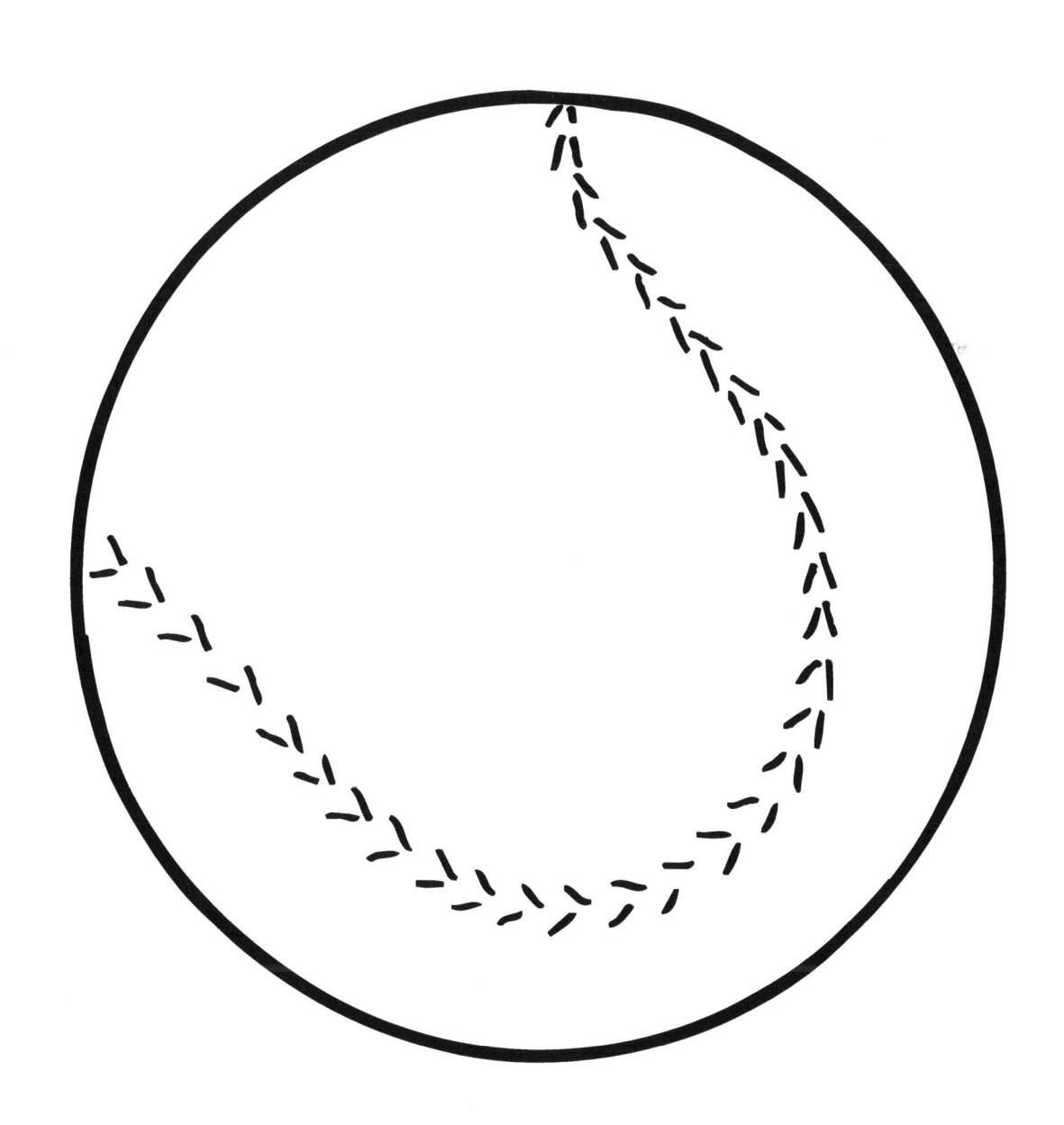

baseball and bat

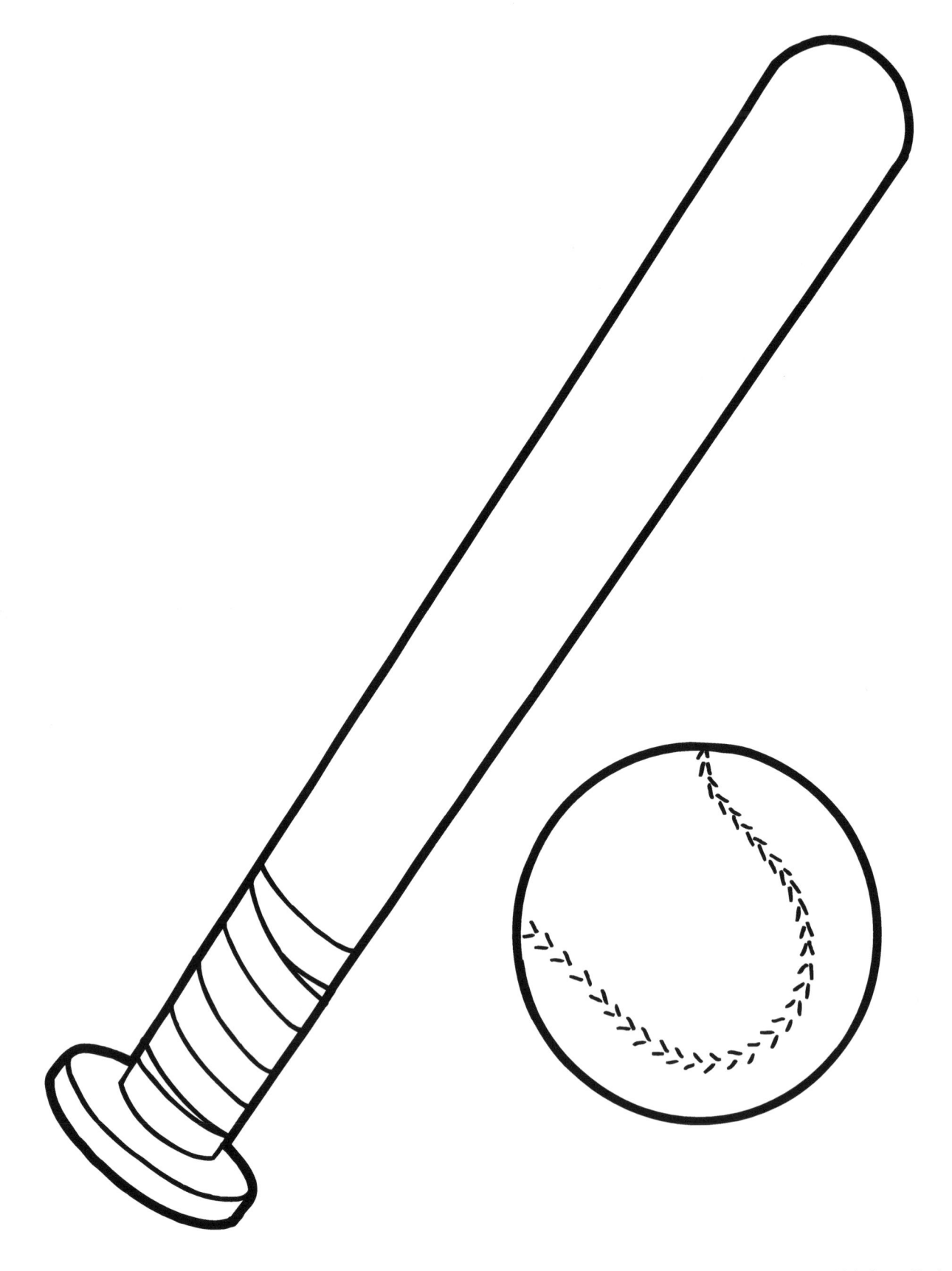

baseball glove

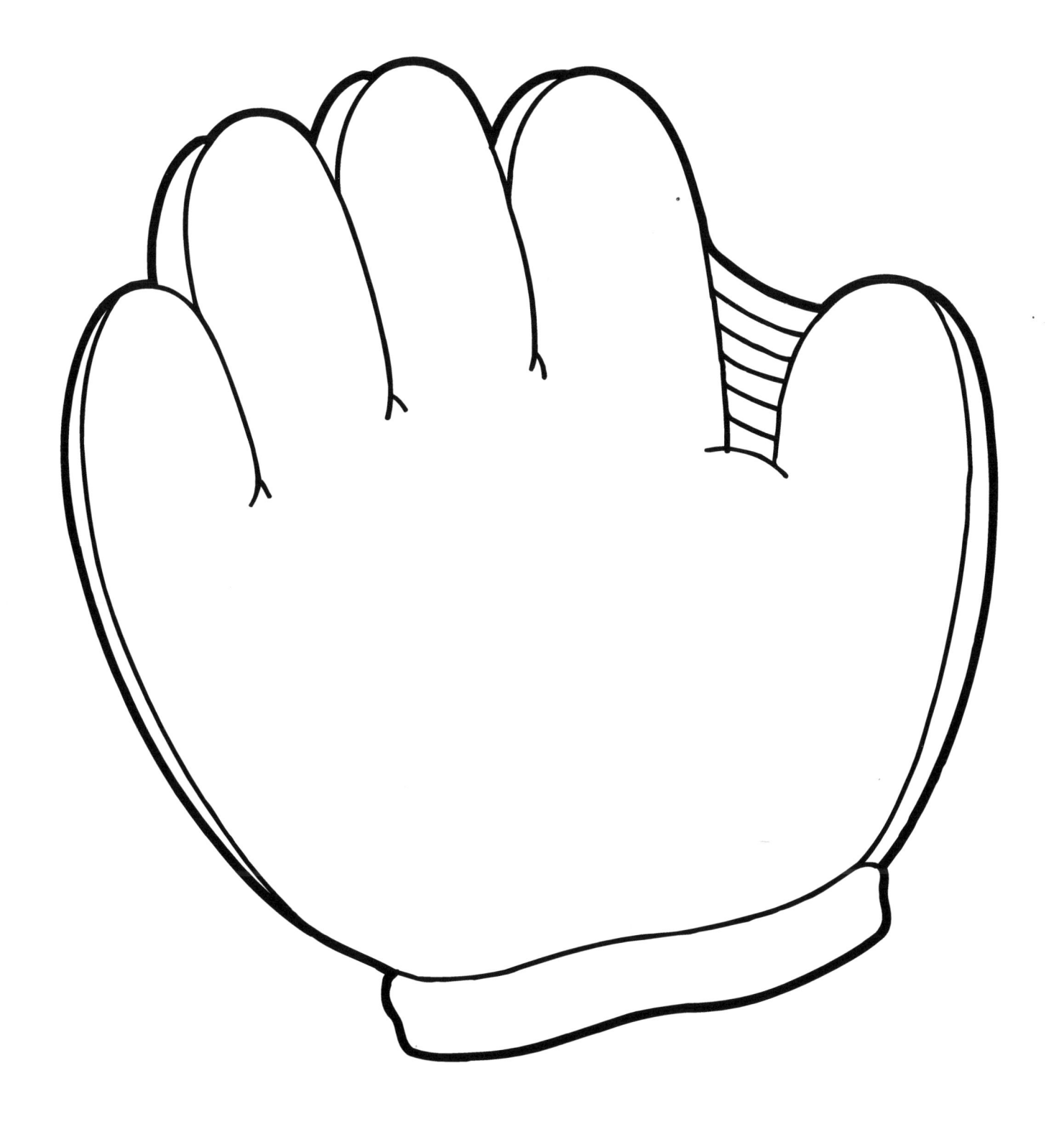

basket (basketball)

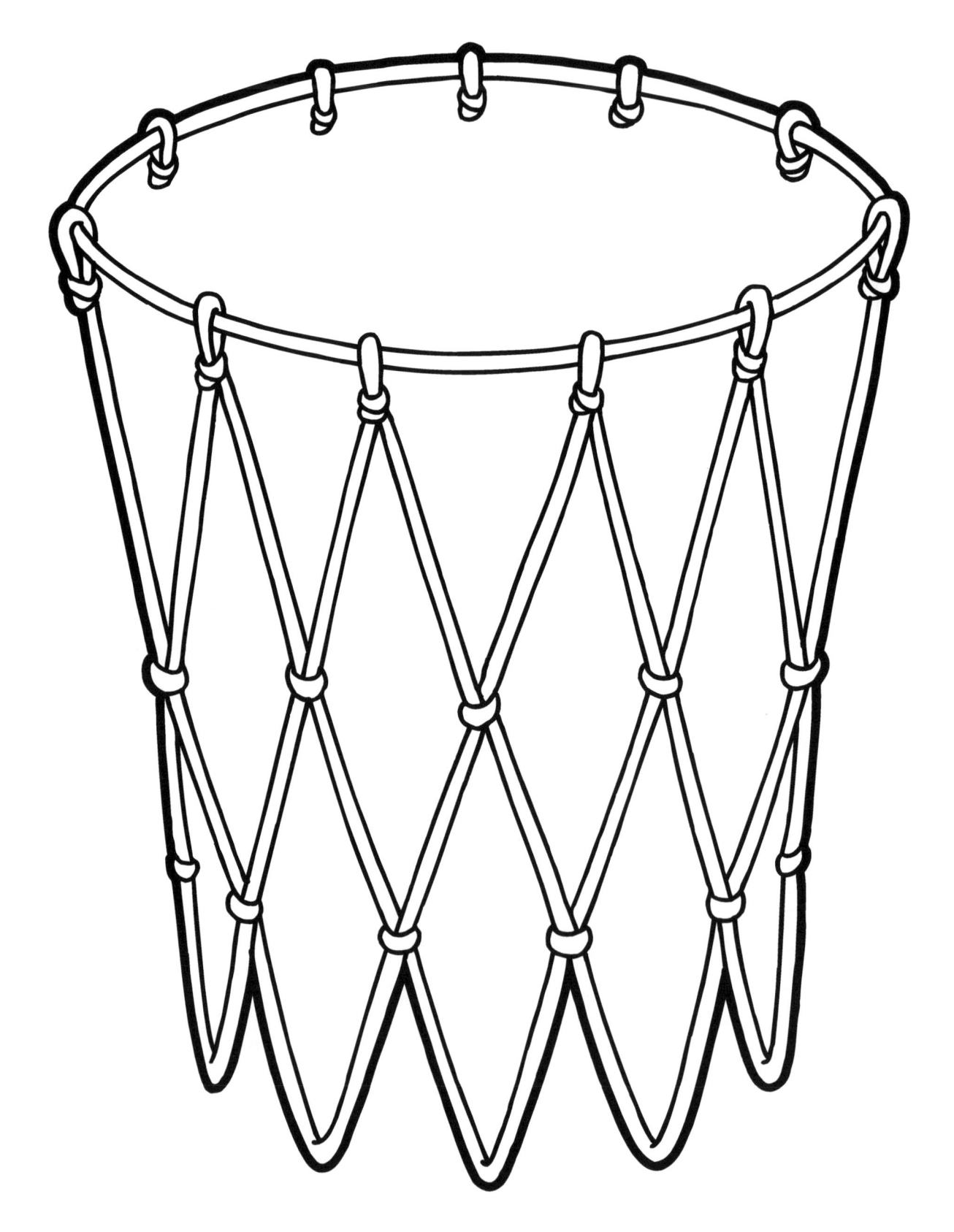

basket (berry)

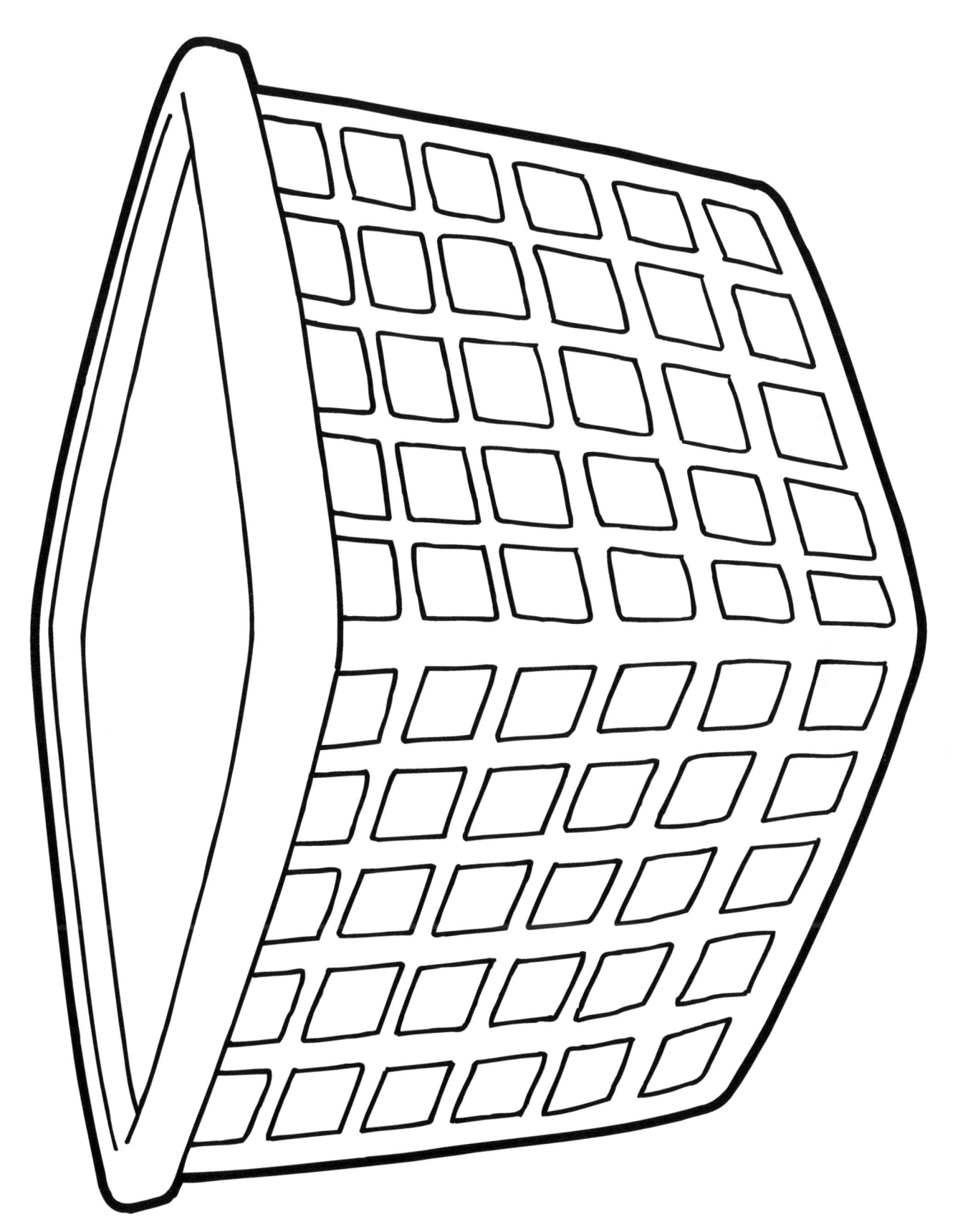

basket (bushel)

basket (hand)

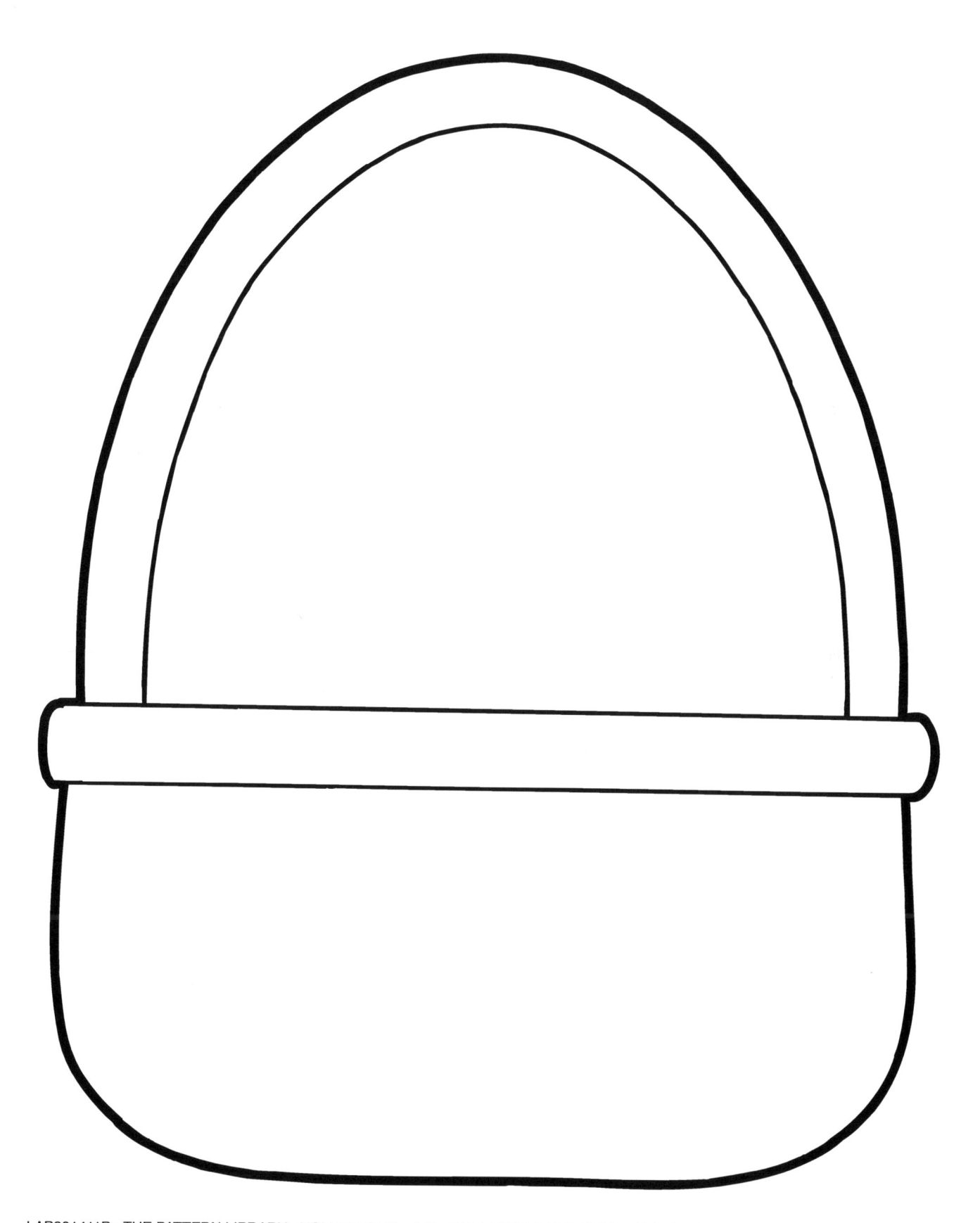

basket (outline)

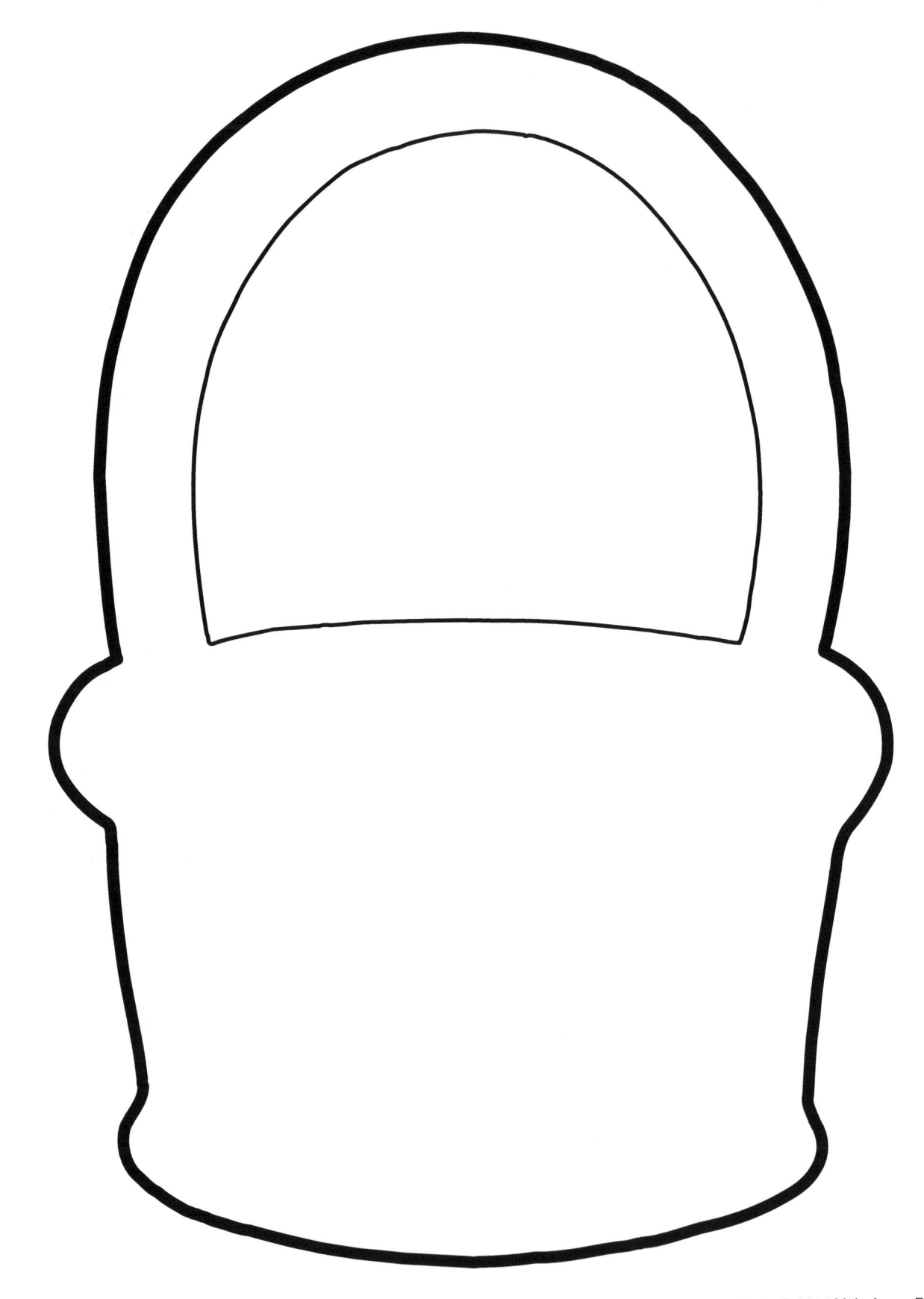

basket (peck)

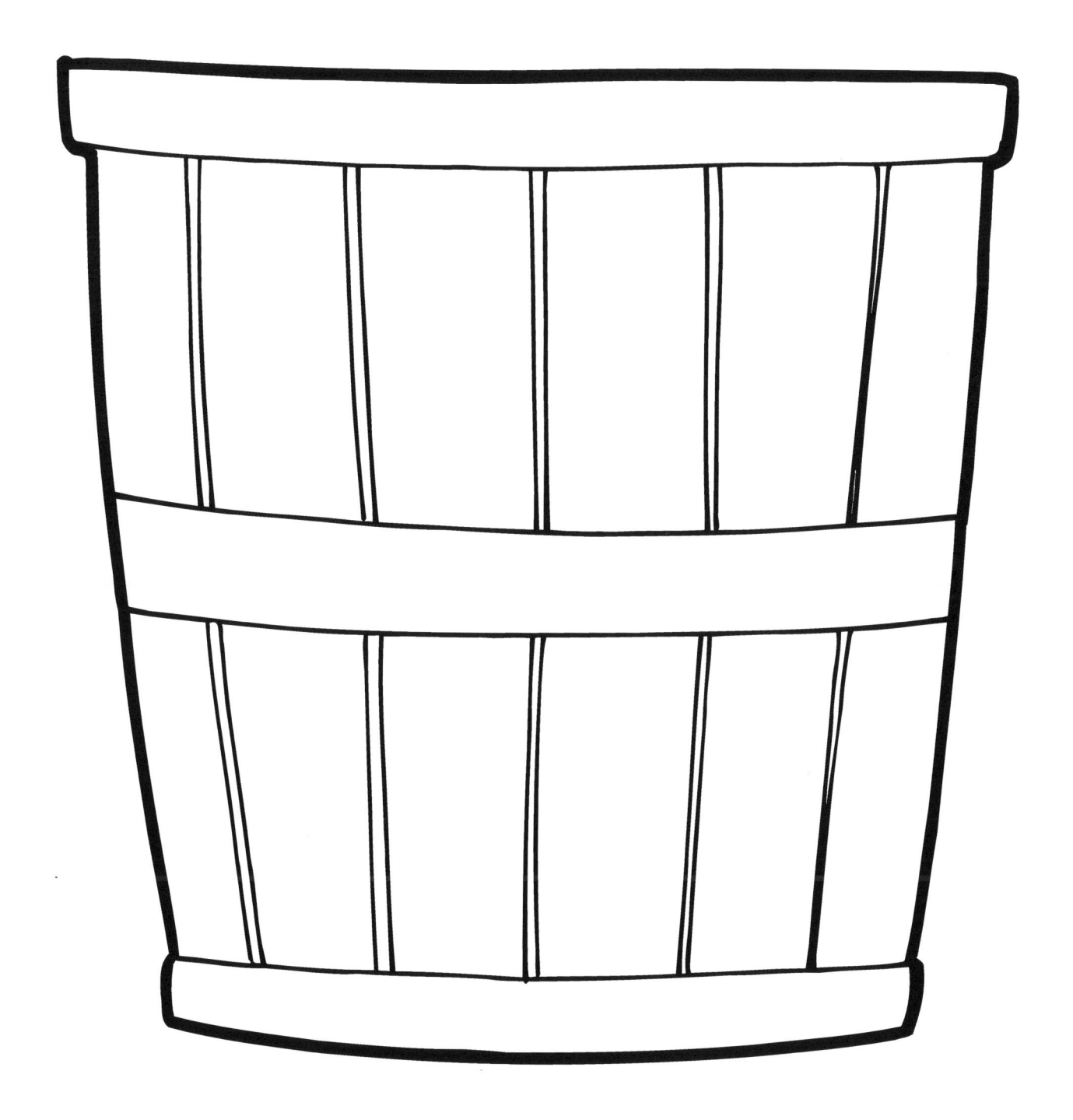

basketball

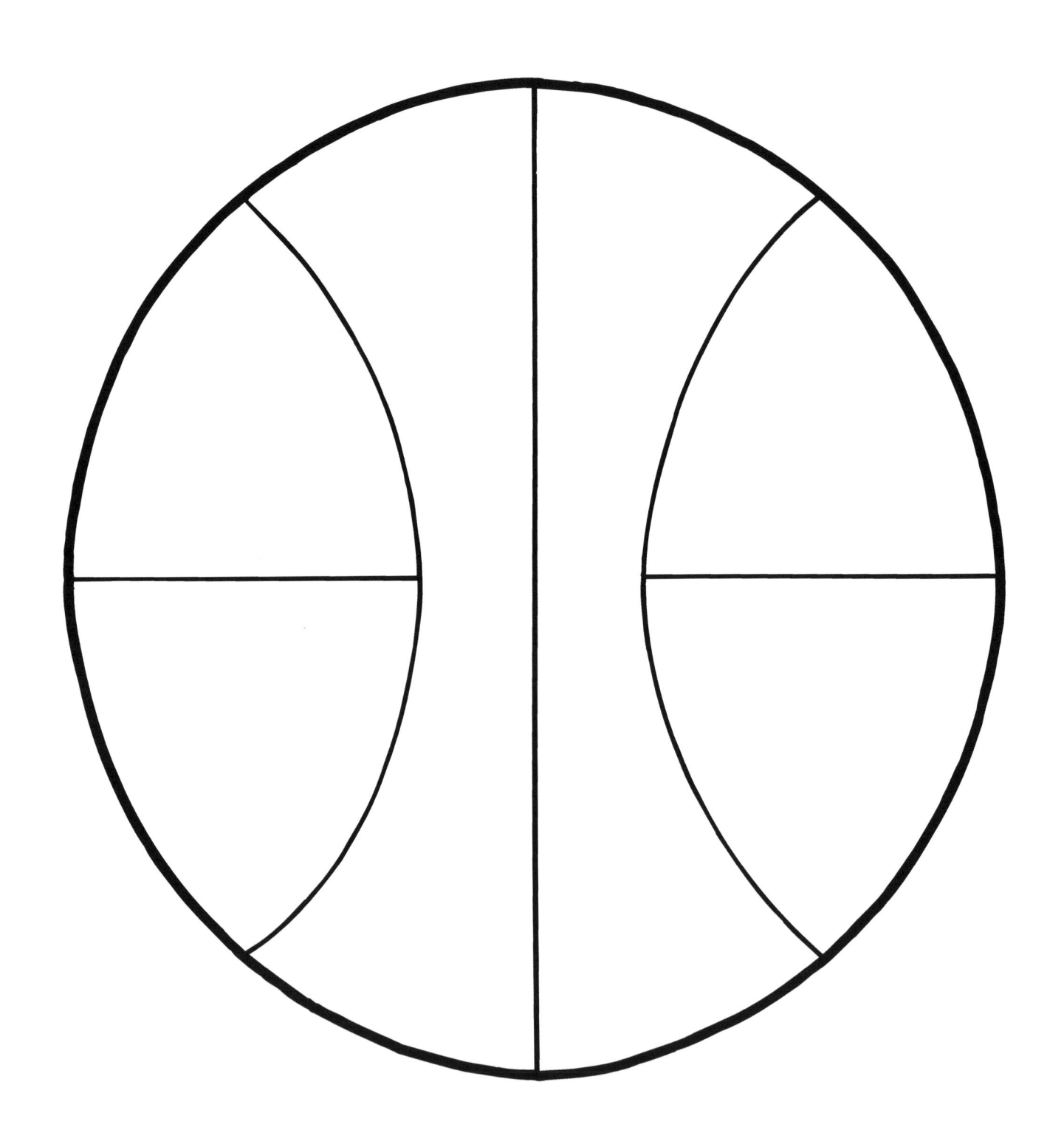

bass (instrument)

bat (animated)

bat (stylized)

bathrobe

bathtub

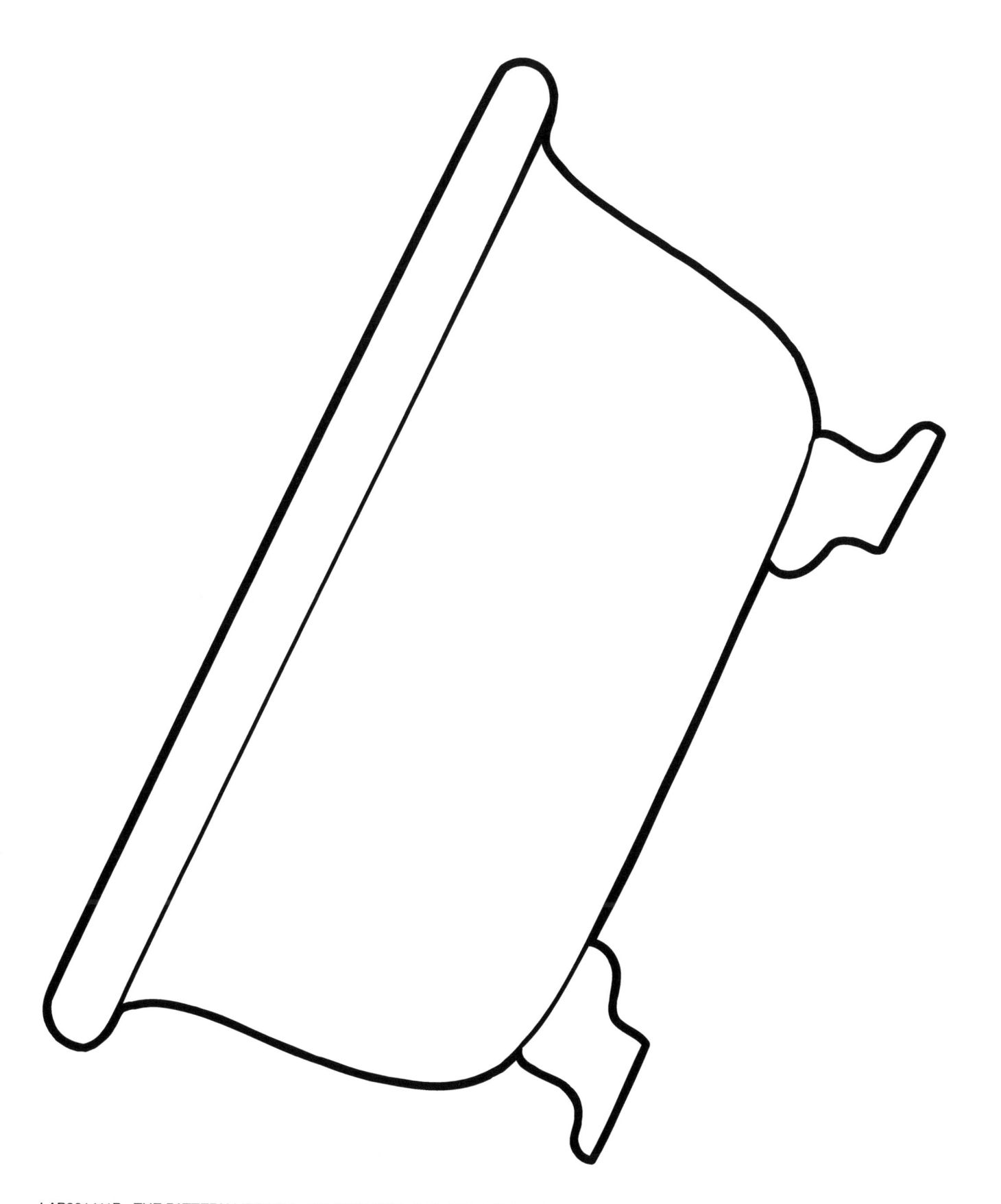

bean

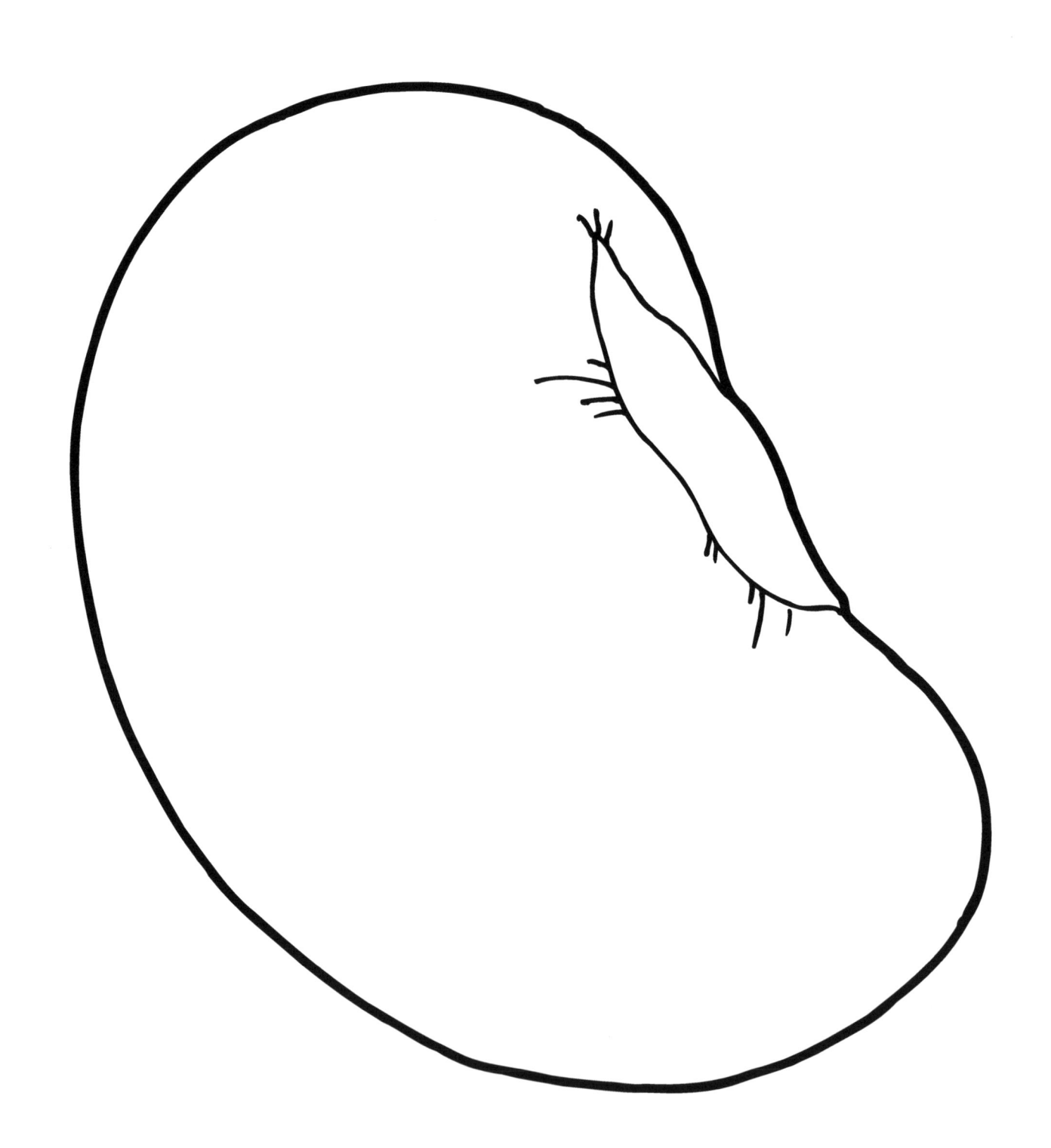

beans

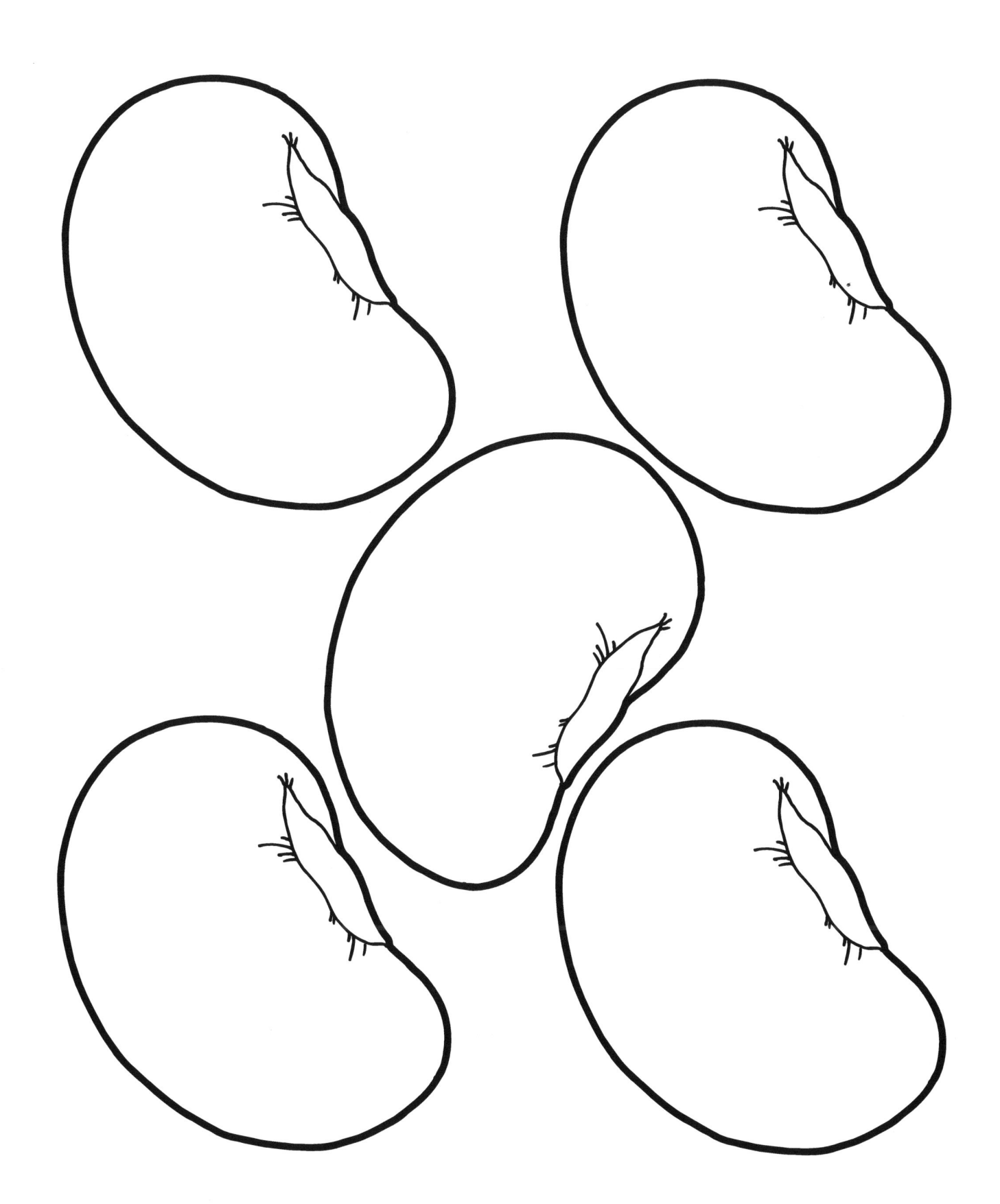

bear (black)

bear (polar)

bear (sloth)

bear (standing)

bear (stuffed, outline)

bear (teddy, with overalls)

bear (with top hat)

beard (pointed)

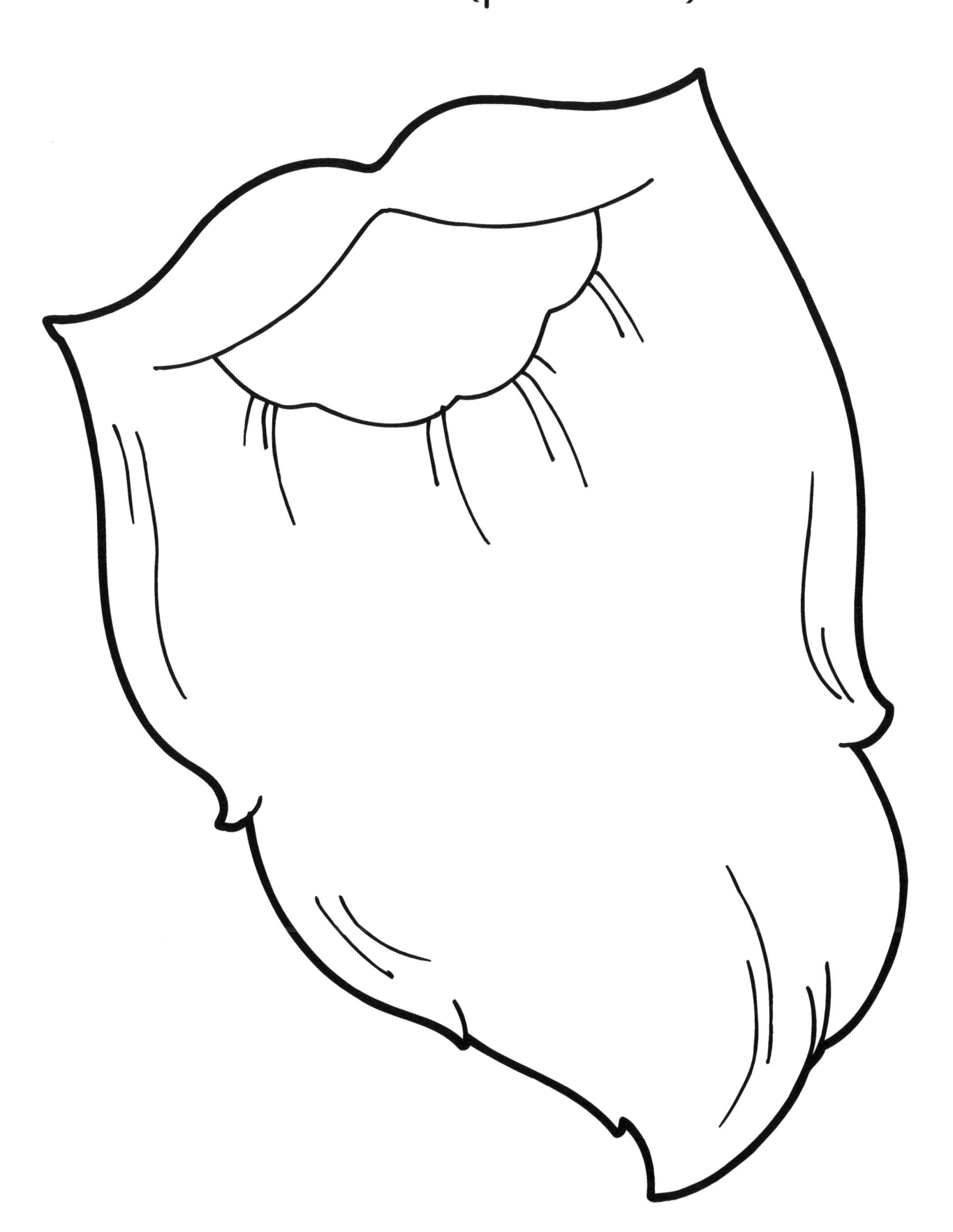

beard (rounded)

beaver (with bowtie)

beaver (walking)

beaver (upright)

beaver (stylized)

bed (frontal view)

bed (side view)

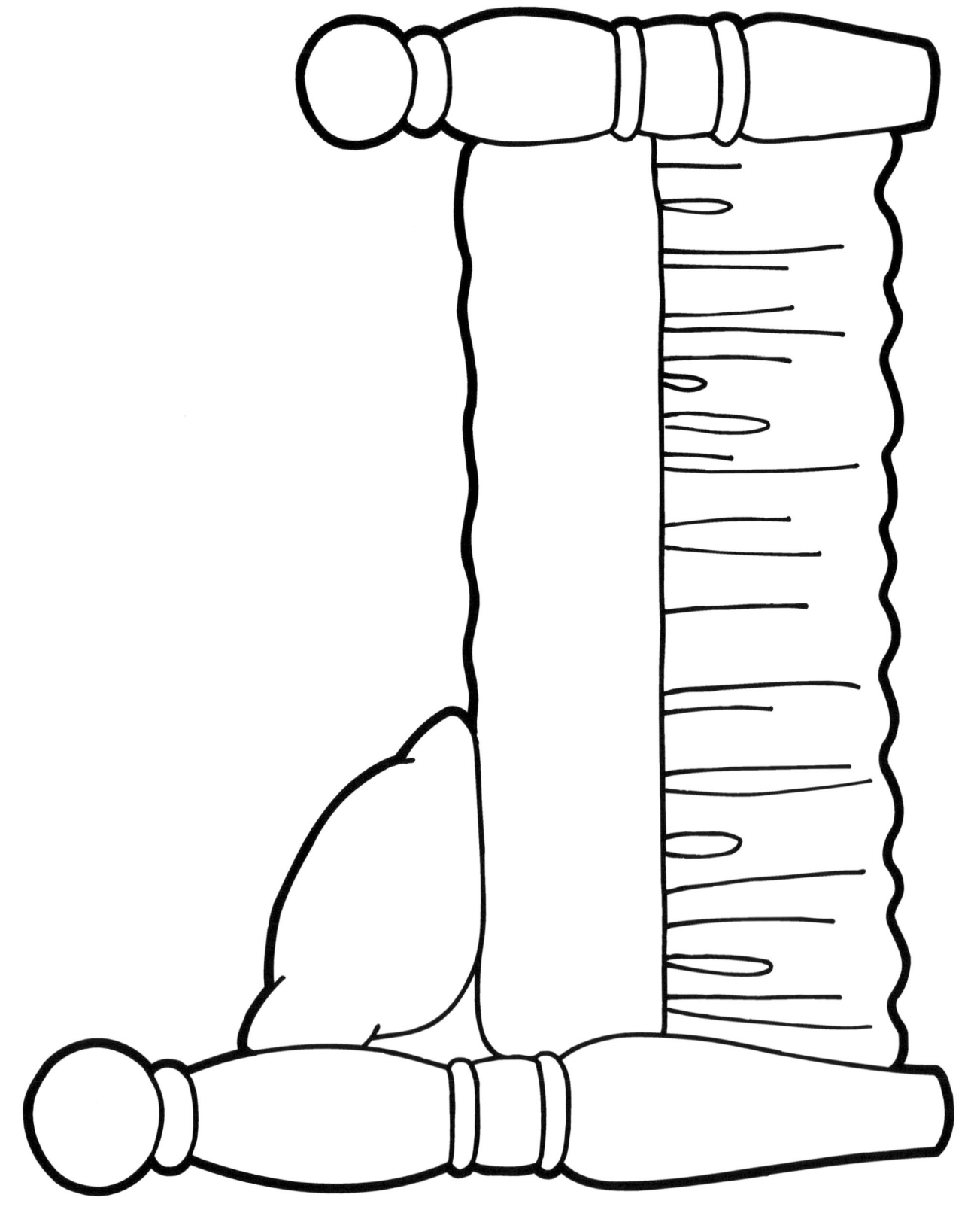

bee (animated)

bee hive

bees (animated)

beetle

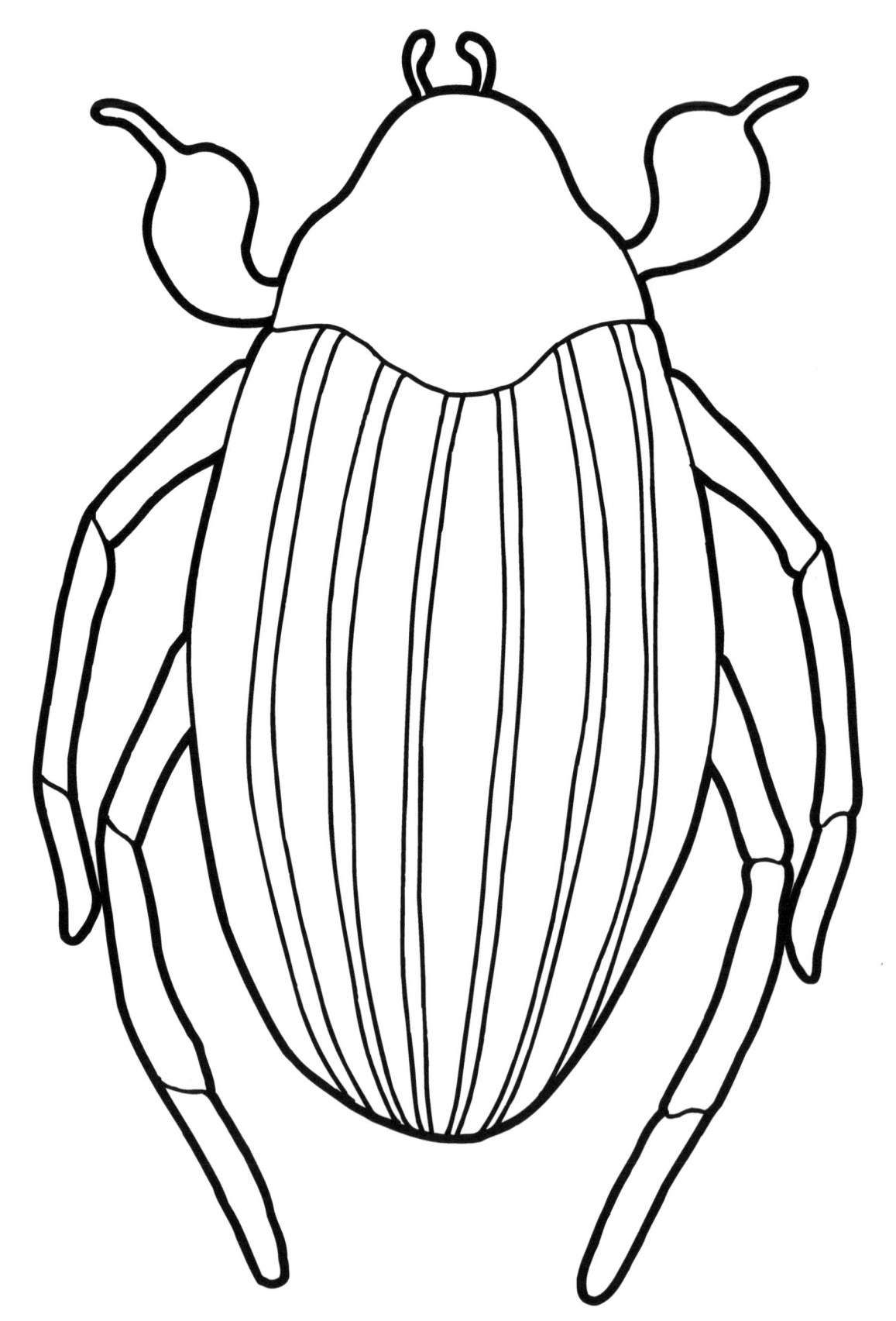

bell (jingle)

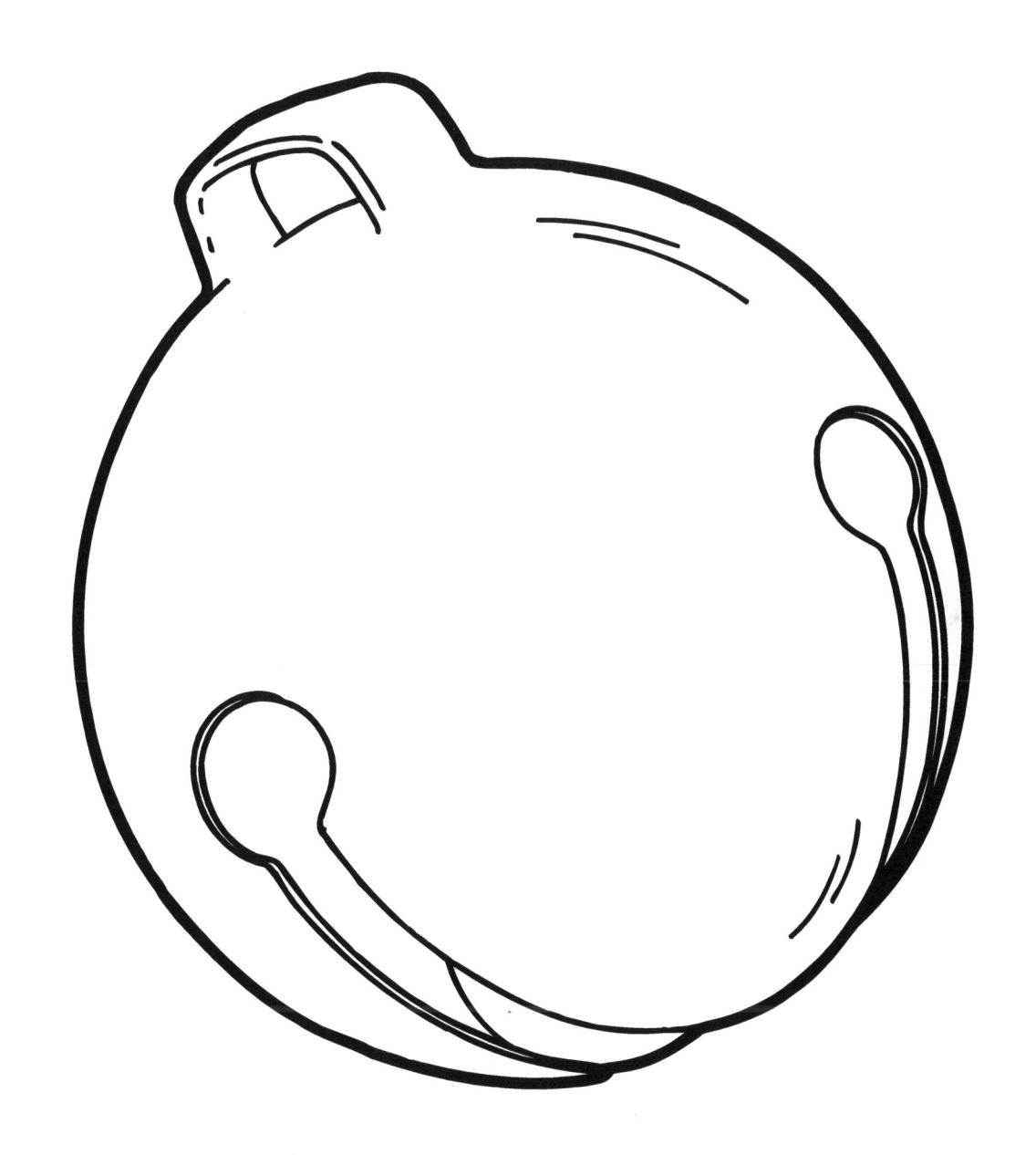

bell (large)

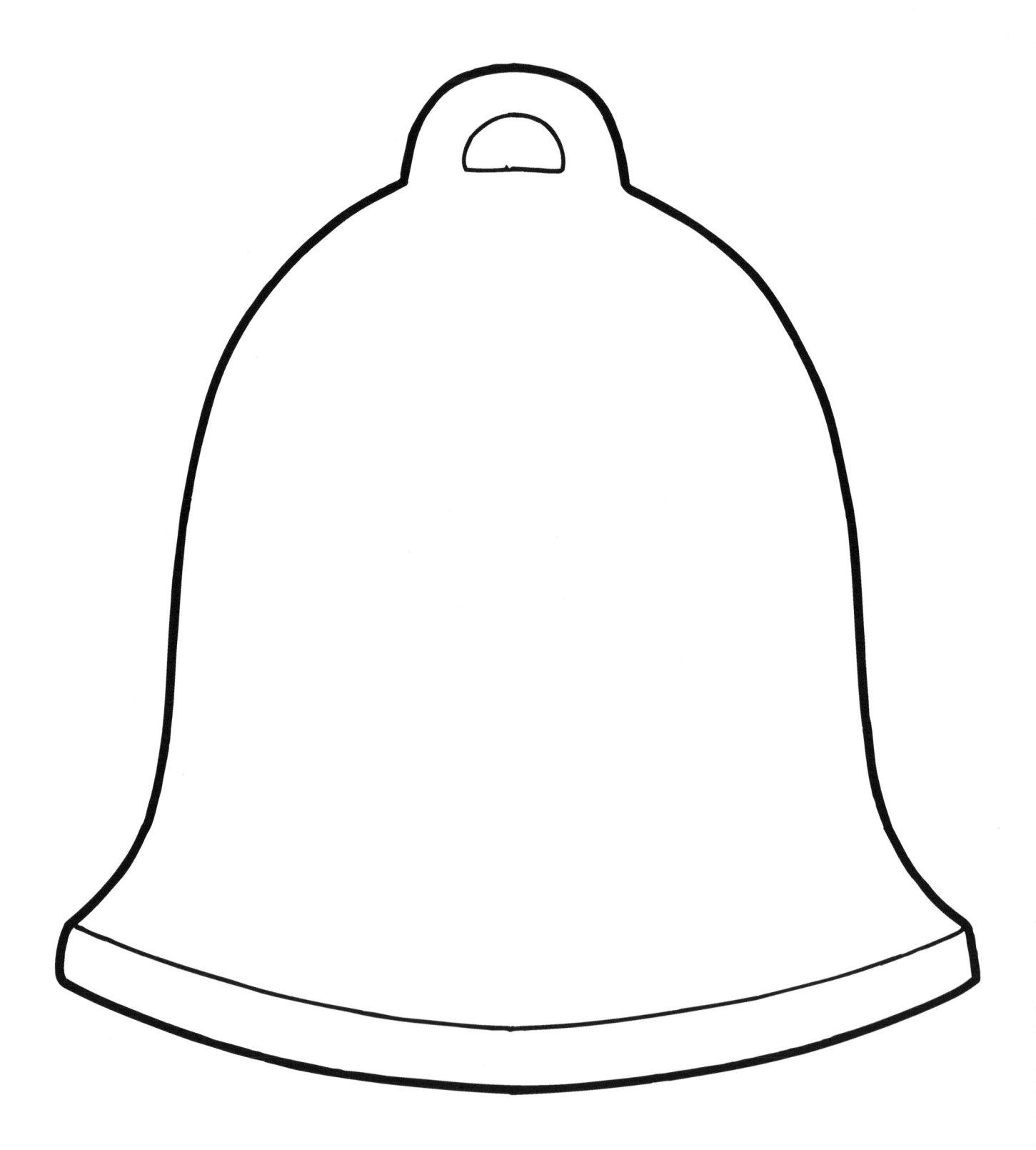

bell (hand)

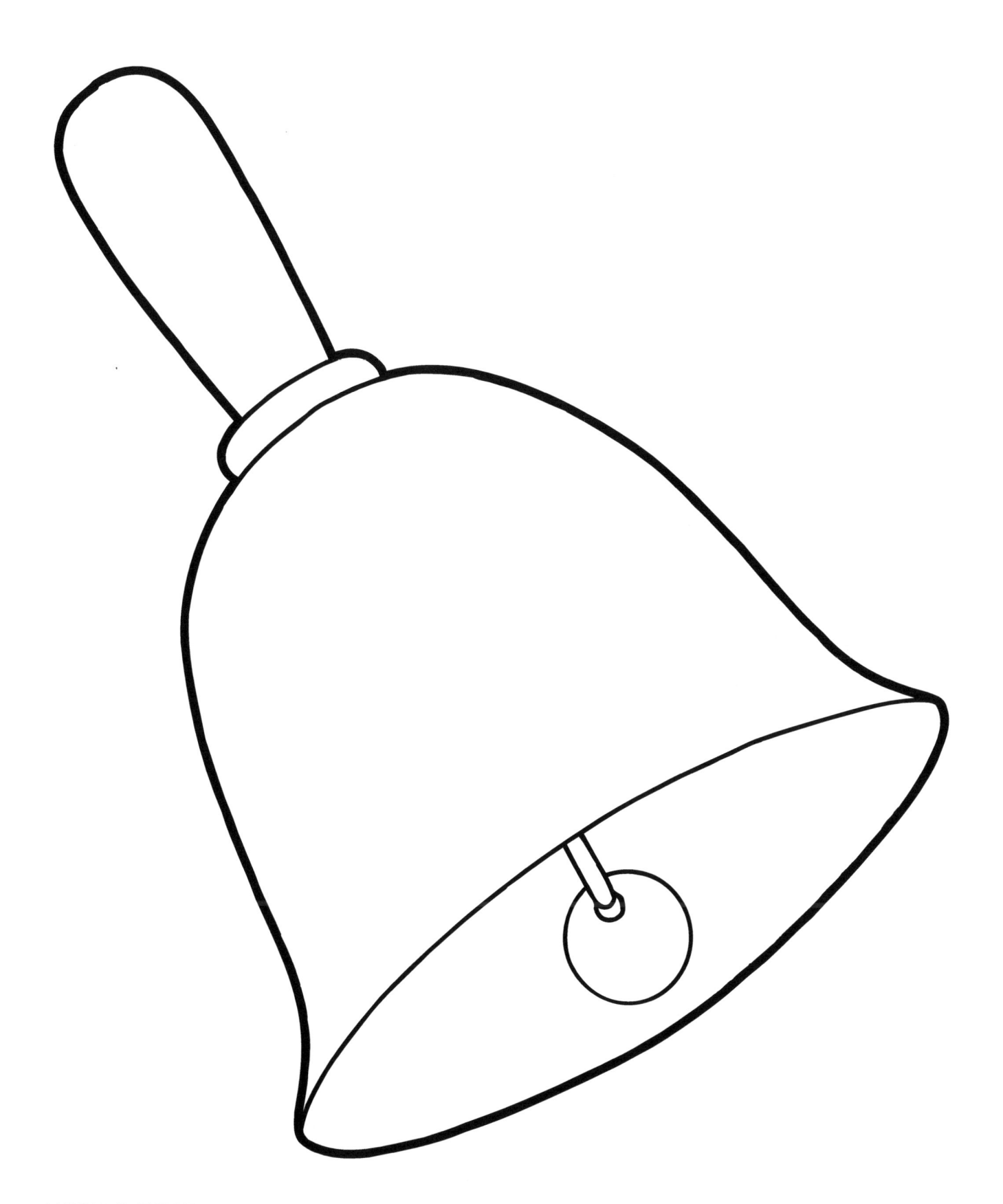

bib

bicycle

billiard balls

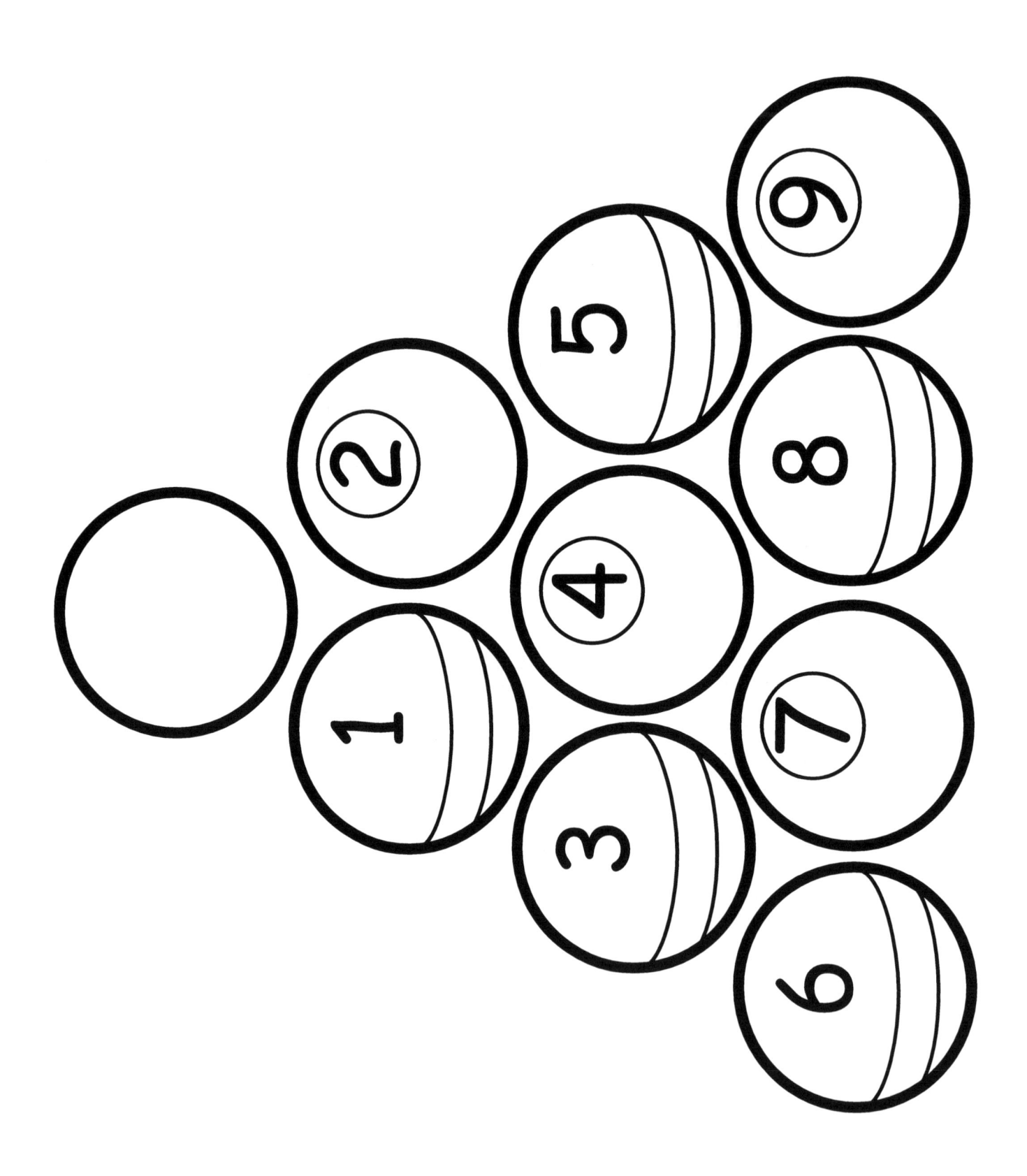

birdbath

birdhouse

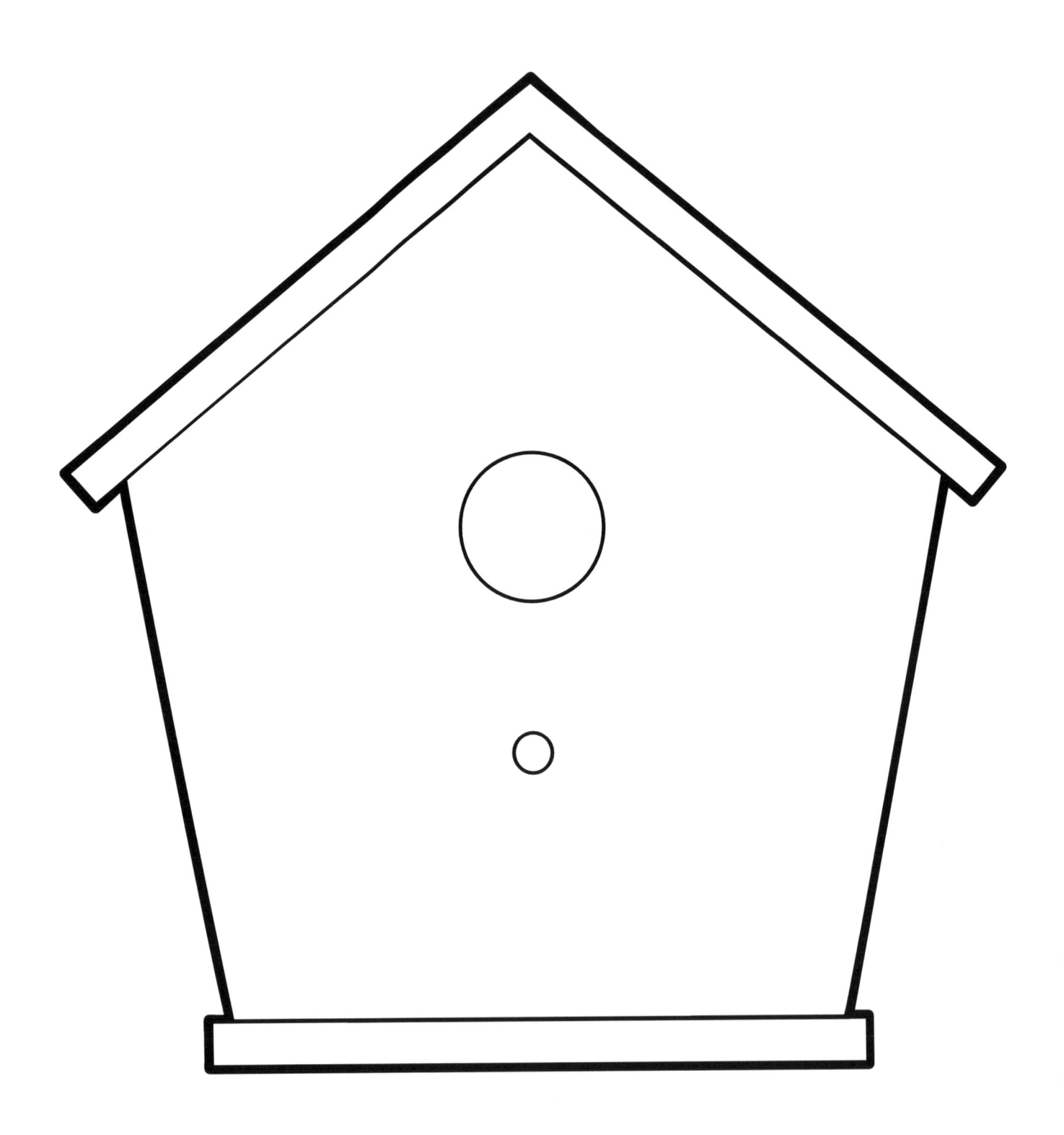

bird of paradise

bird (in flight)

birds

bird (stylized)

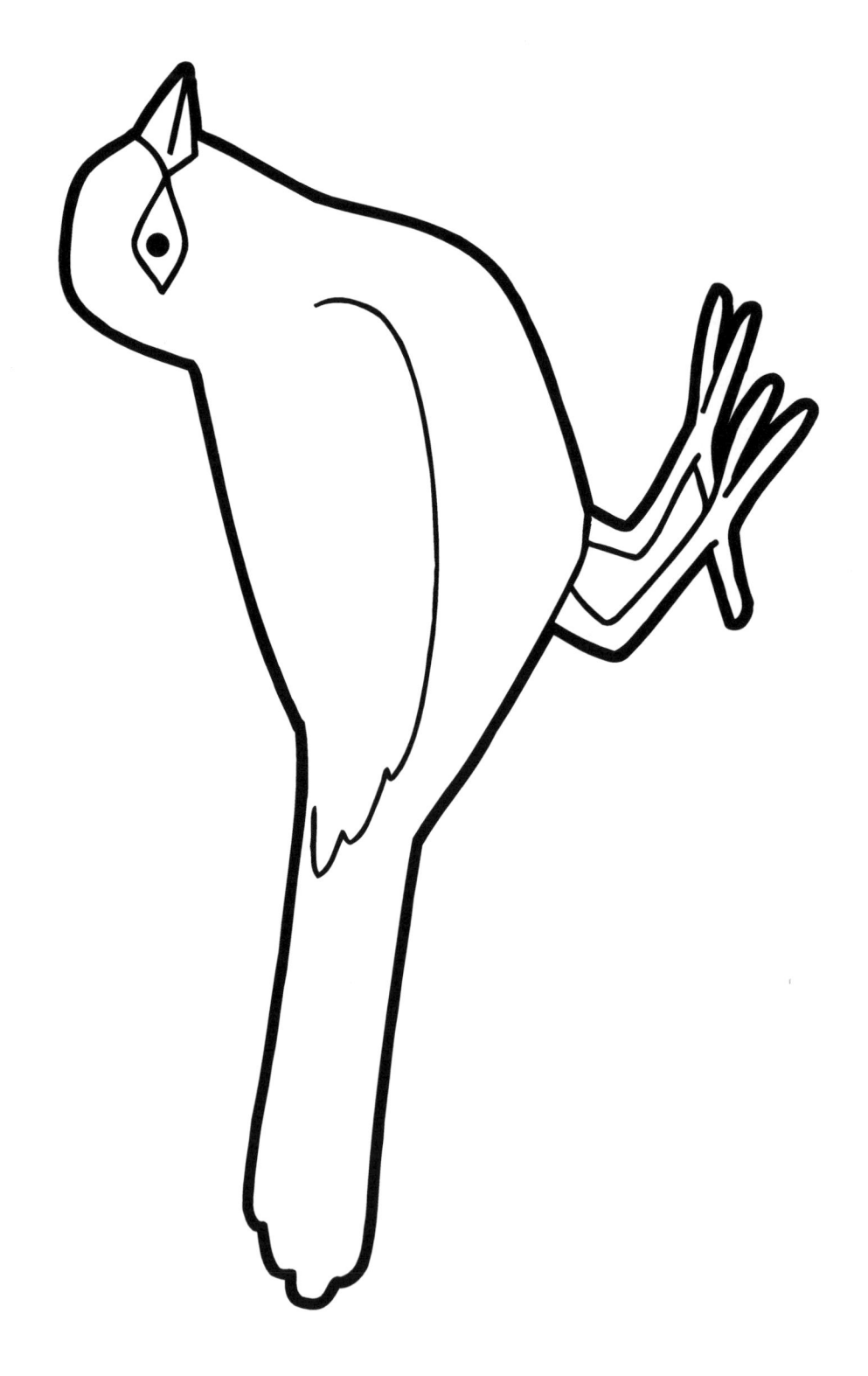

black (crayon)

Black

blanket

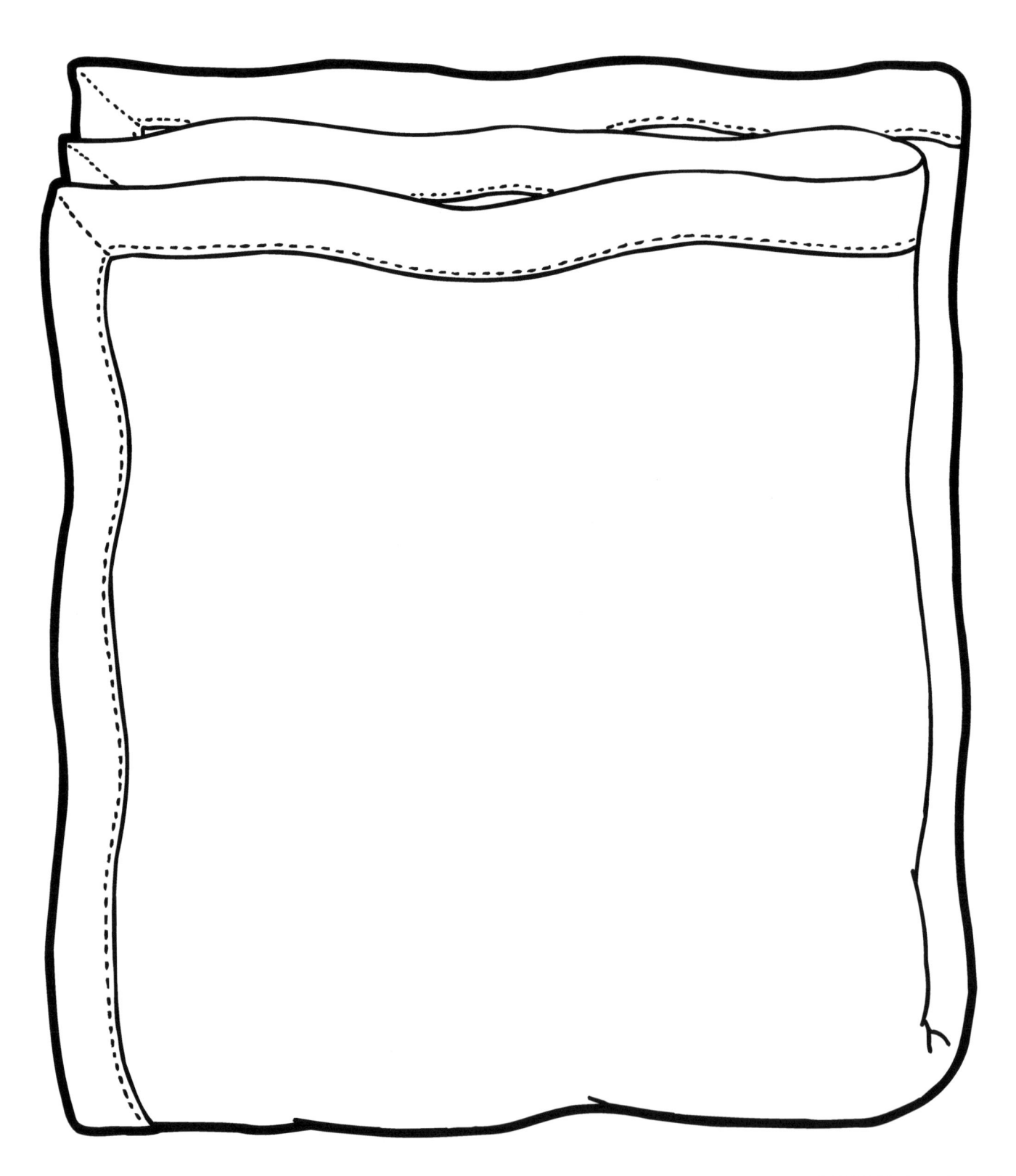

blender

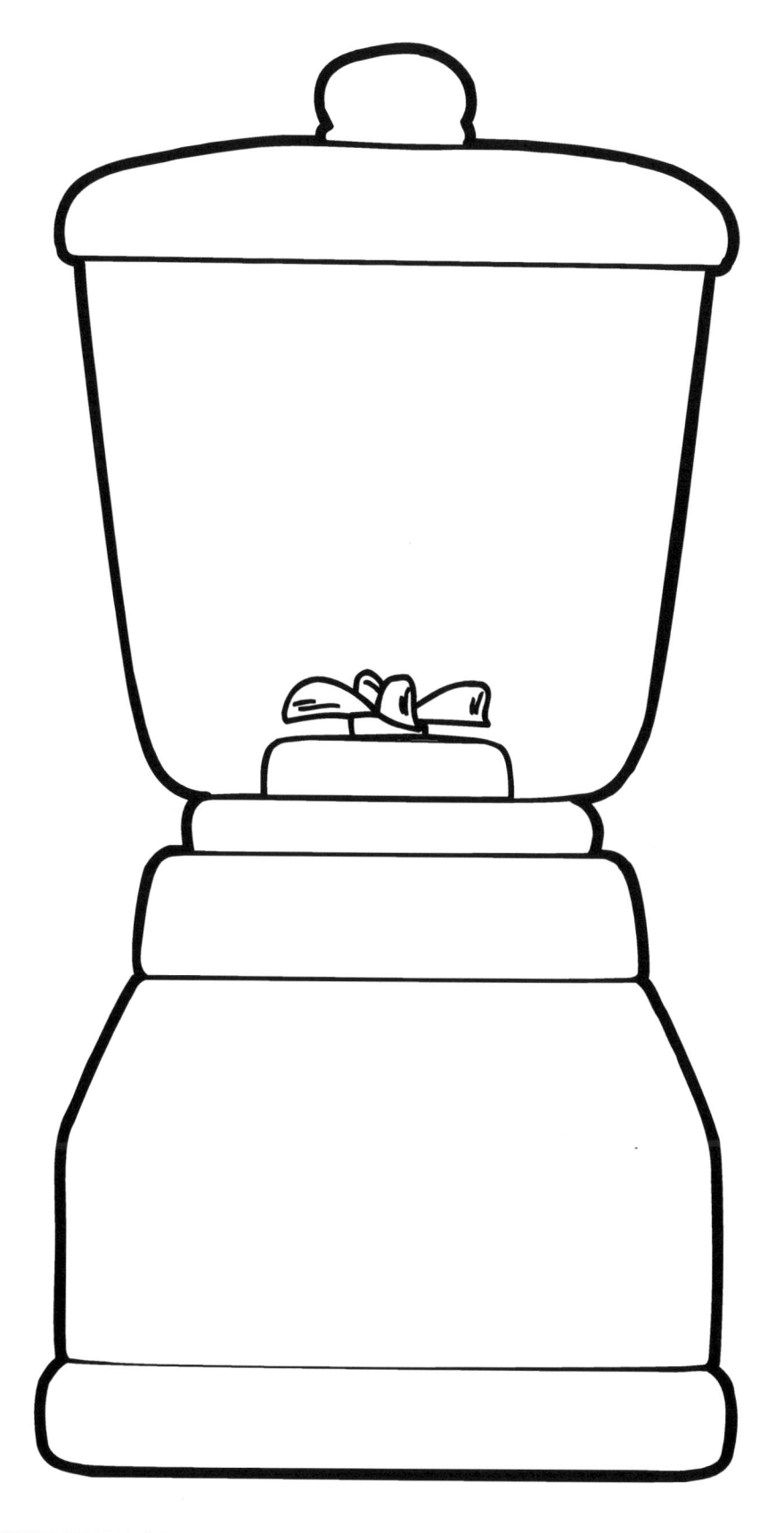

blimp

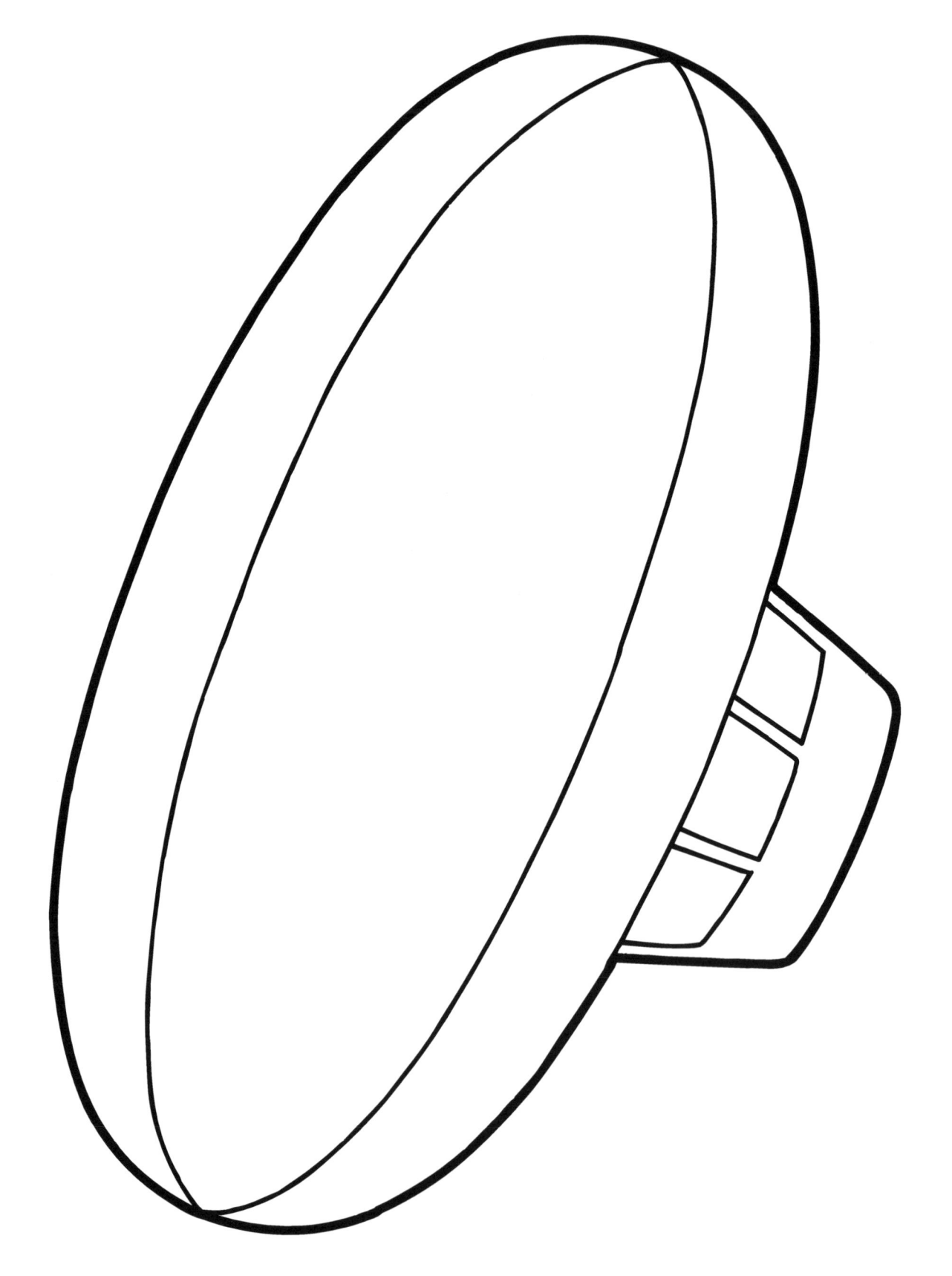

block

blouse

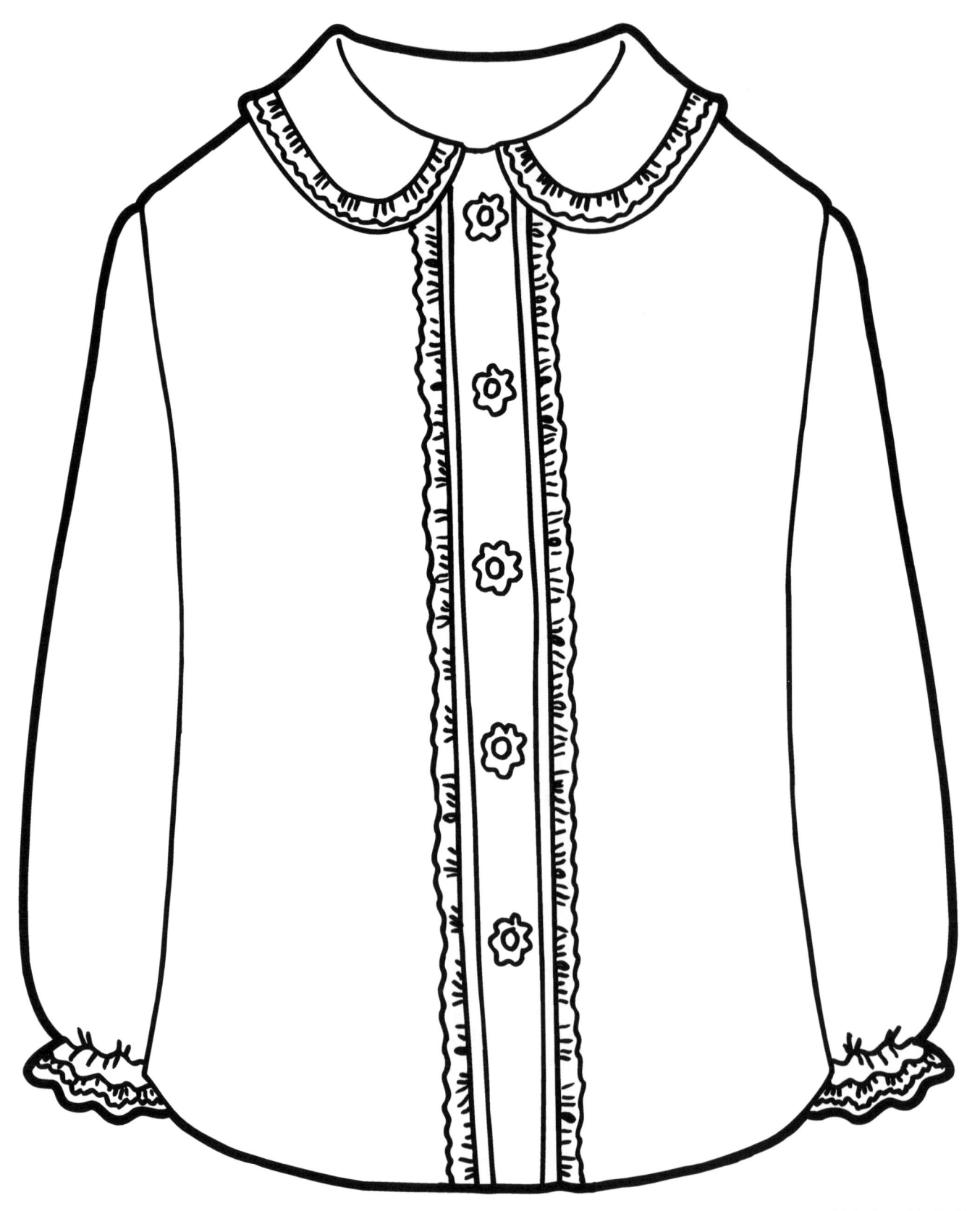

blue (crayon)

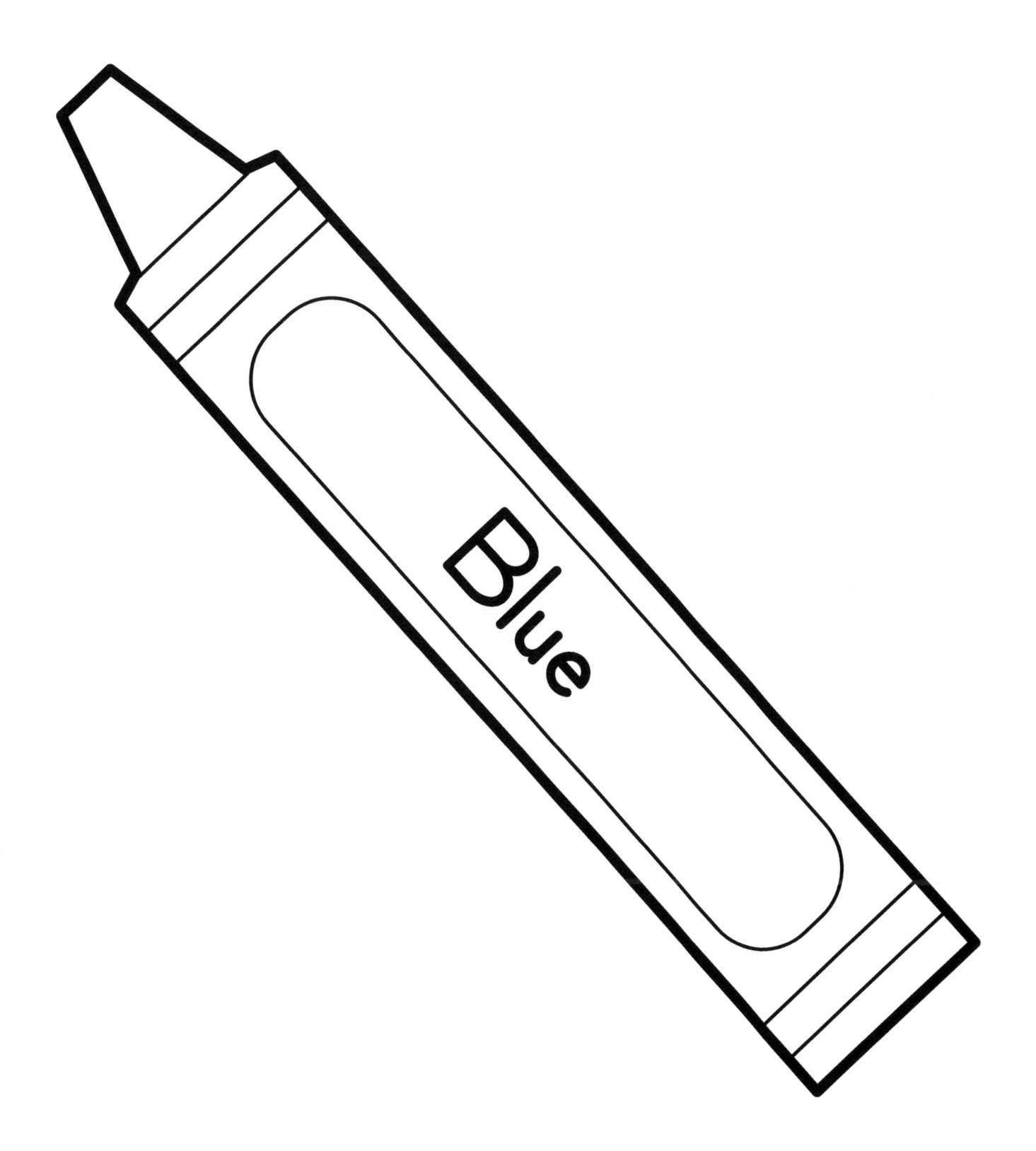

Blue

blueberries

boar

boat

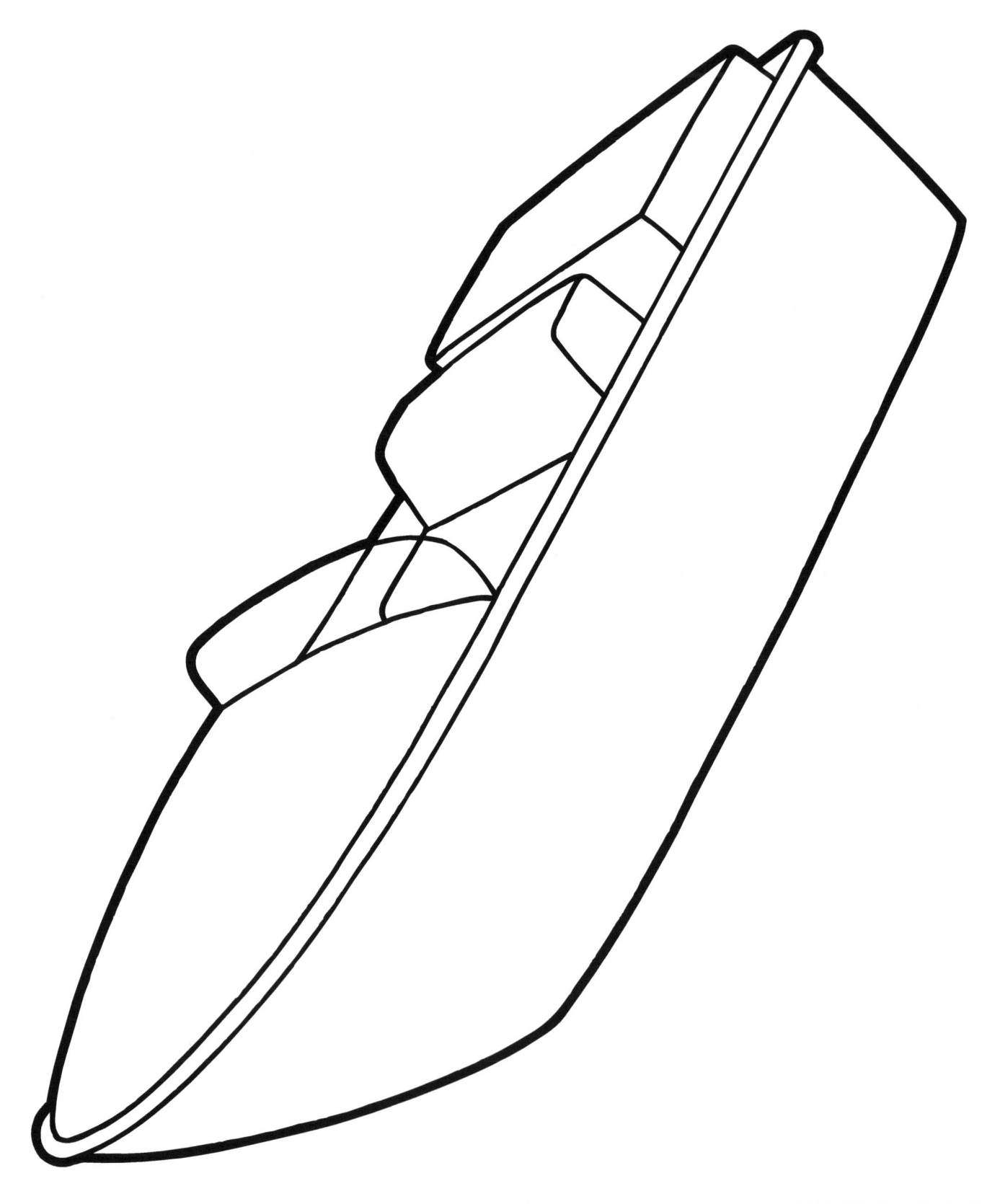

bone

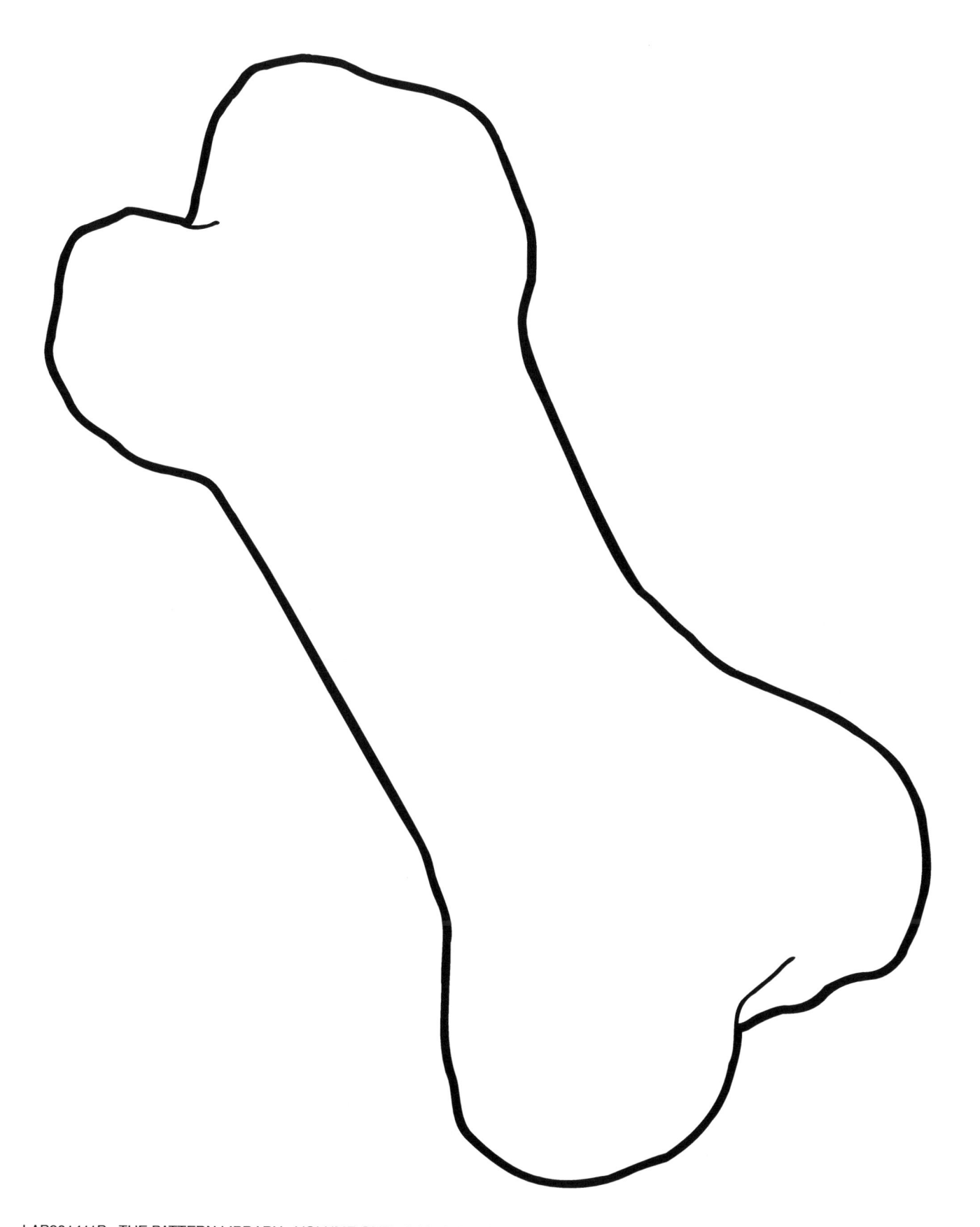

bongos

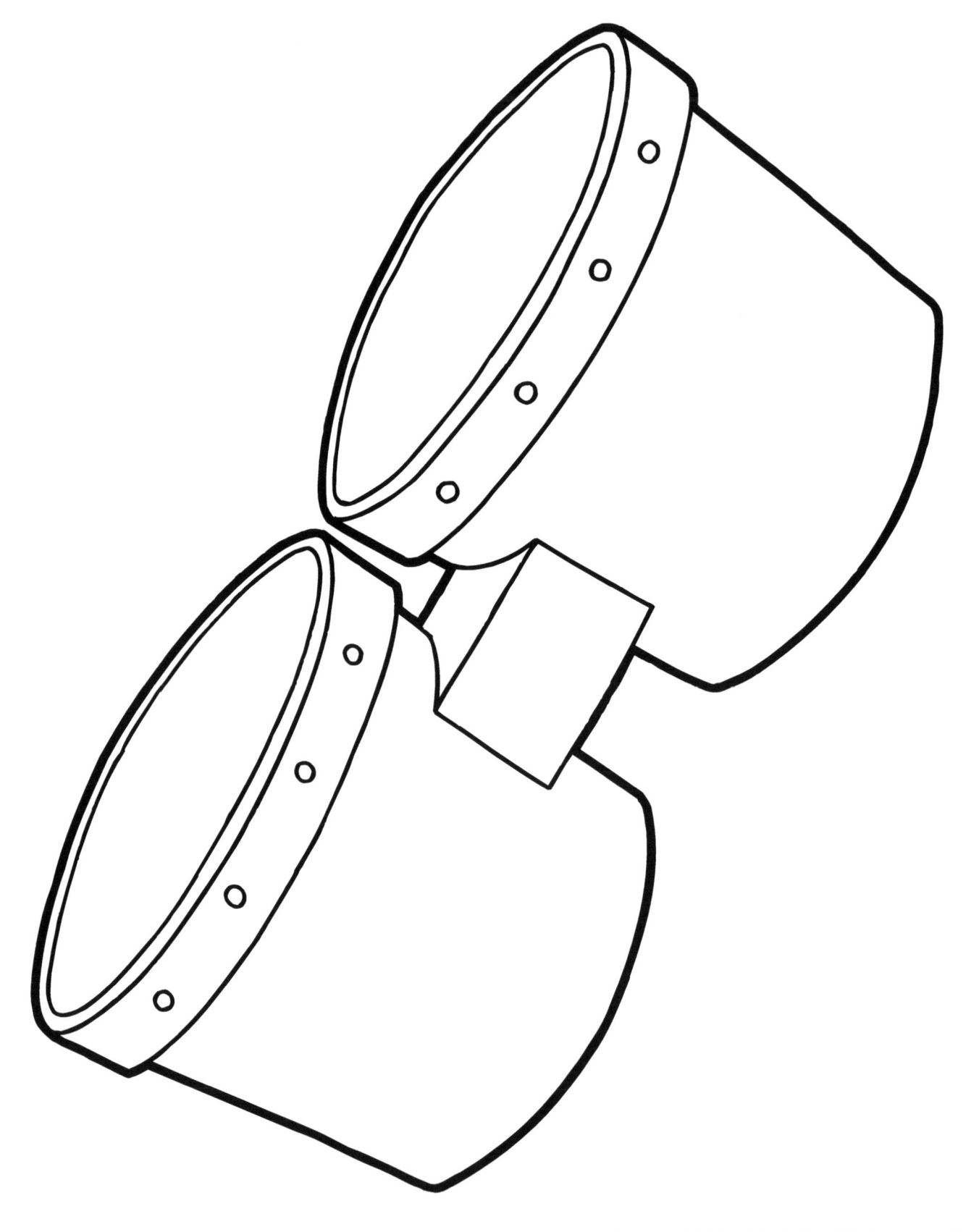

bonnet

book (closed)

book (open)

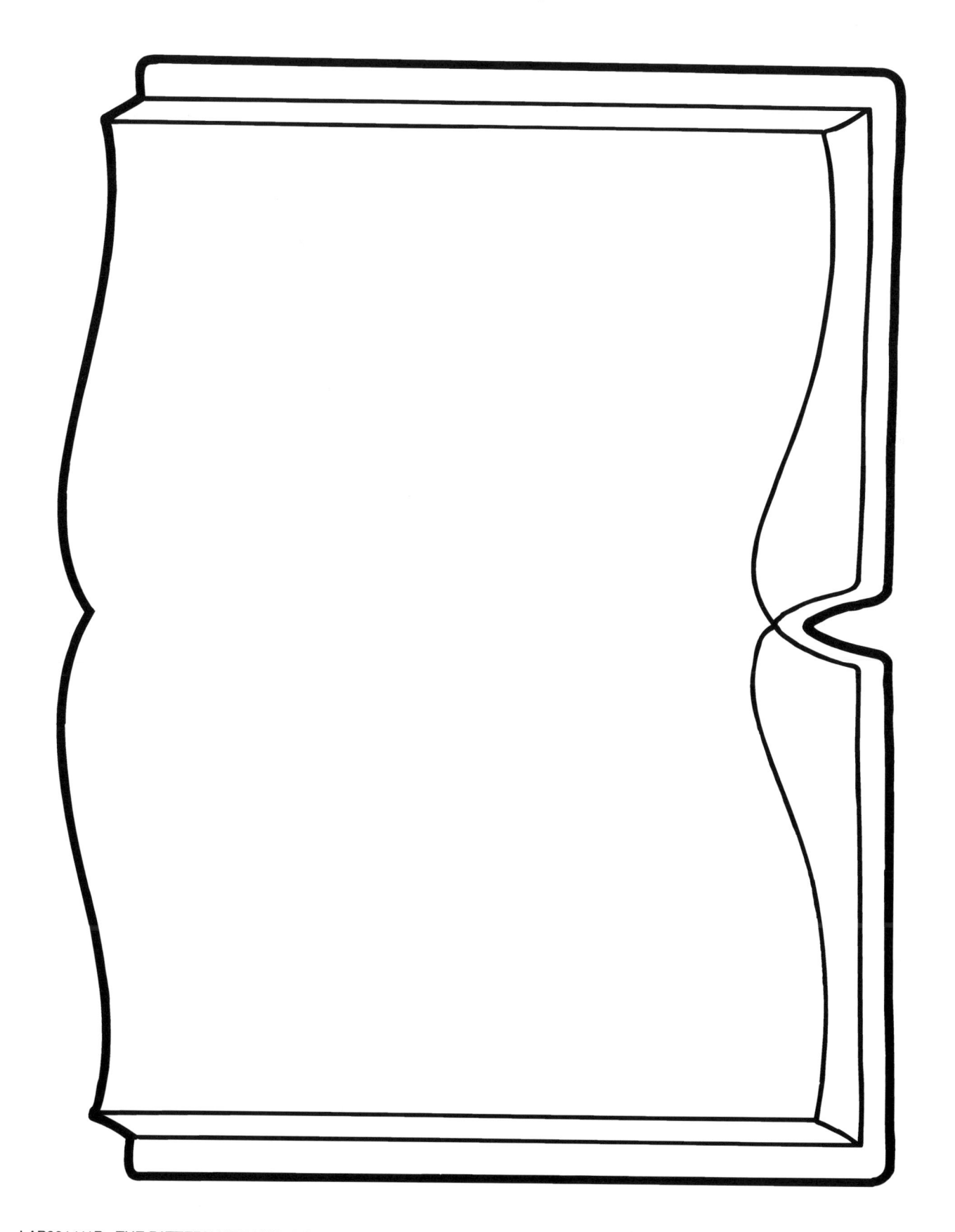

bookcase

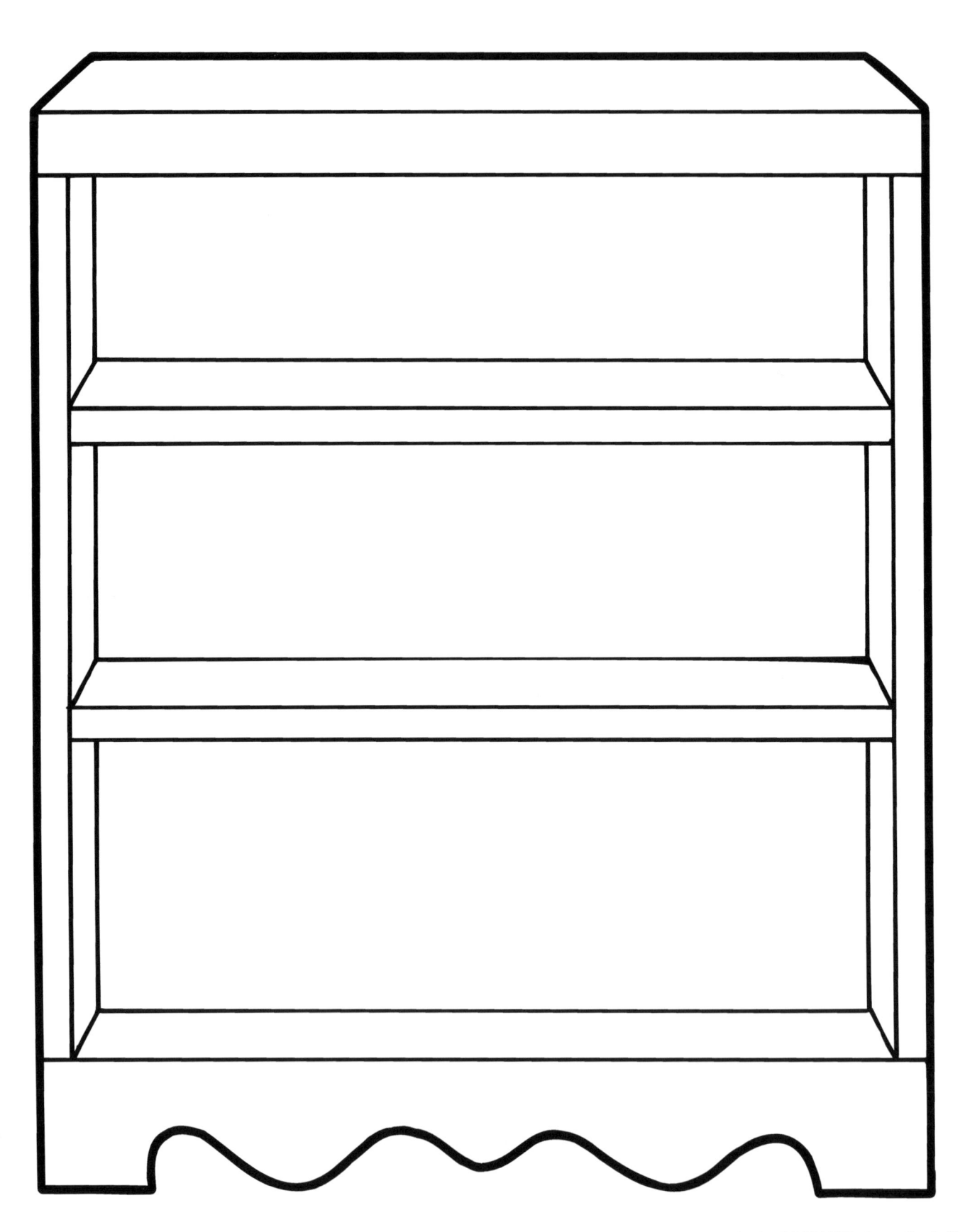

boomerang

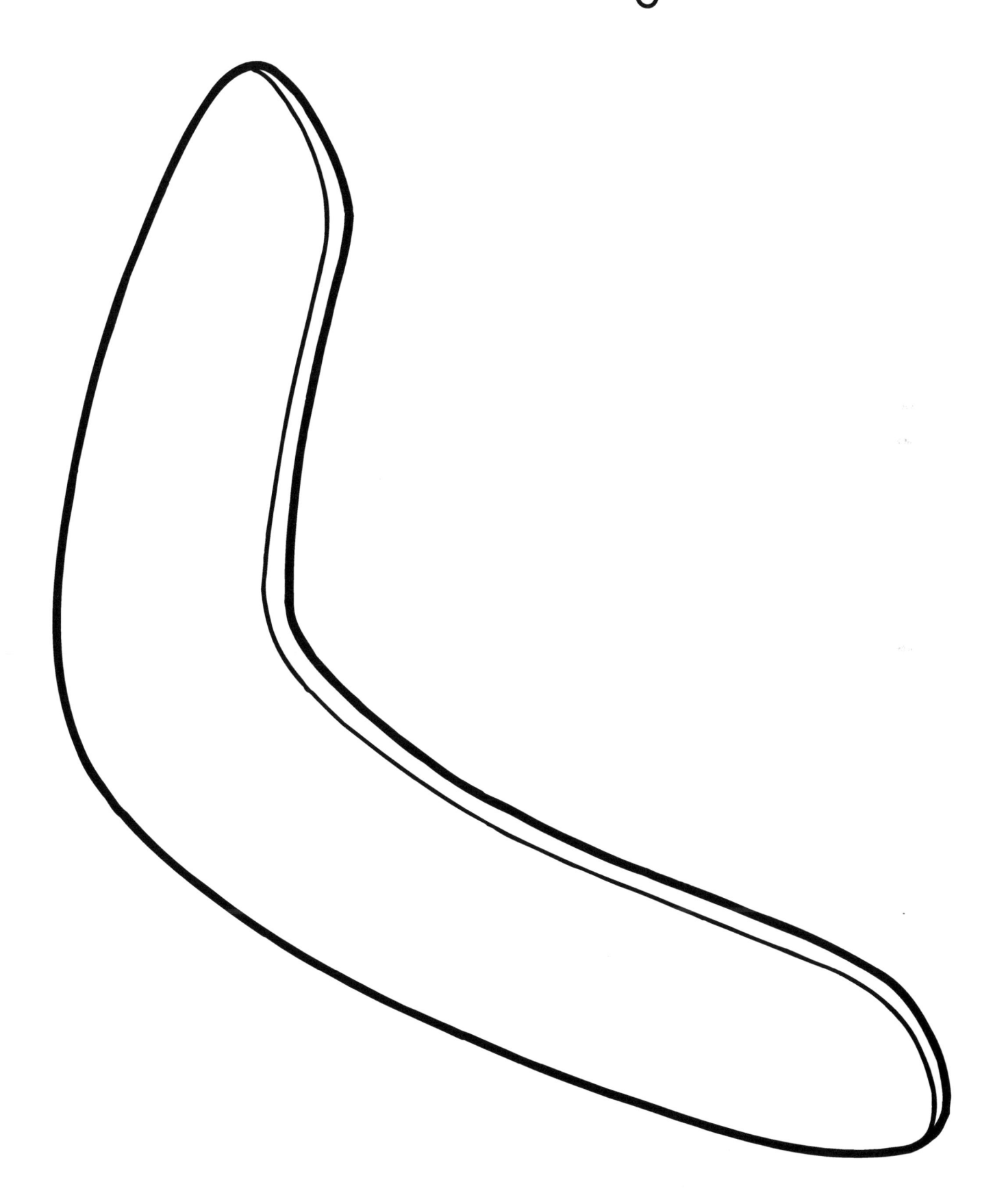

boot (rain-left)

boot (rain-right)

boot (Western-left)

boot (Western-right)

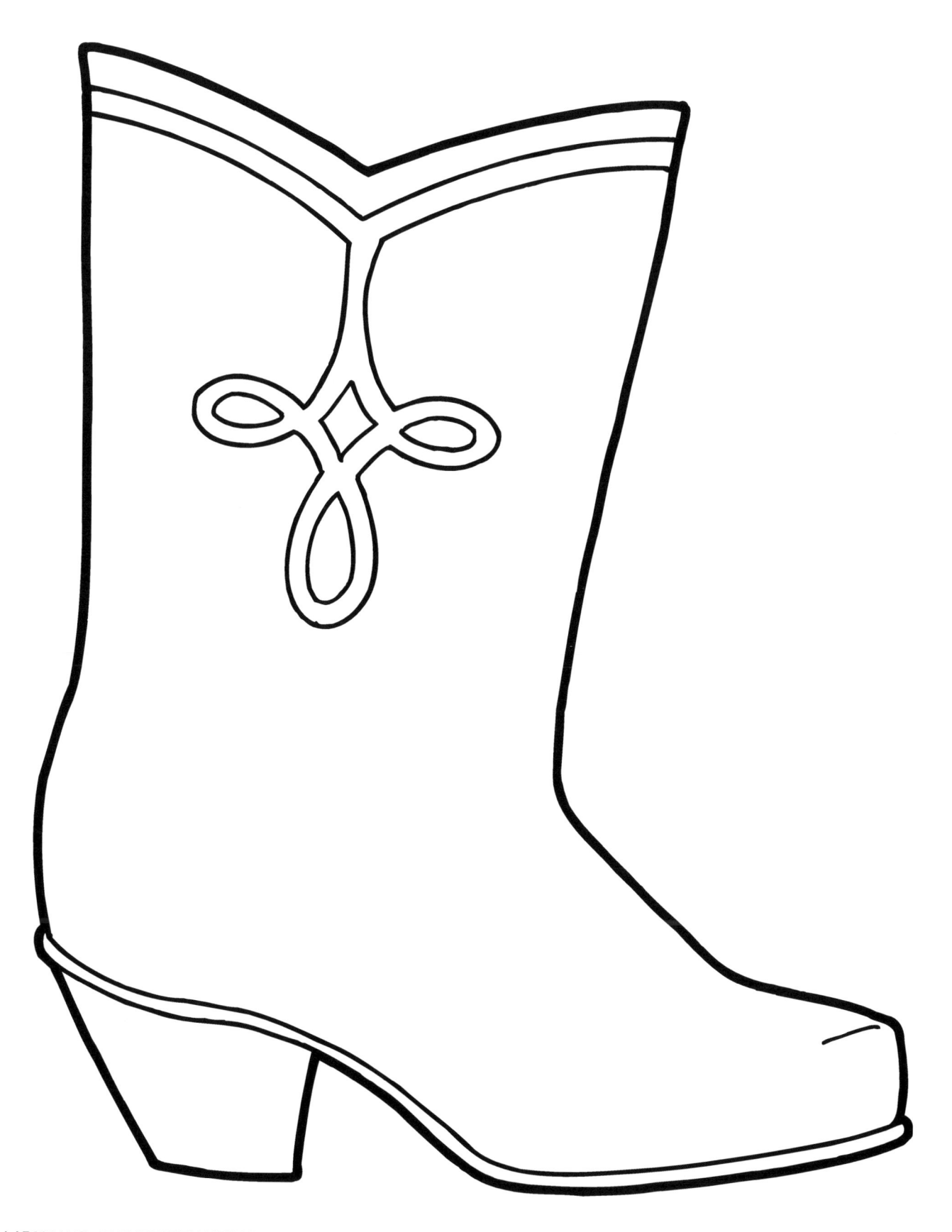

boot (work-left)

boot (work-right)

boot (child-left)

boot (child-right)

boot (ladies-left)

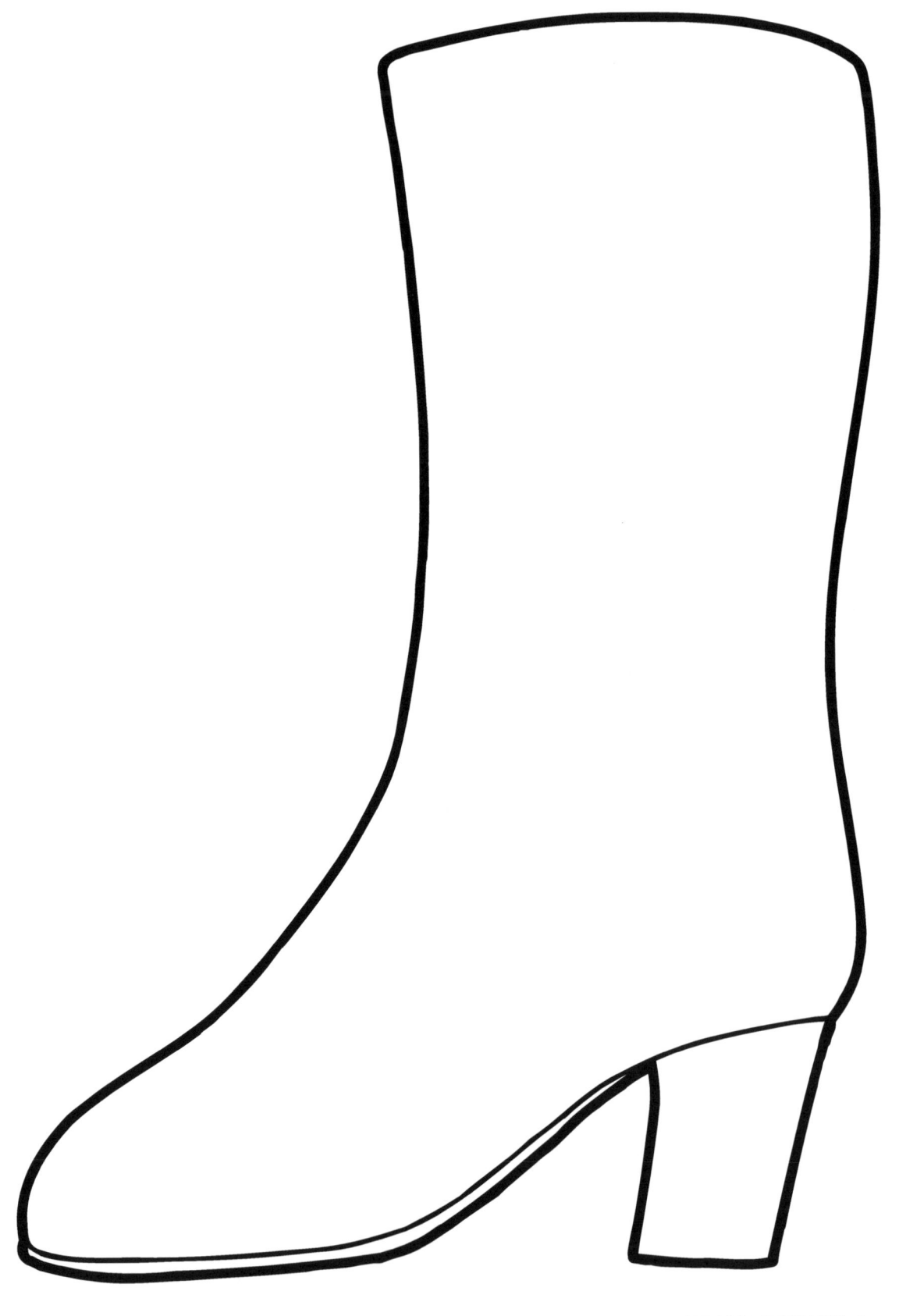

boot (ladies-right)

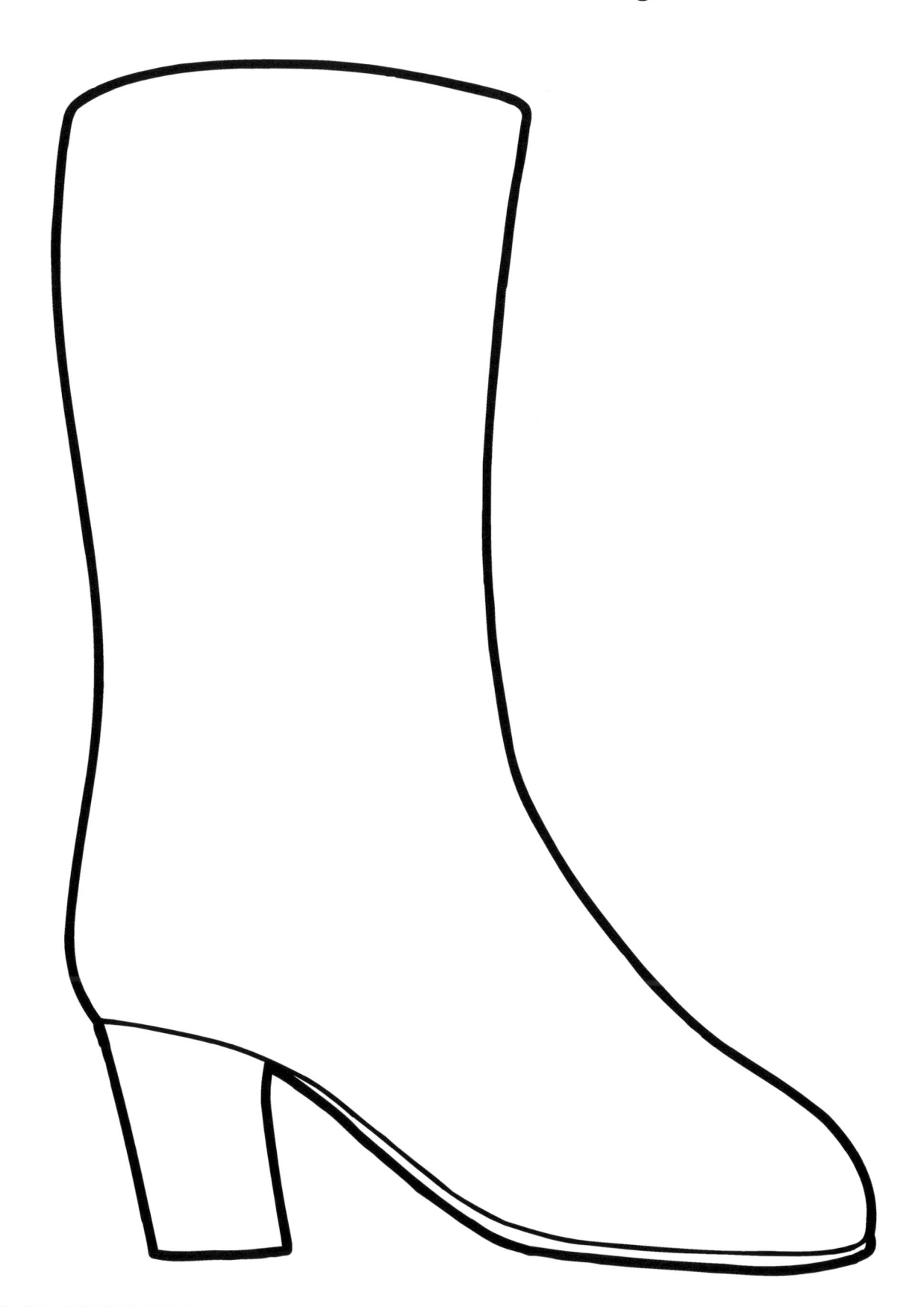

boot (ski-left)

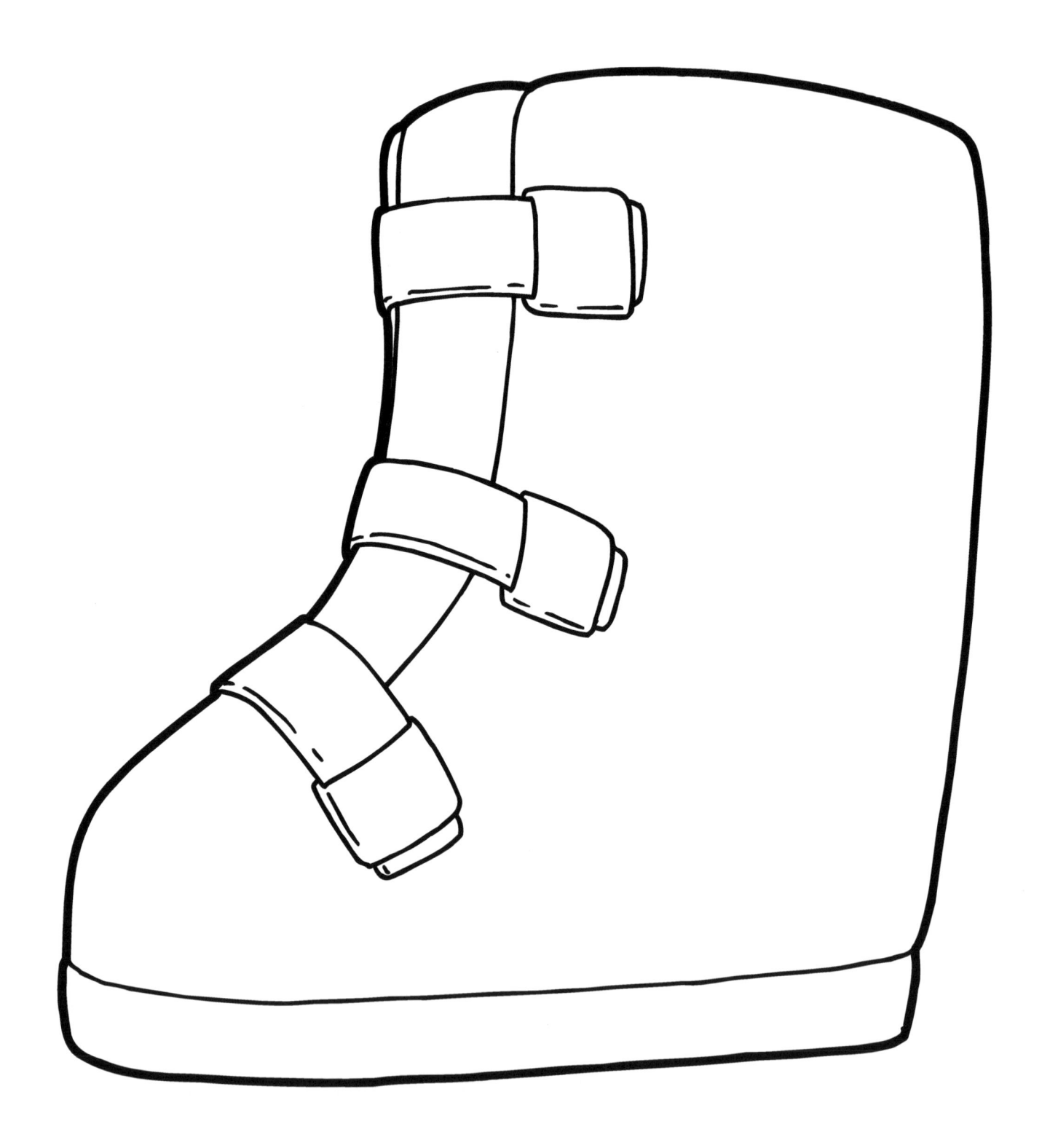

boot (ski-right)

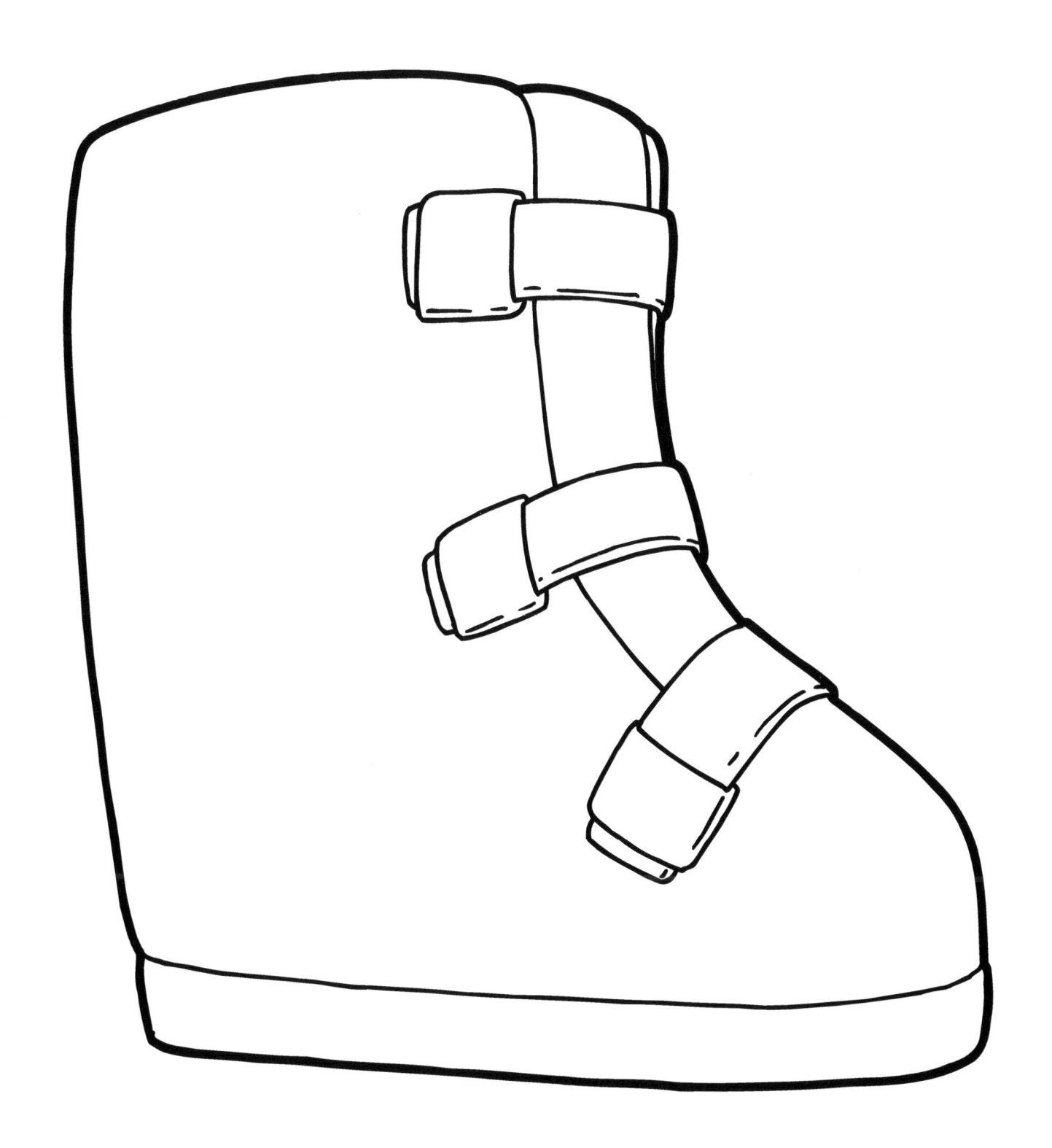

bottle (juice)

bottle (milk)

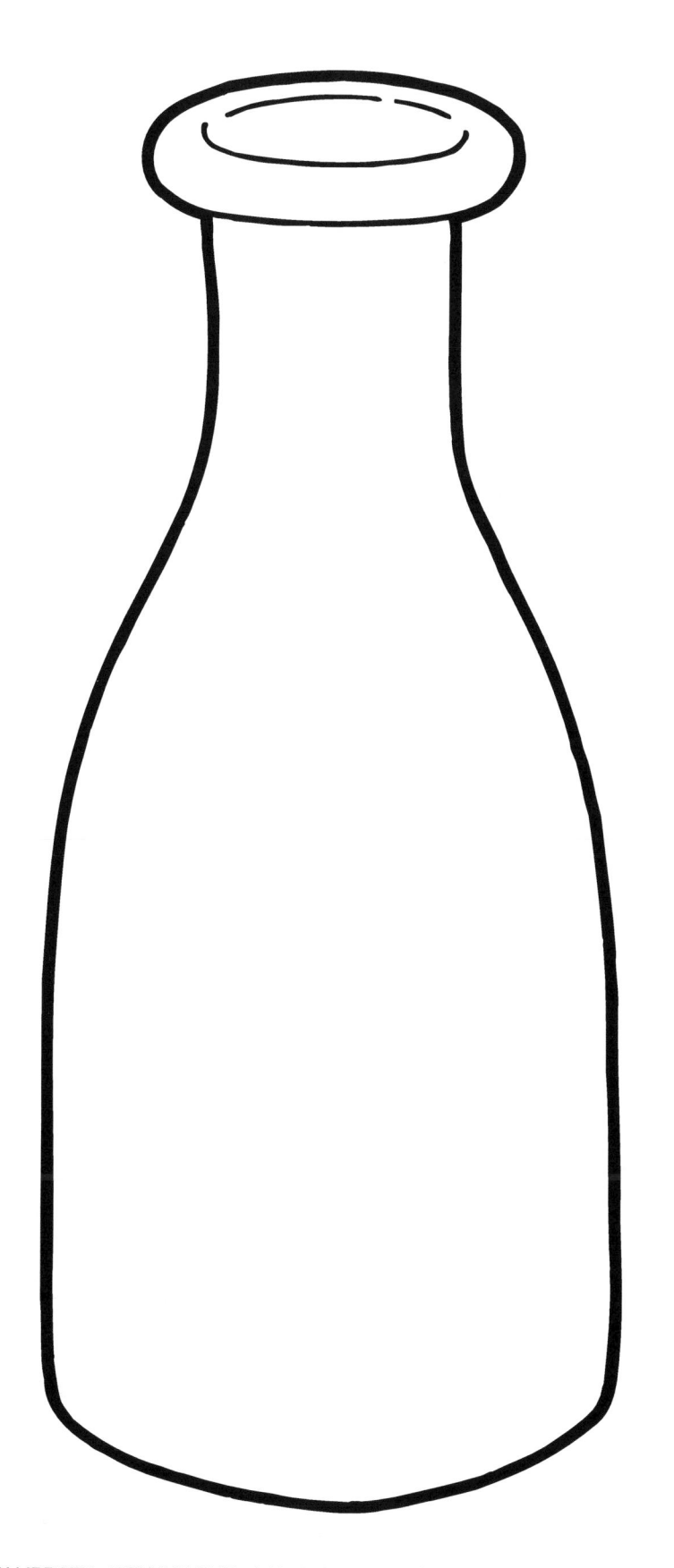

bottle (pop)

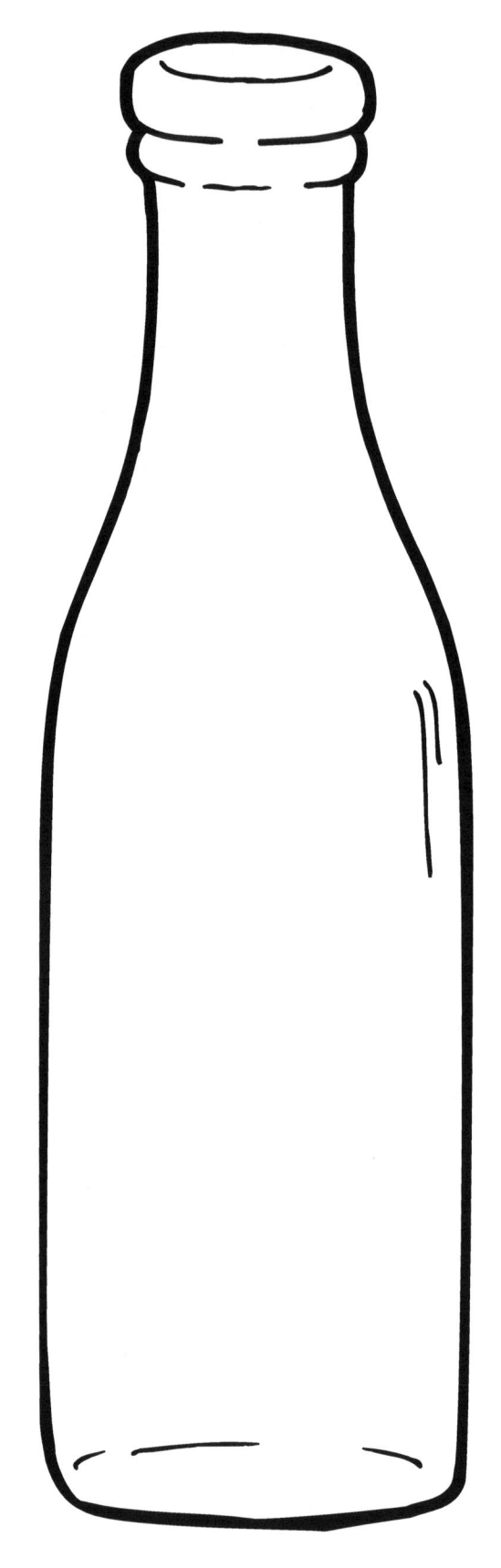

bow (archer's)

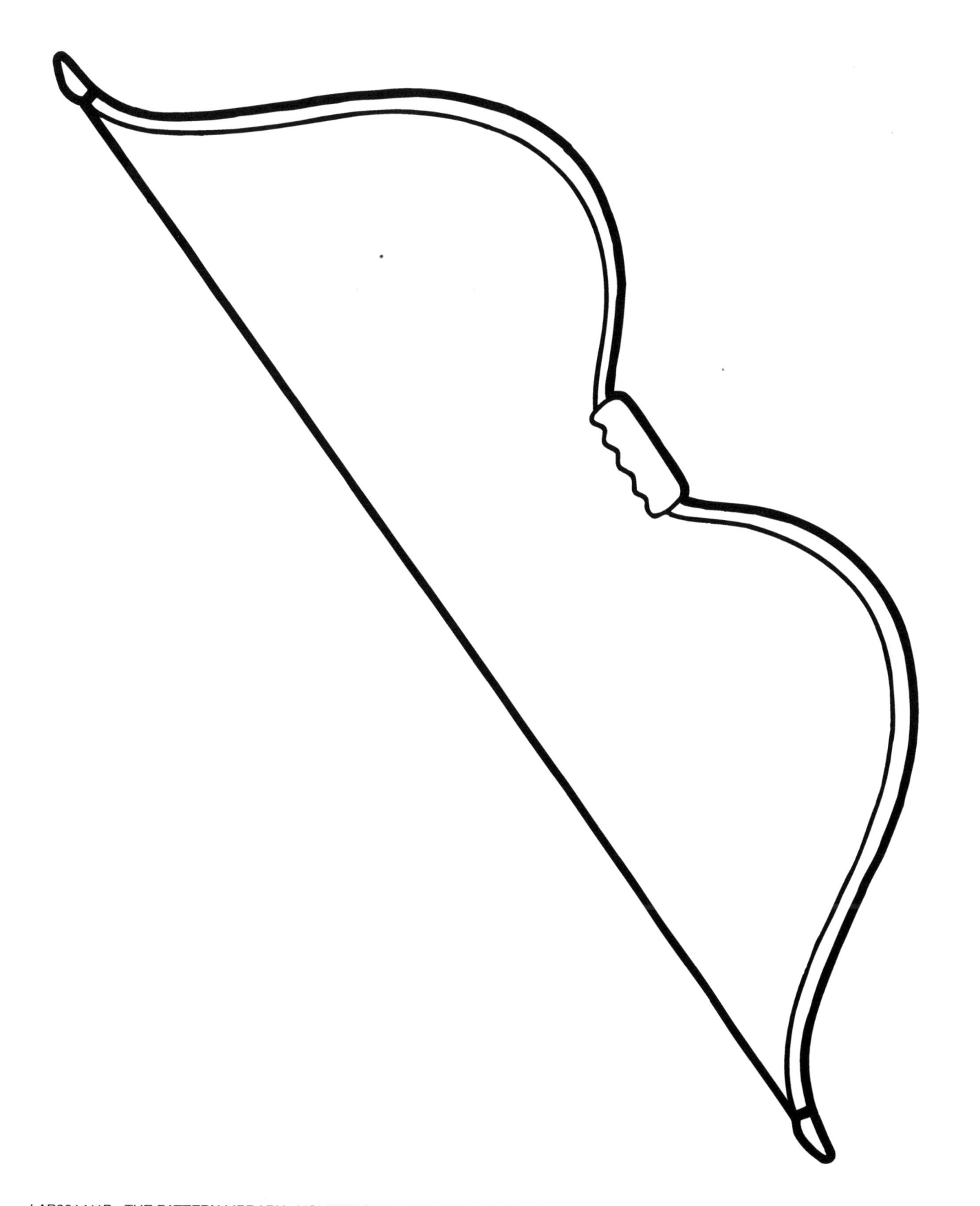

bow (knot)

bow (pompom)

bowl

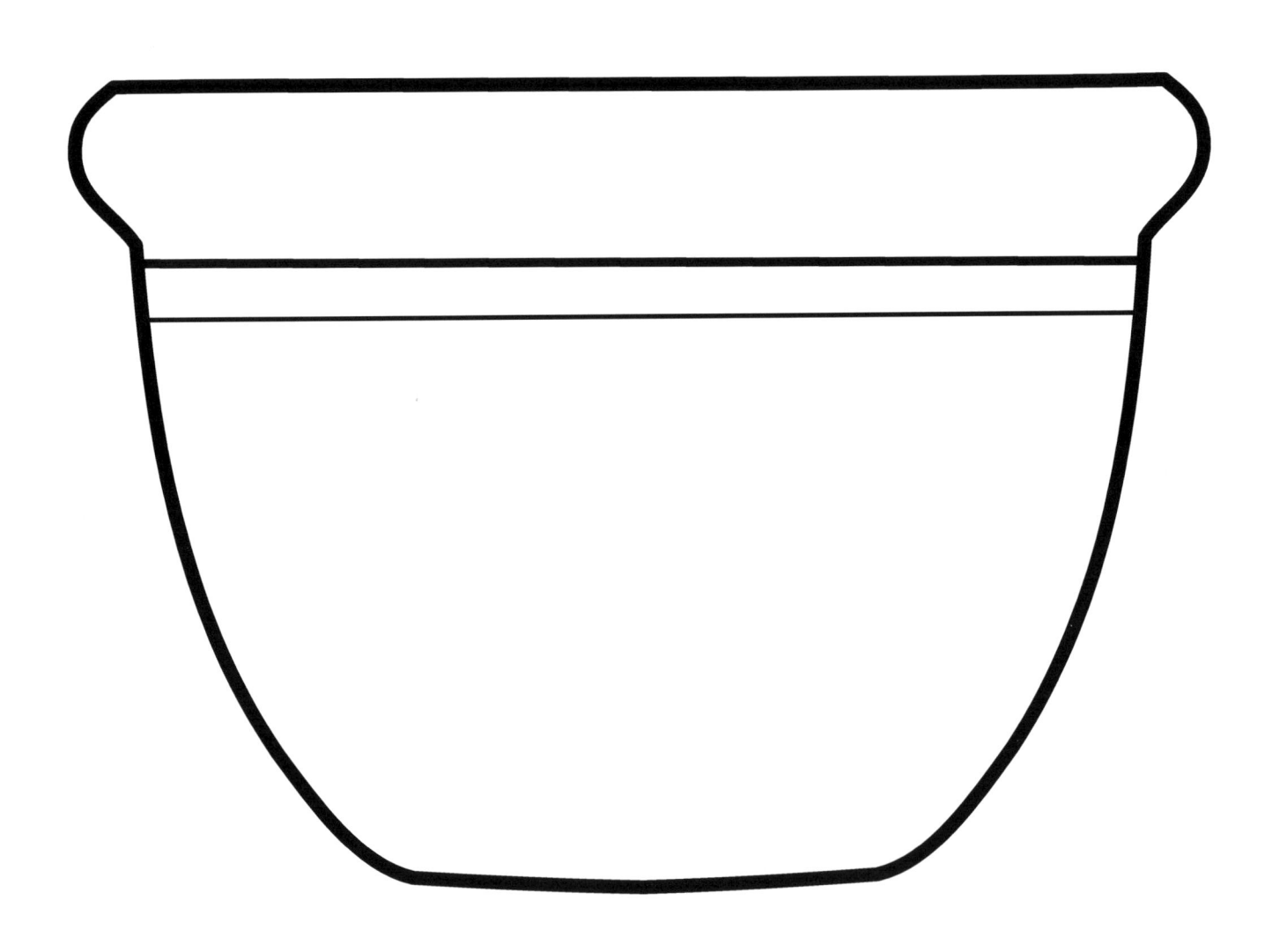

bowling ball

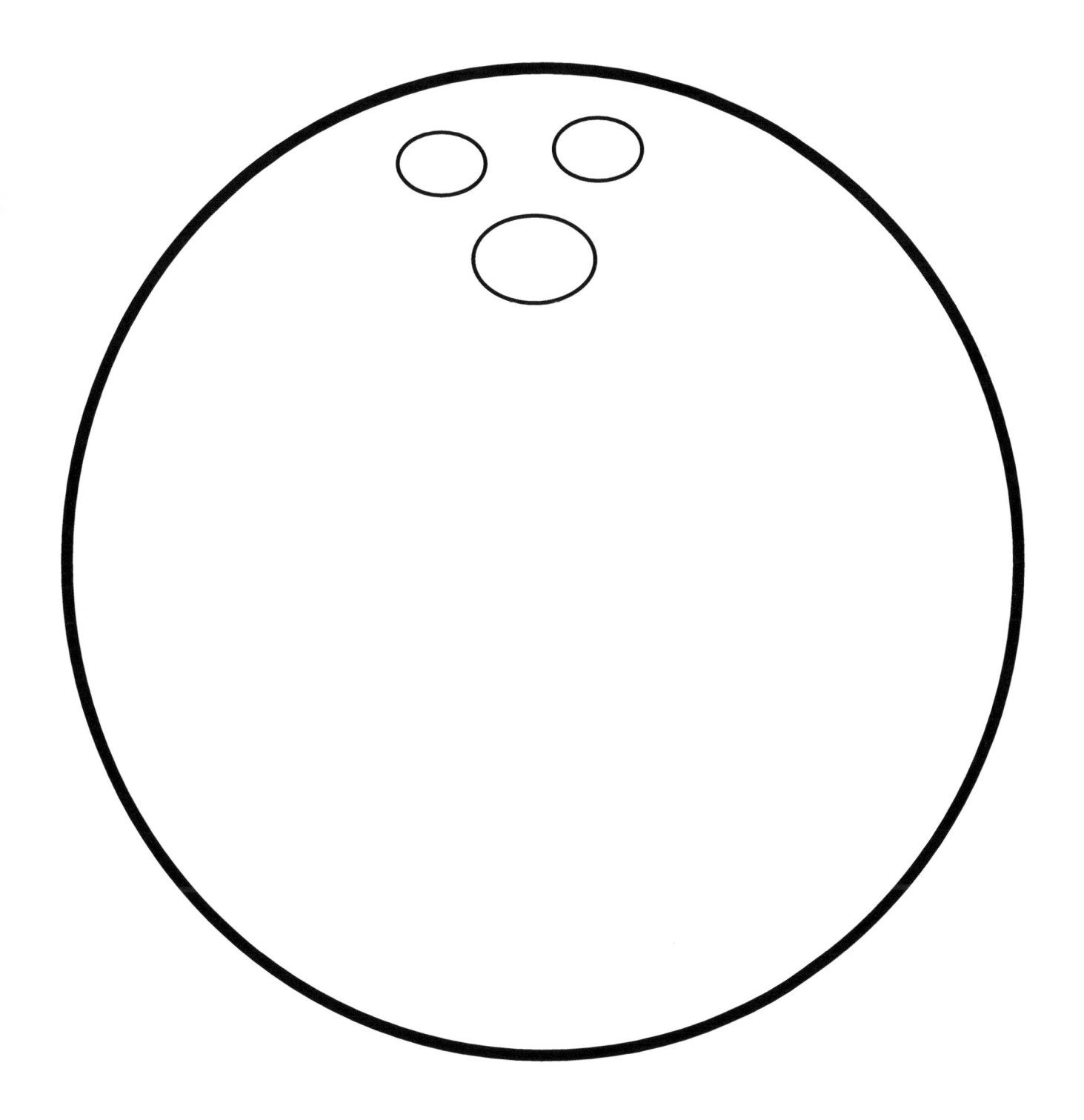

bowling pin

bowling pins

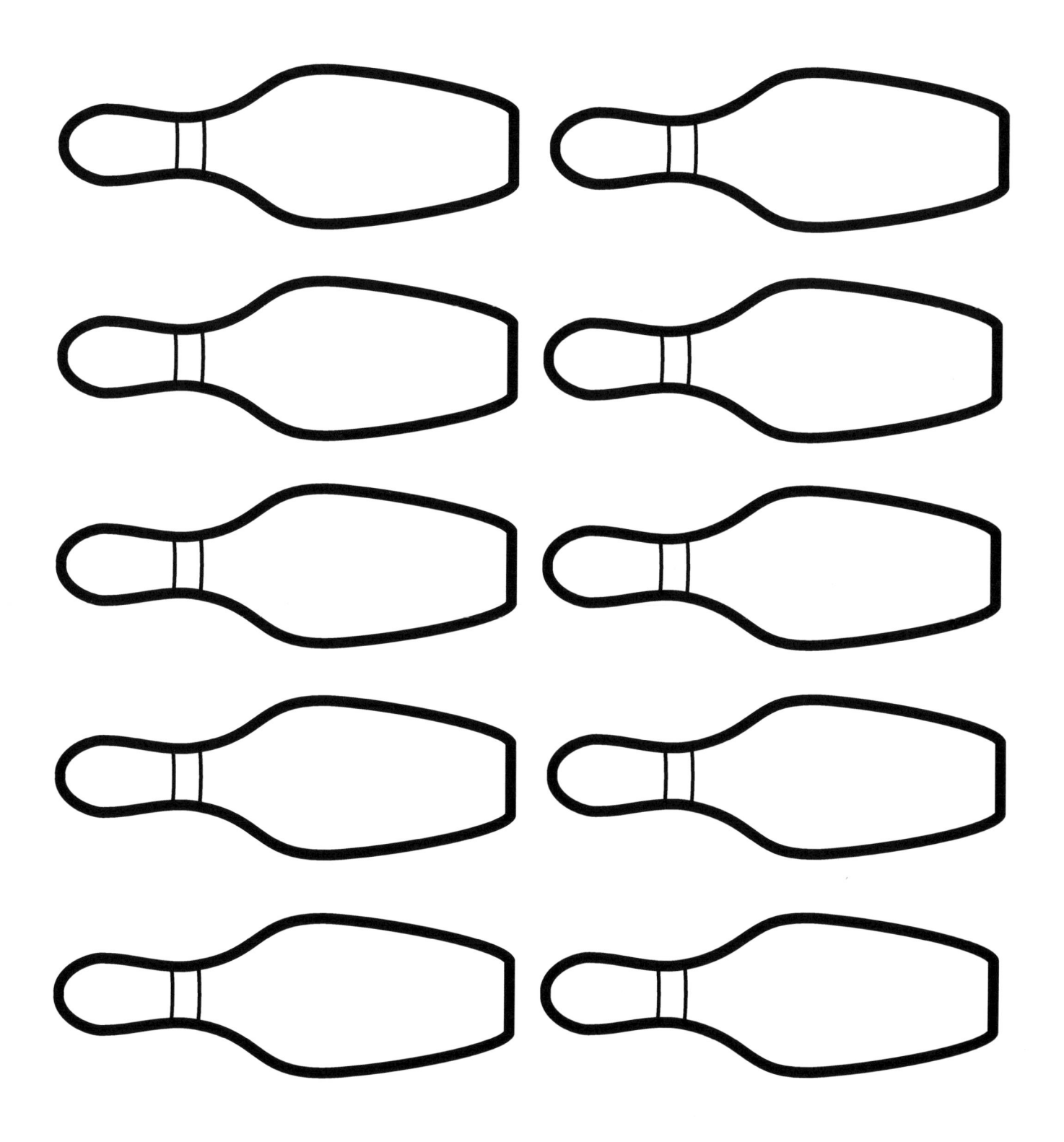

bowtie

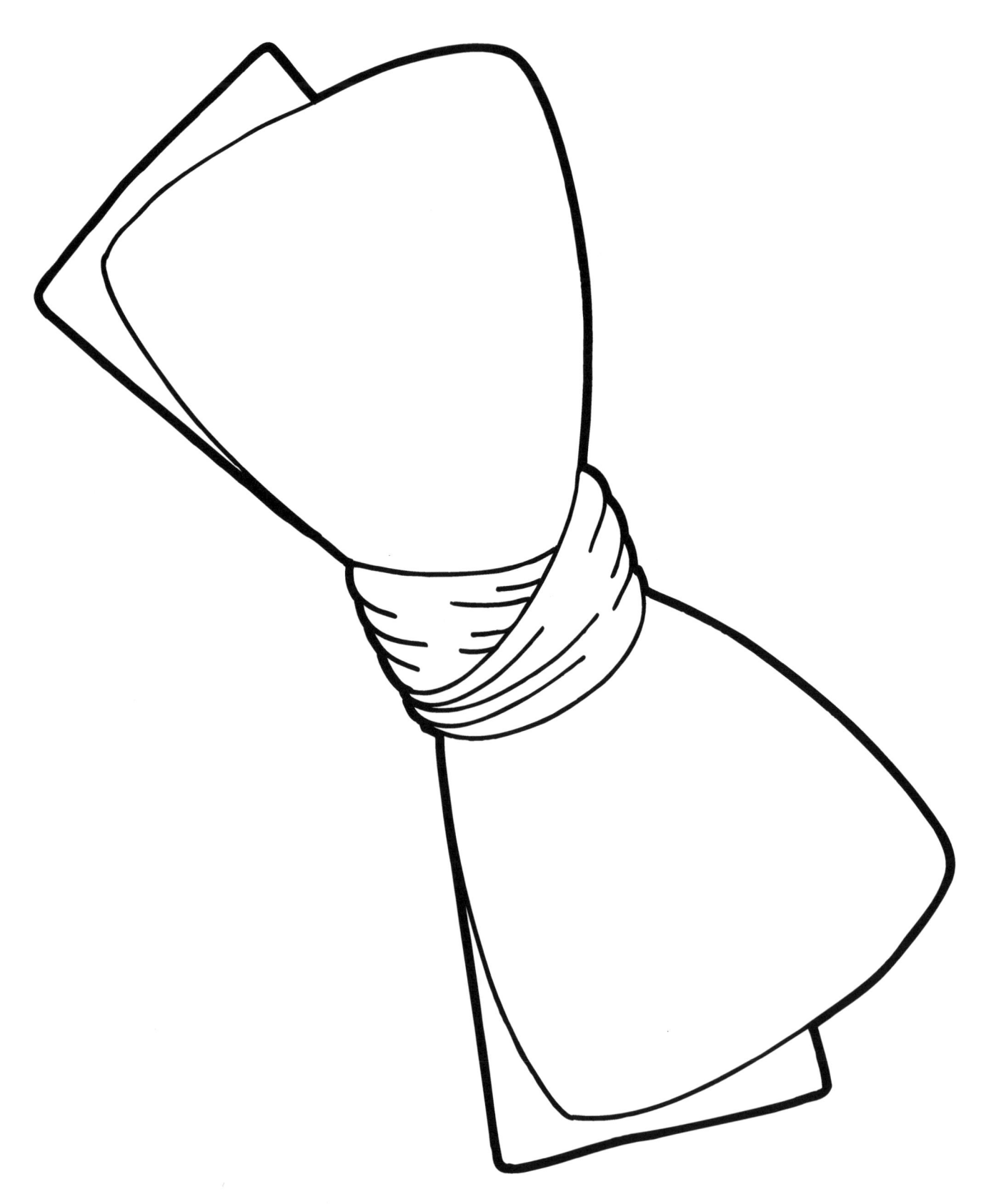

box

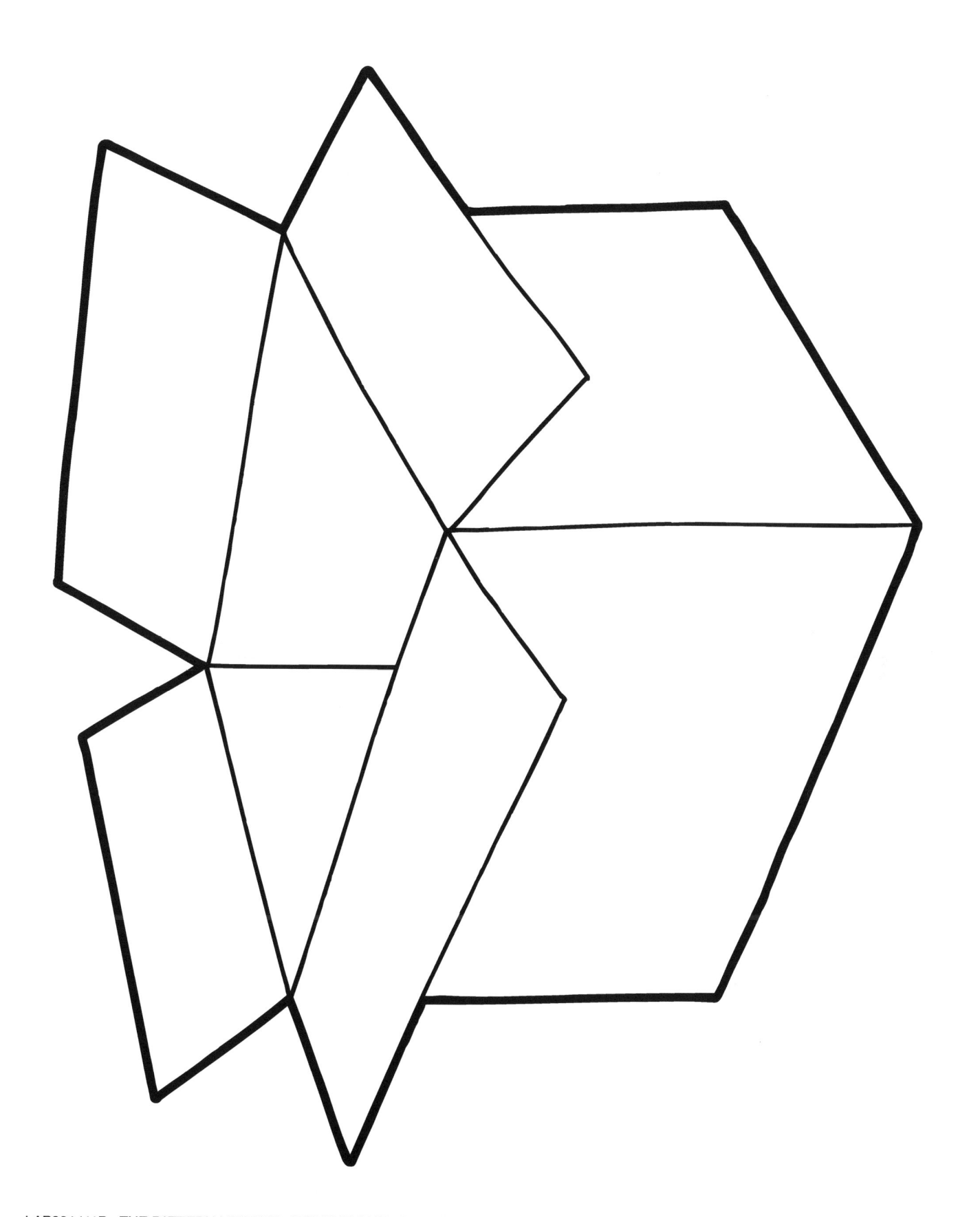

boxers

boy

boy

boy

boy

Braille alphabet chart

Braille Alphabet Chart

	a	b	c	
d	e	f	g	h
i	j	k	l	m
n	o	p	q	r
s	t	u	v	w
	x	y	z	

brain

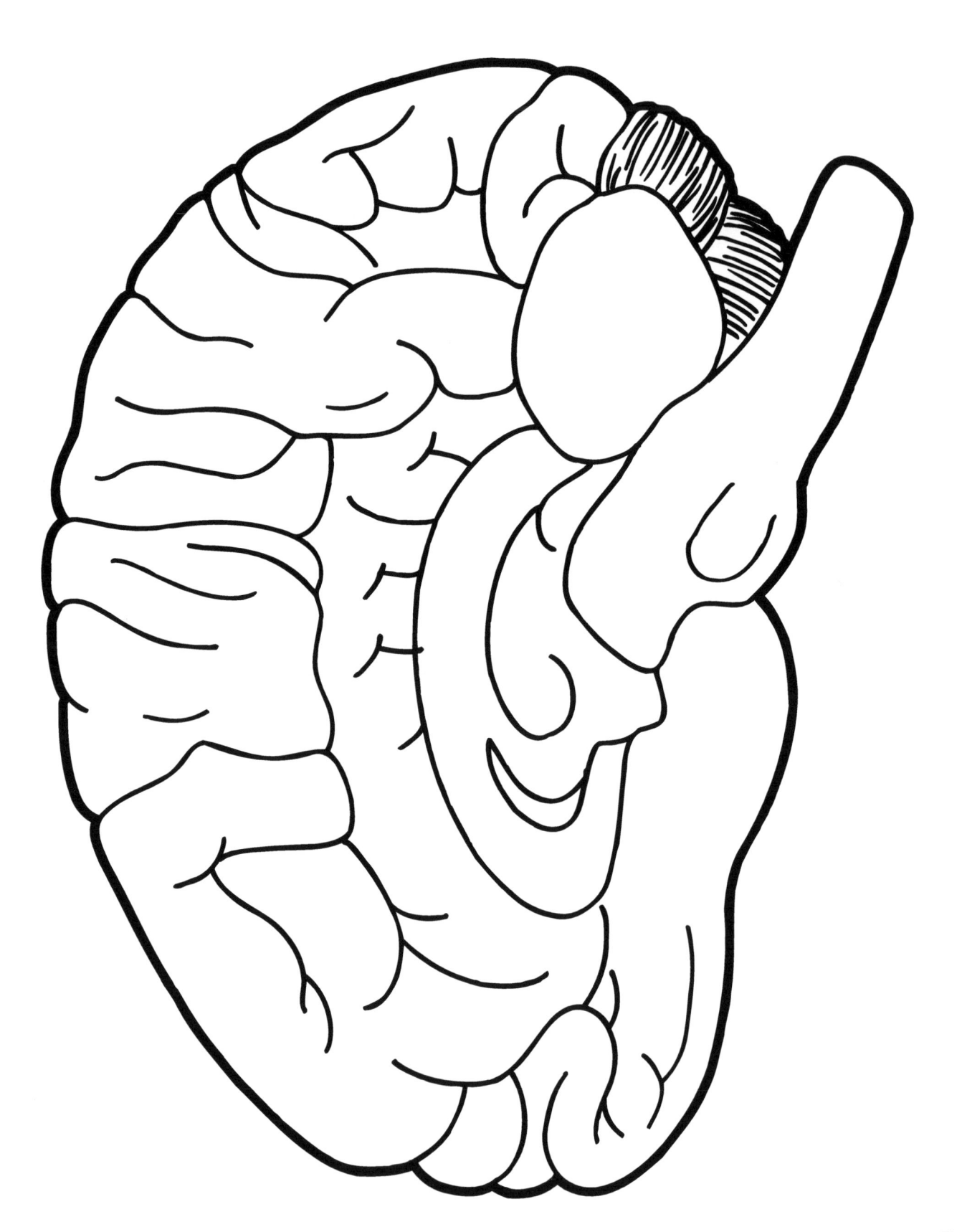

branch

bread (loaf)

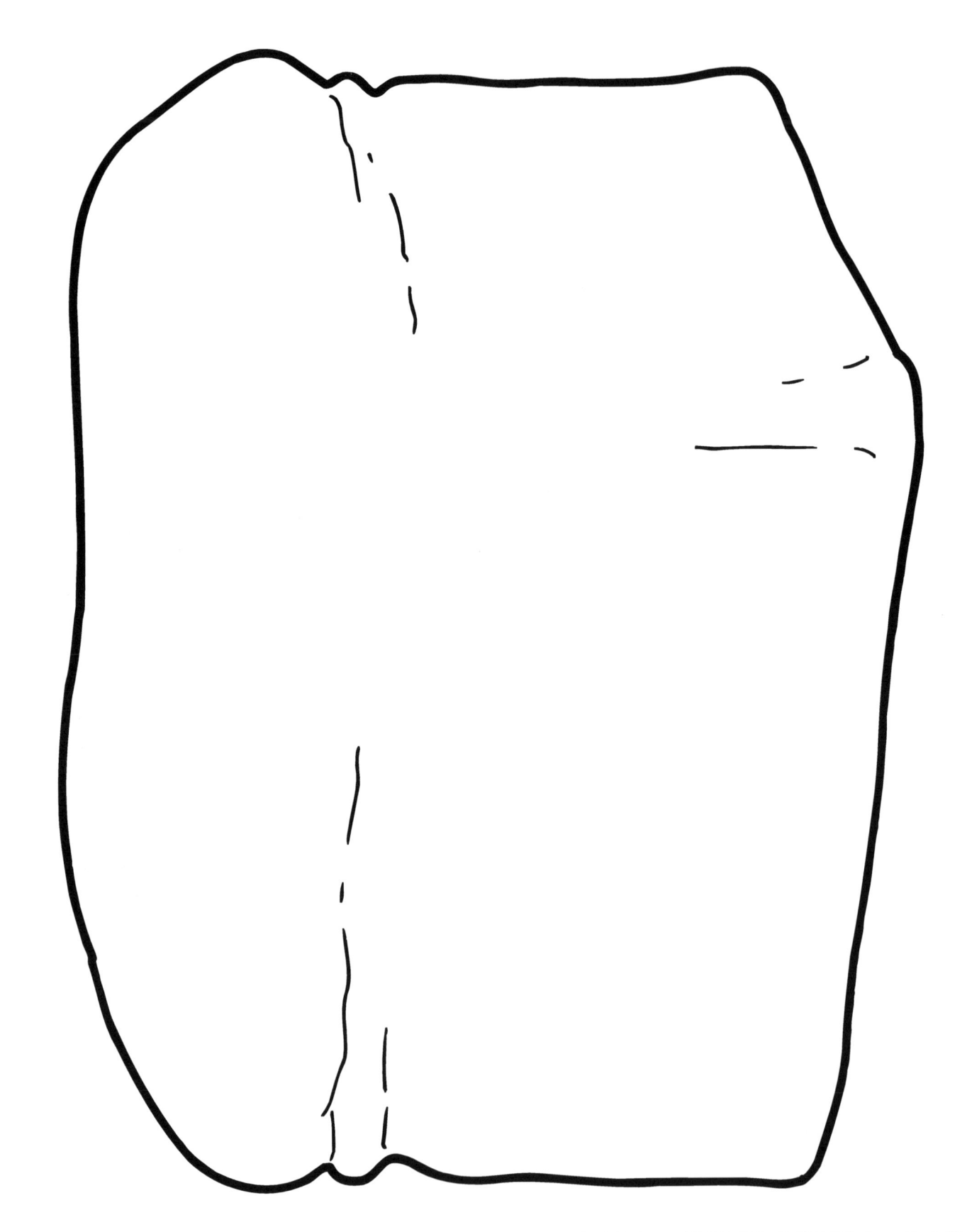

bread (slice)

brick (side view)

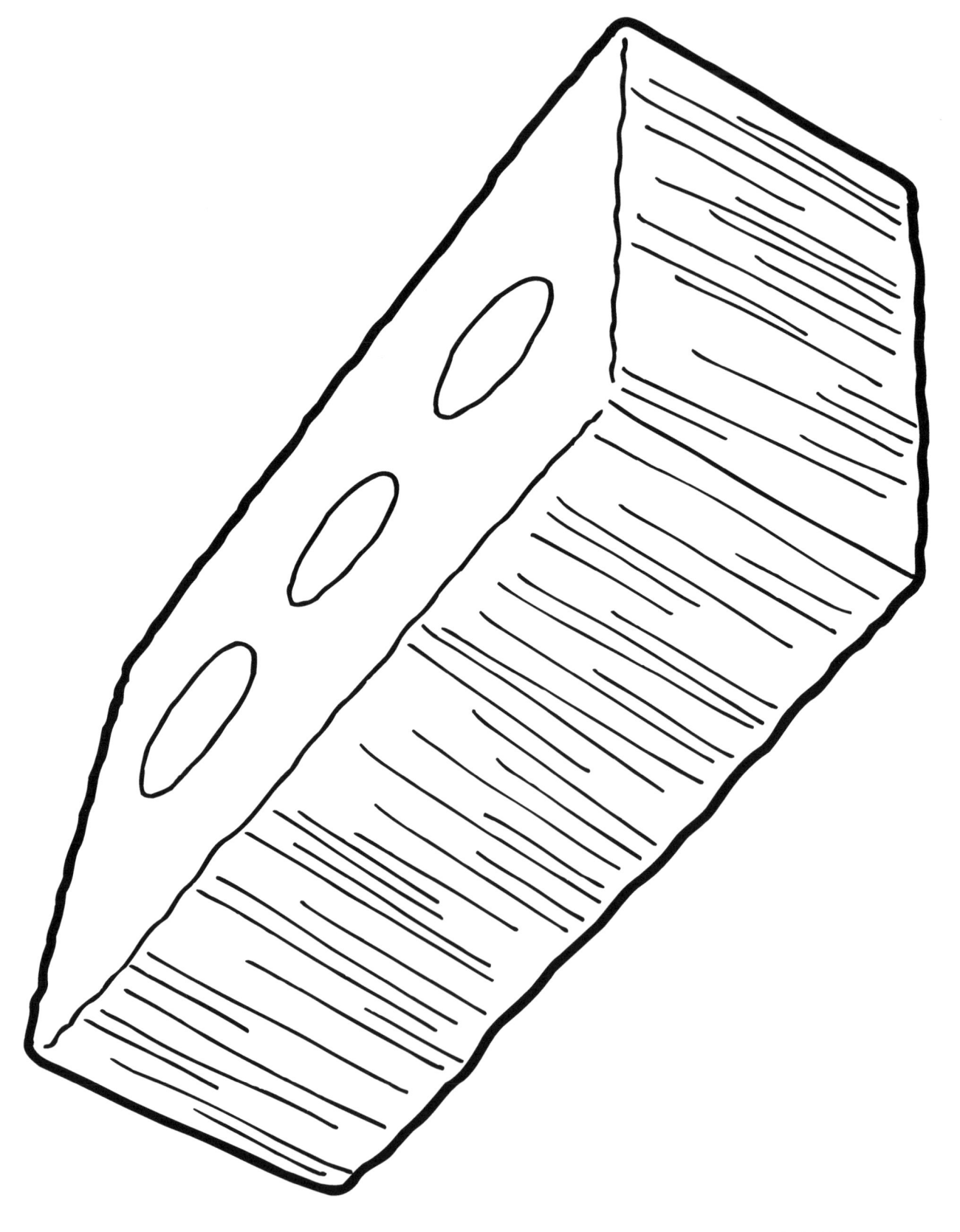

brick (top)

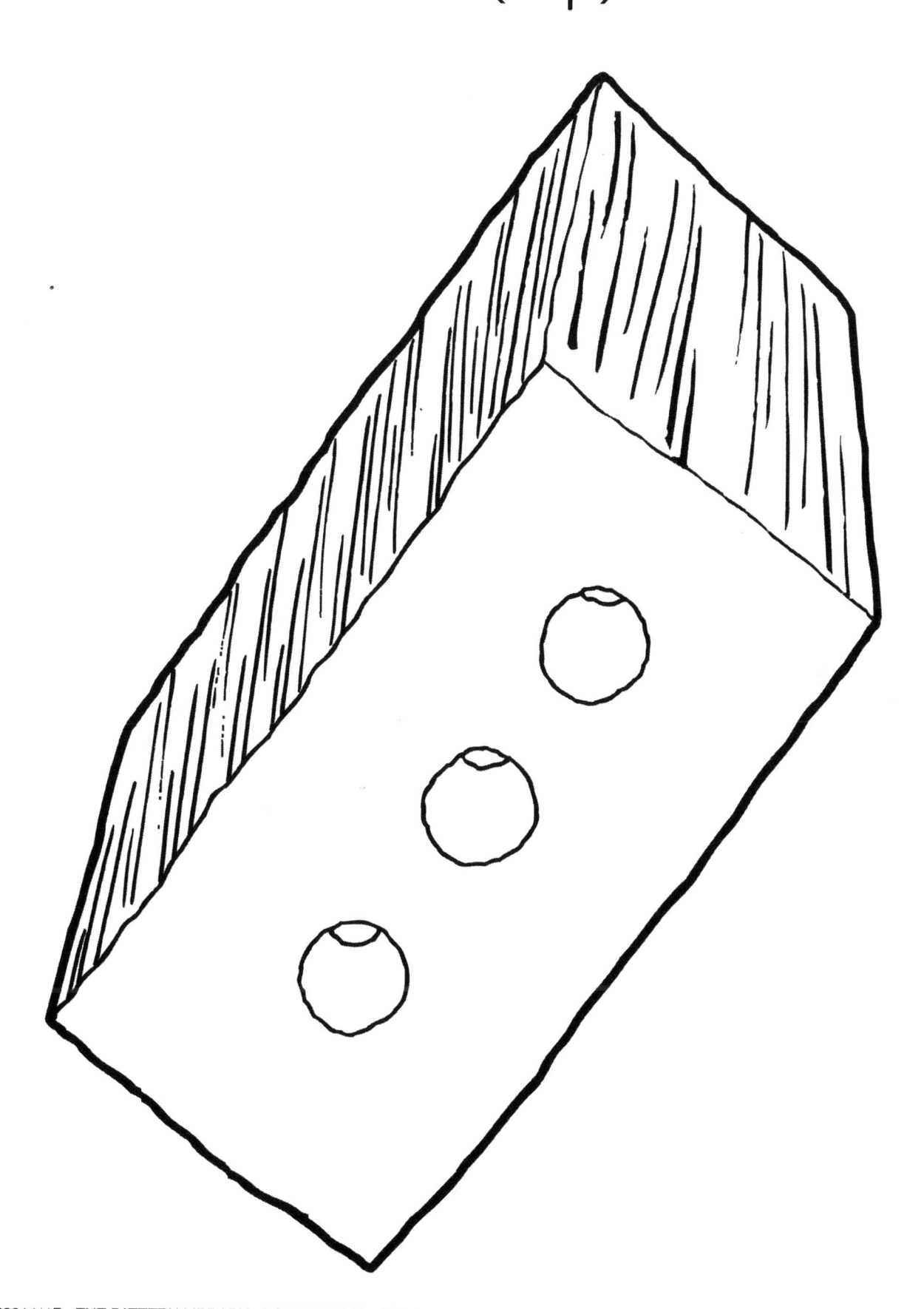

bride

bridge (suspension)

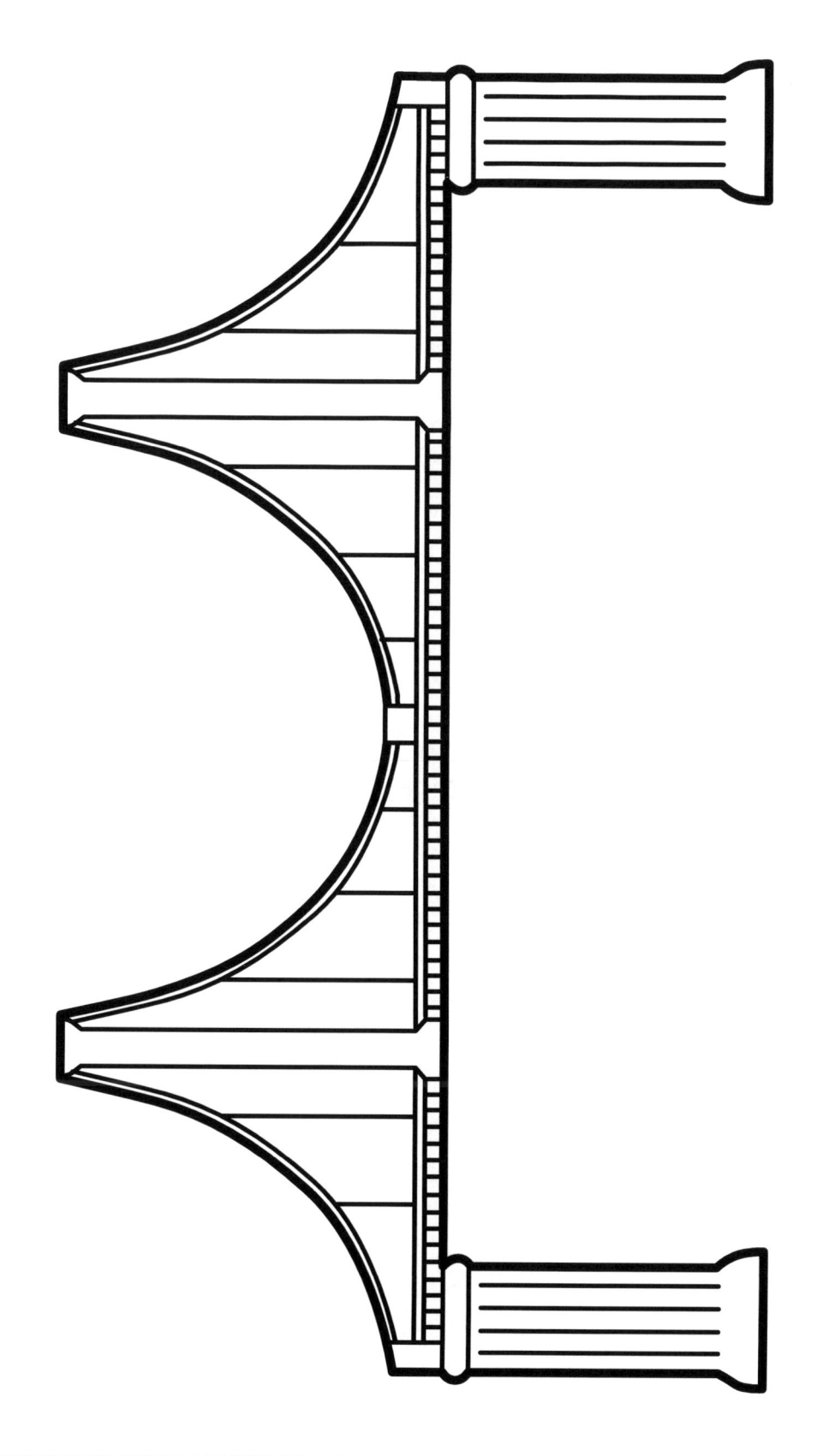

bridge (walking)

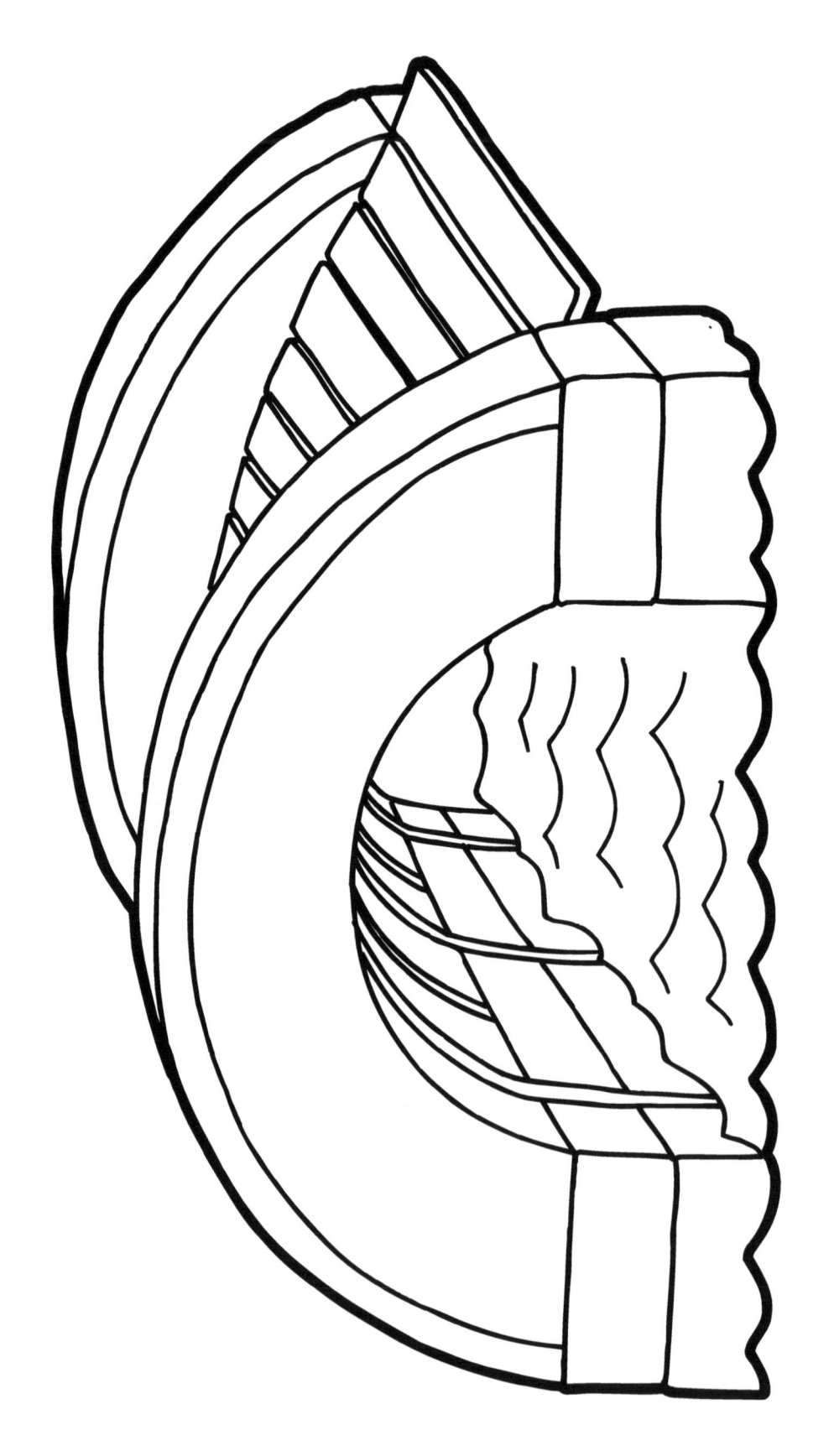

British Columbia, Canada

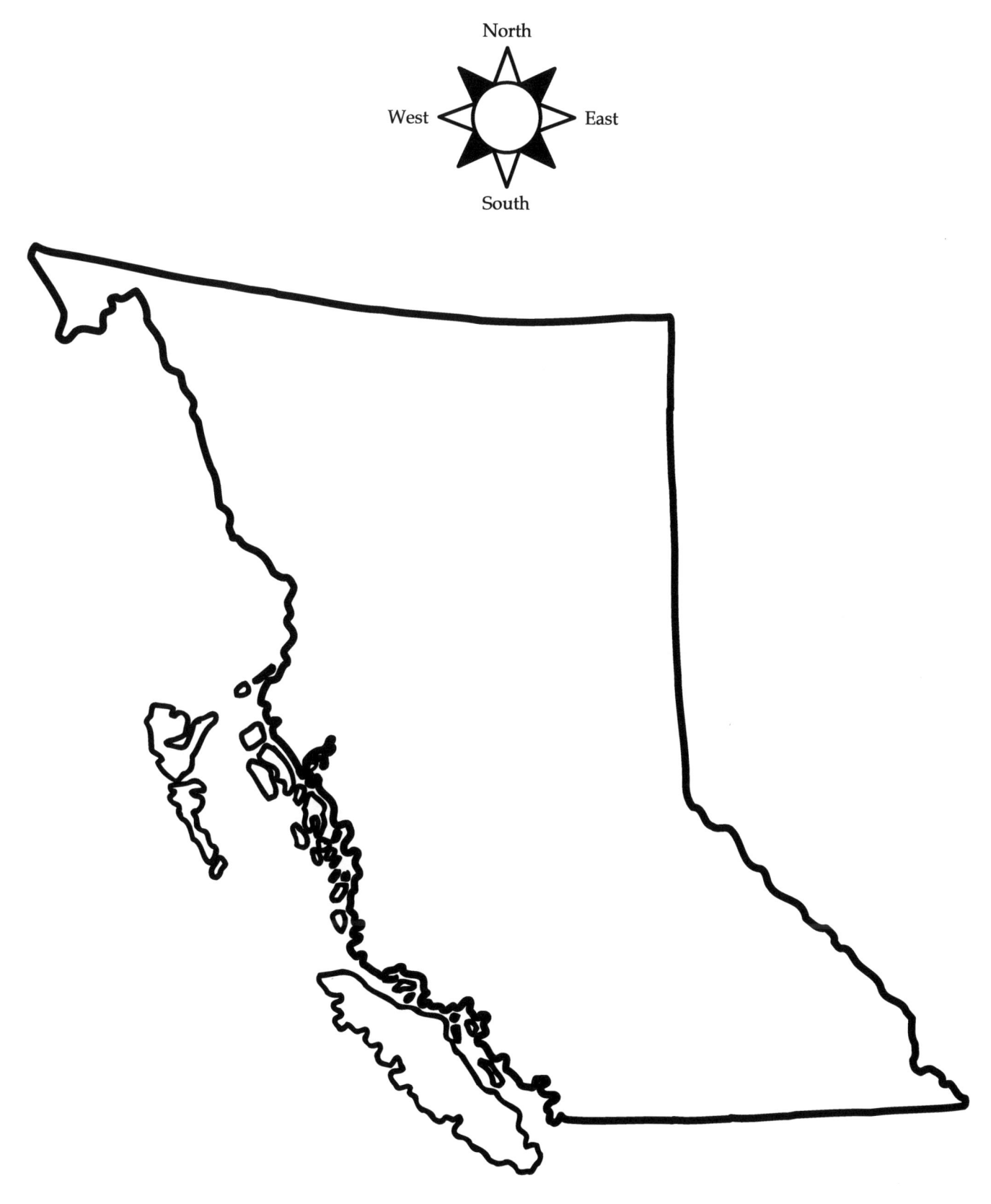

Maps are representations and boundaries are not exact.

LAB201411P • THE PATTERN LIBRARY • VOLUME ONE • A-H • 978-1-937257-62-0 • © 2014 Little Acorn Books™

171

broccoli

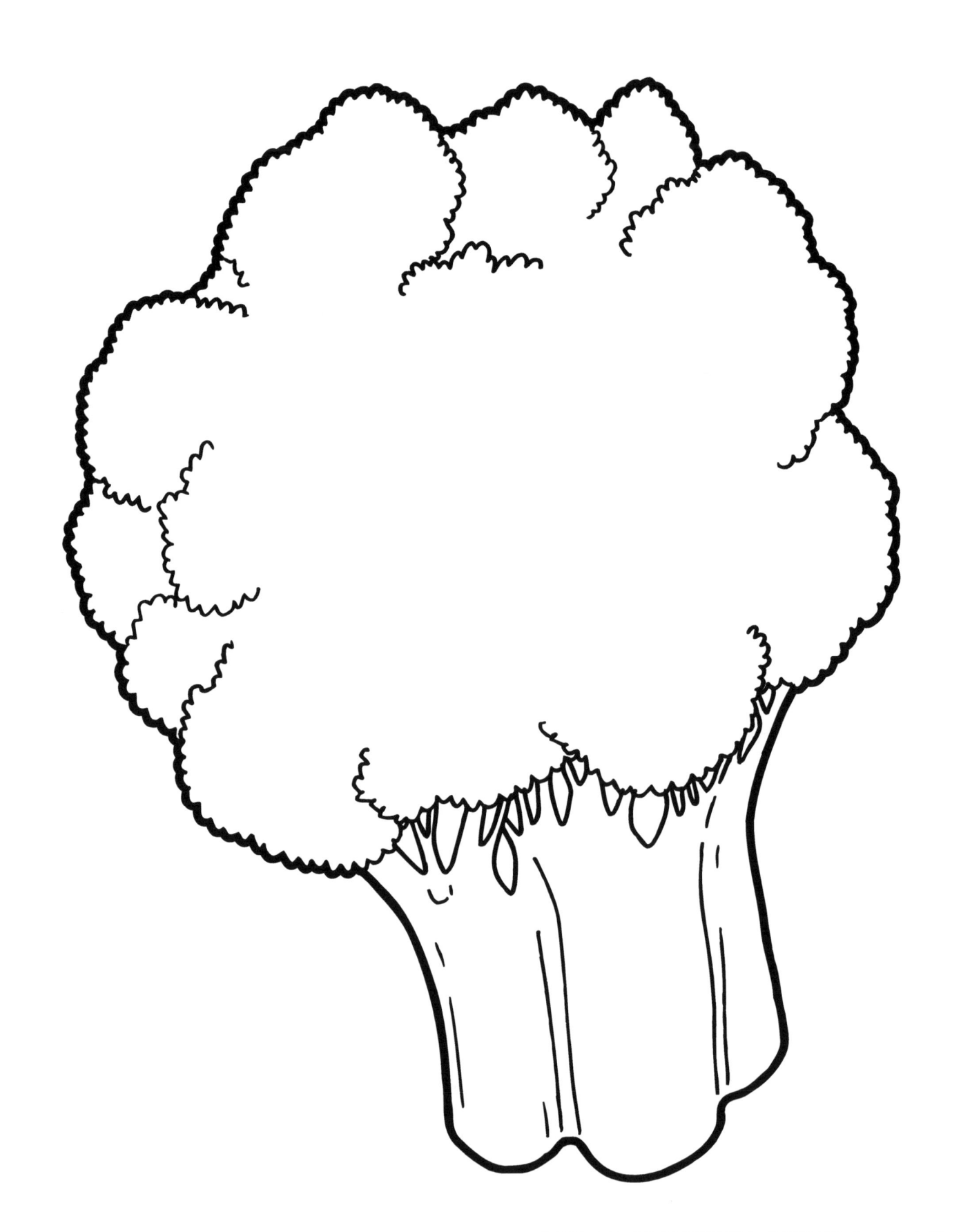

brontosaurus

broom (push)

broom (swish)

broom (whisk)

brown (crayon)

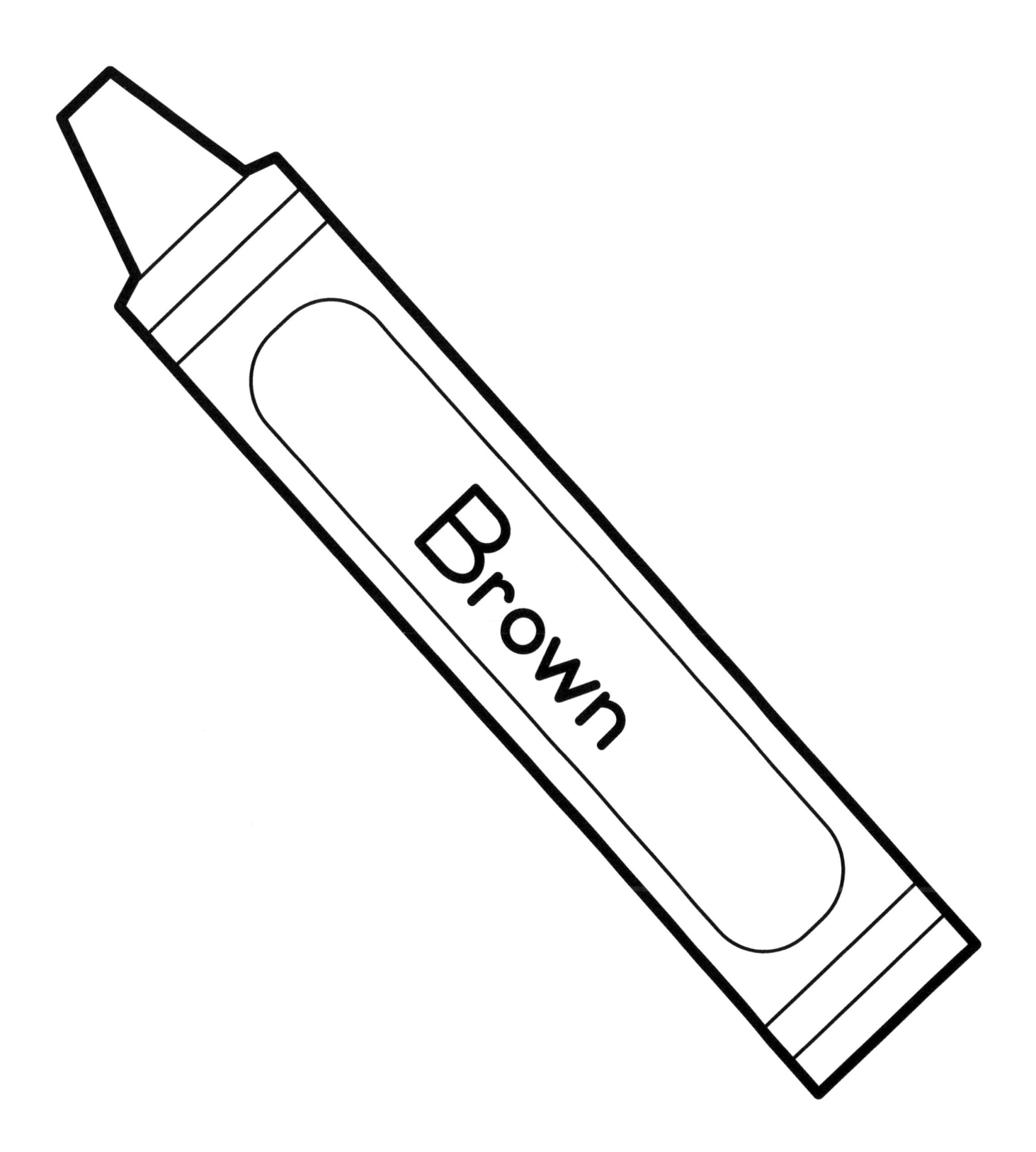

brush (grooming)

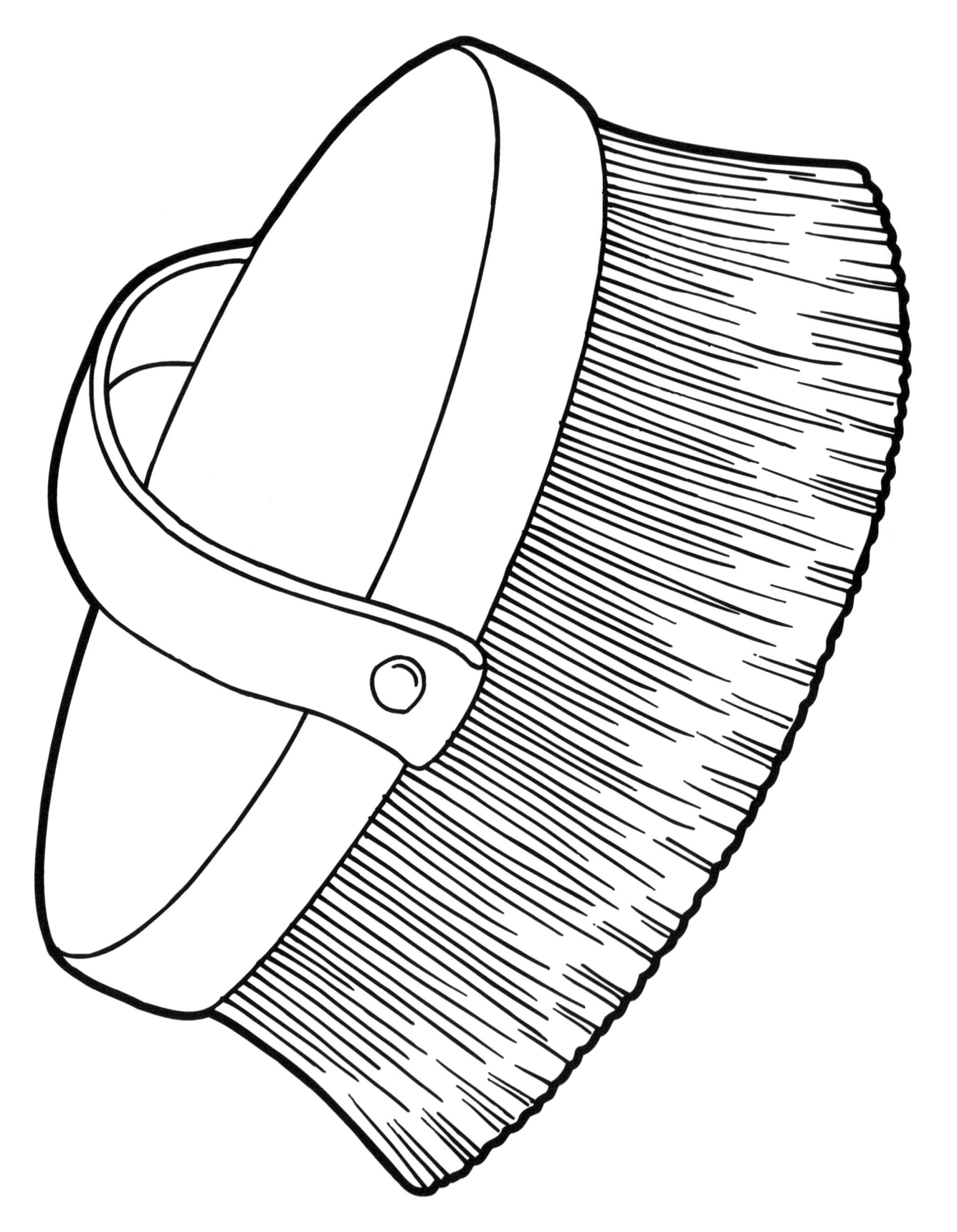

brush (hair)

brush (scrub)

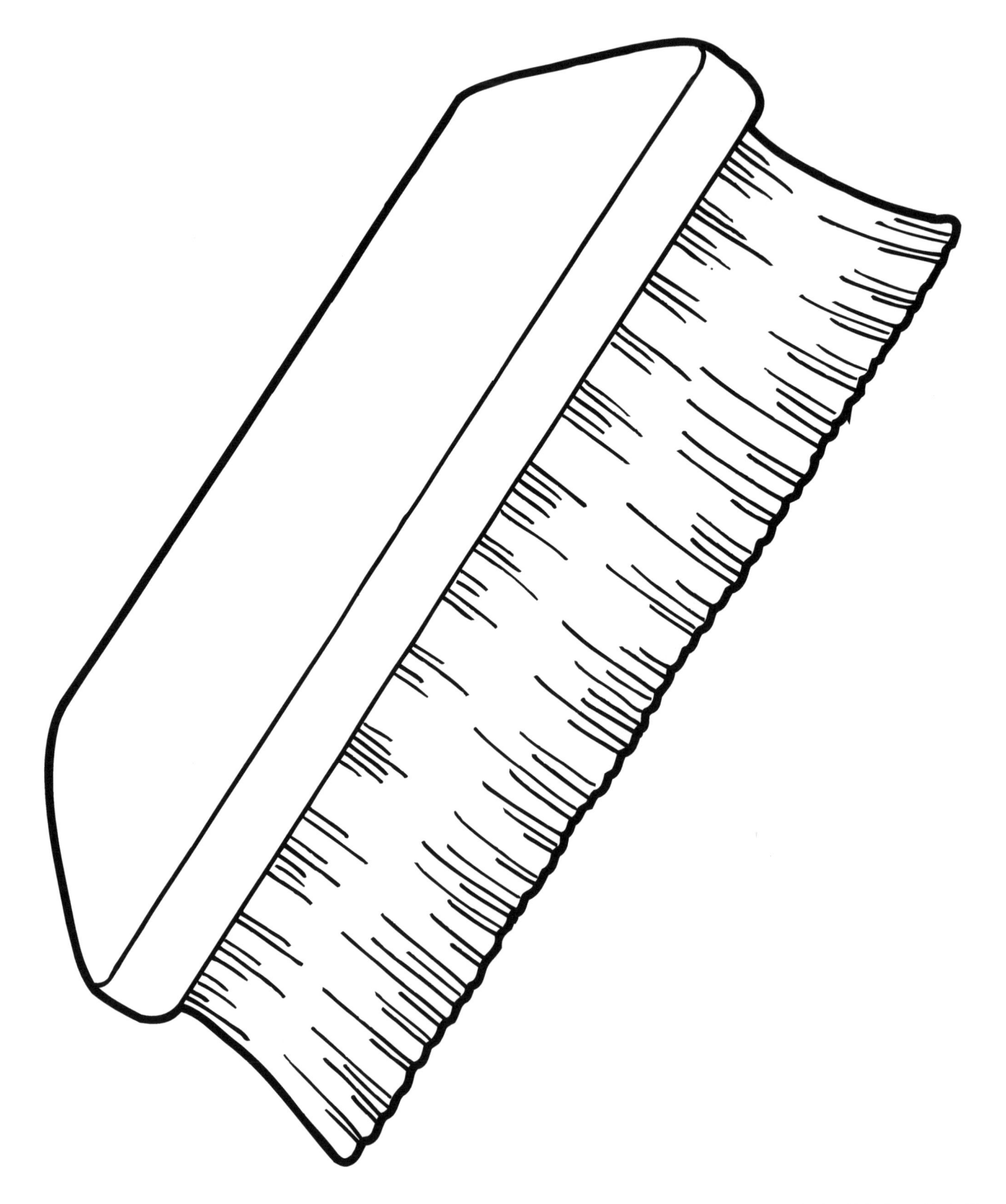

bubbles

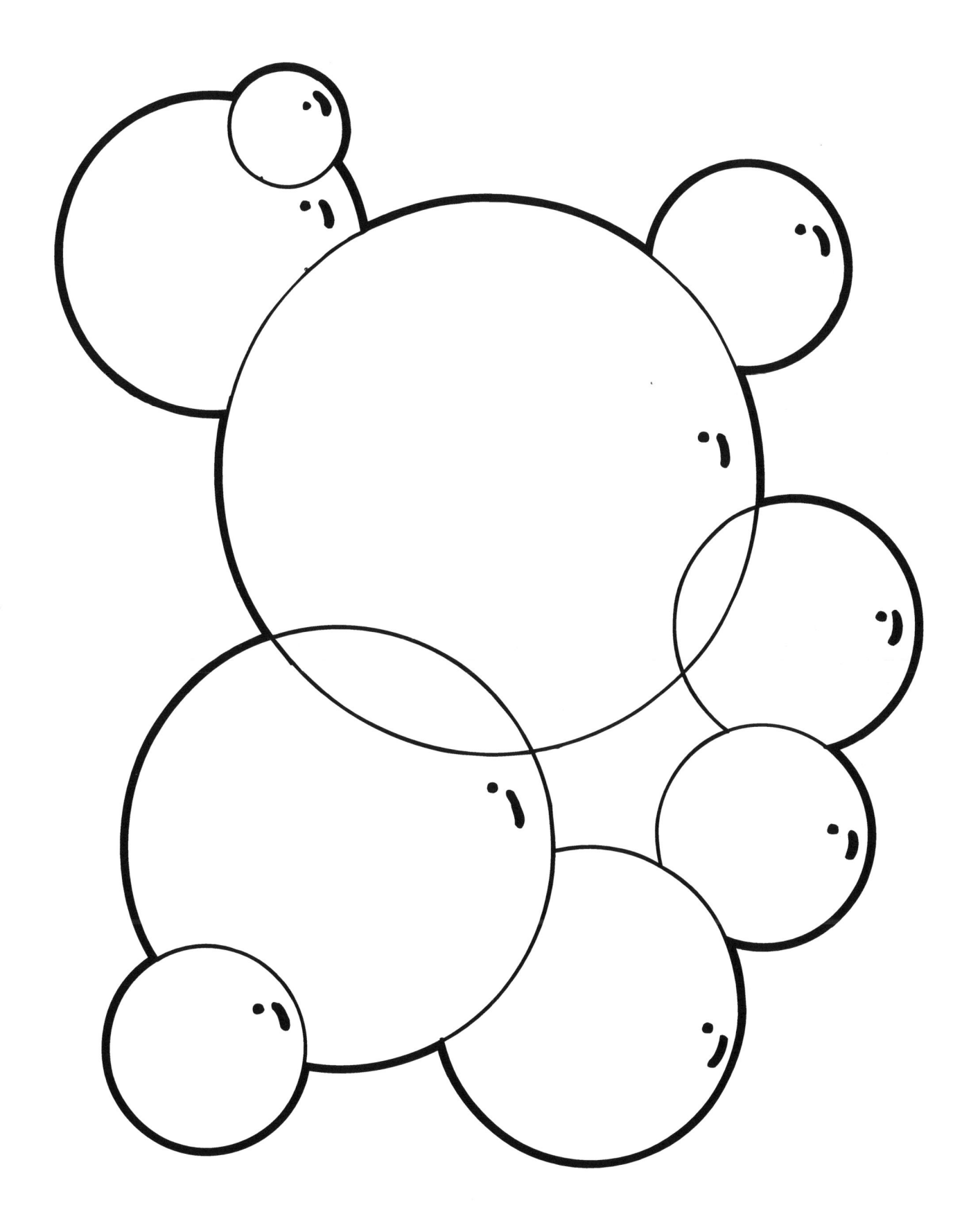

bucket (wire handle)

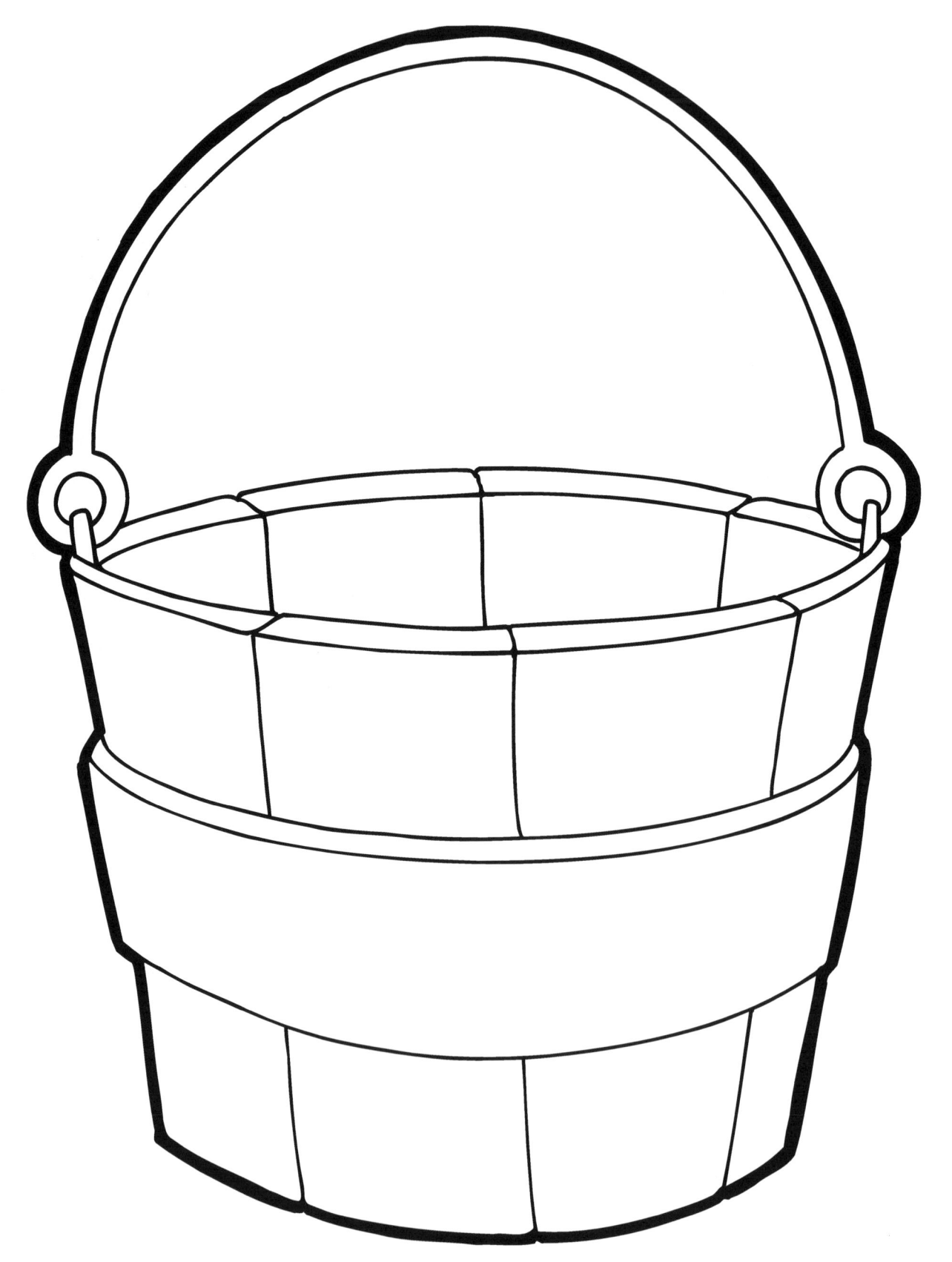

bucket (rustic)

buckle

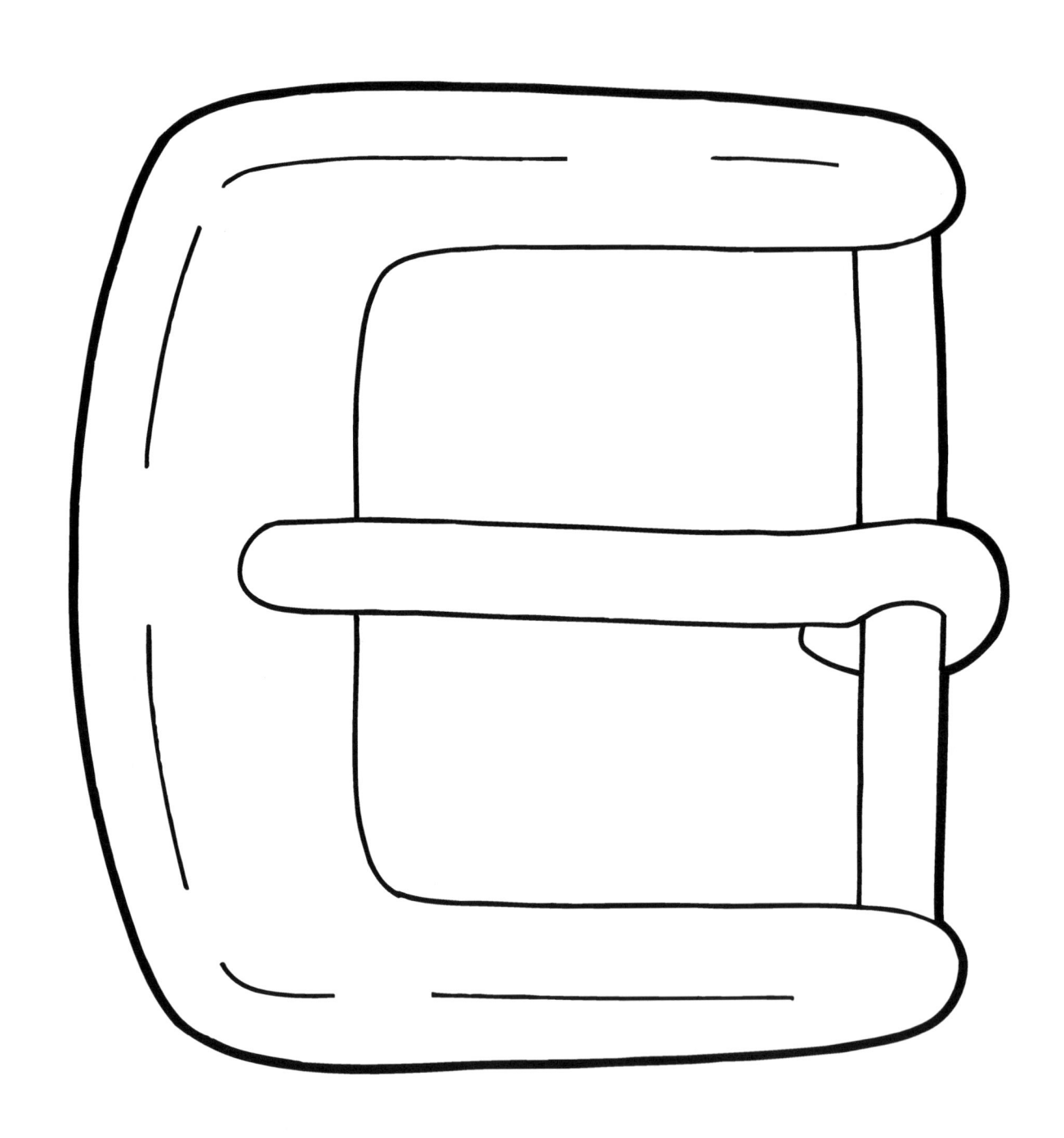

buffalo

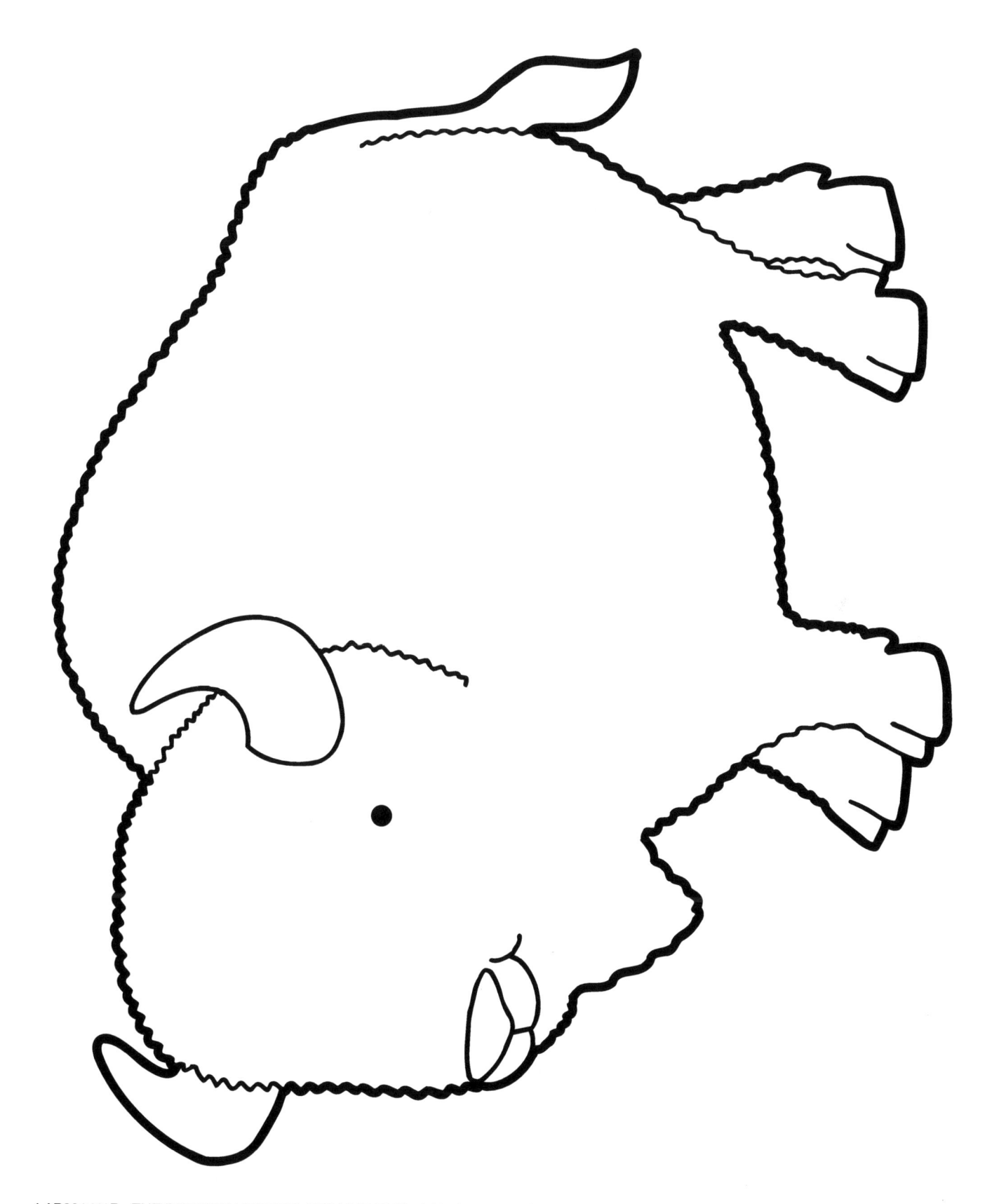

bun (hotdog)

bunny

bunny (outline)

bus (city)

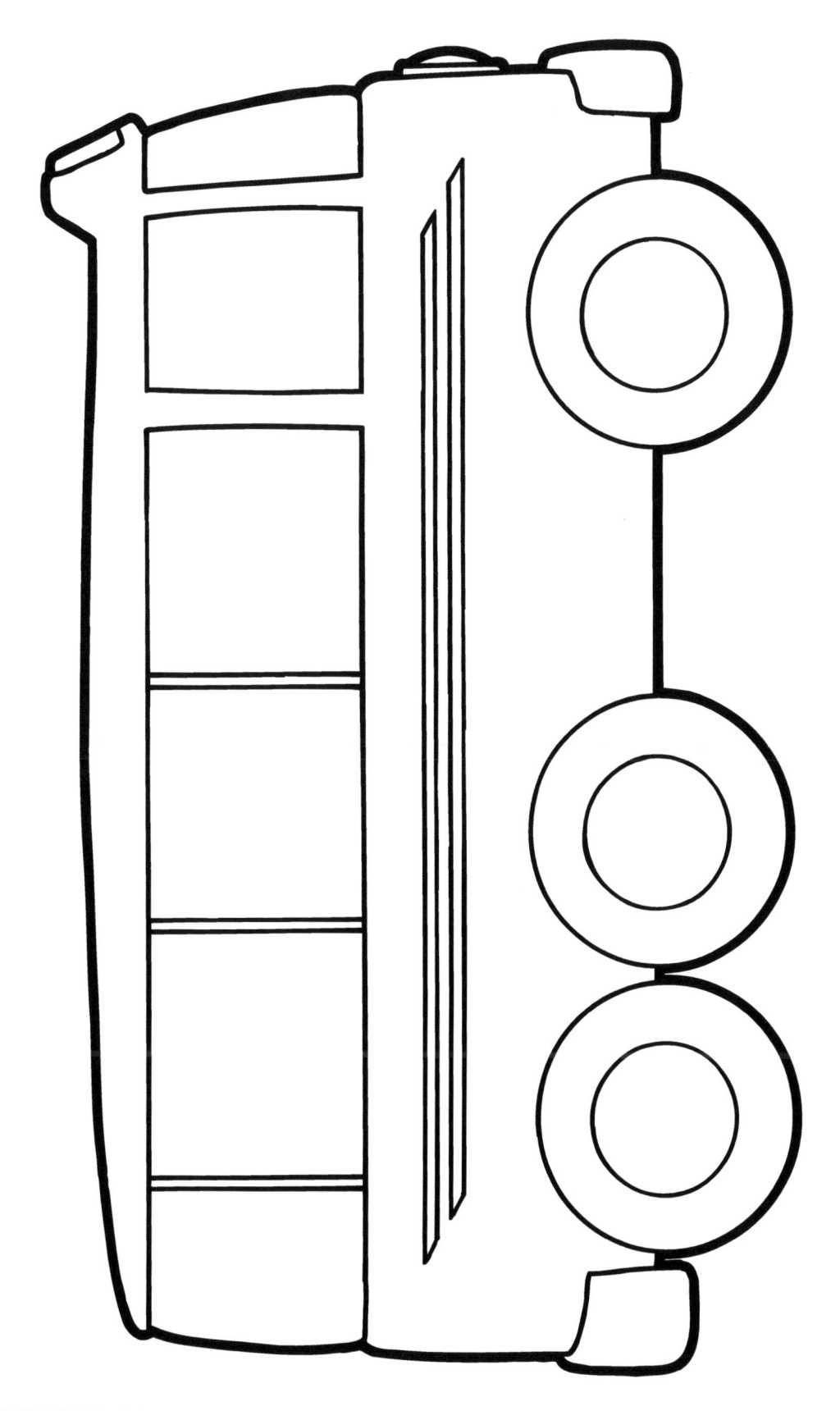

bus (school)

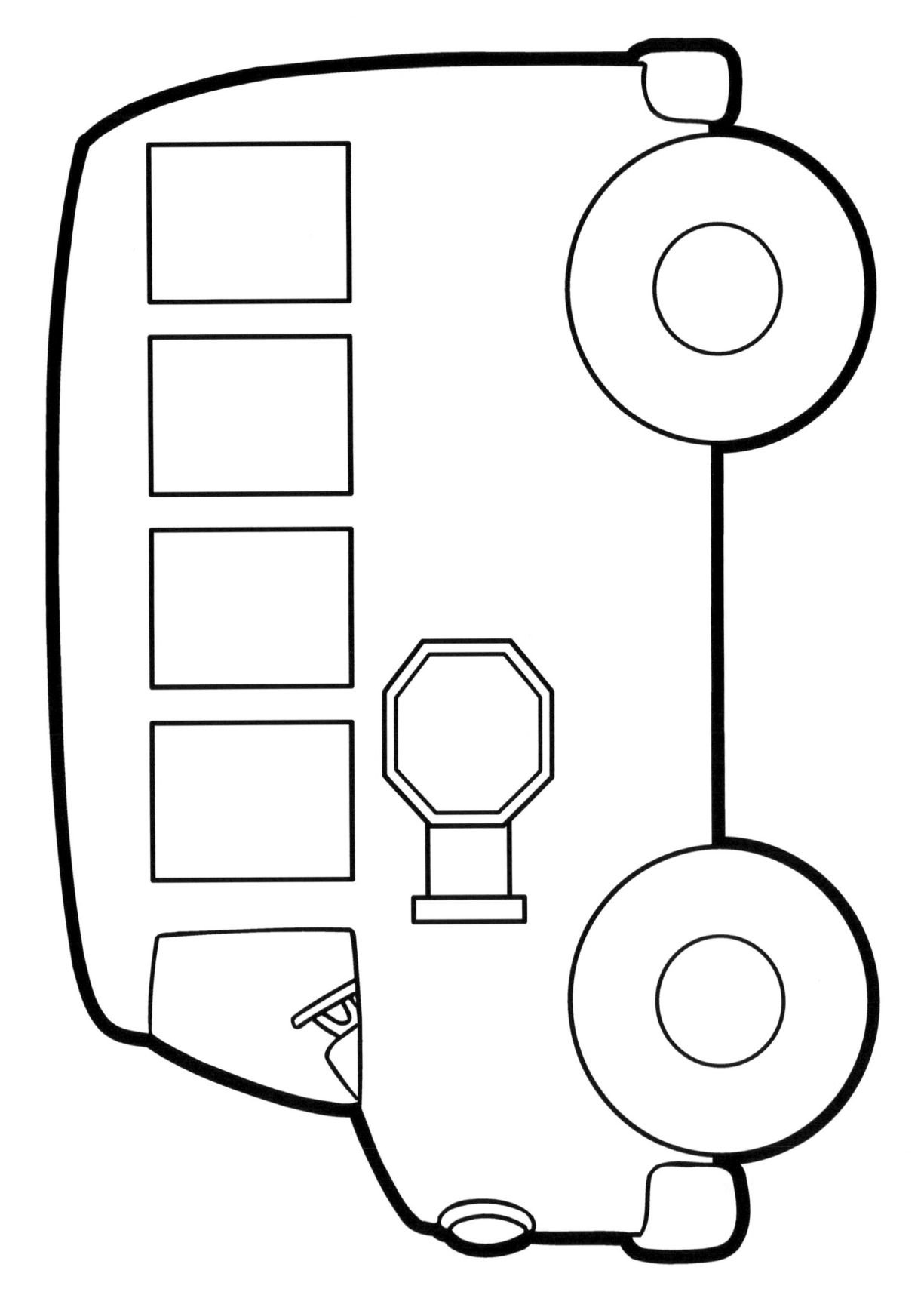

butter

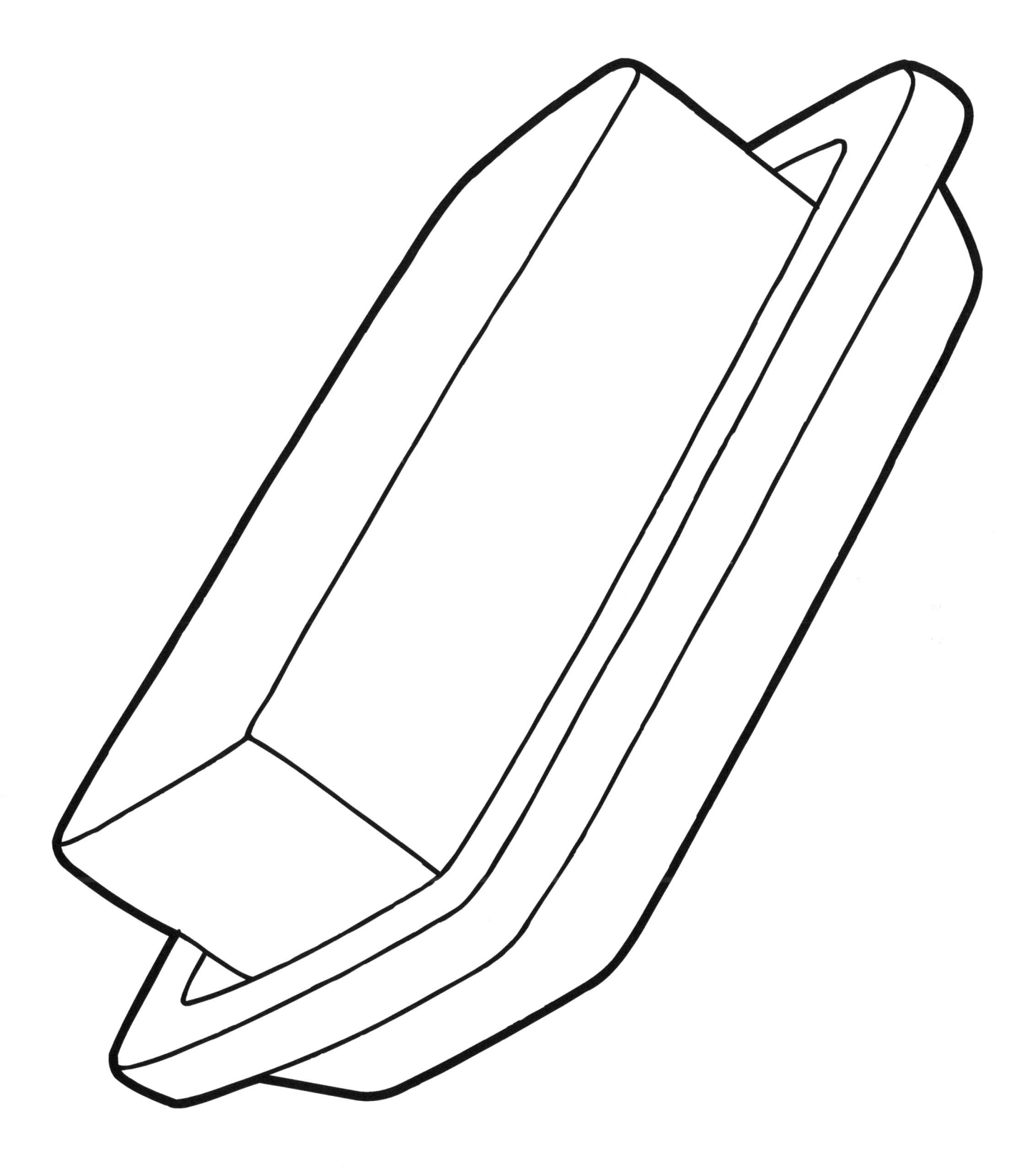

butter churn

butterfly (animated)

butterfly (full view)

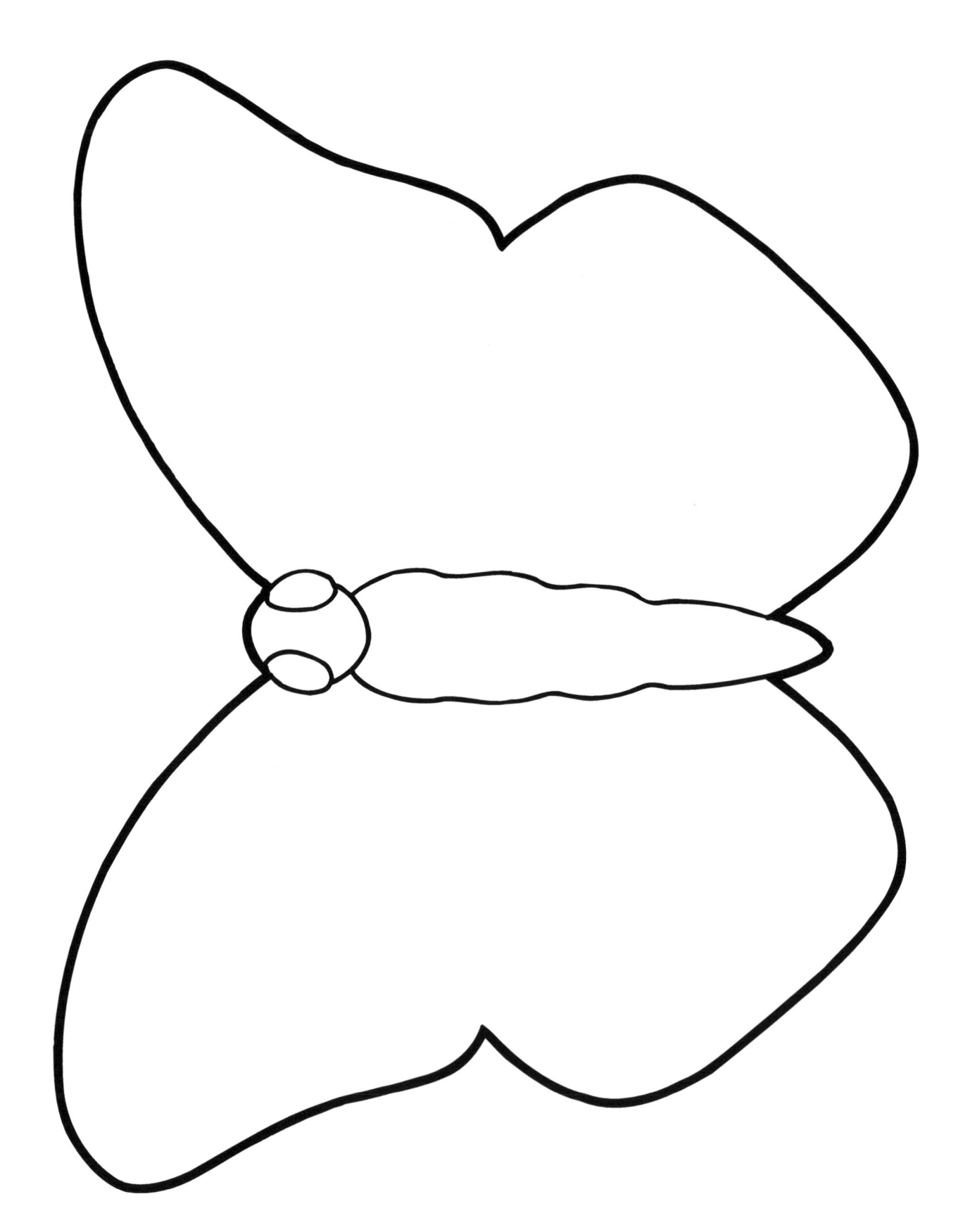

butterfly (side view)

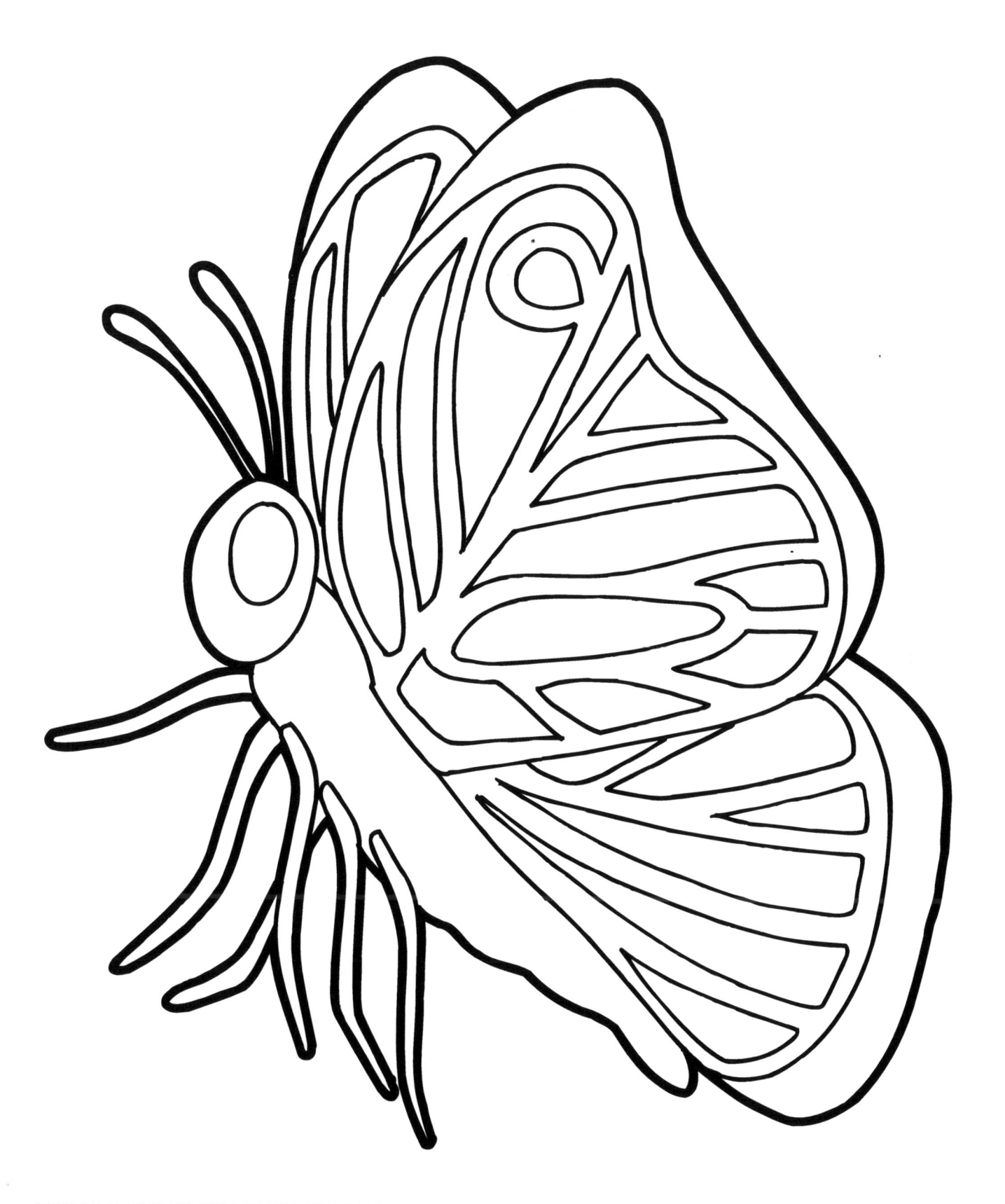

butterfly (outline)

cactus

cage (bird)

cage (circus train)

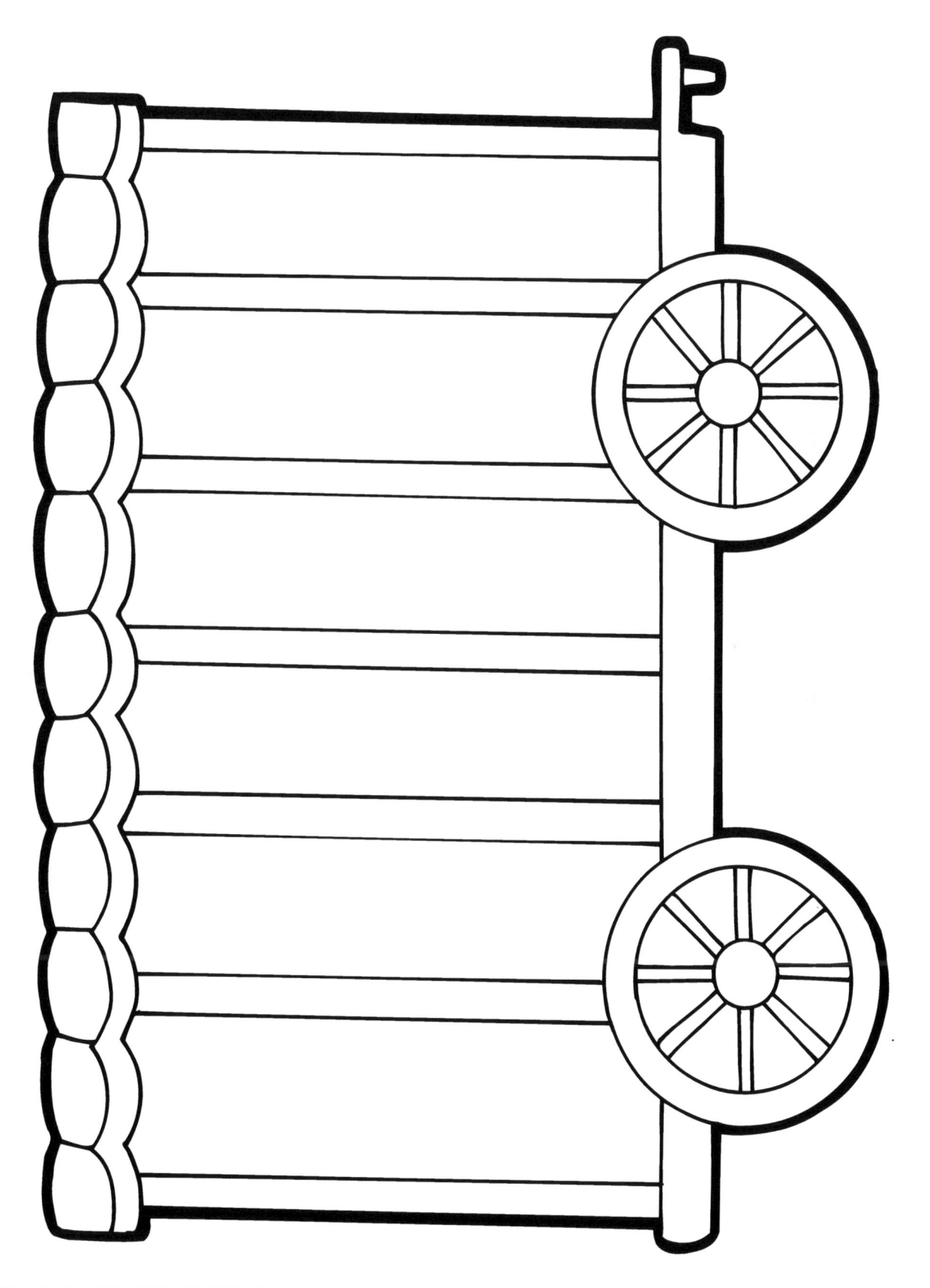

cage (hamster)

cake

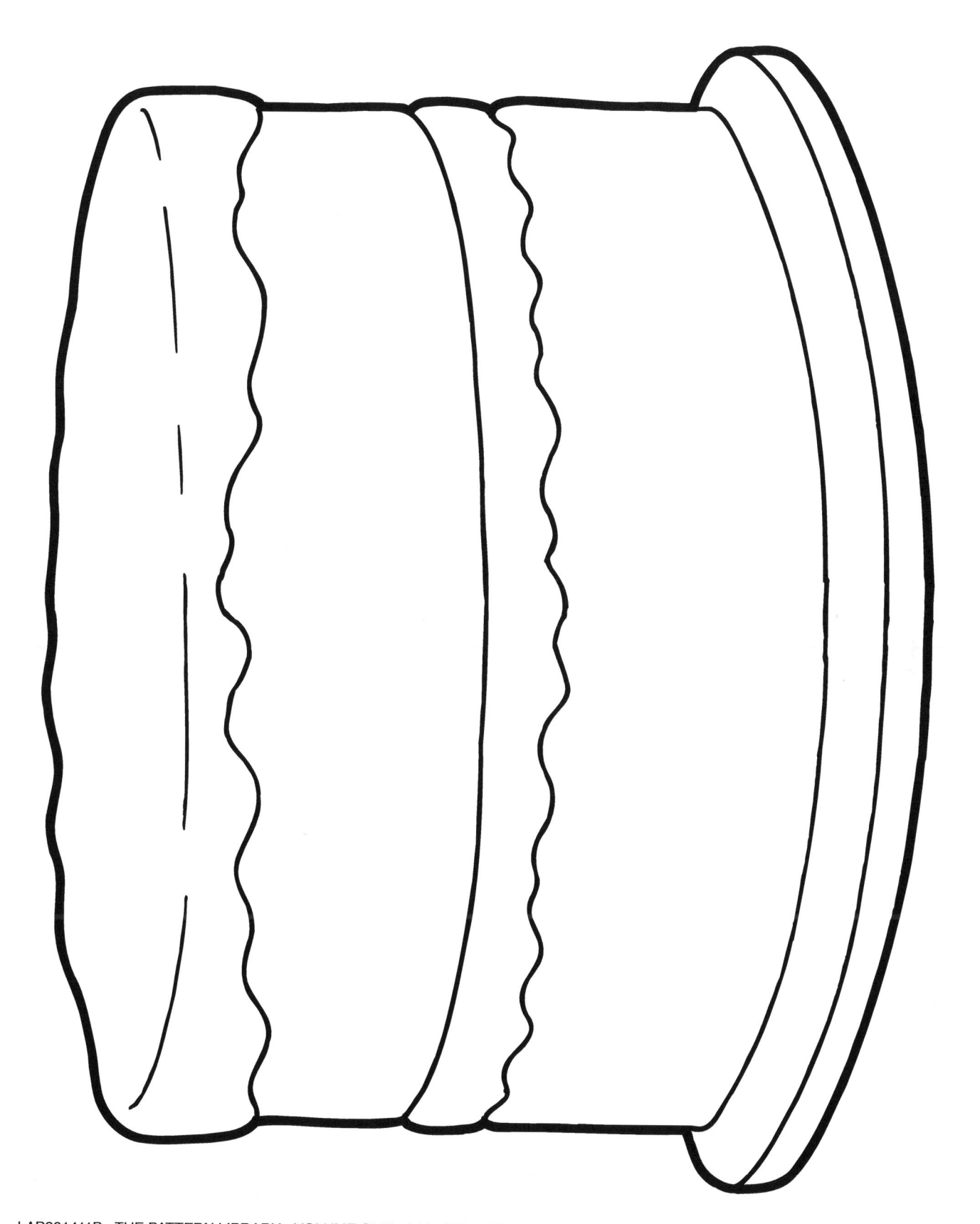

California, USA

Maps are representations and boundaries are not exact.

camel (dromedary)

camera

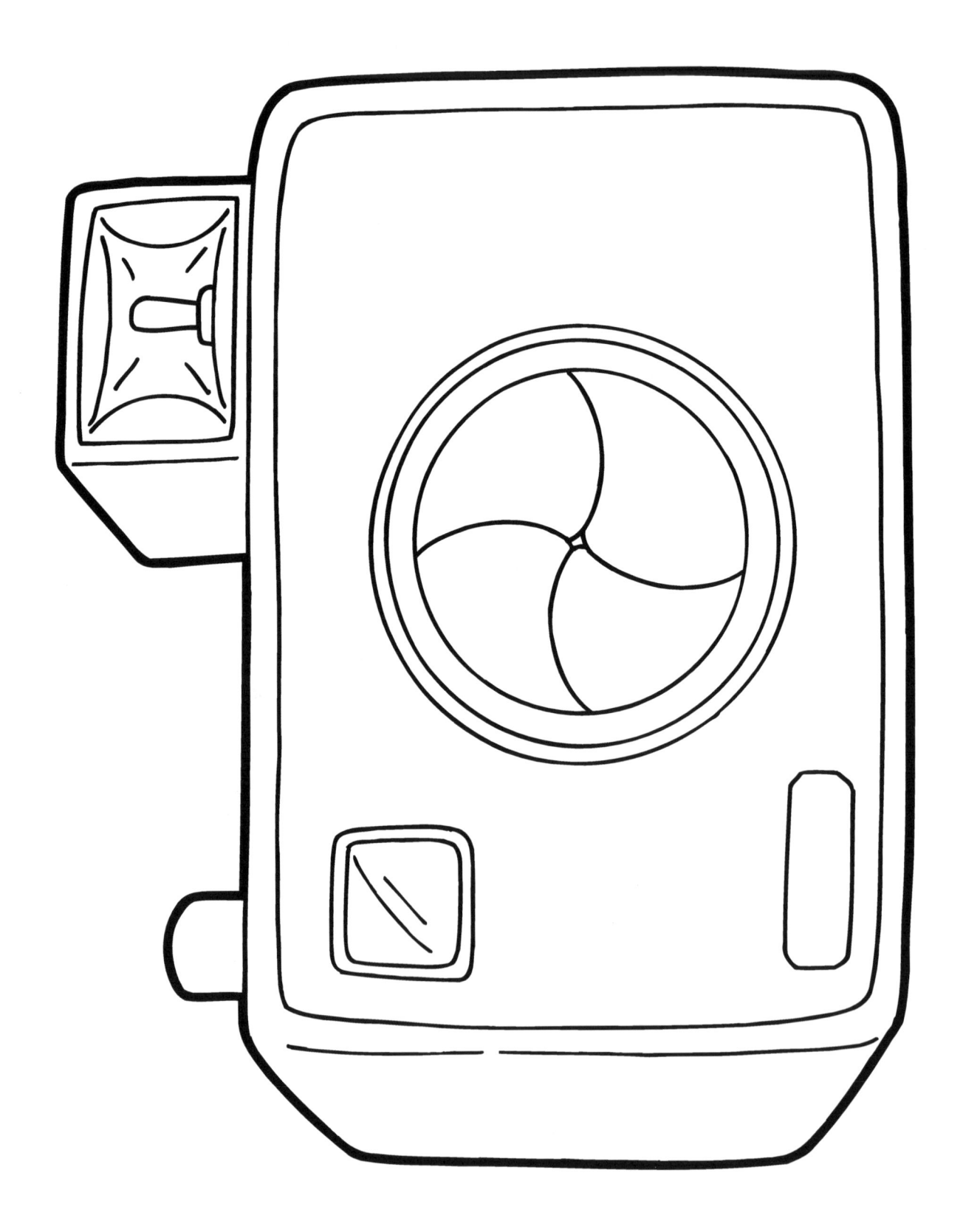

can (coffee)

can (tuna)

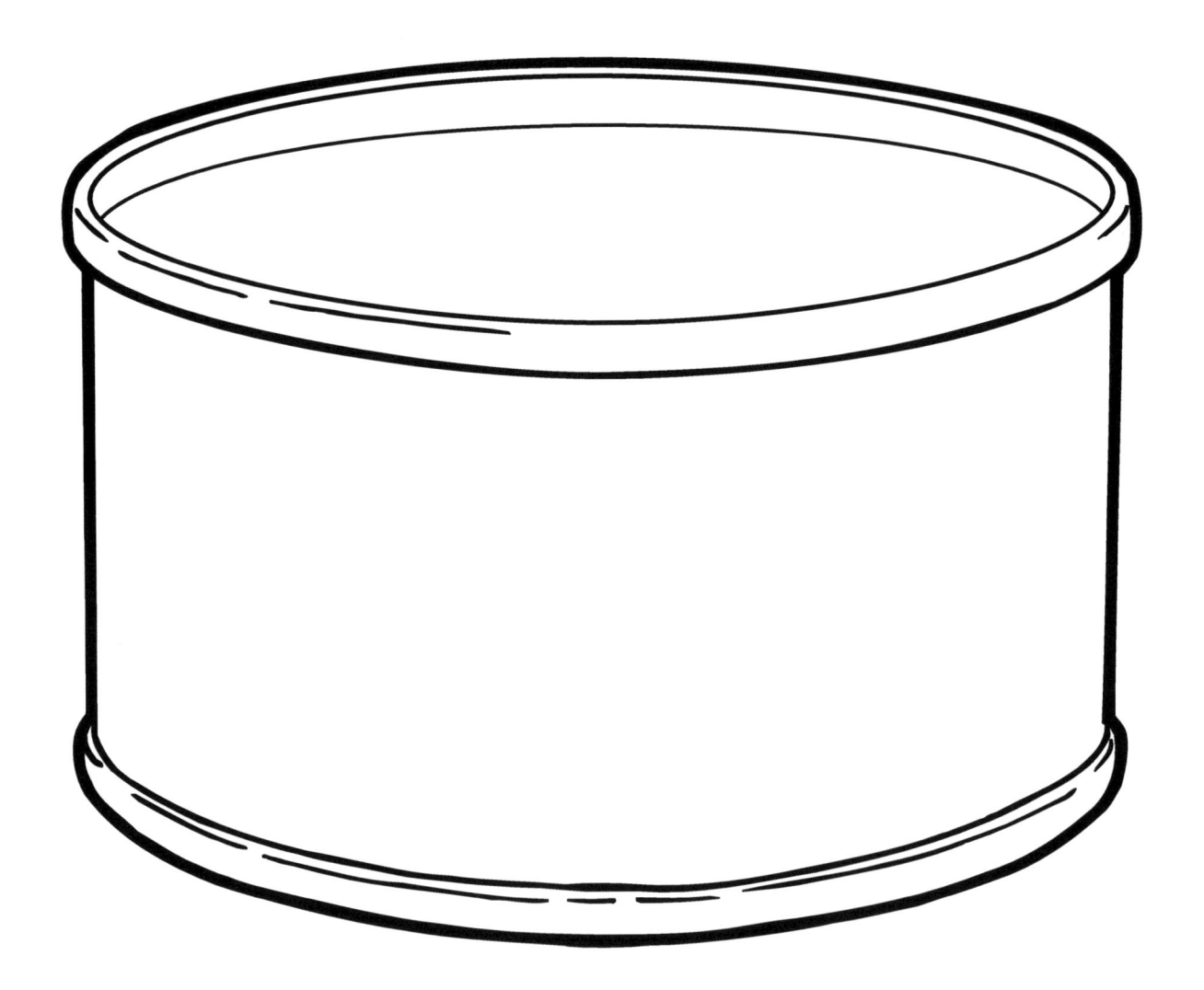

Canada

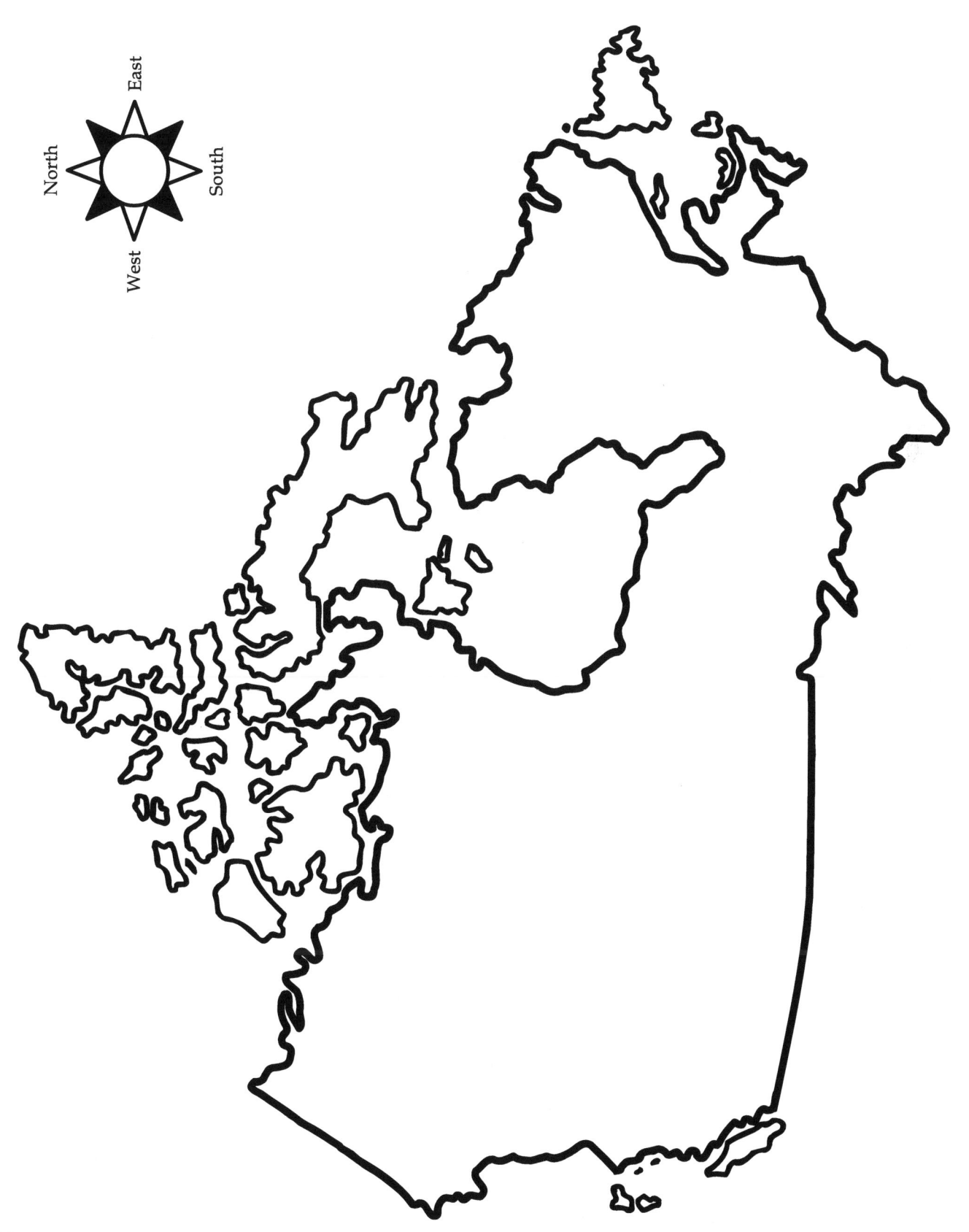

North East South West

Maps are representations and boundaries are not exact.

Canada (boundaries)

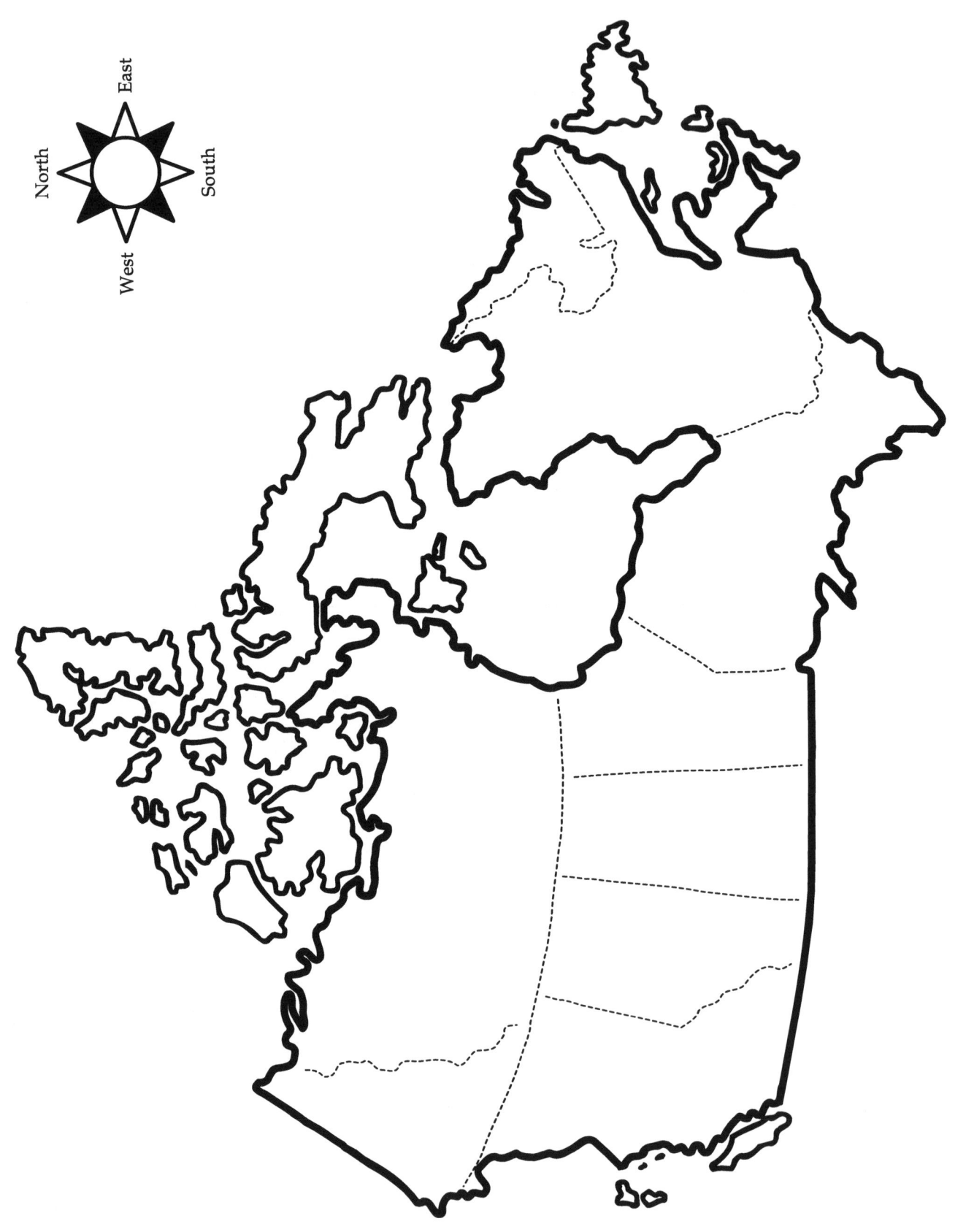

Maps are representations and boundaries are not exact.

candle (pillar)

candle (thumb candle holder)

candles

candy cane

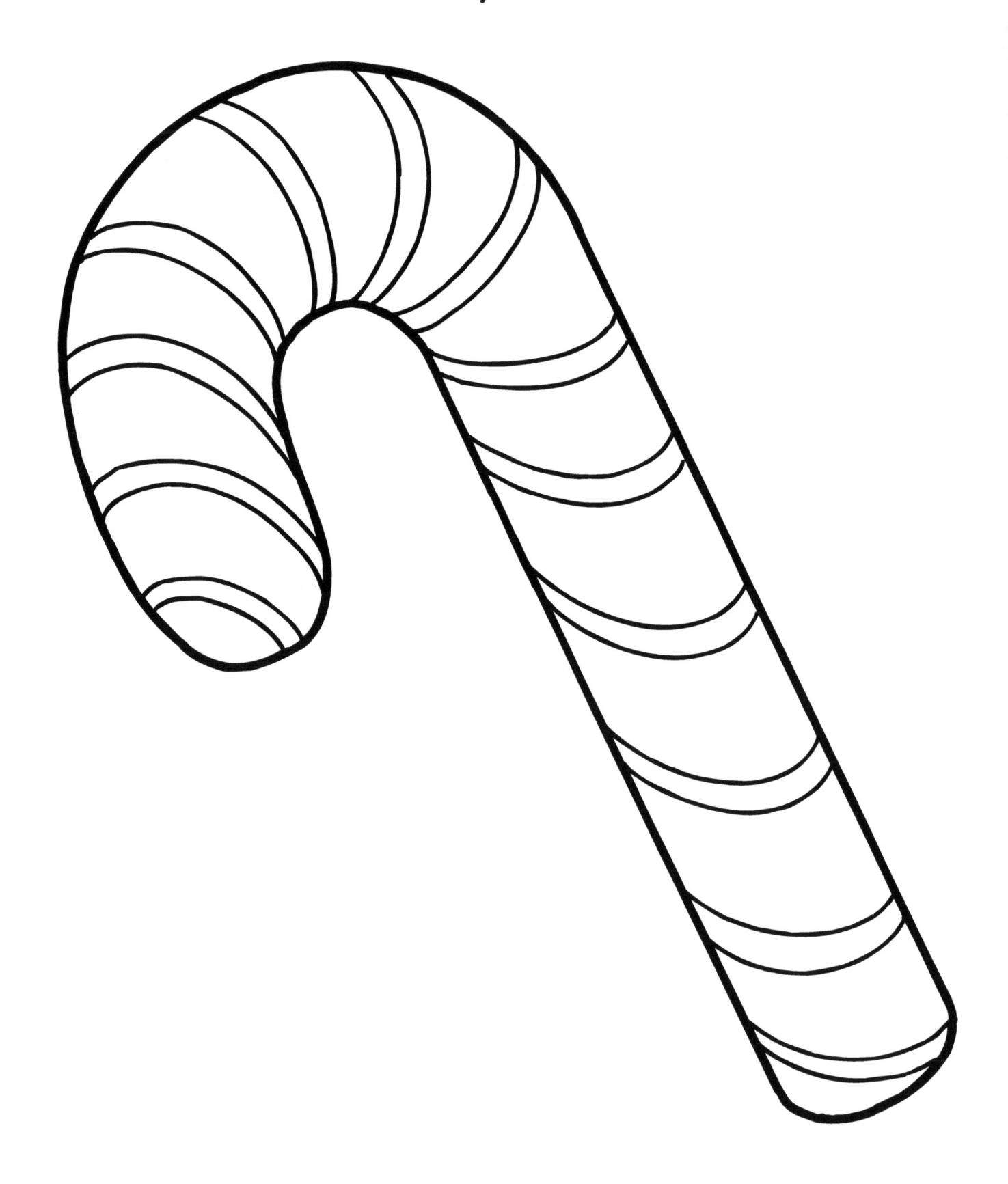

candy (cherry cordial)

candy corn

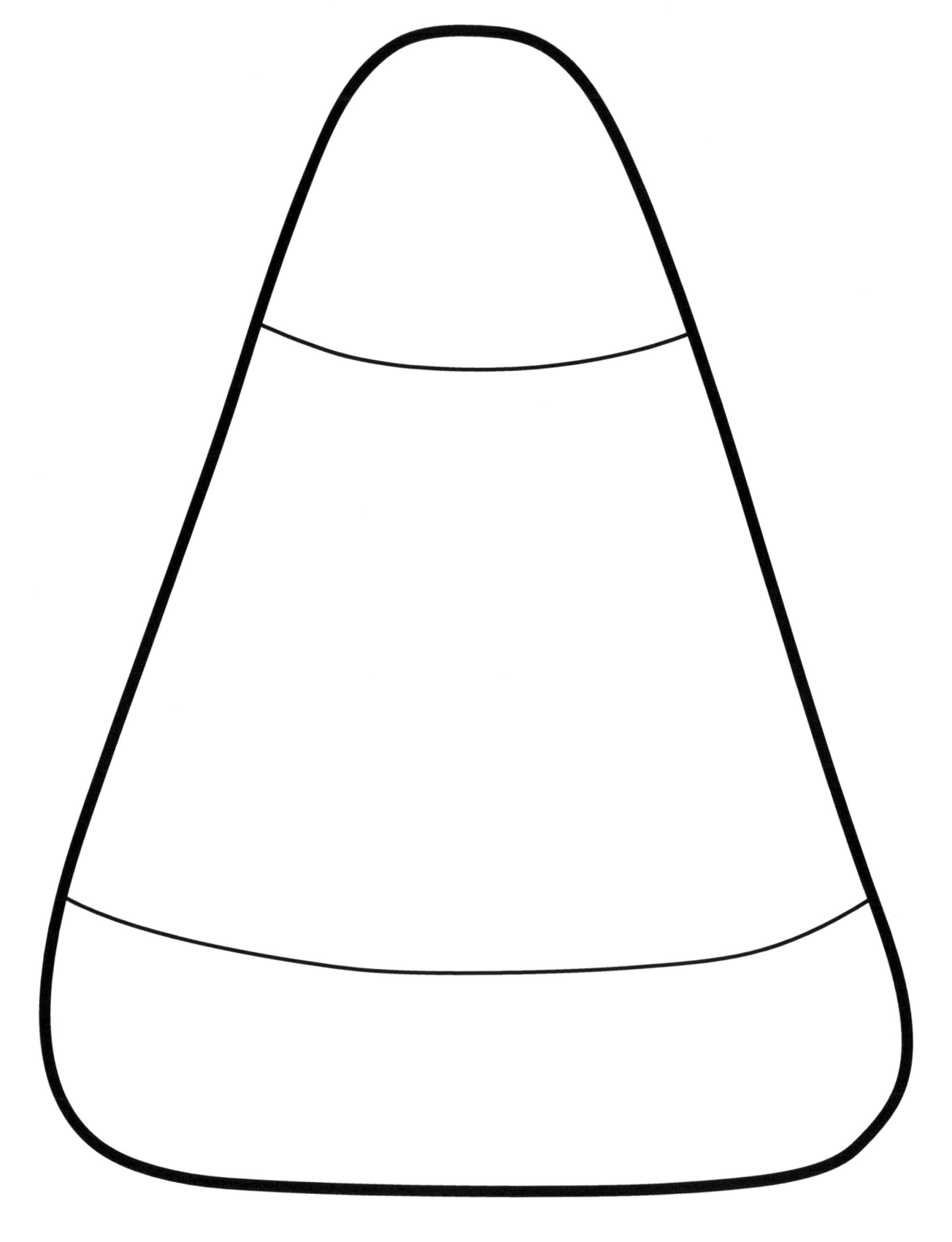

candy hearts

candy (peppermint)

cane

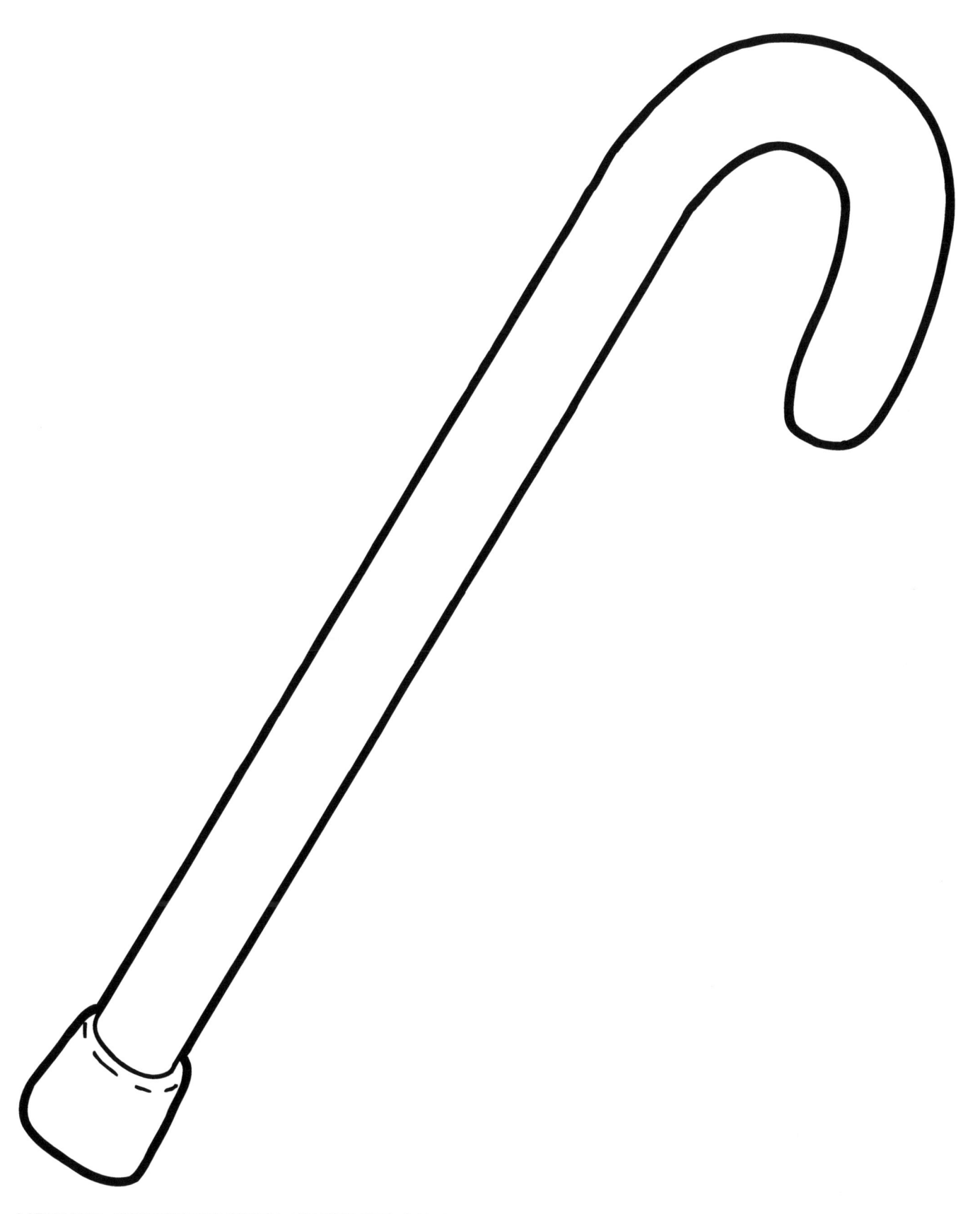

canoe

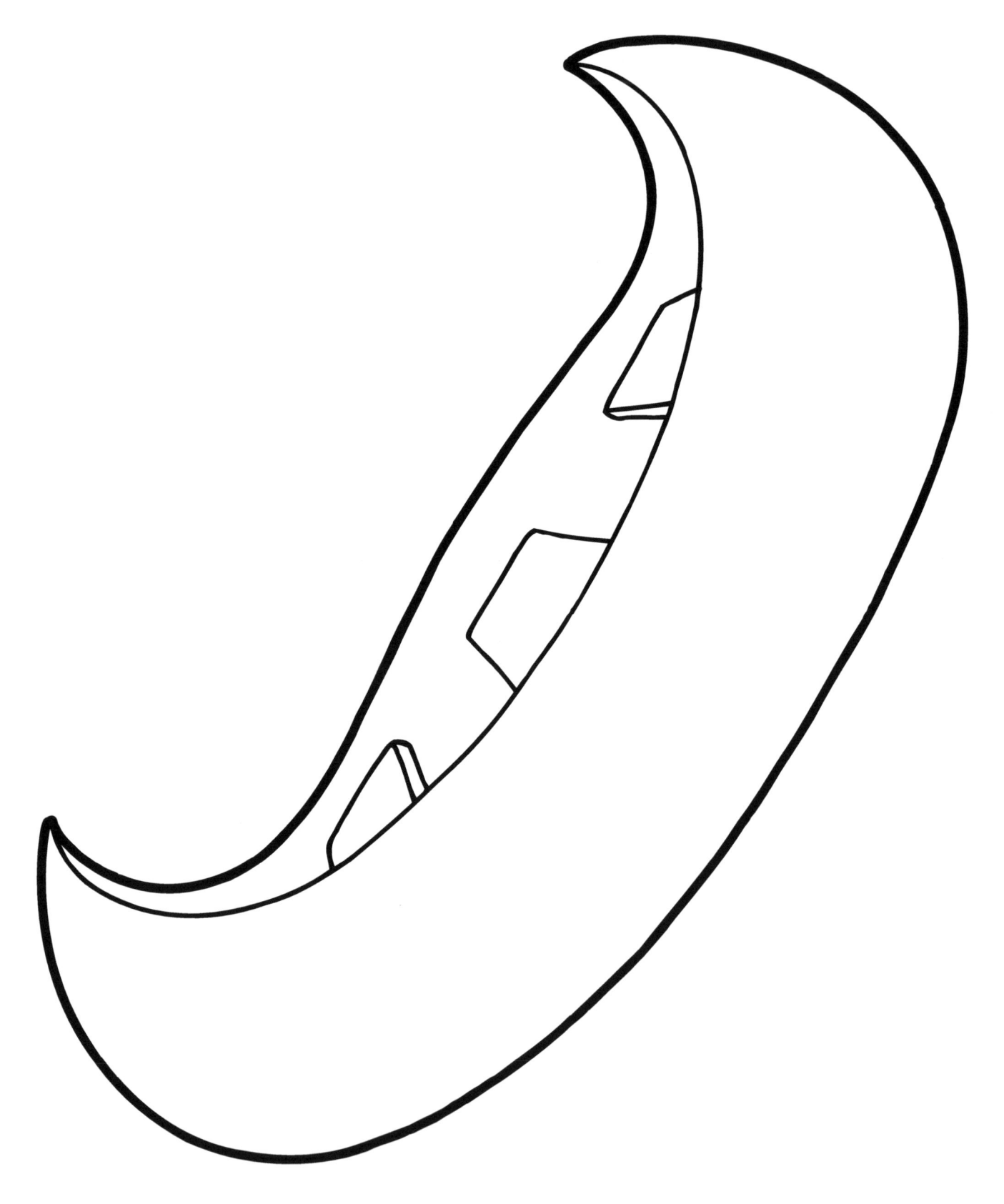

cap (plain)

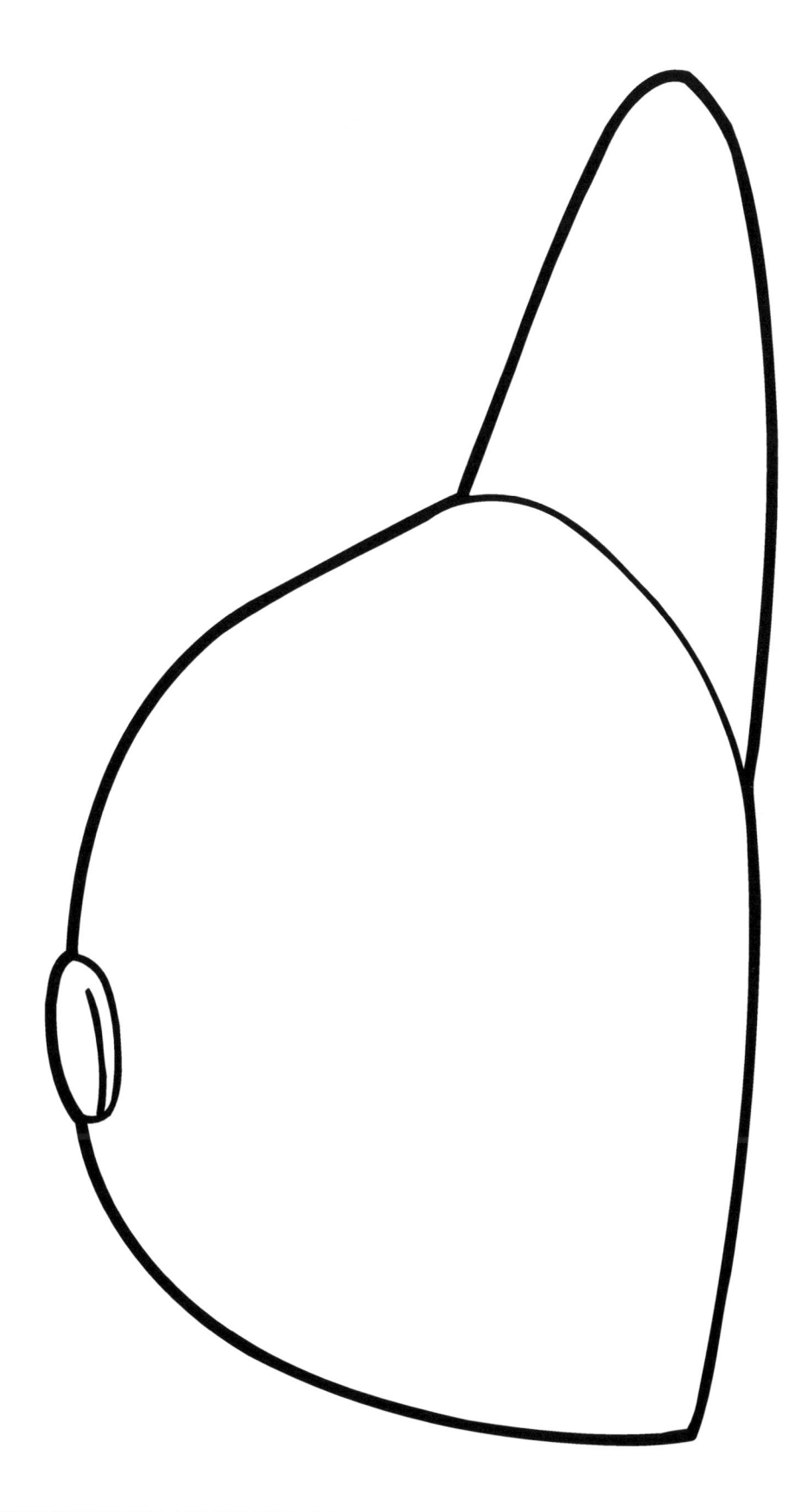

cap (with stiches)

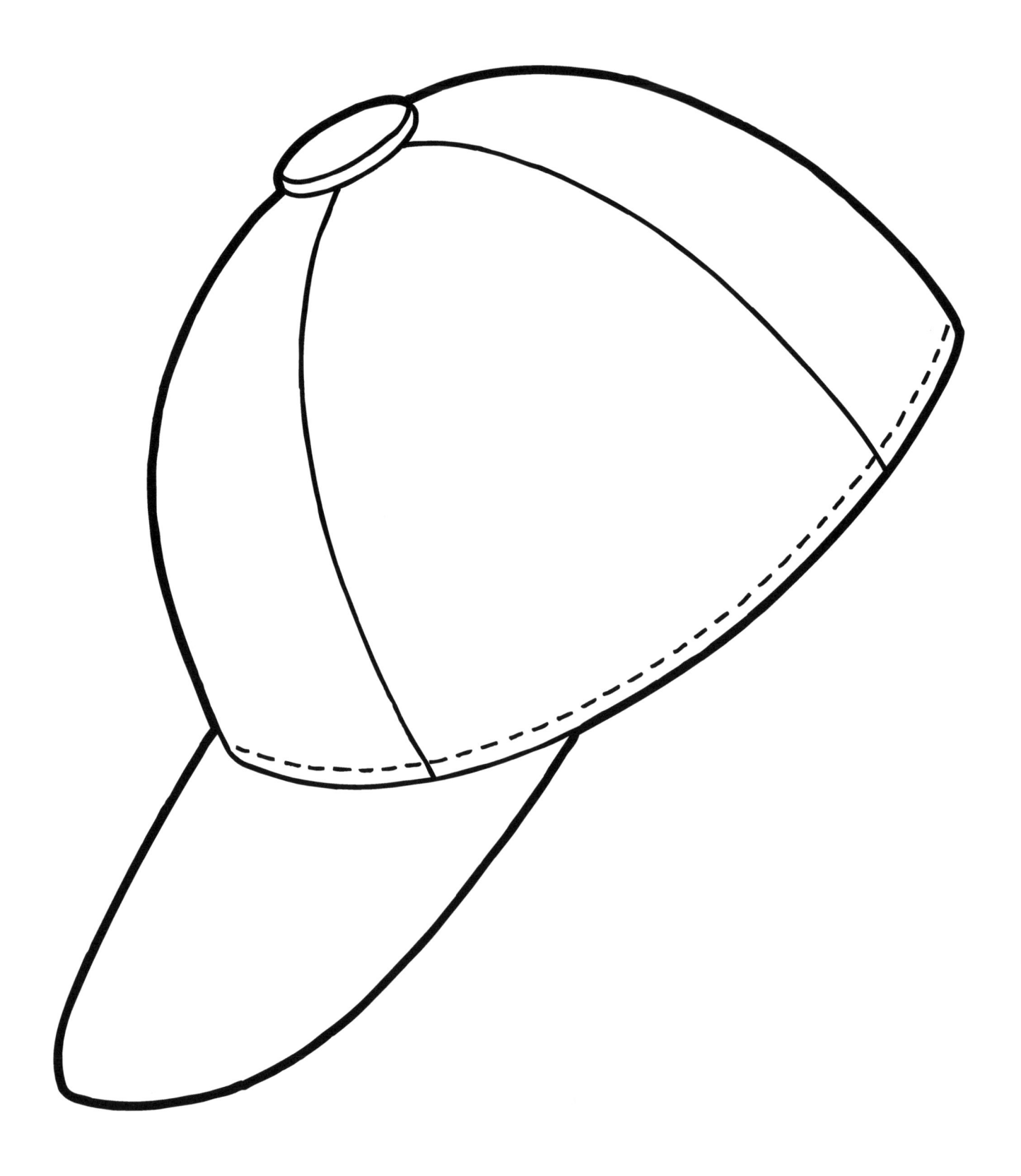

cape

Capital Building

(Washington, DC, USA)

car

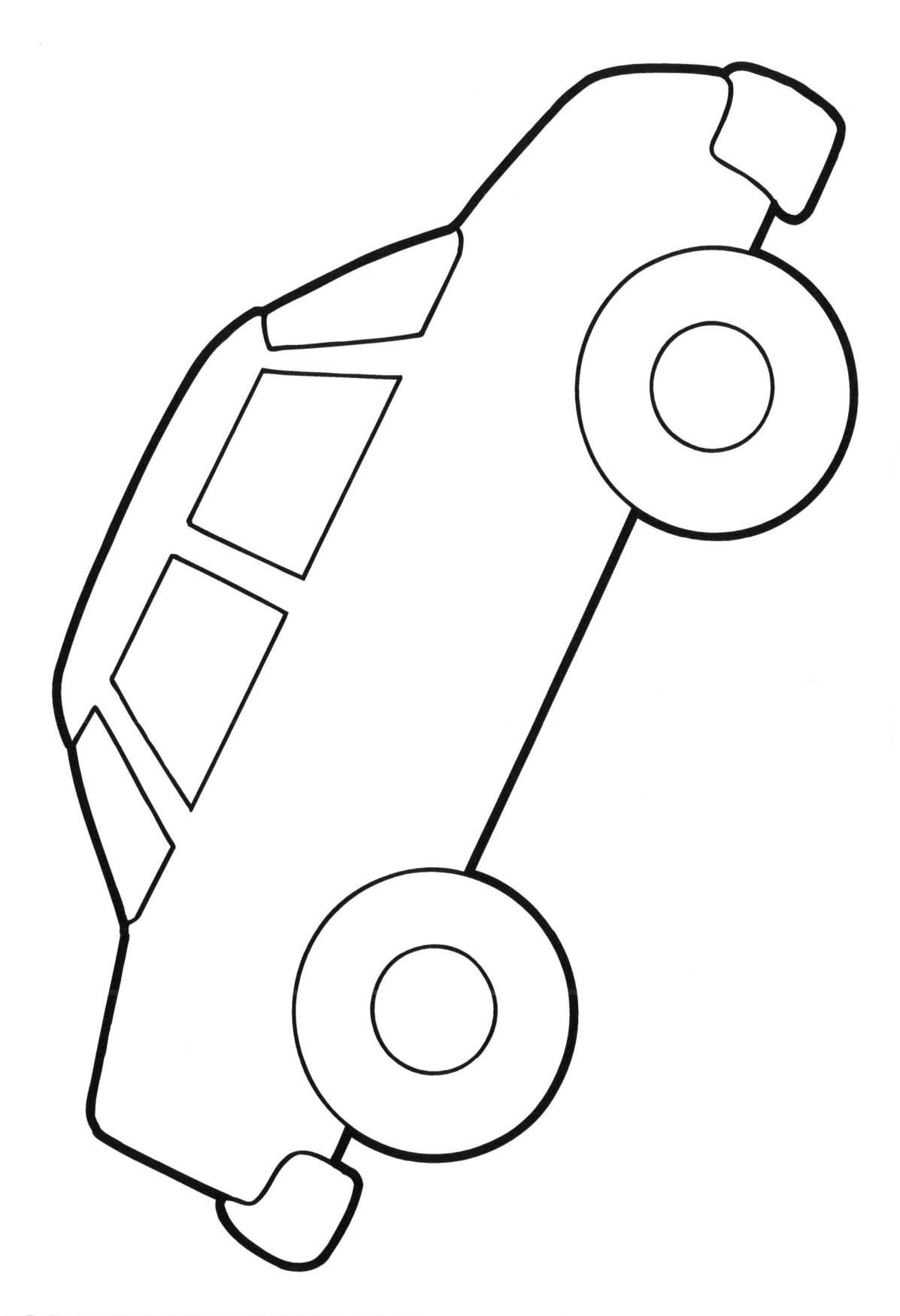

car (Model-T)

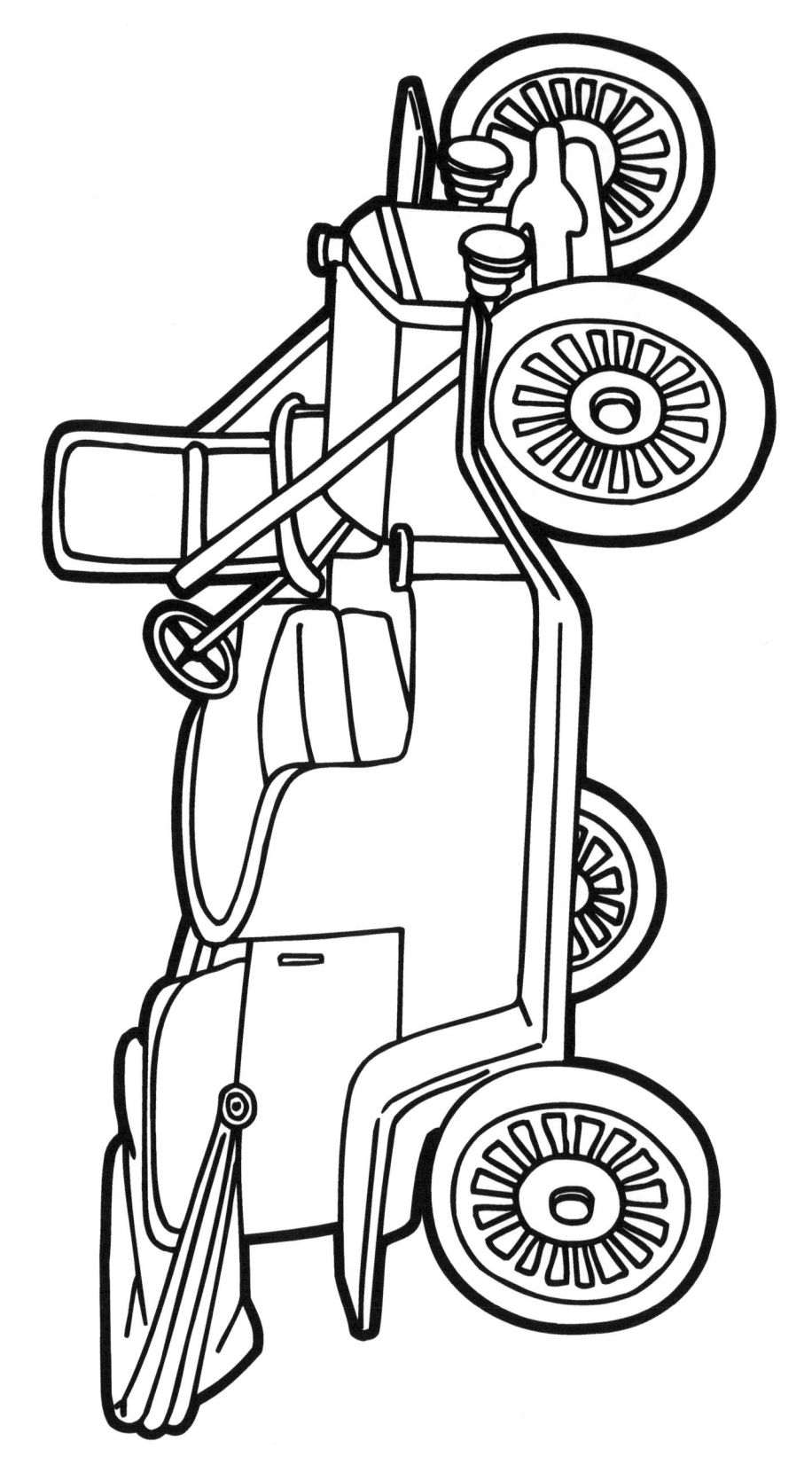

carafe

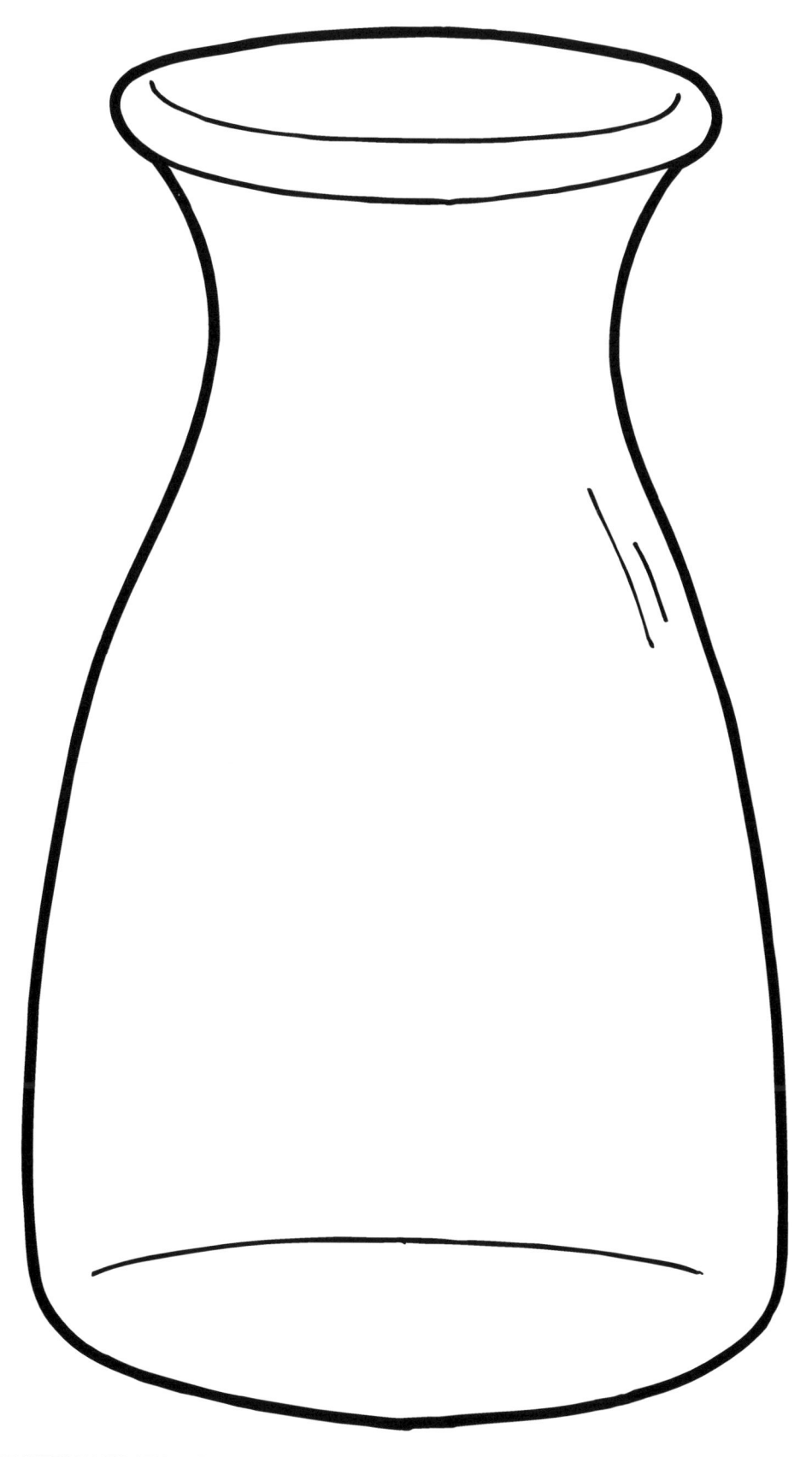

card (playing)

carousel

carrots

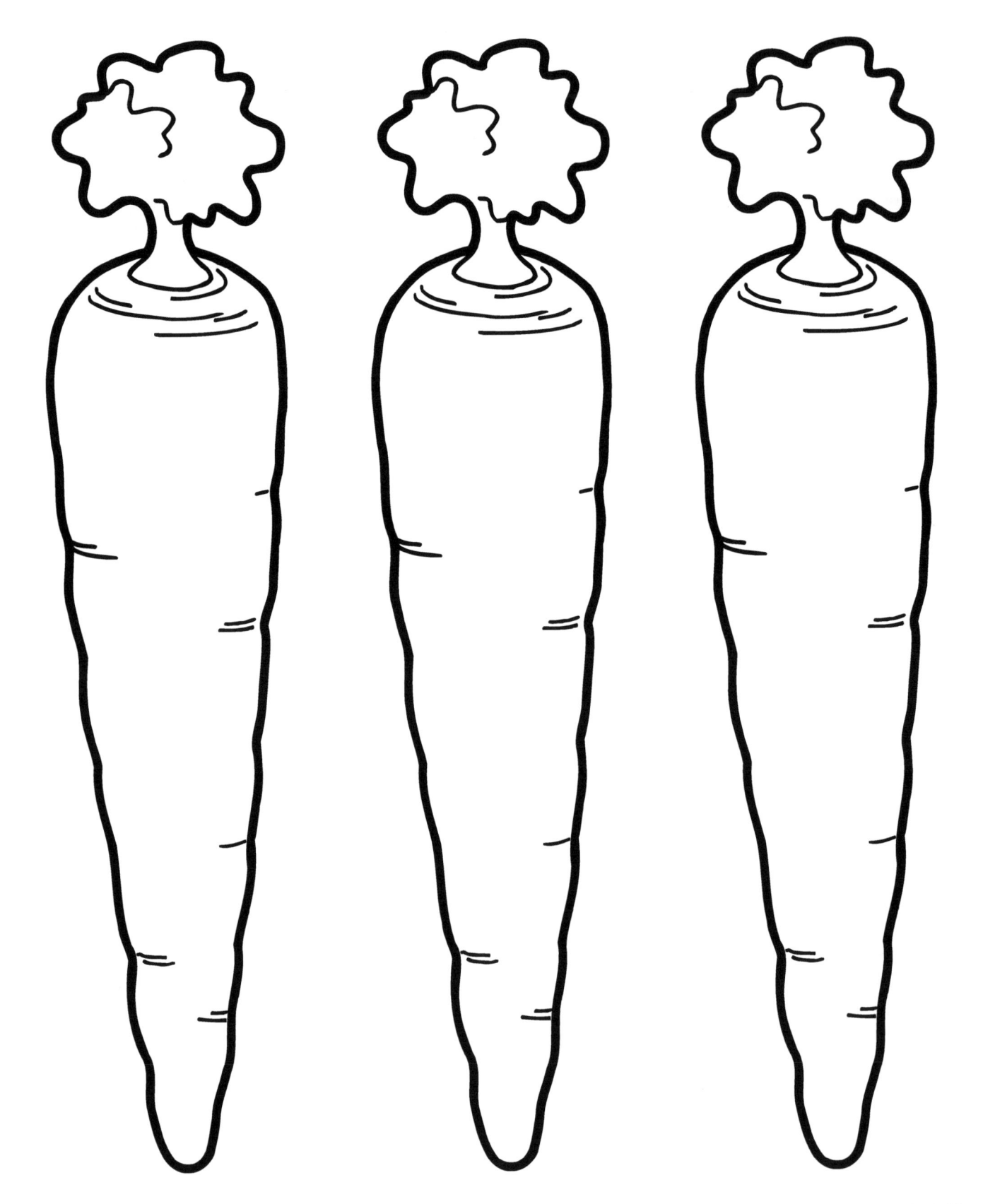

castañet

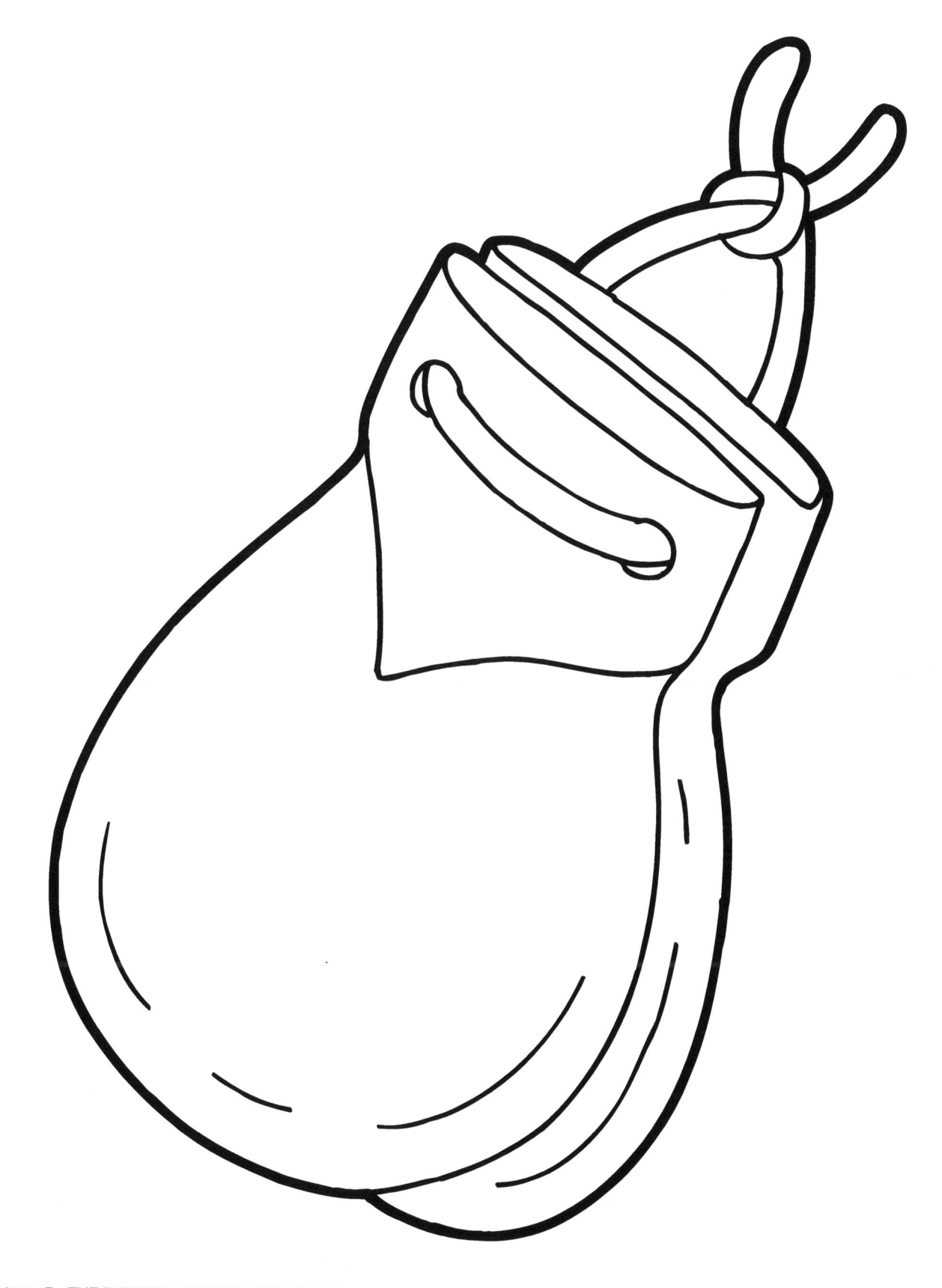

castle

cat (laying)

cat (outline)

caterpillar

cattail

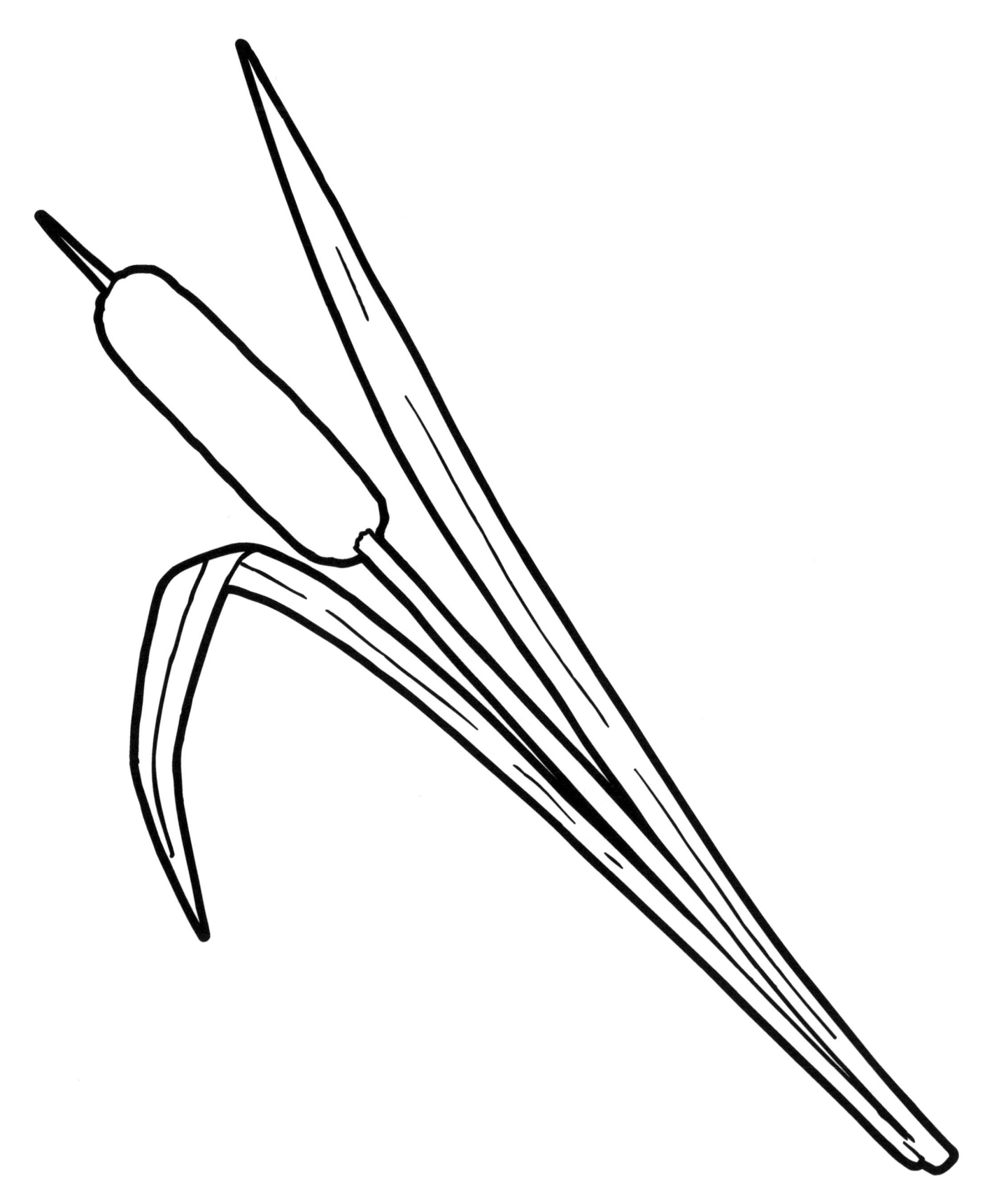

cello

cereal (in bowl)

chain (links)

chair

chameleon

cheese (Swiss)

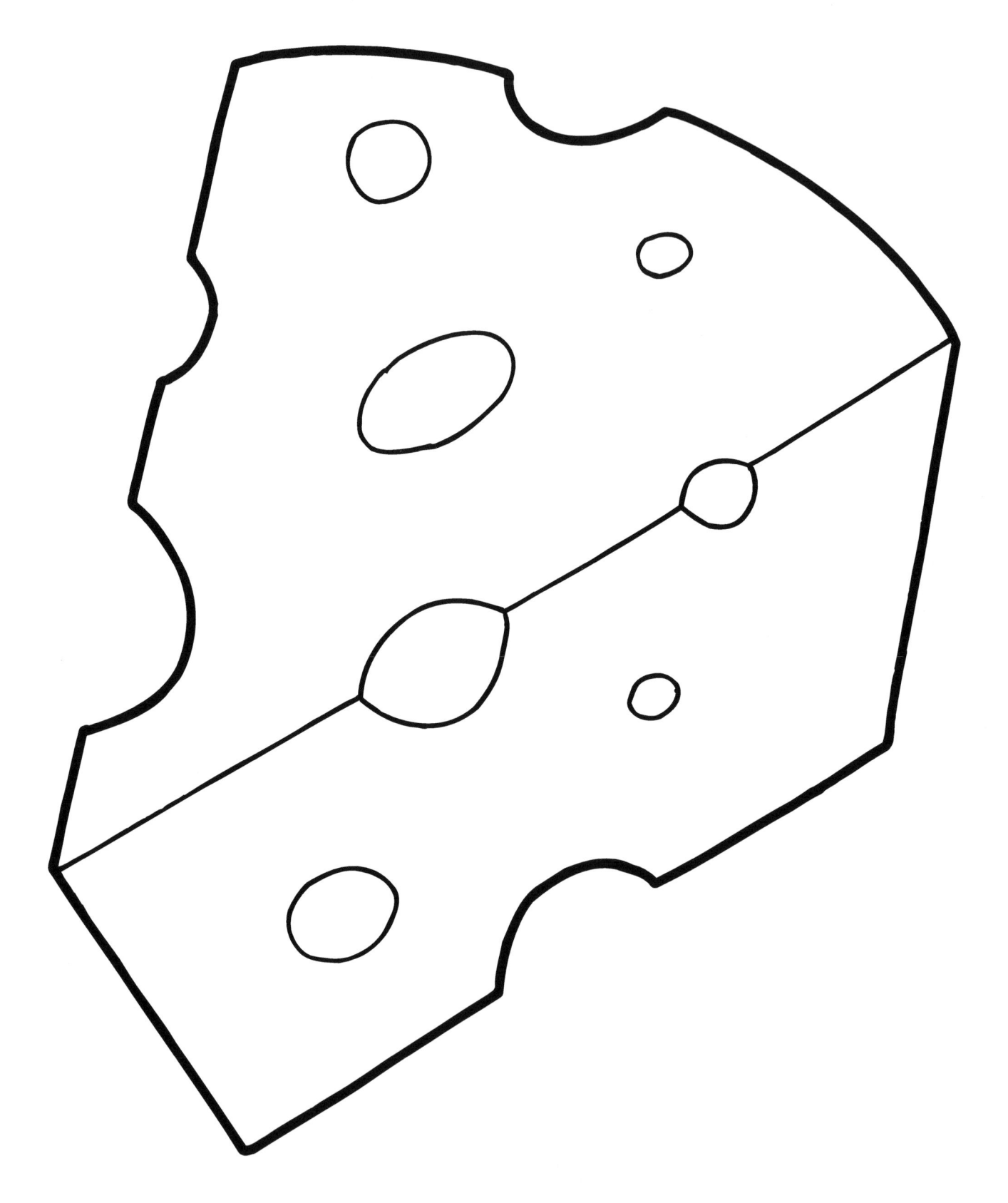

cherries

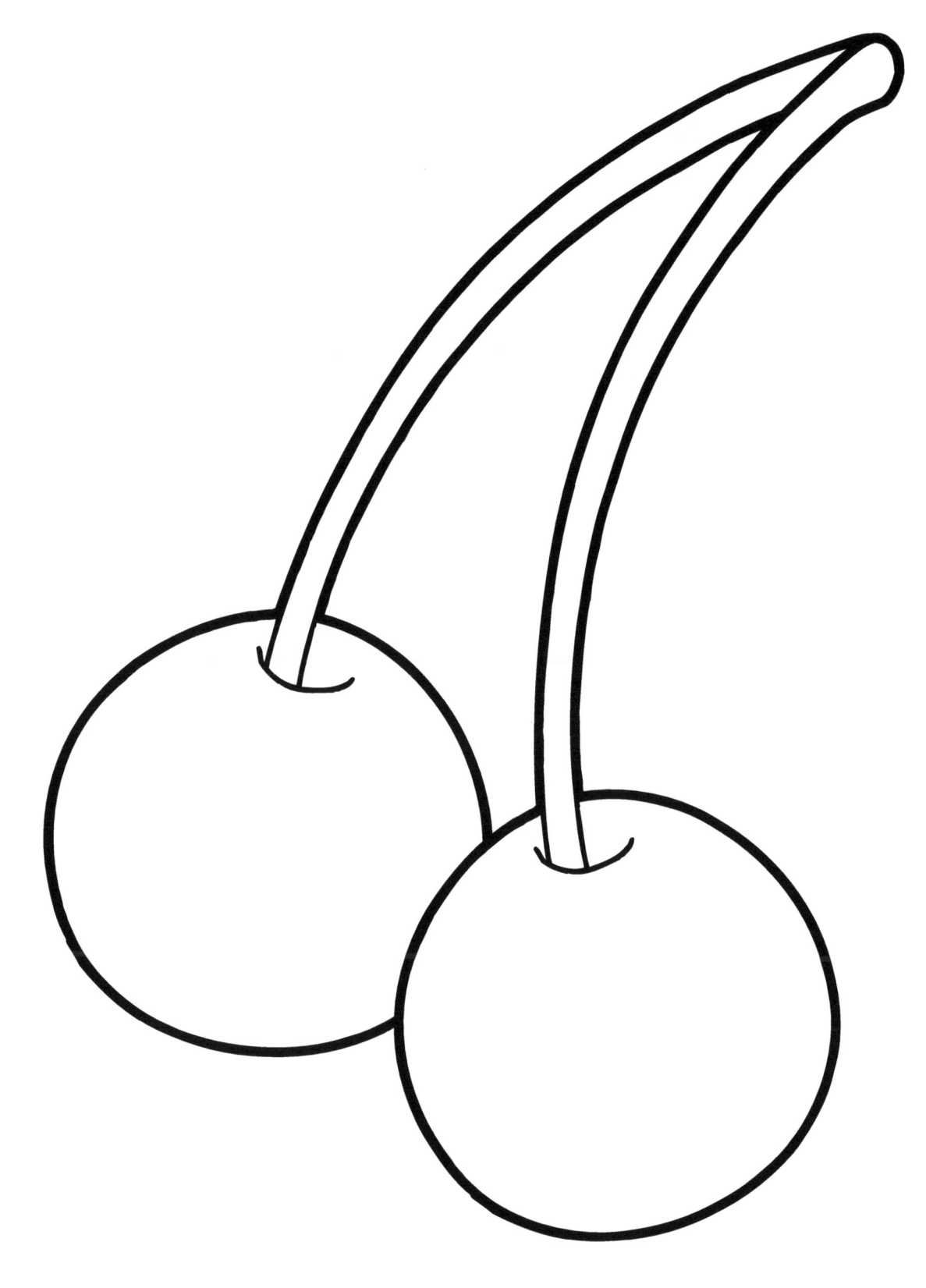

chick

chicken (outline)

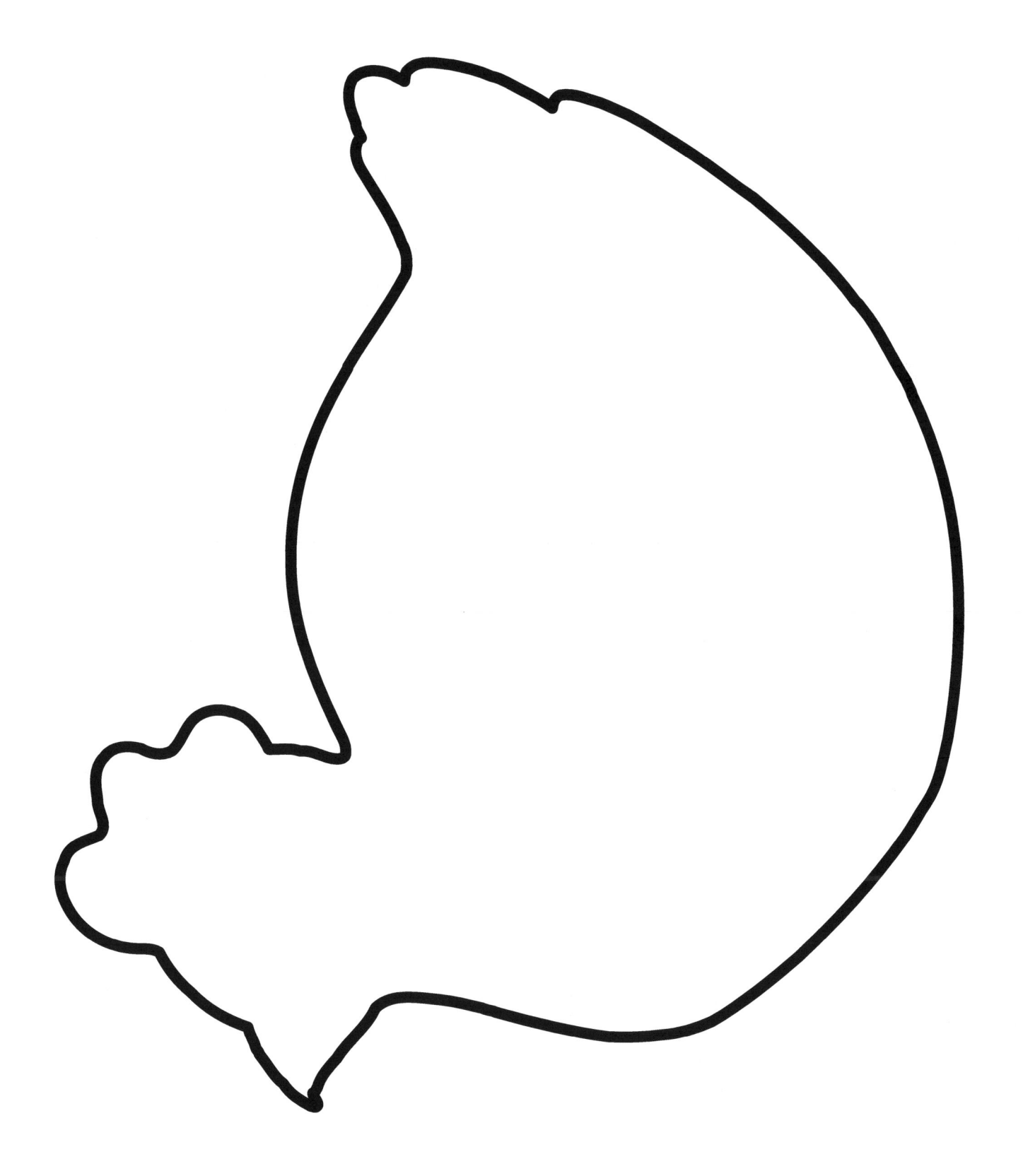

chicken (nesting)

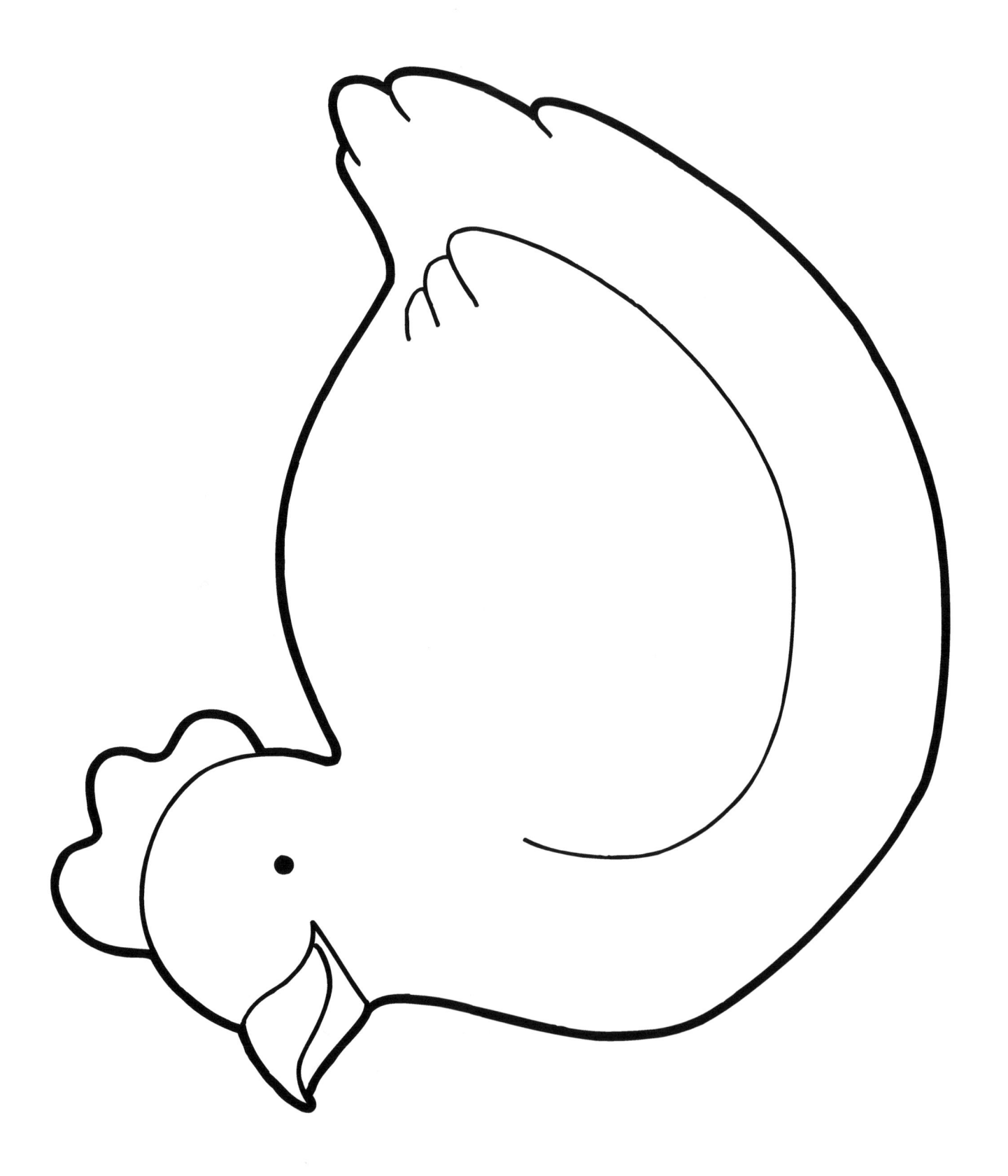

chicken (standing)

chimney

chimpanzee

chipmunk (animated)

chisel

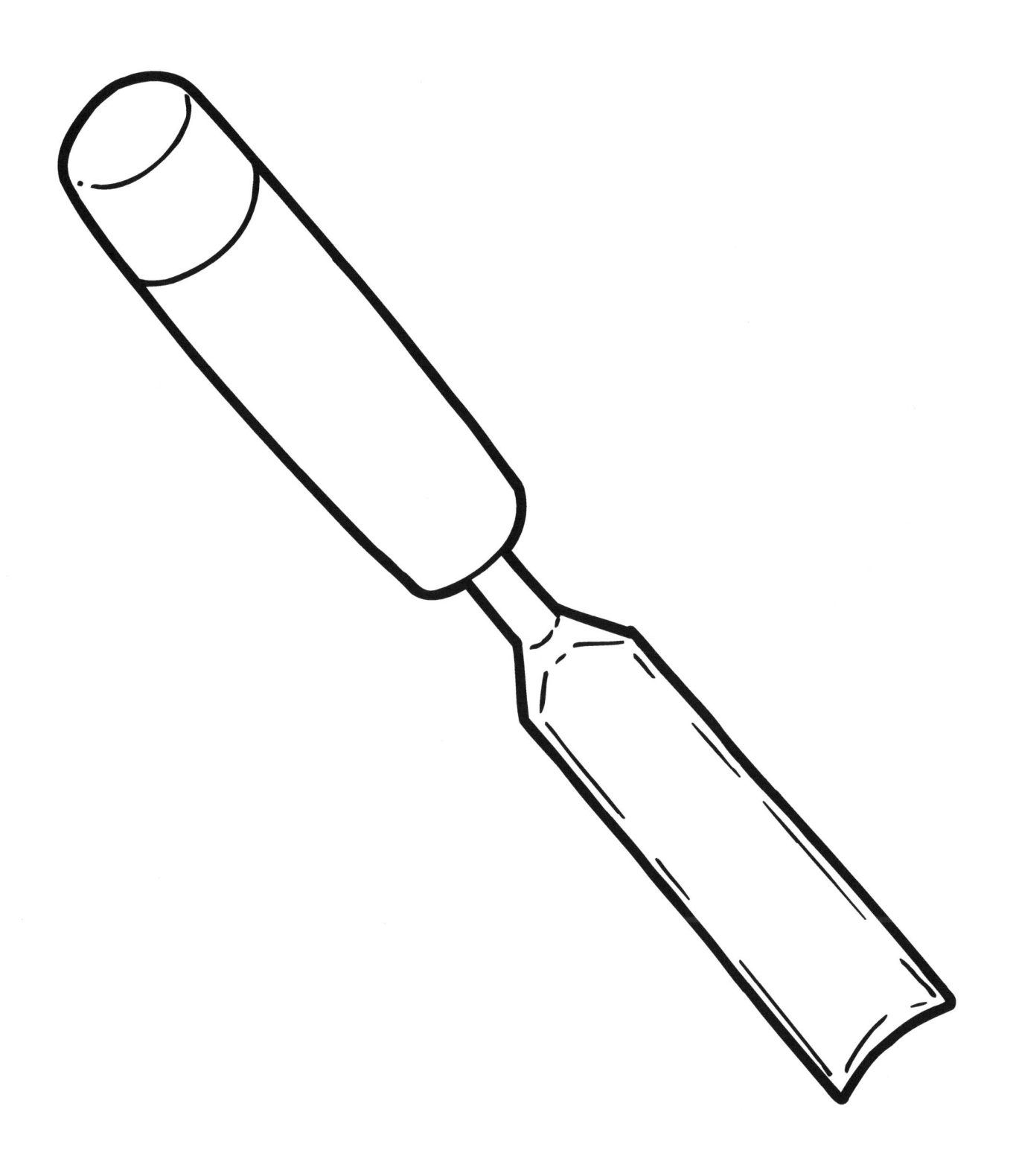

chocolate kiss

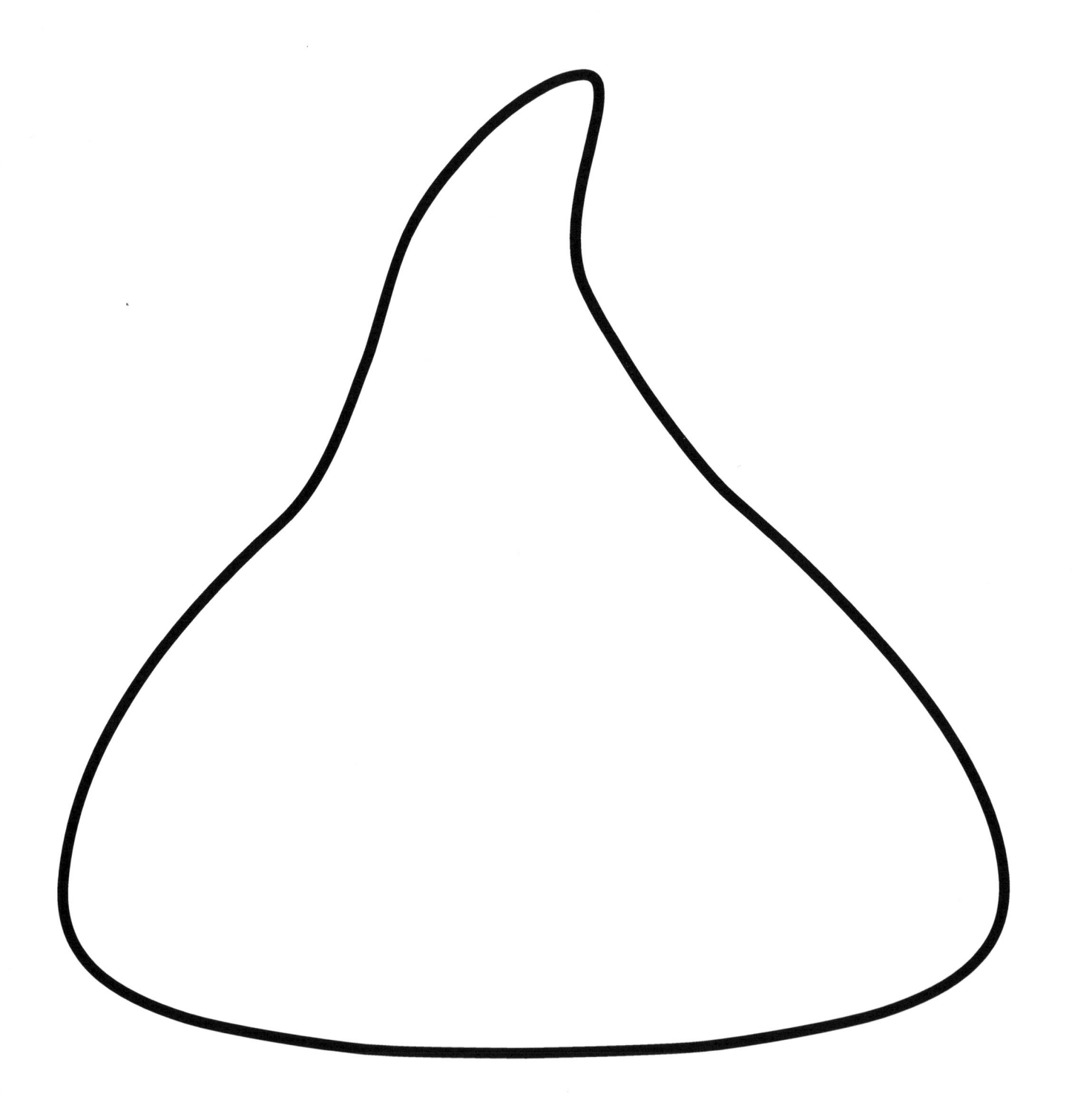

Christmas stocking

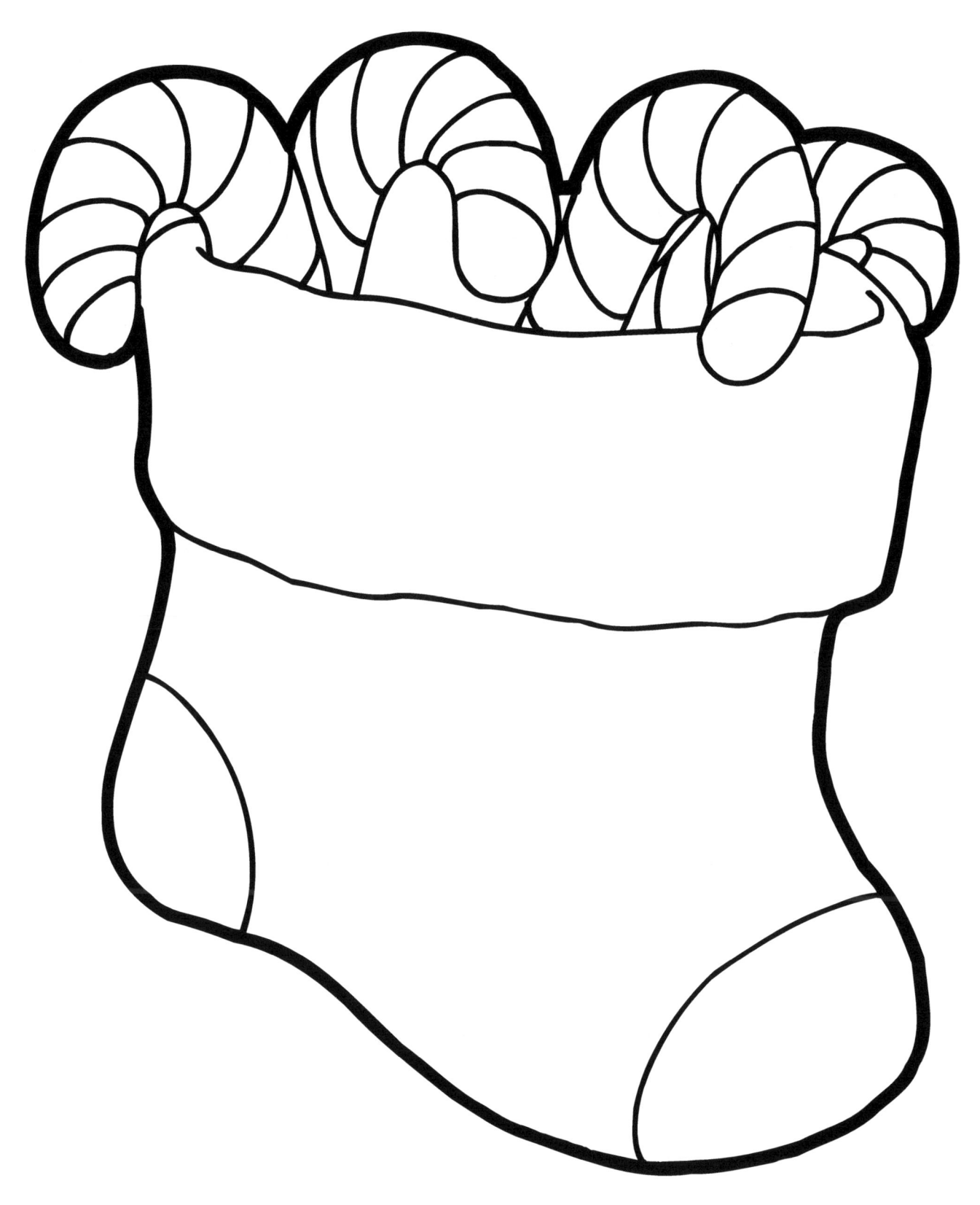

church

circle

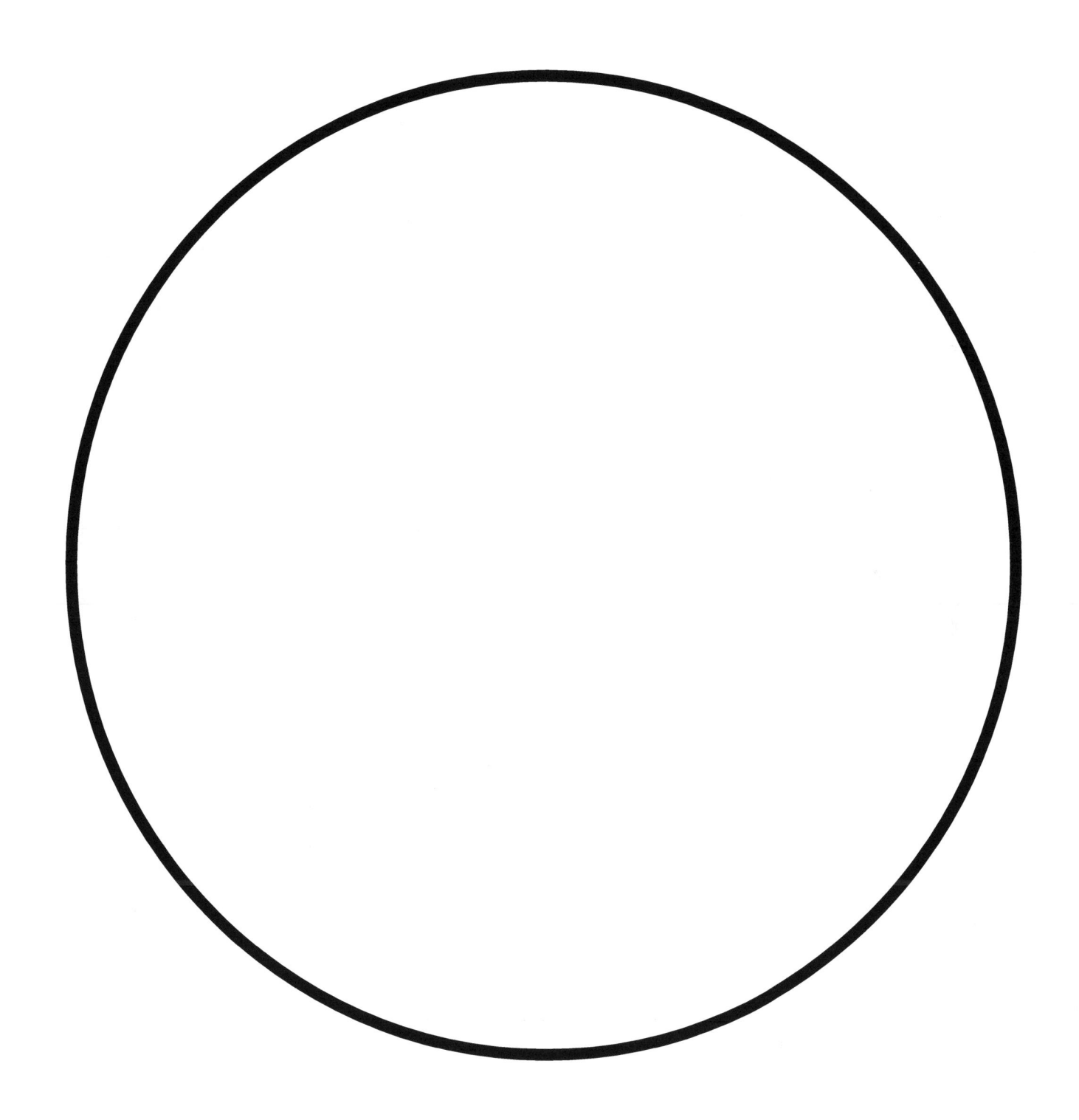

clipboard

clock

clothespin (spring)

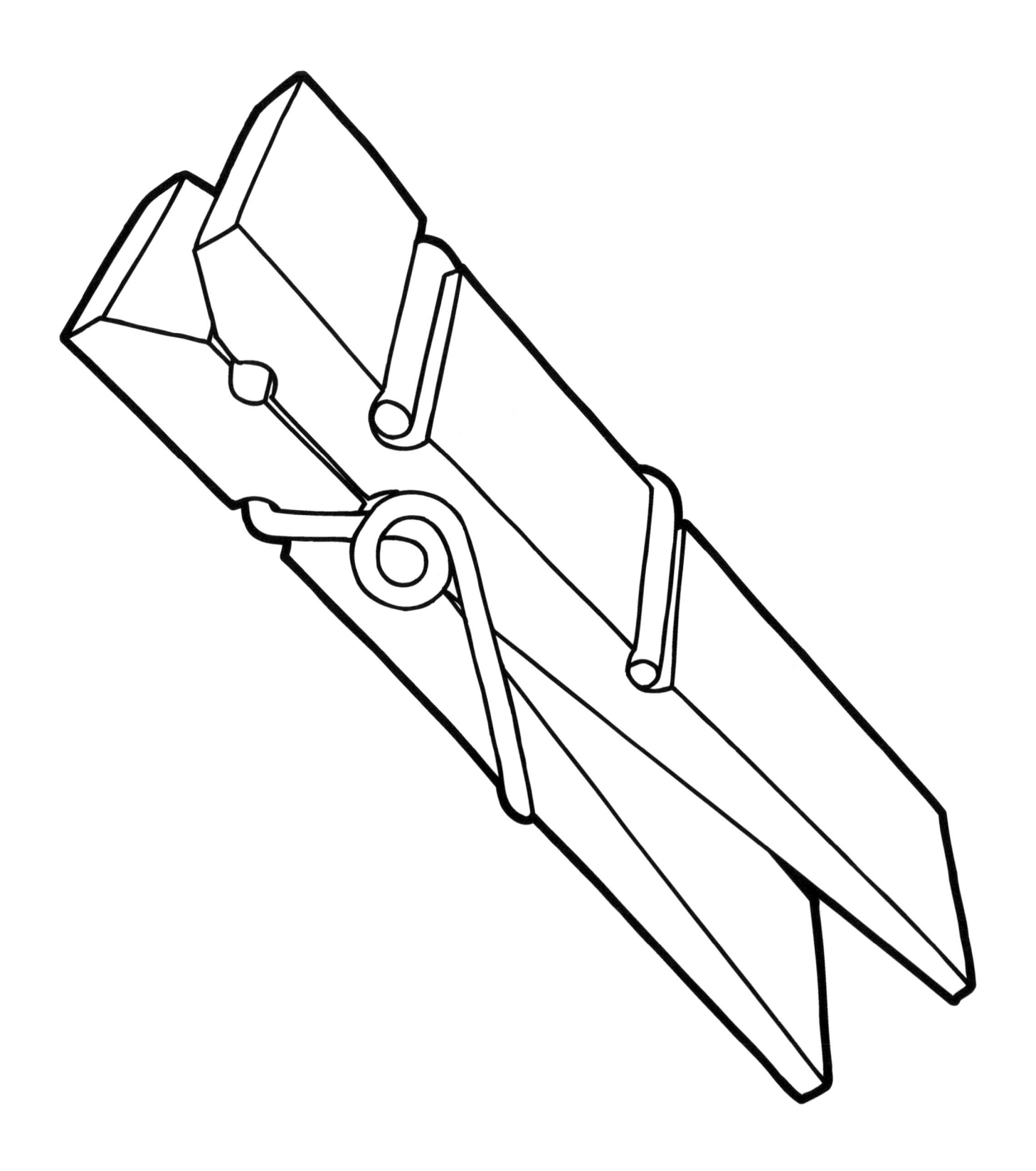

clothespin

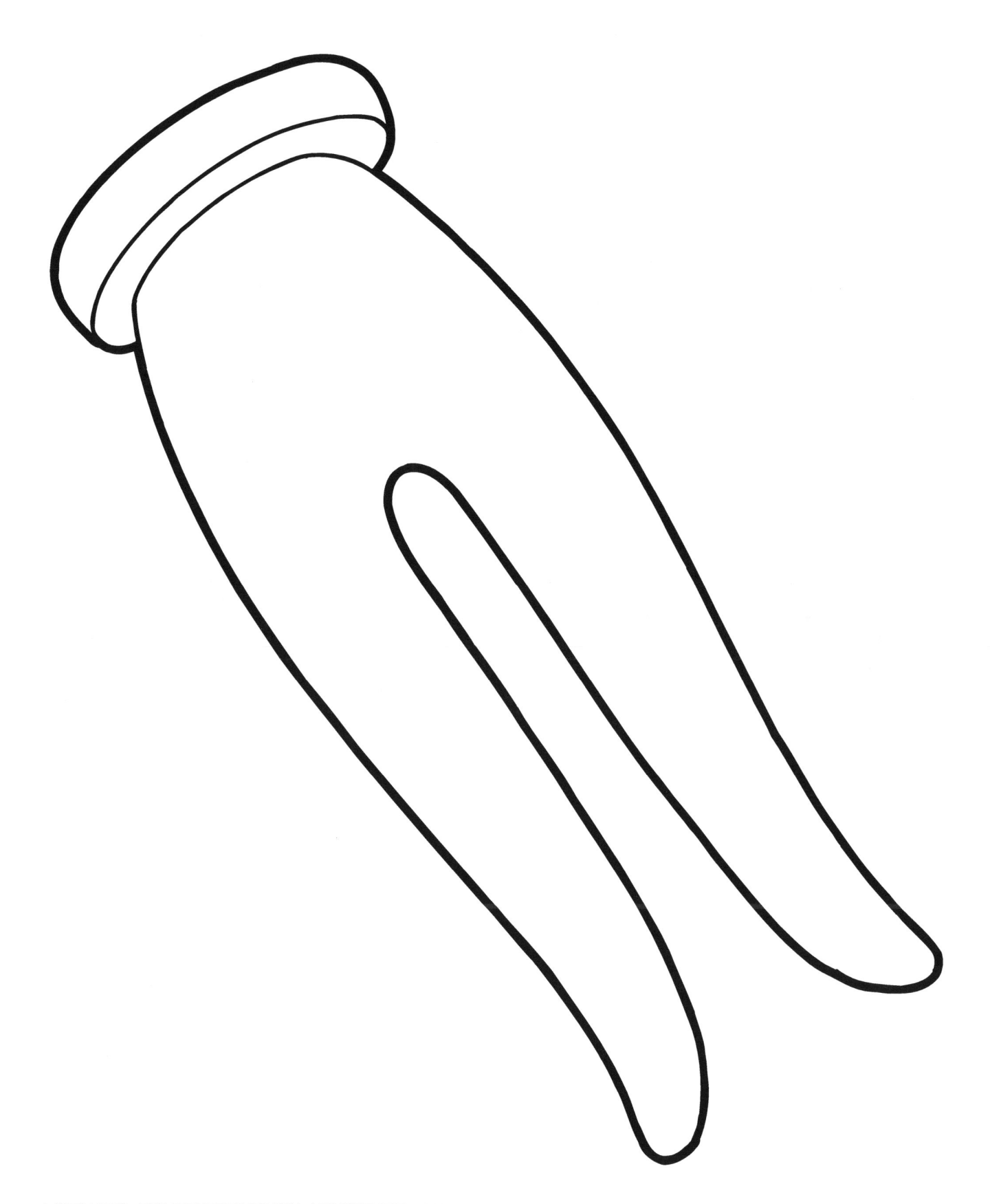

cloud

clown

club (symbol)

coat

collar (pointed)

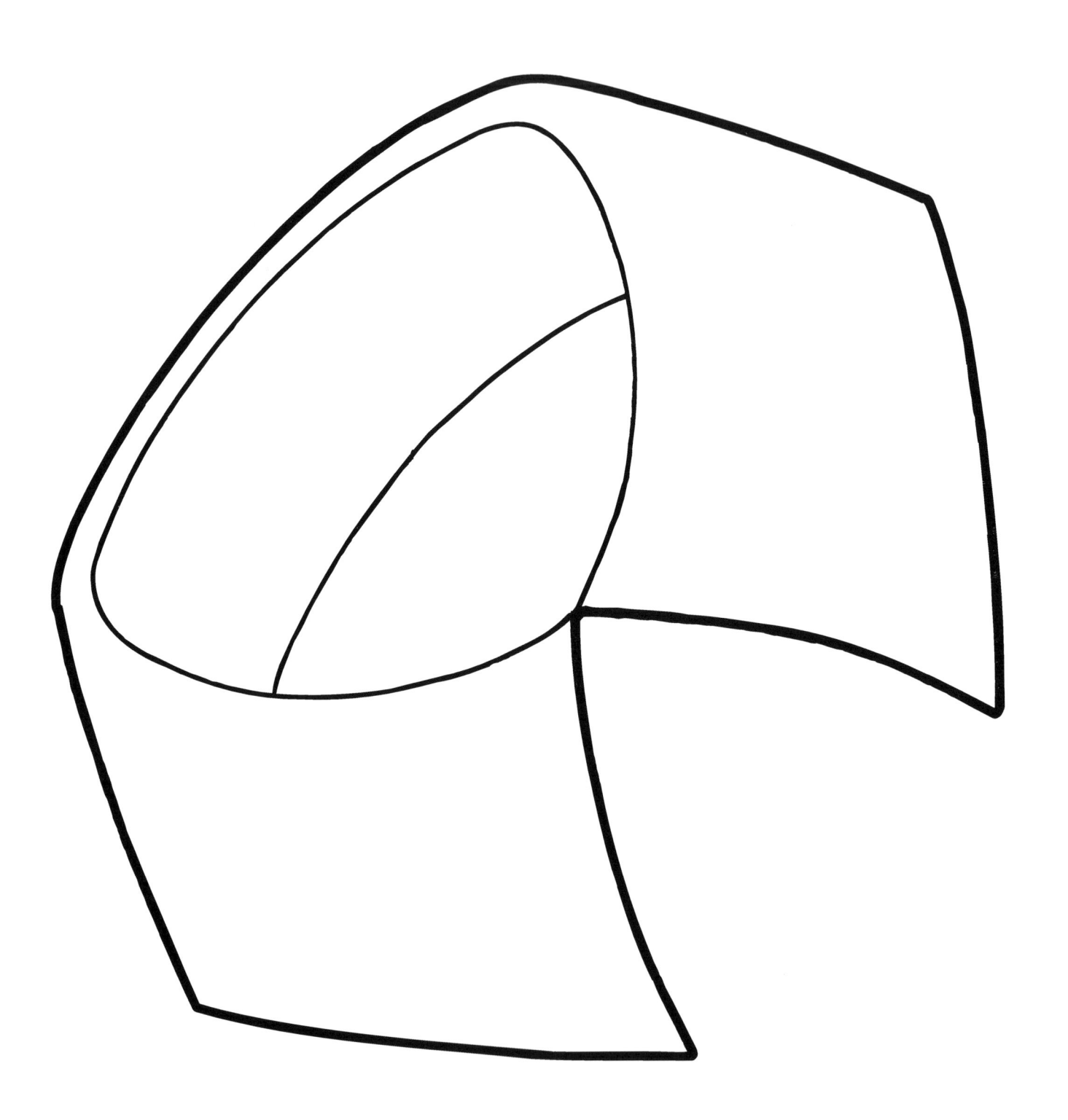

collar (rounded)

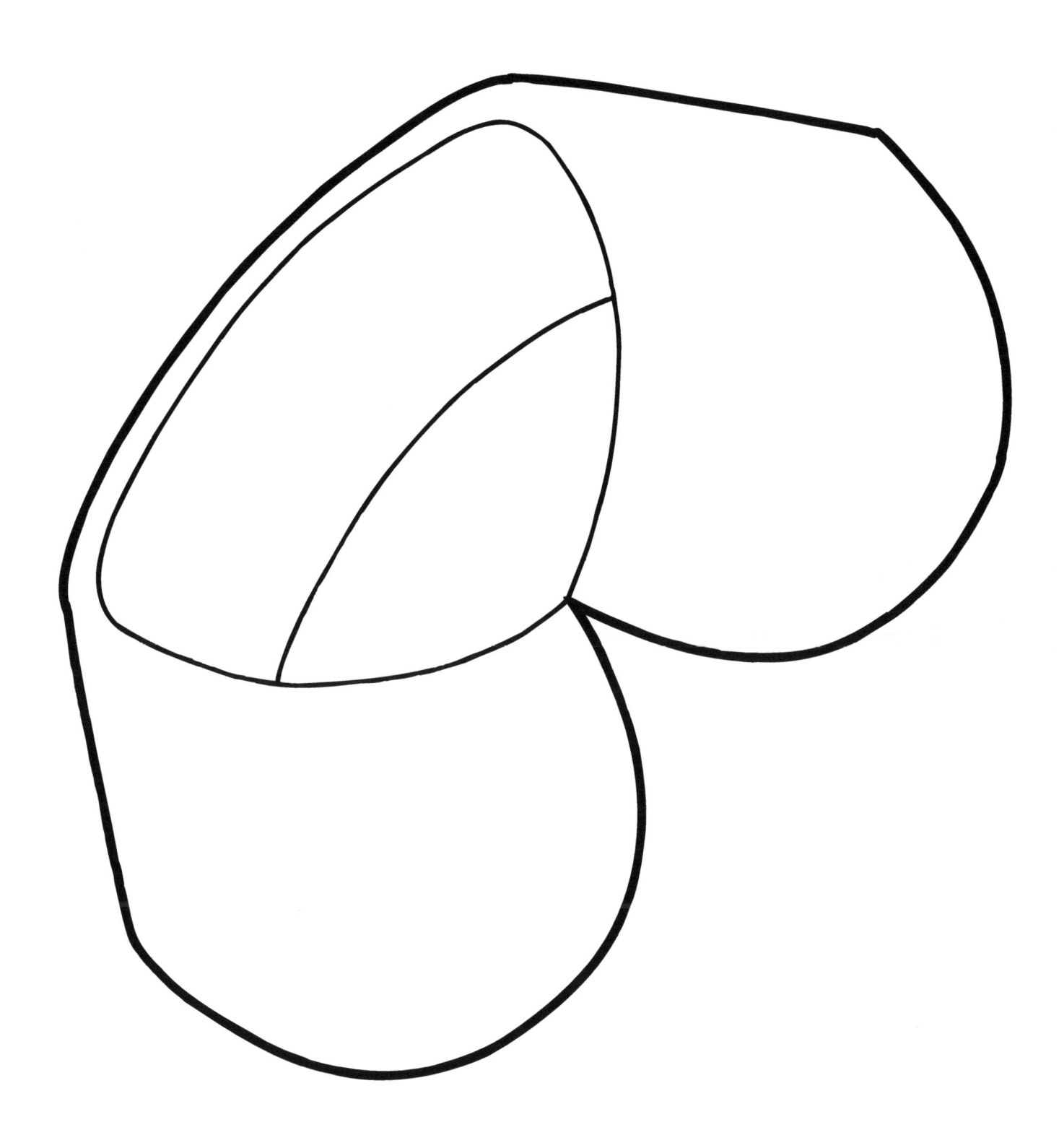

Colorado, USA

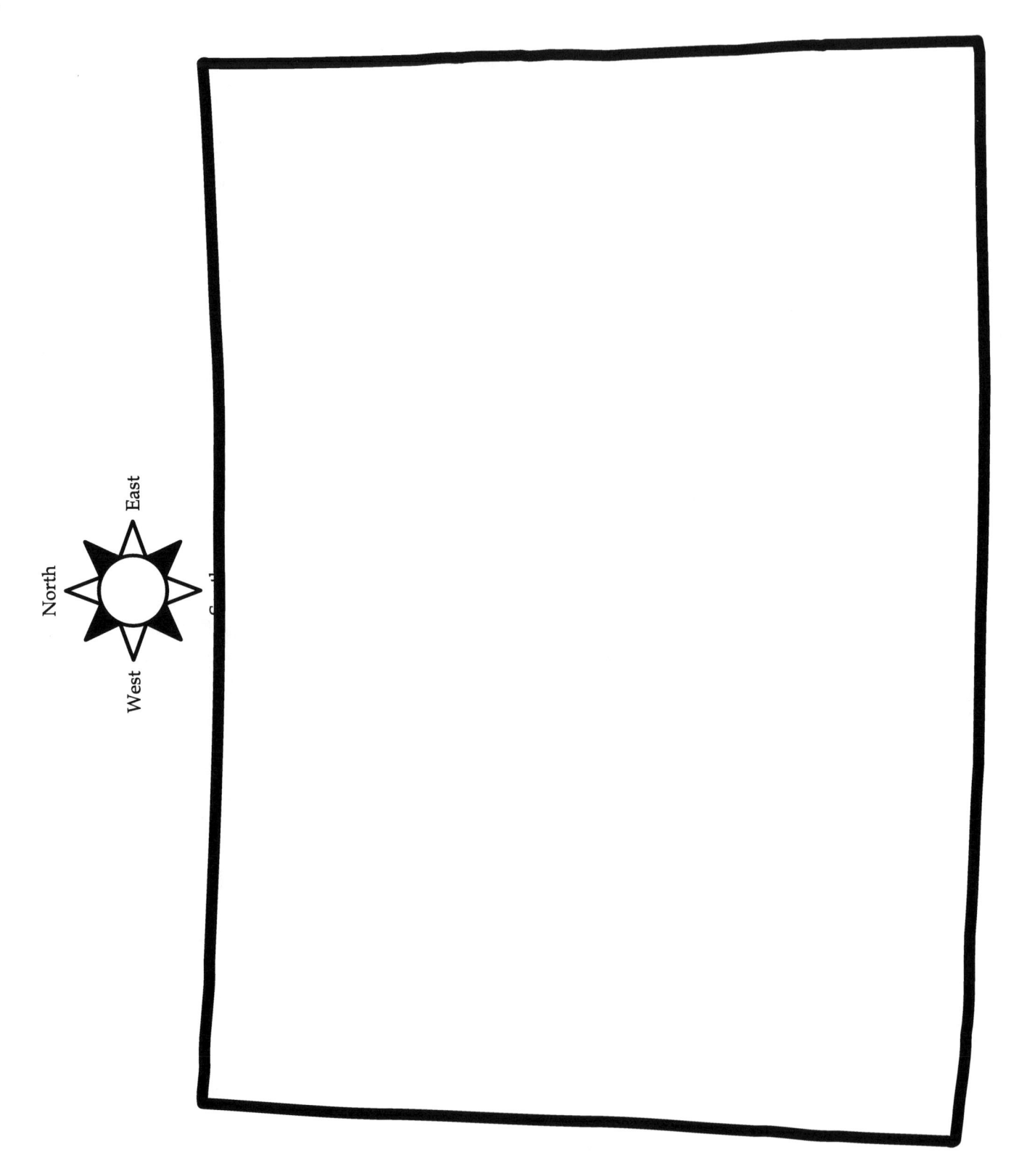

North · East · South · West

Maps are representations and boundaries are not exact.

comb

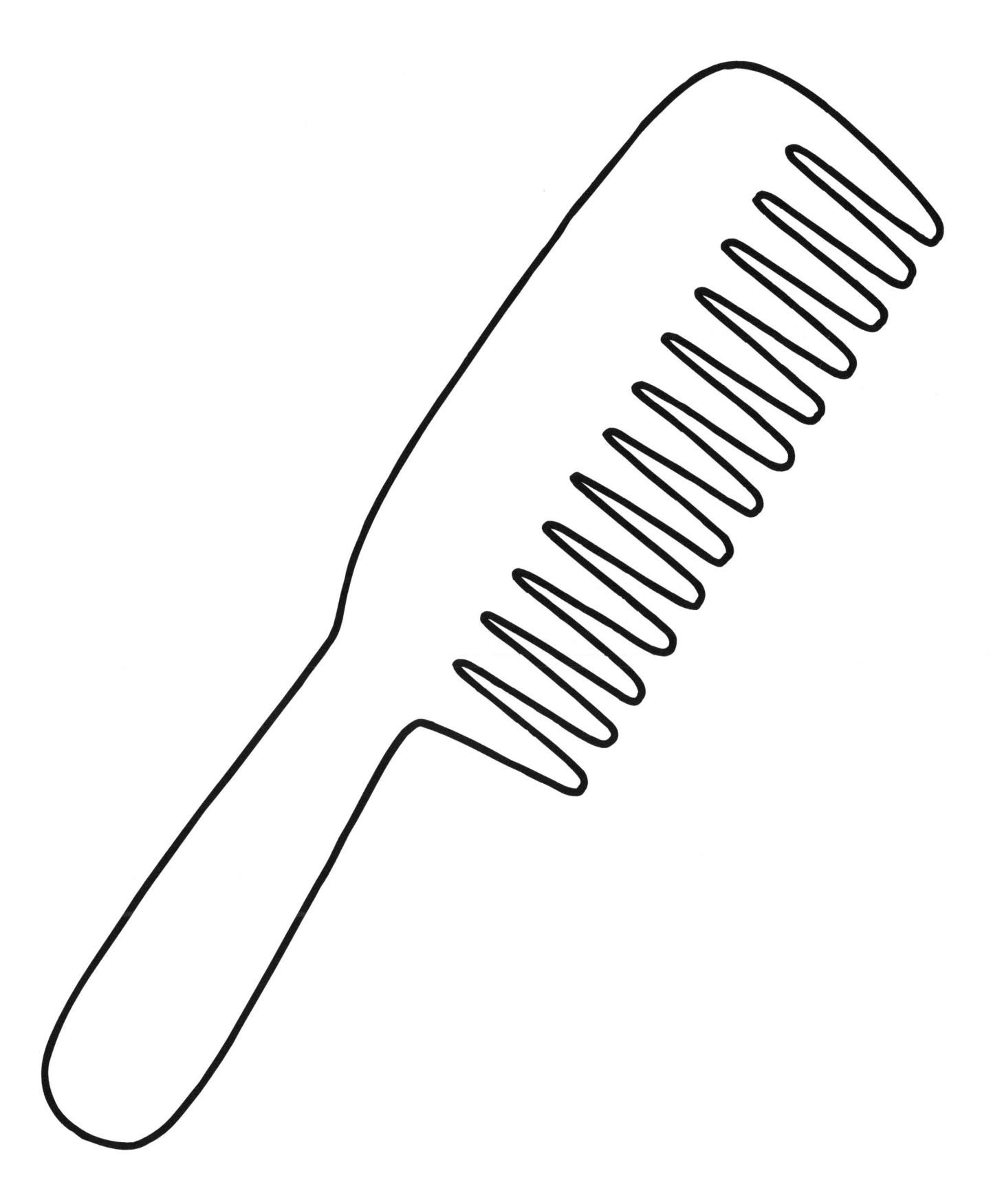

computer

cone

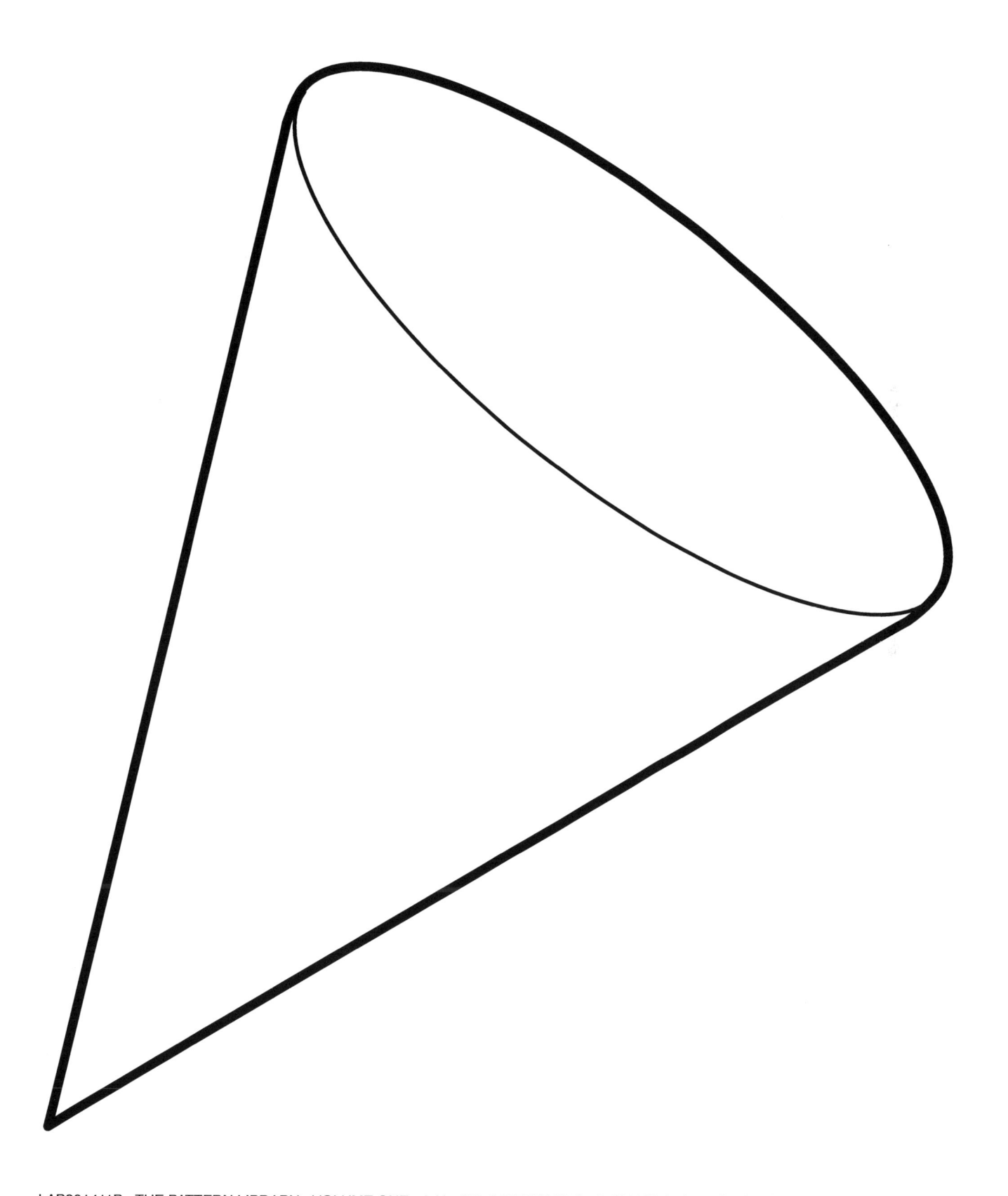

Connecticutt, USA

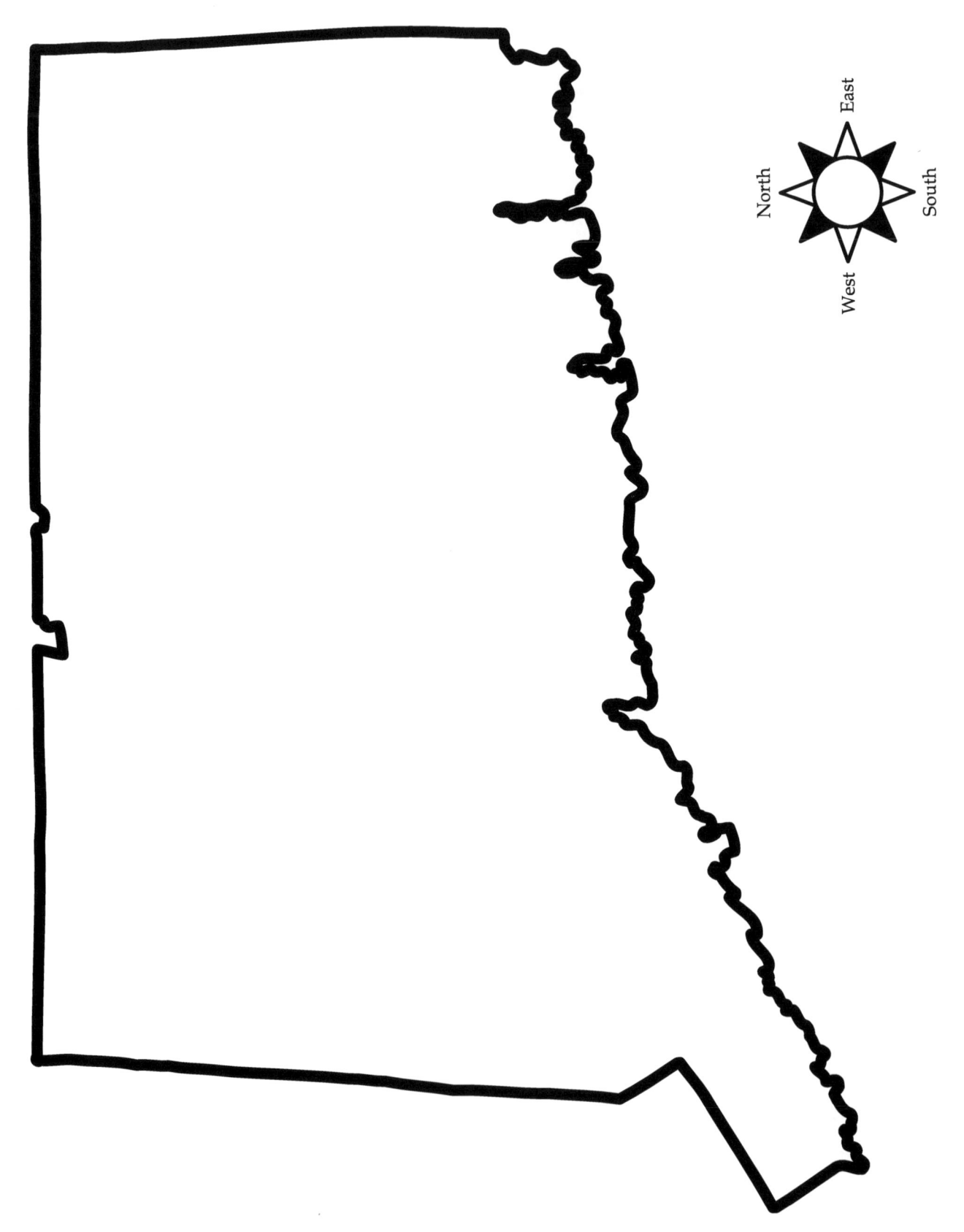

Maps are representations and boundaries are not exact.

cookie jar

cookies

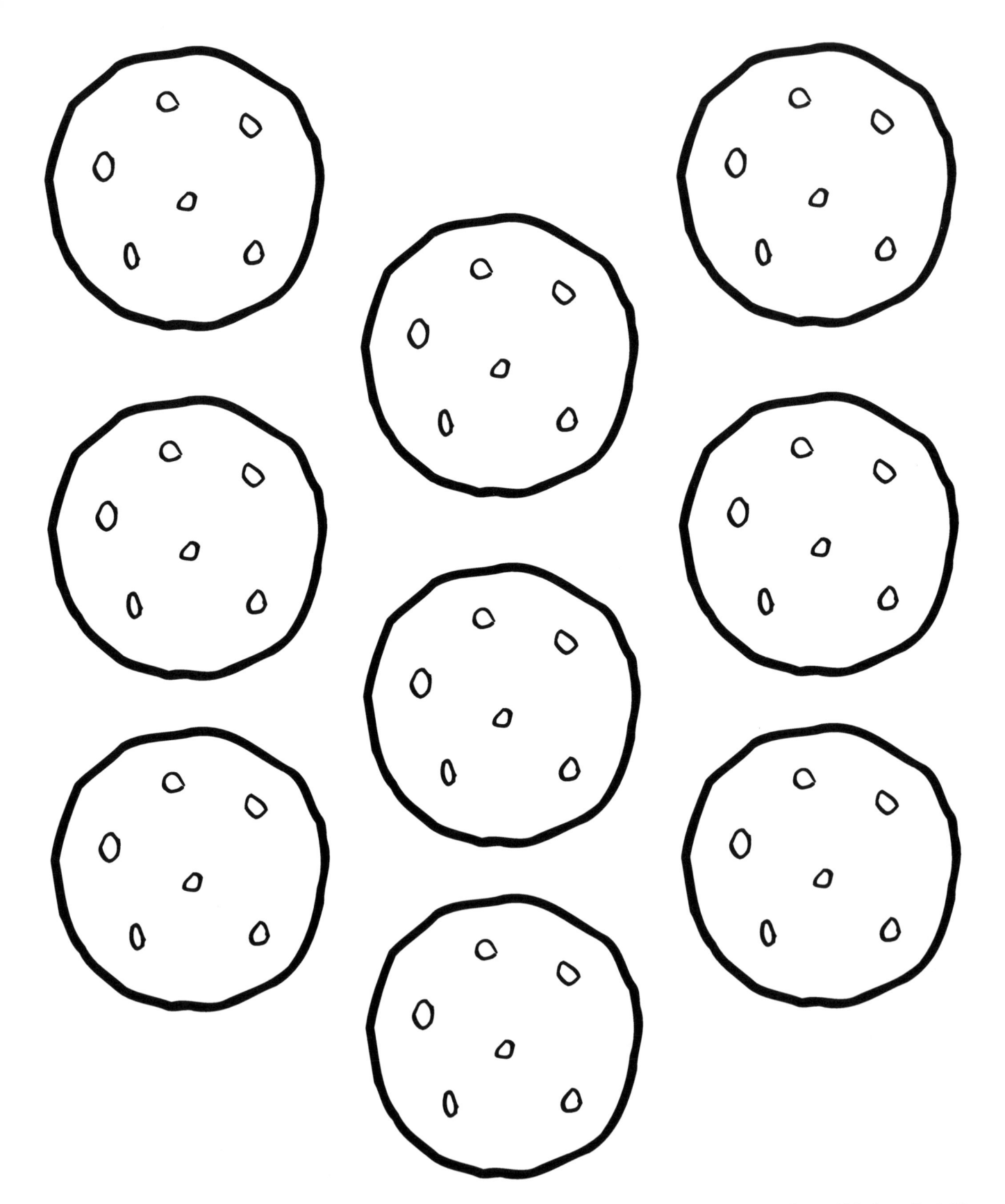

corn

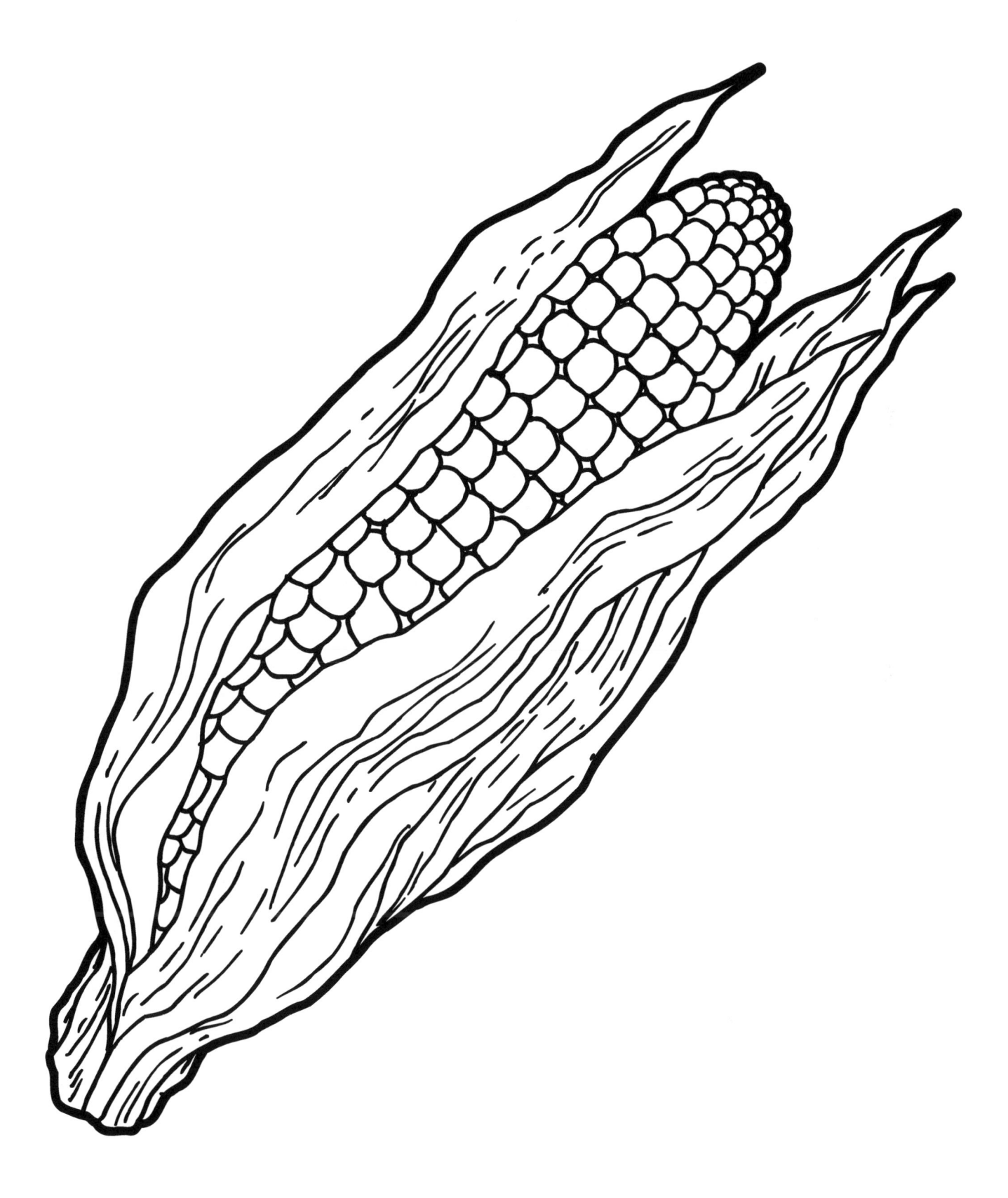

cornucopia

couch

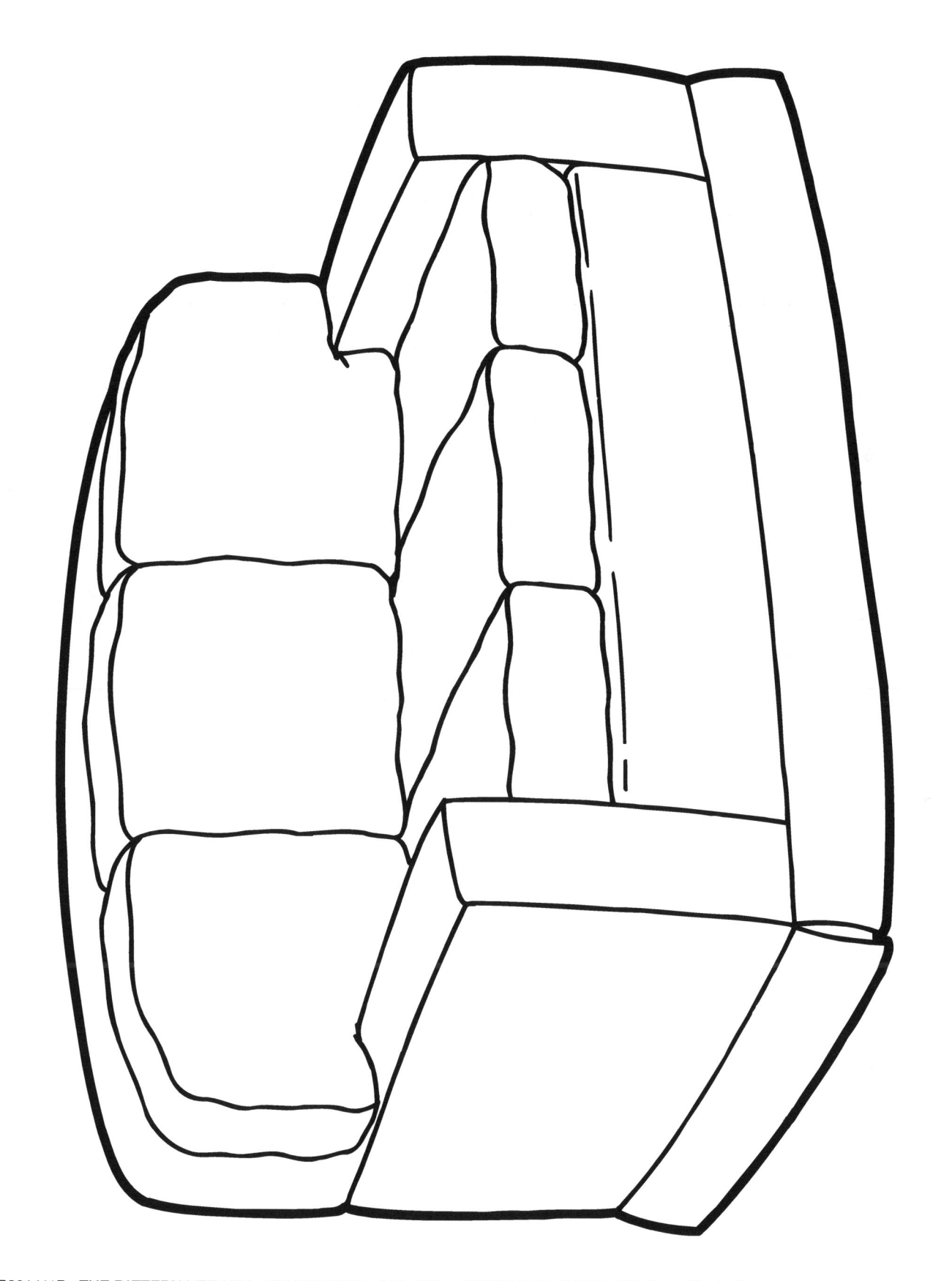

cow (frontal view)

cow (side view)

cowbell

cowboy

cowgirl

crab

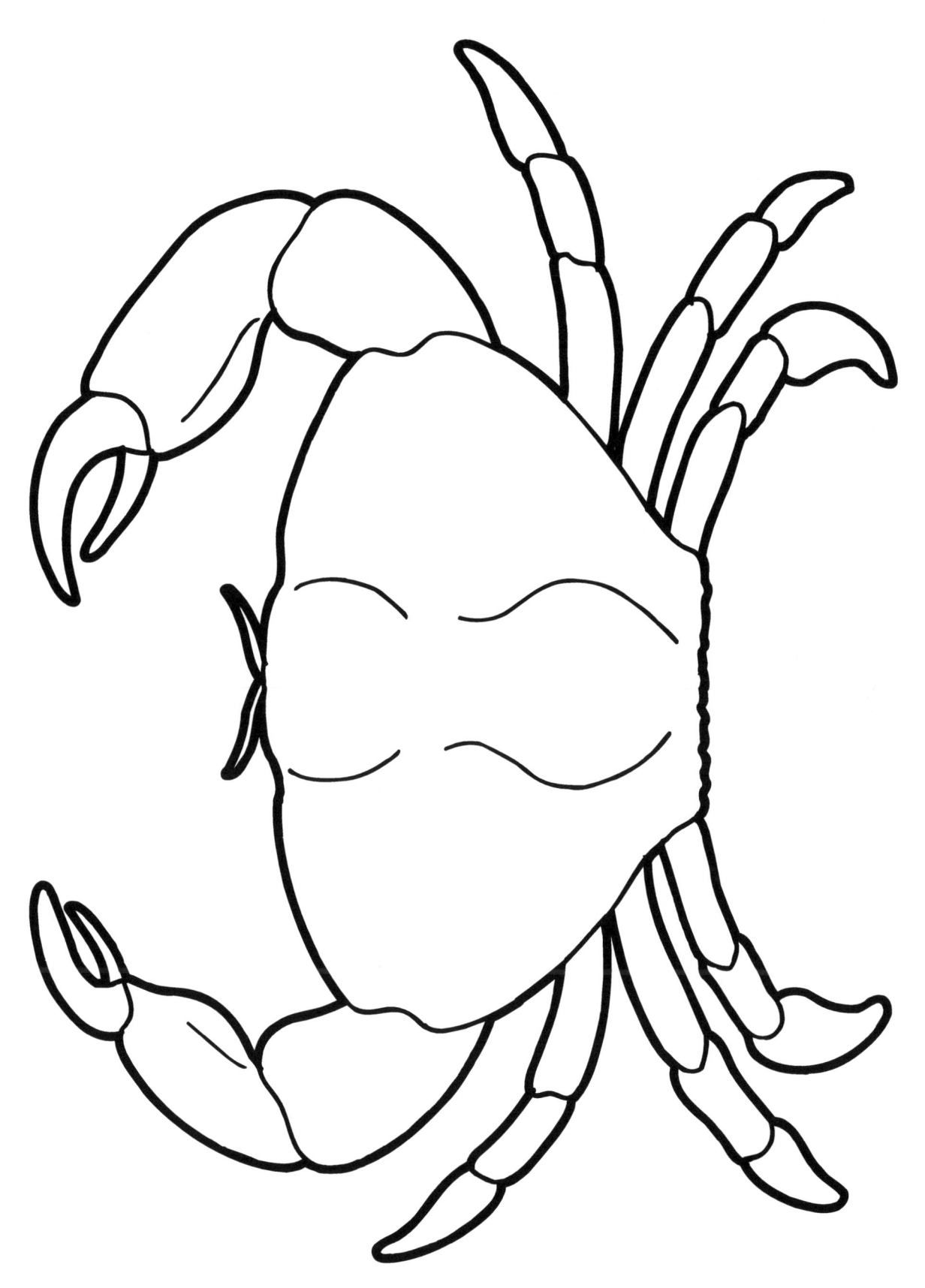

cracker

cradle

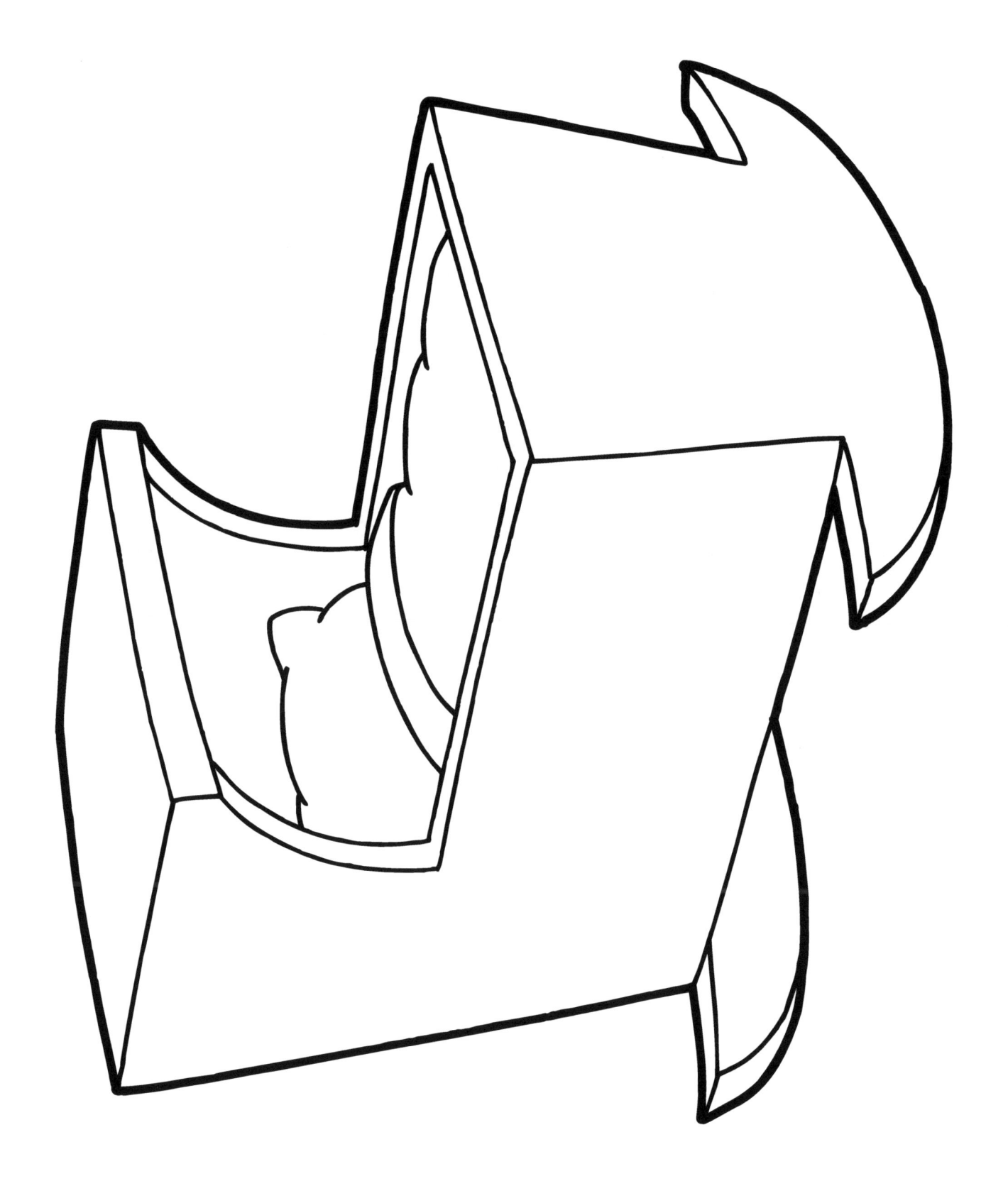

crate (wood)

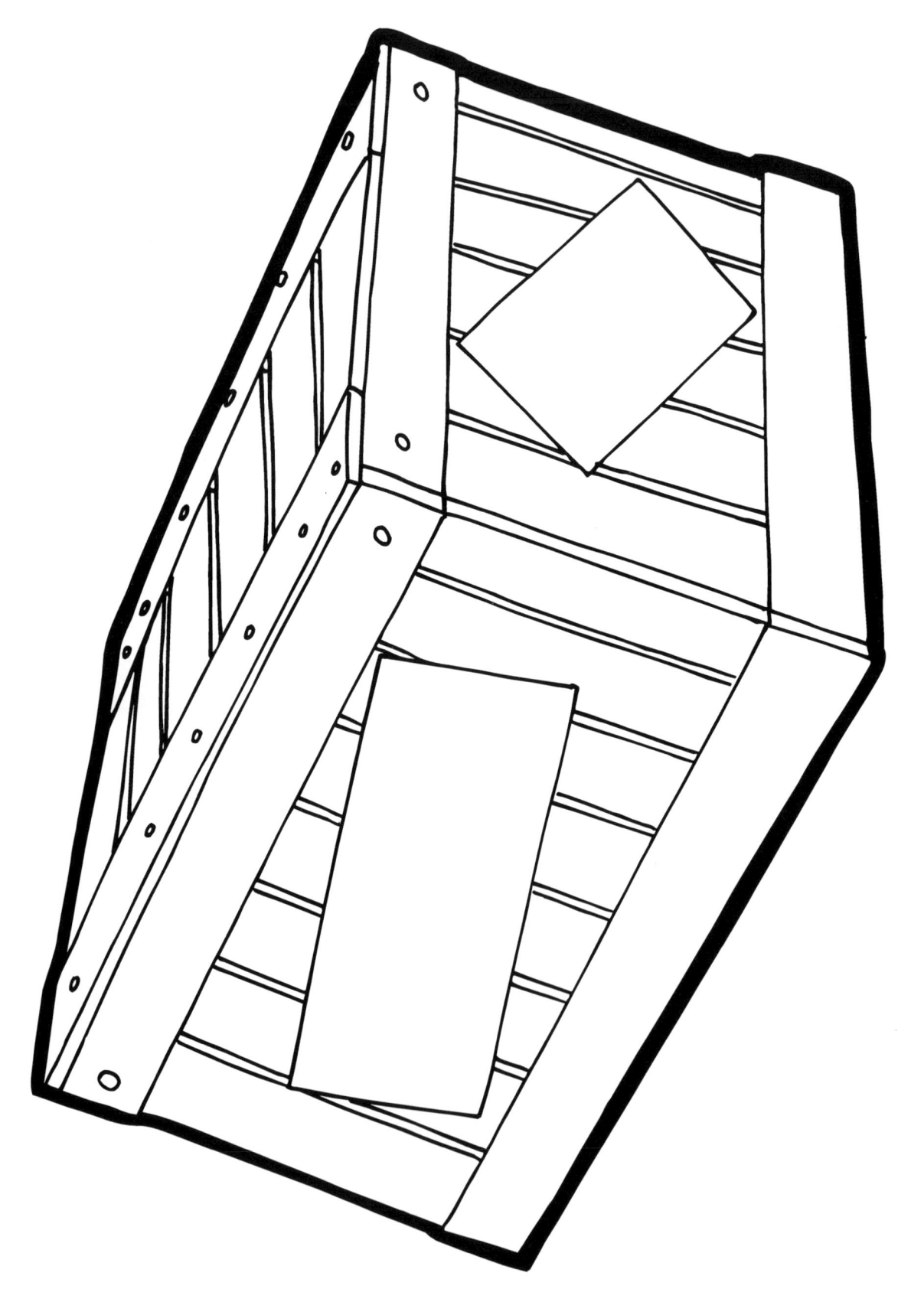

crayons

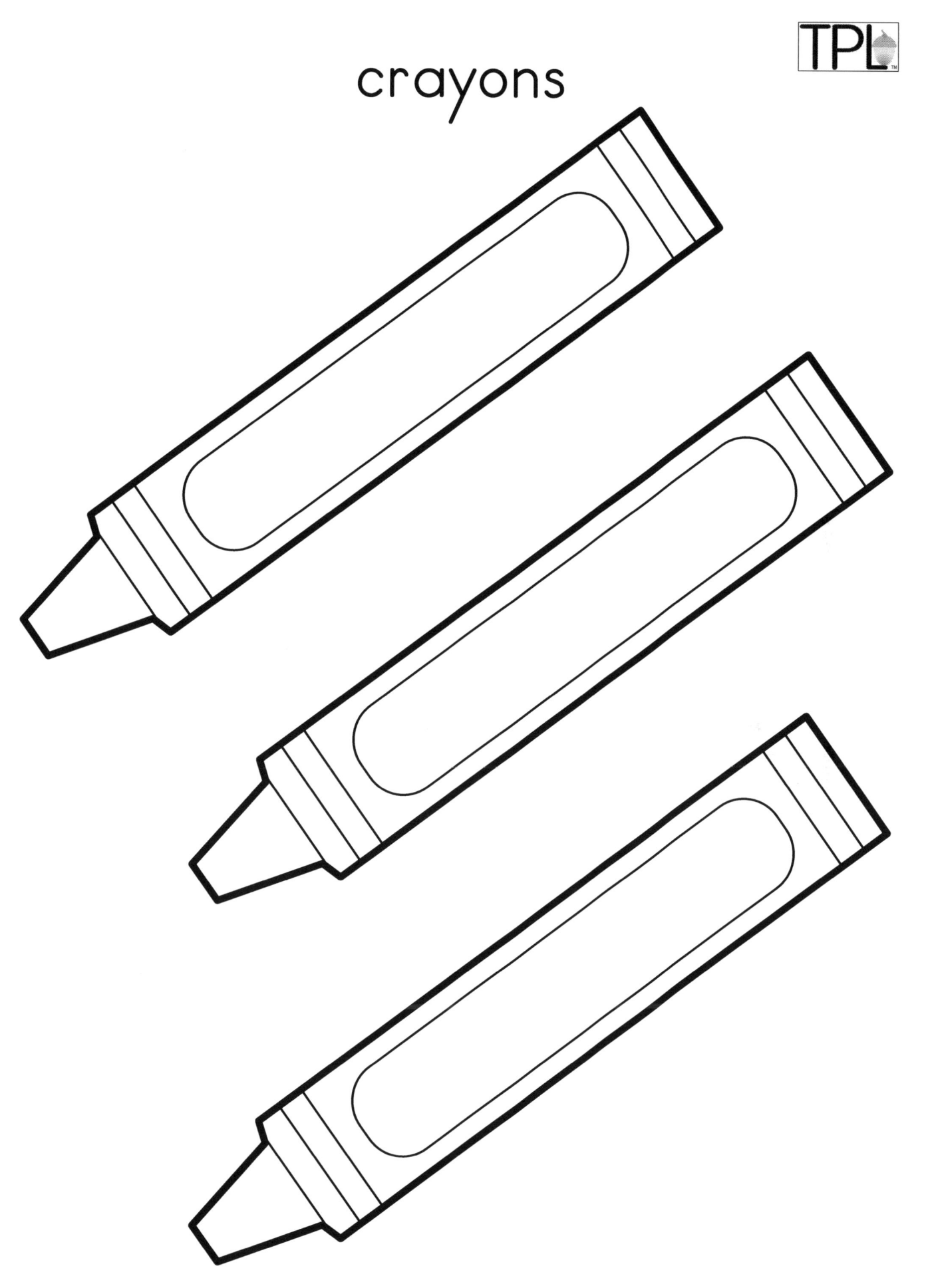

crayon box

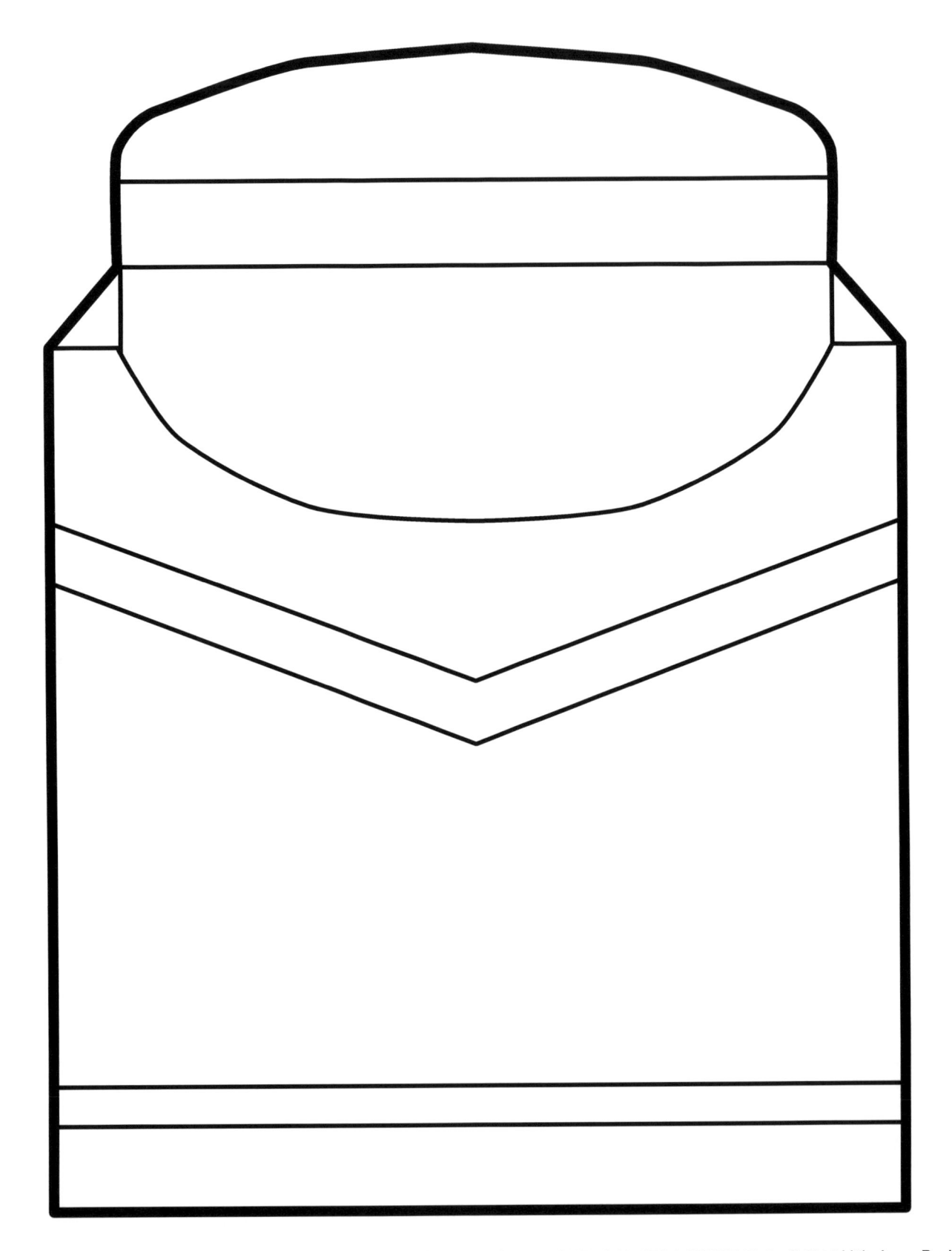

crown (short)

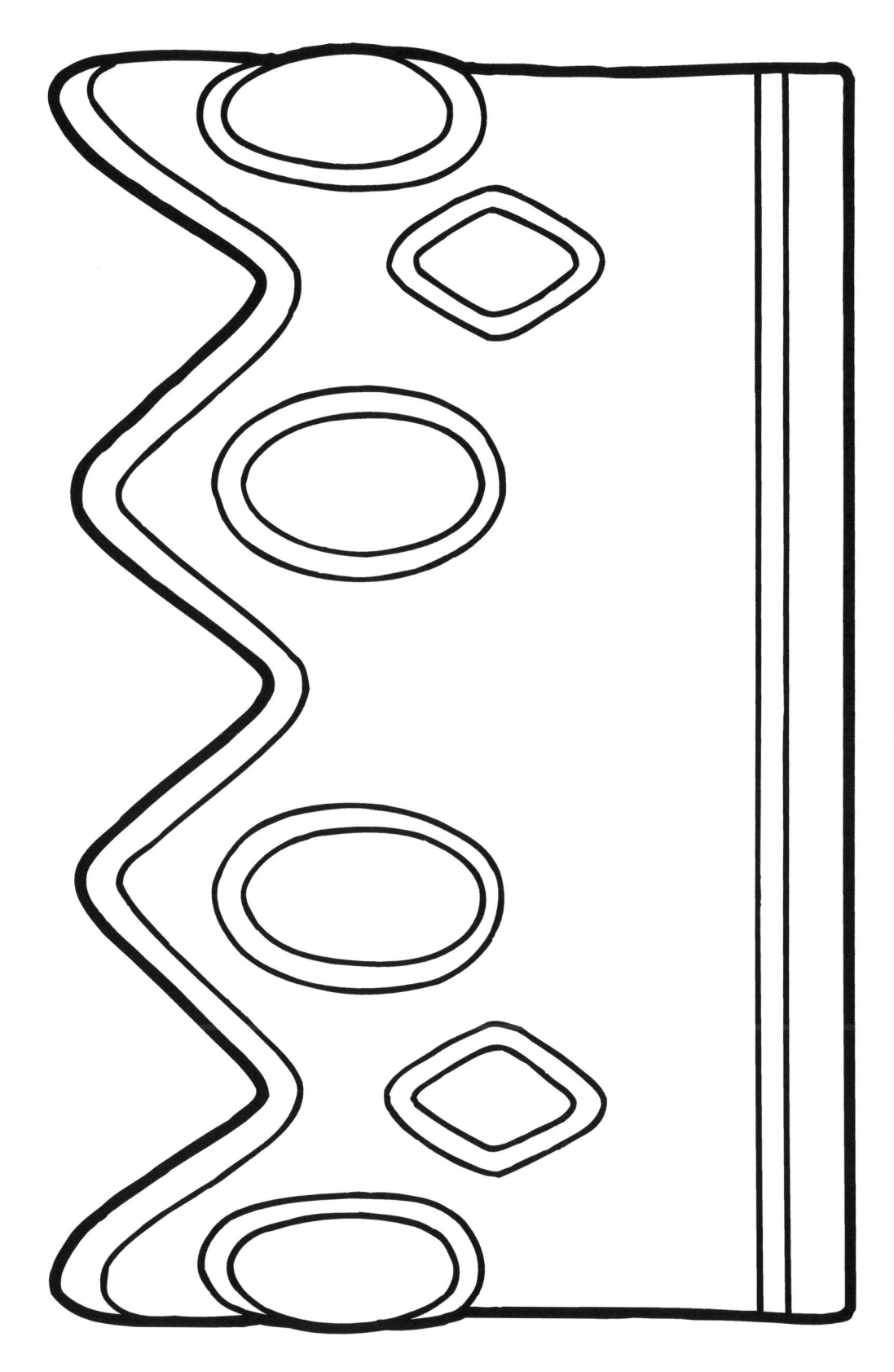

crown (tall)

cube

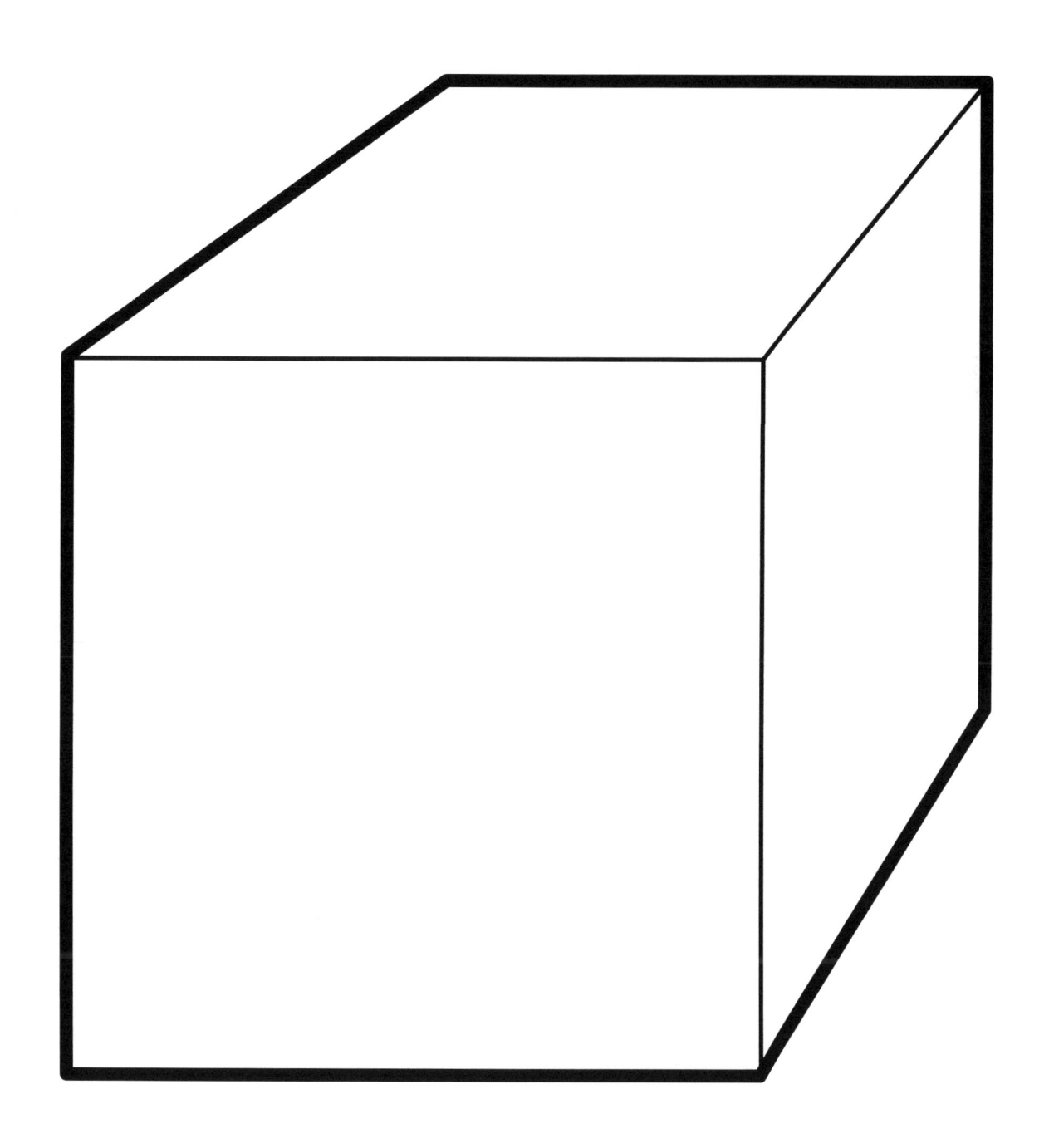

cucumber

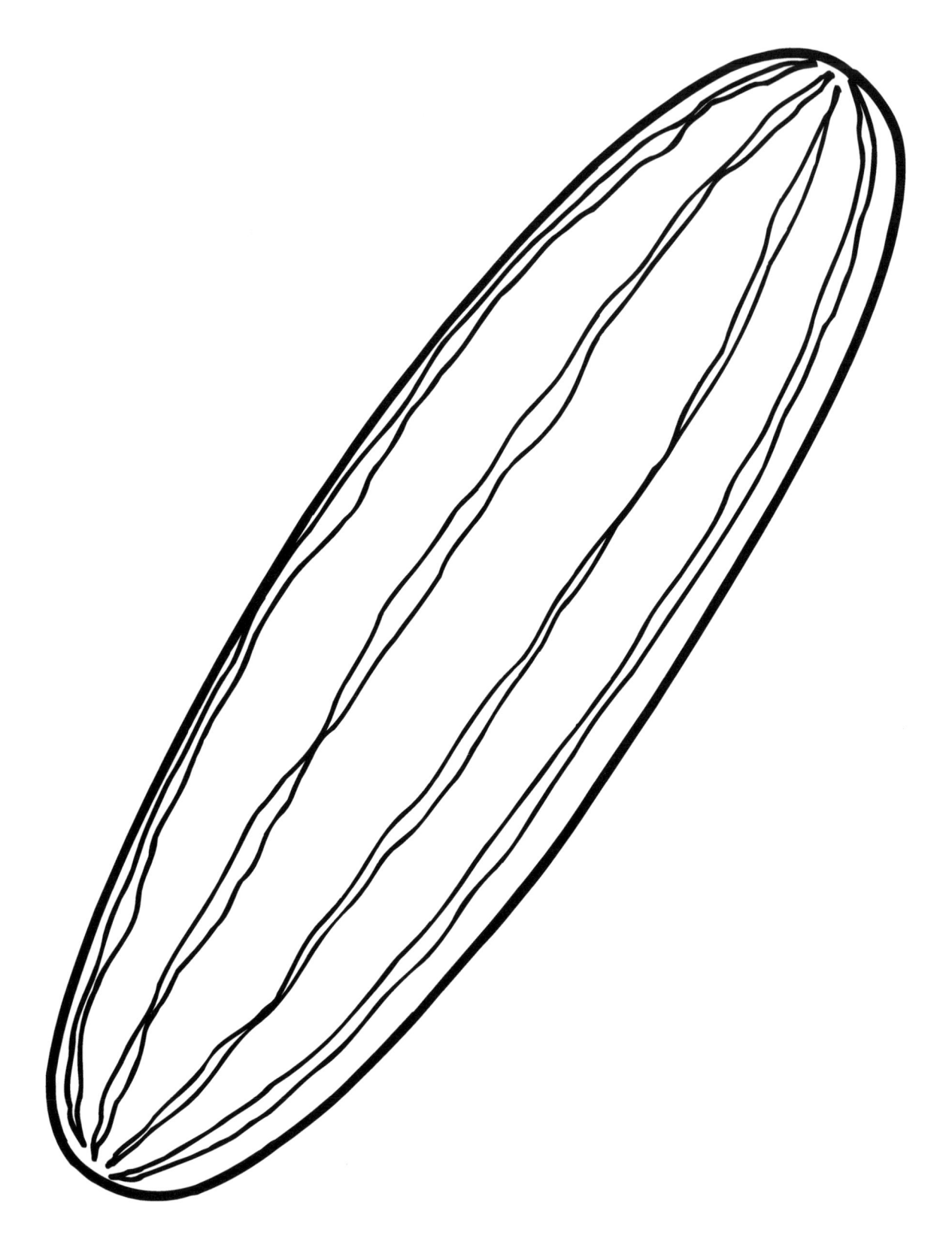

cup

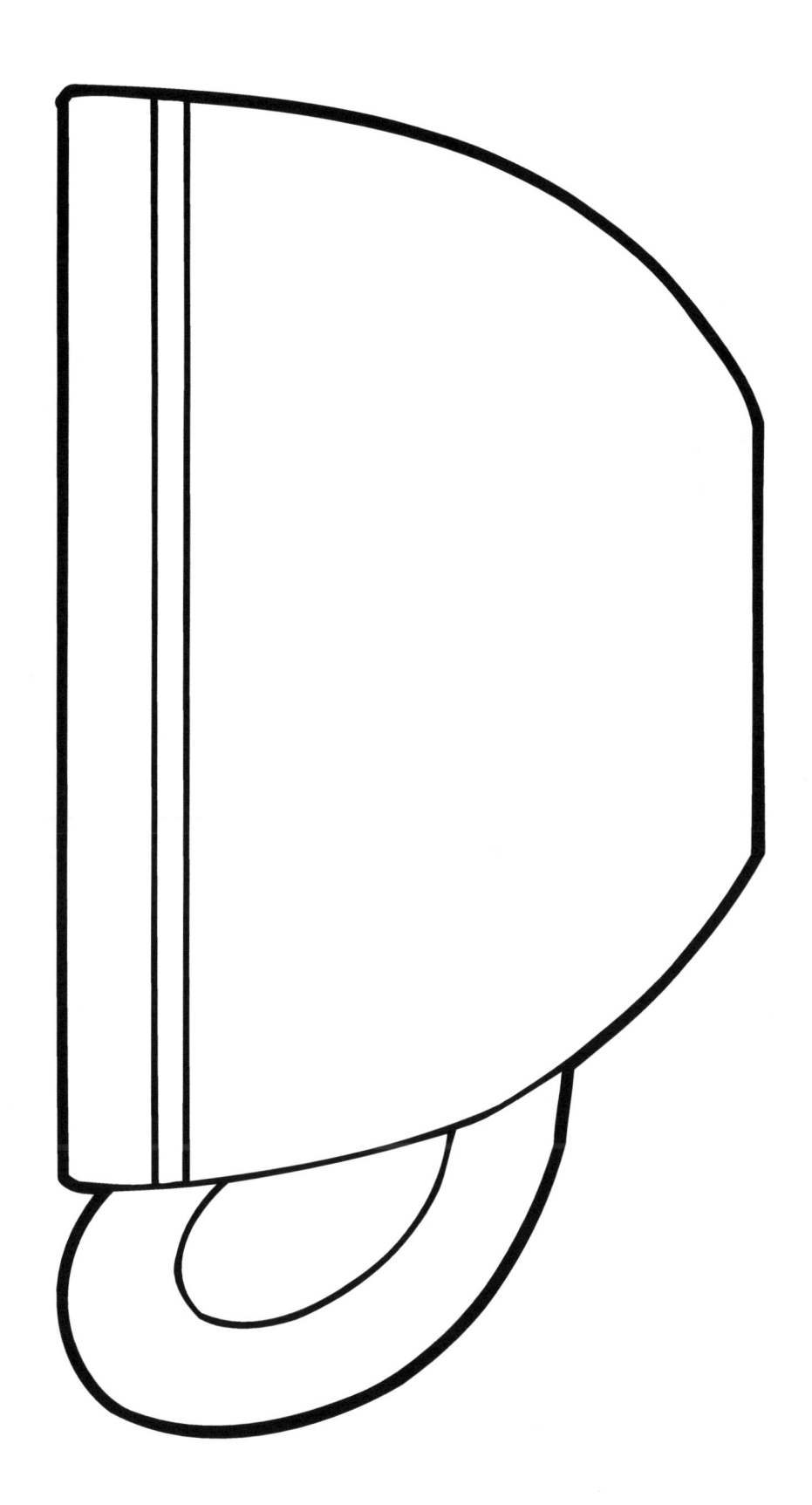

cupcake

cups

cylinder

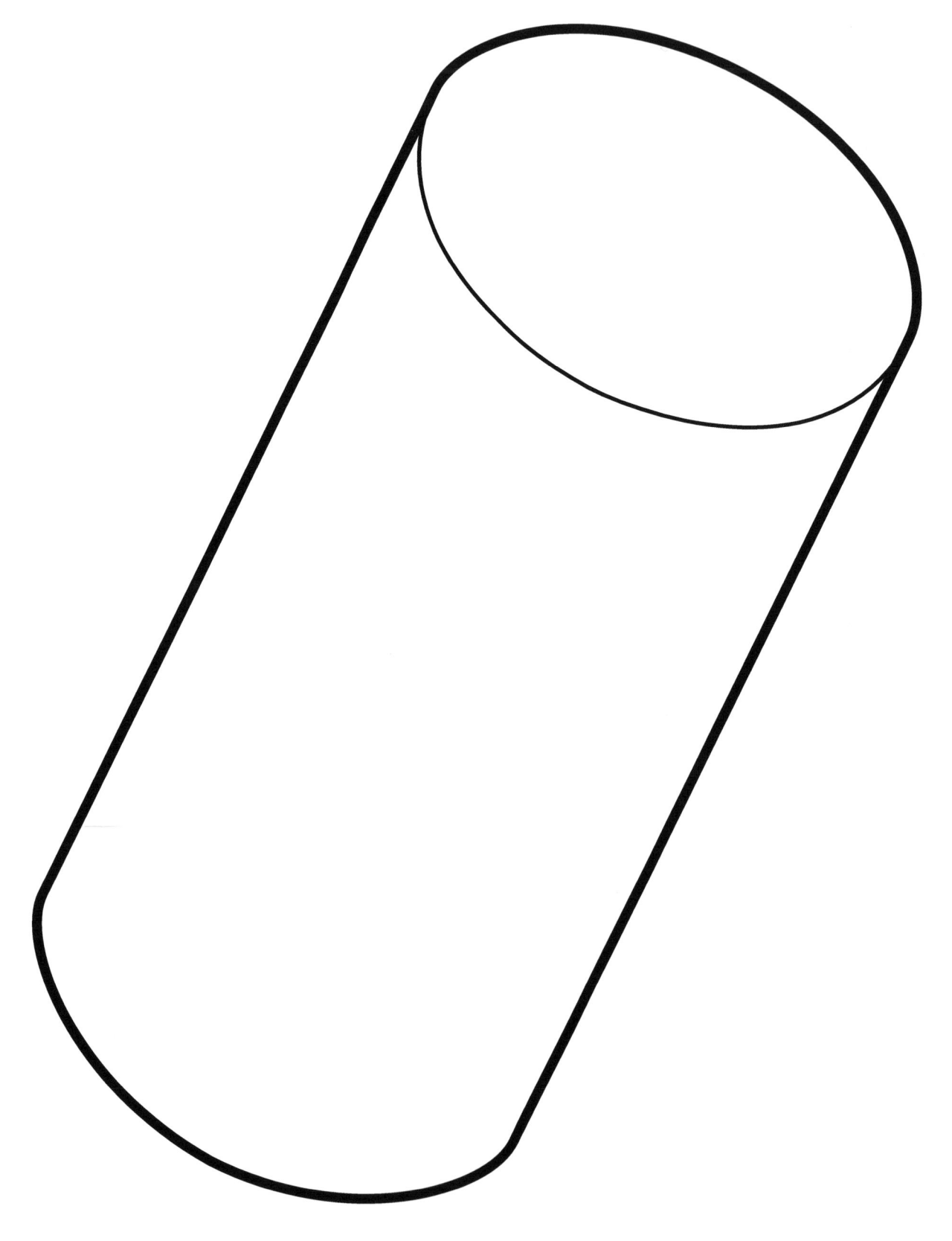

cymbal

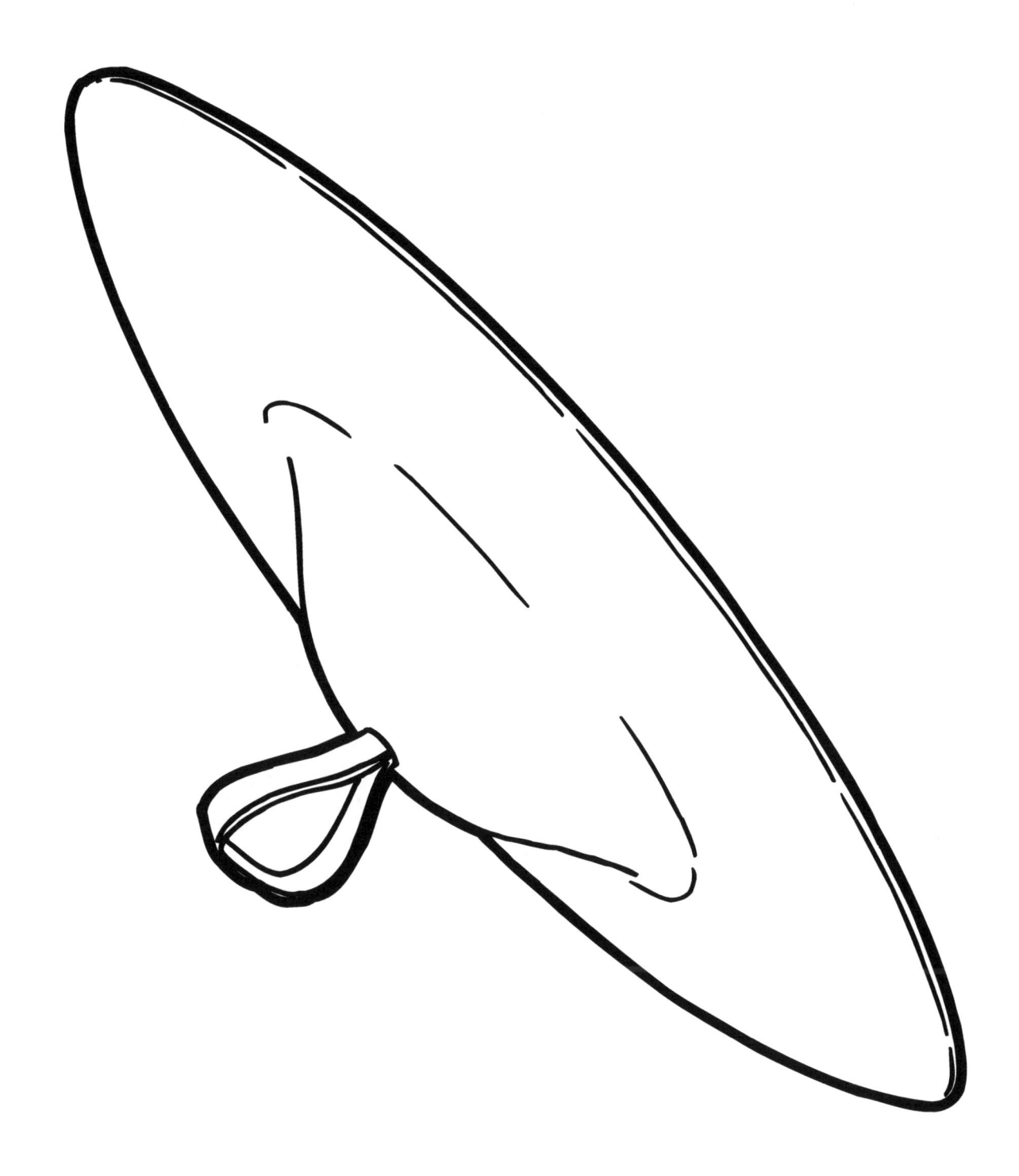

dart

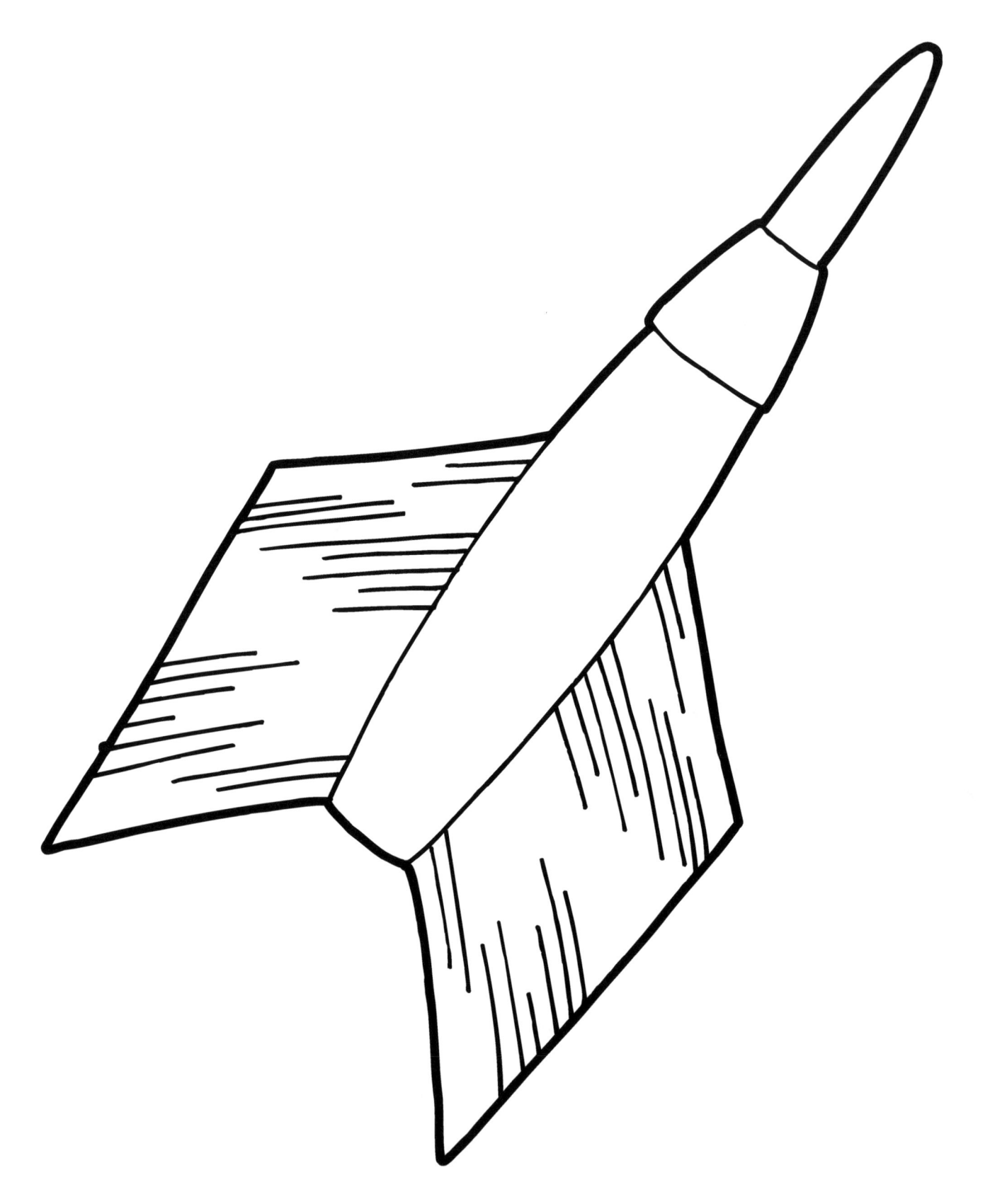

deer (buck)

deer (doe)

Delaware, USA

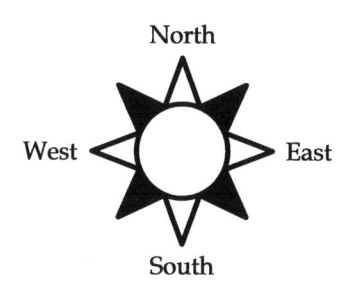

West — North — East — South

Maps are representations and boundaries are not exact.

LAB201411P • THE PATTERN LIBRARY • VOLUME ONE • A-H • 978-1-937257-62-0 • © 2014 Little Acorn Books™

297

diamond (baseball)

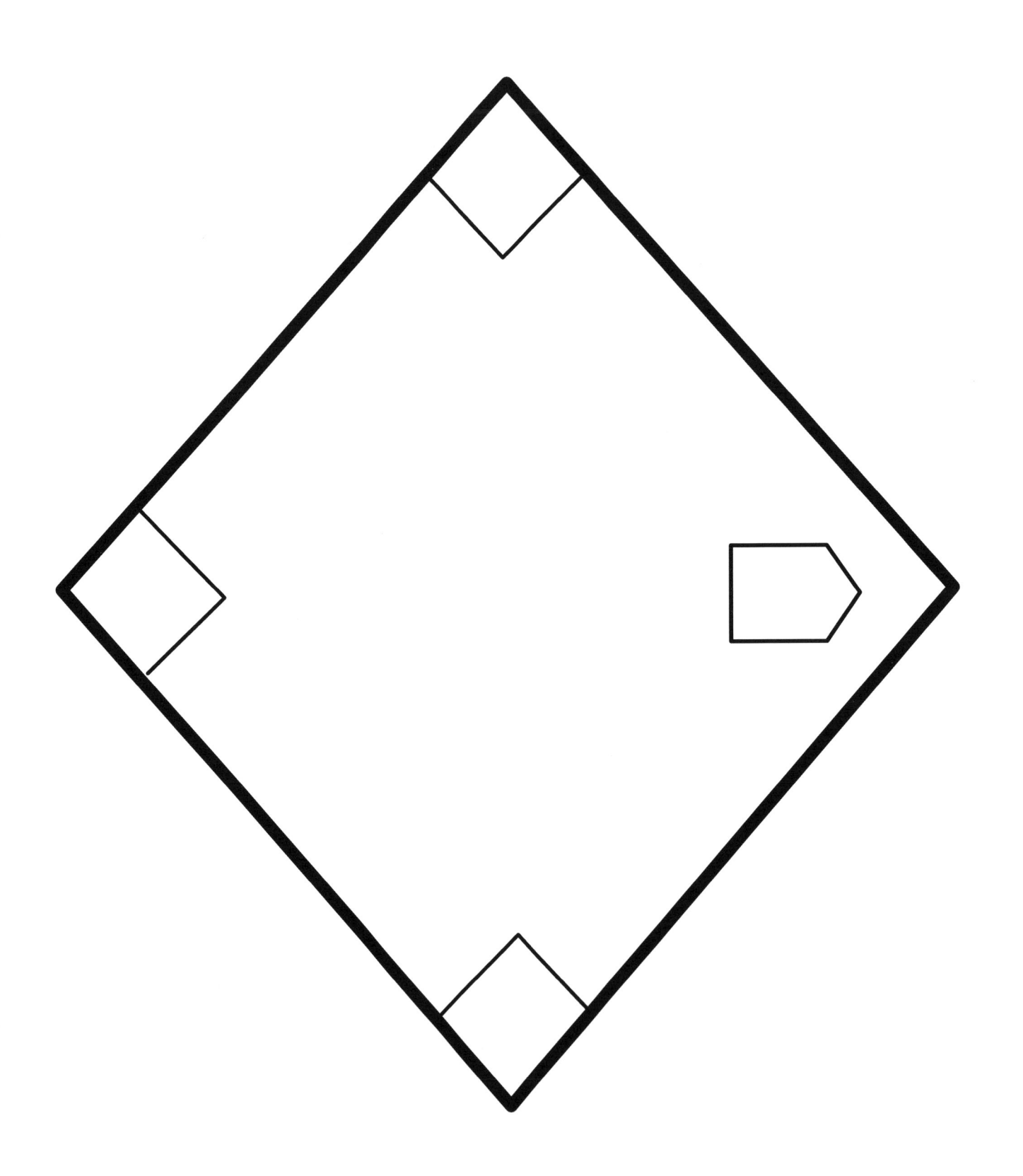

diamond (jewel)

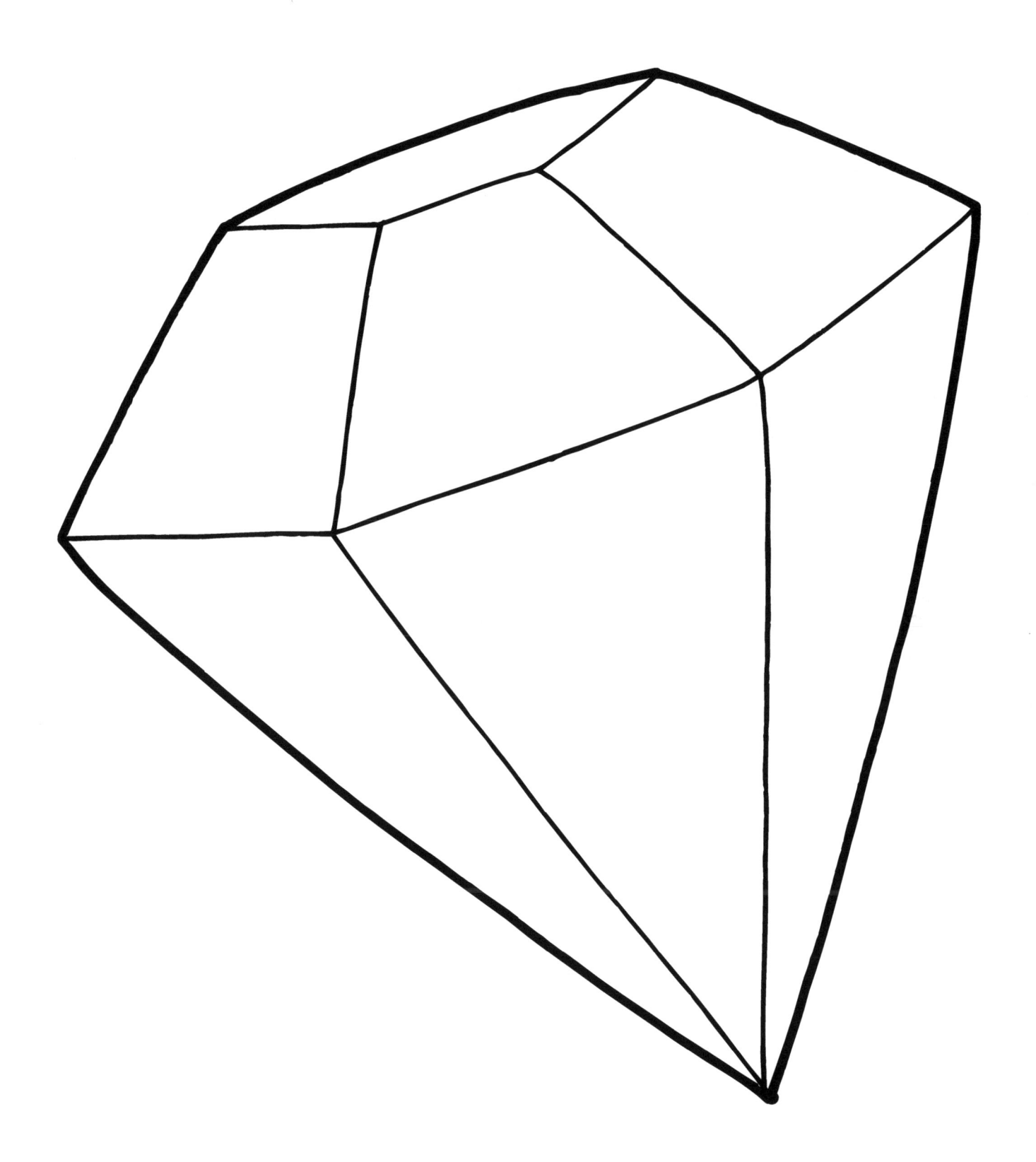

diamond (shape)

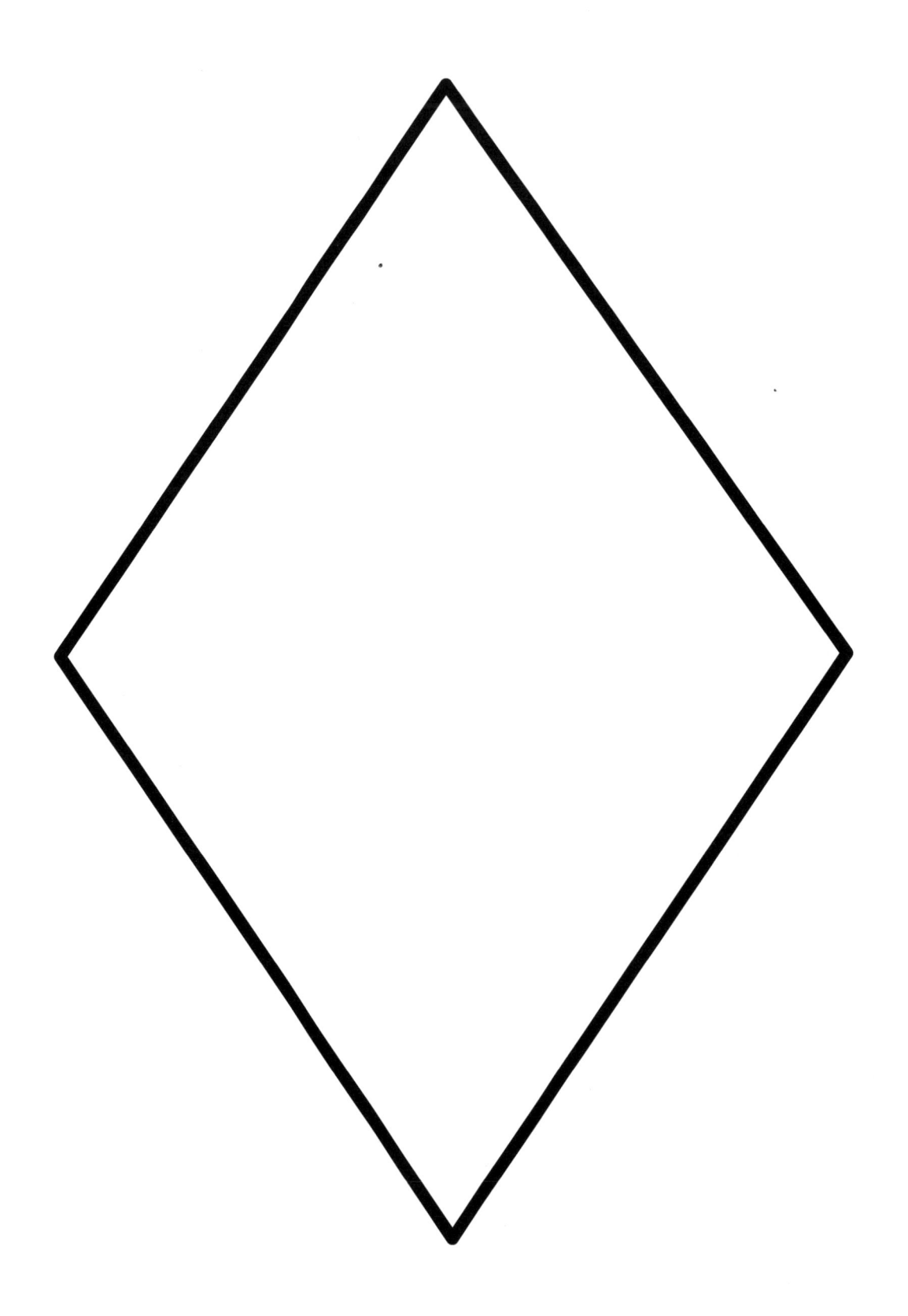

diaper

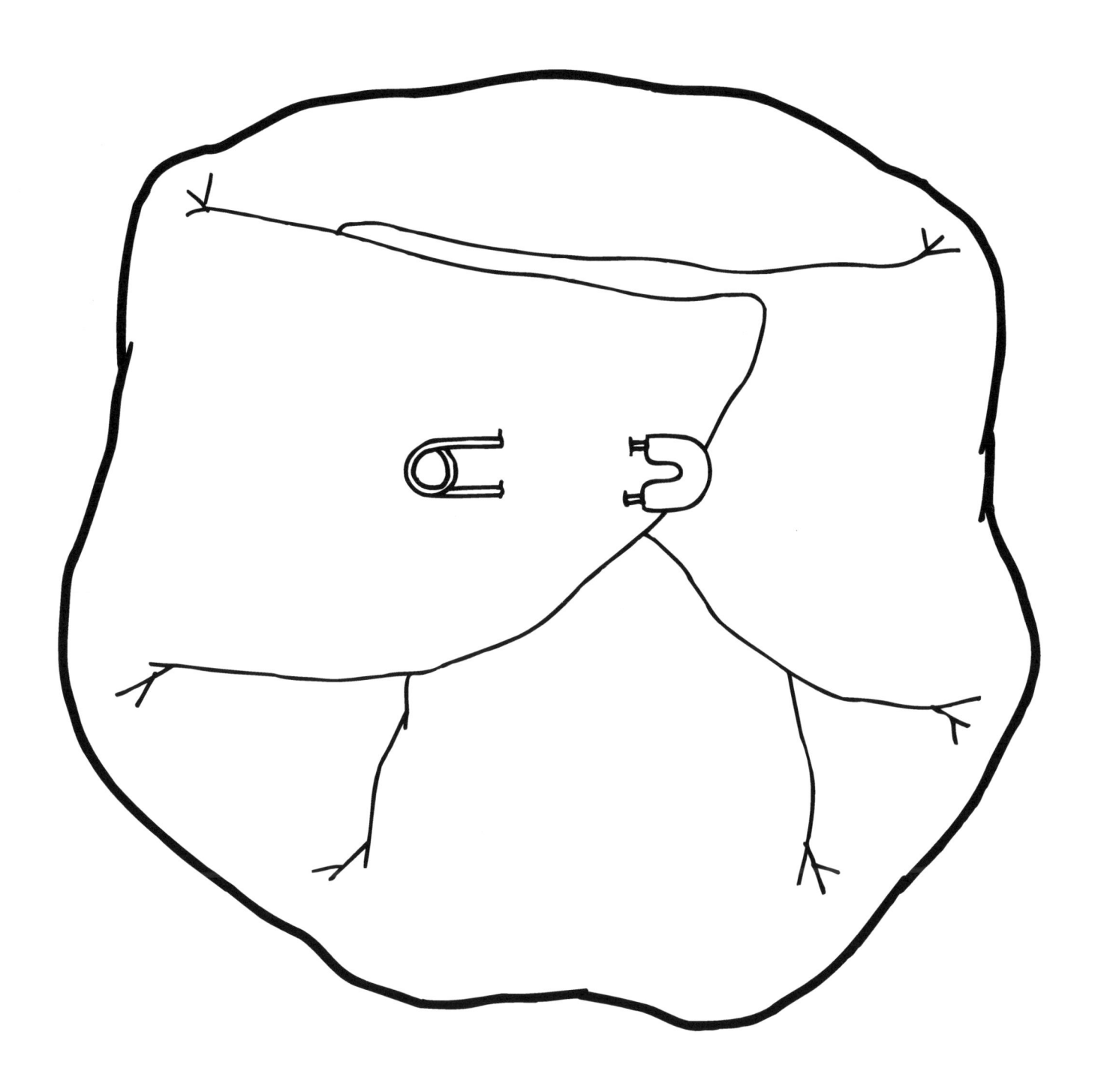

dice

die

dimes

dingo

dinosaur (animated)

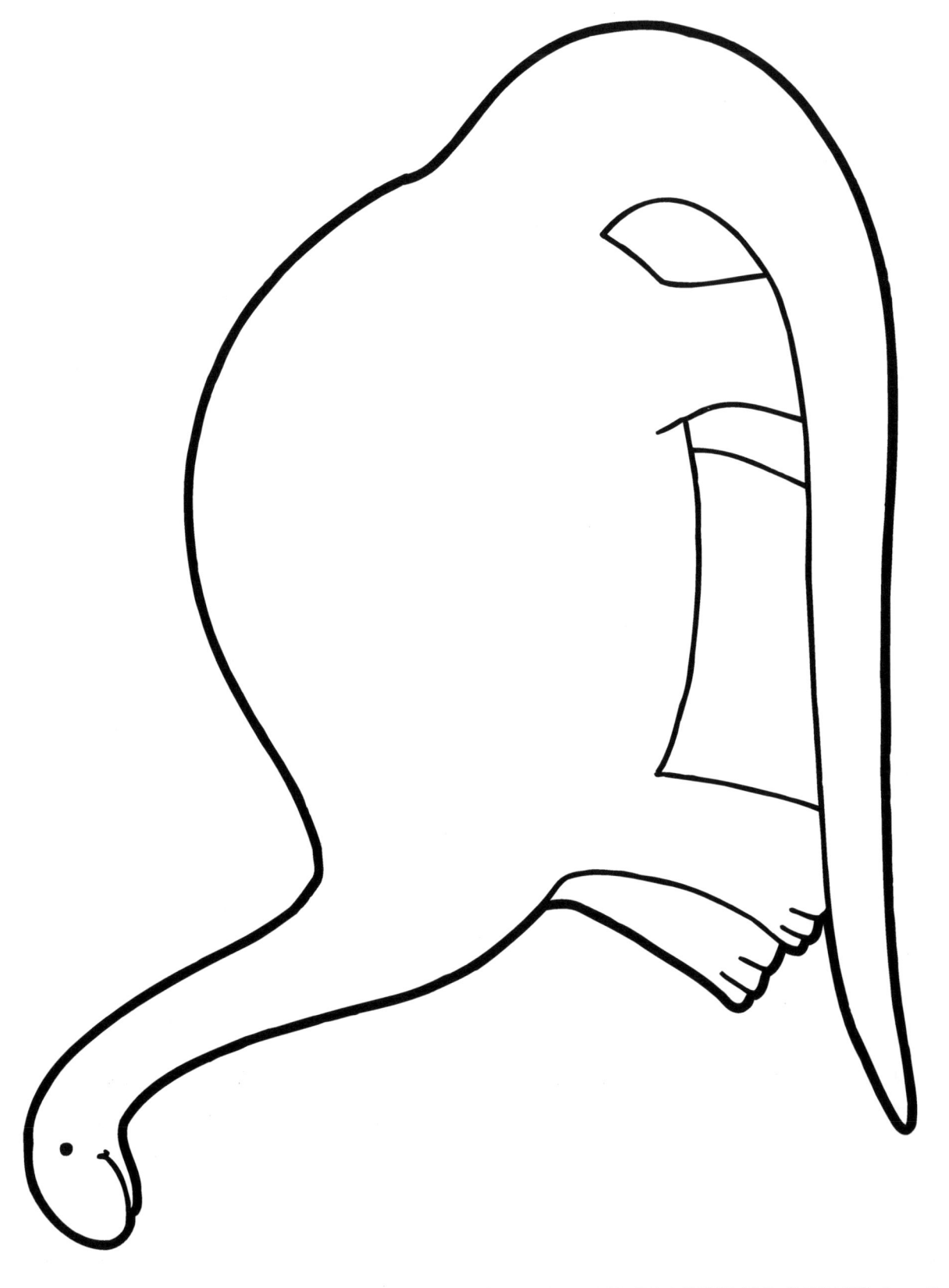

dog (Basset)

dog (outline)

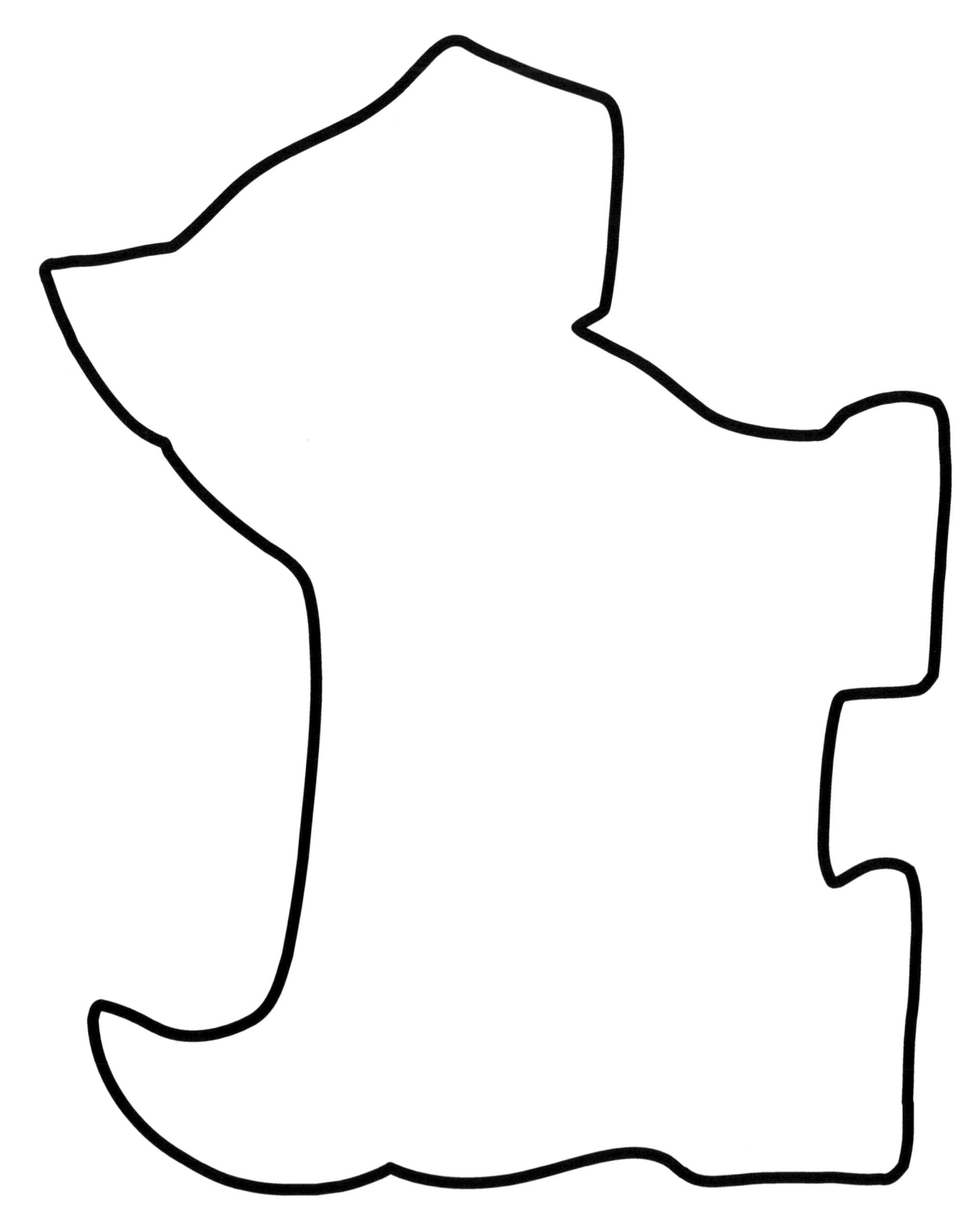

dog (Scotty)

doghouse

doll

dollar (20th c.)

dollar (play)

dollars (Susan B. Anthony)

dolphin

donkey

door

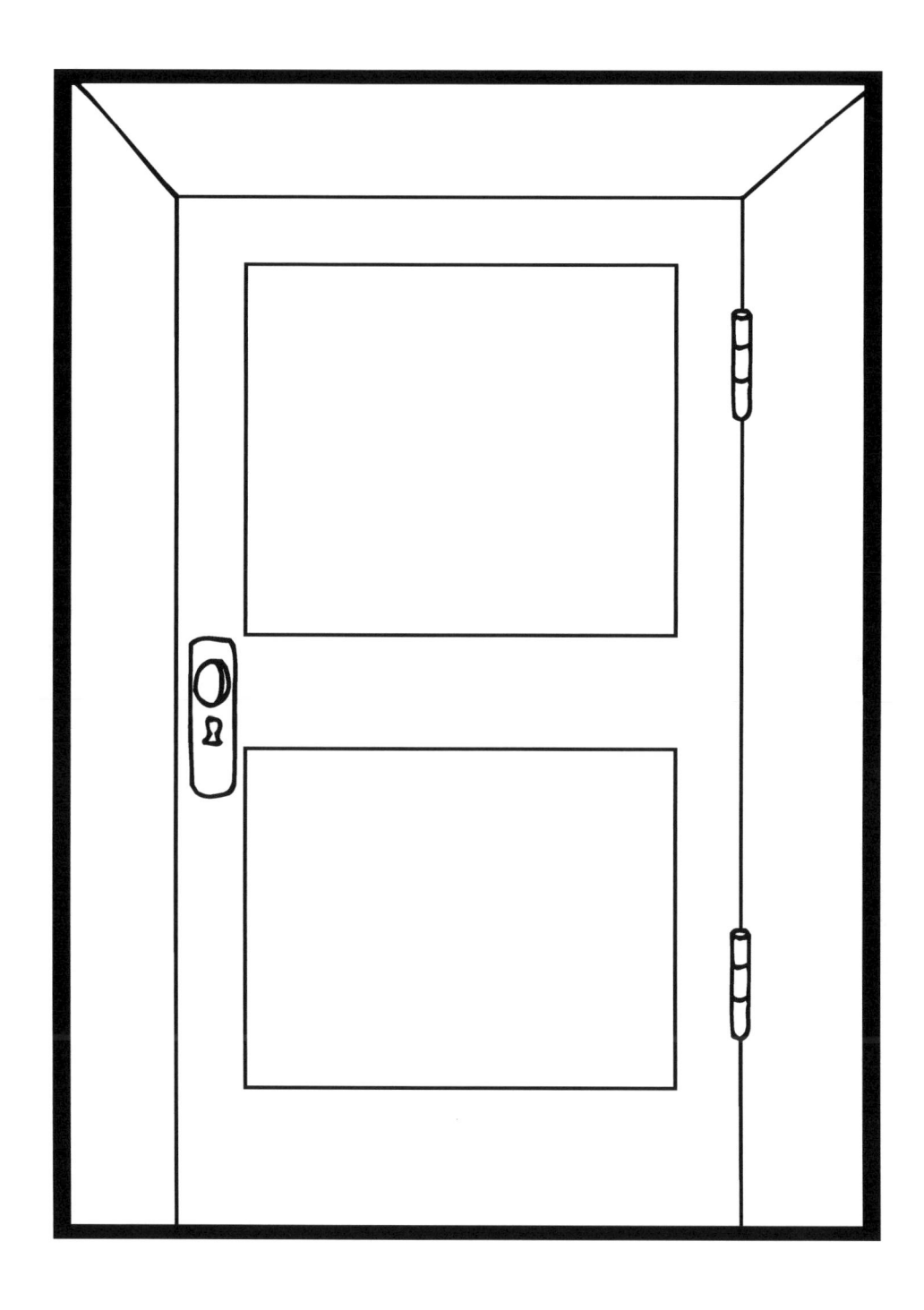

doorknob

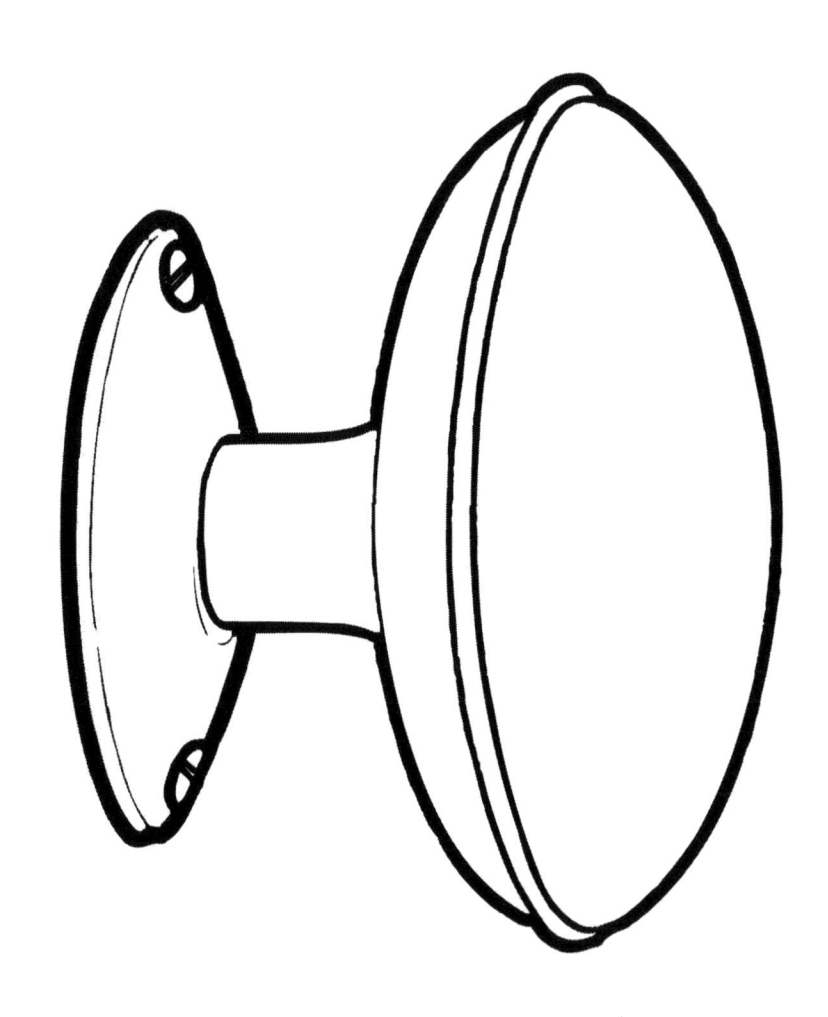

doughnut

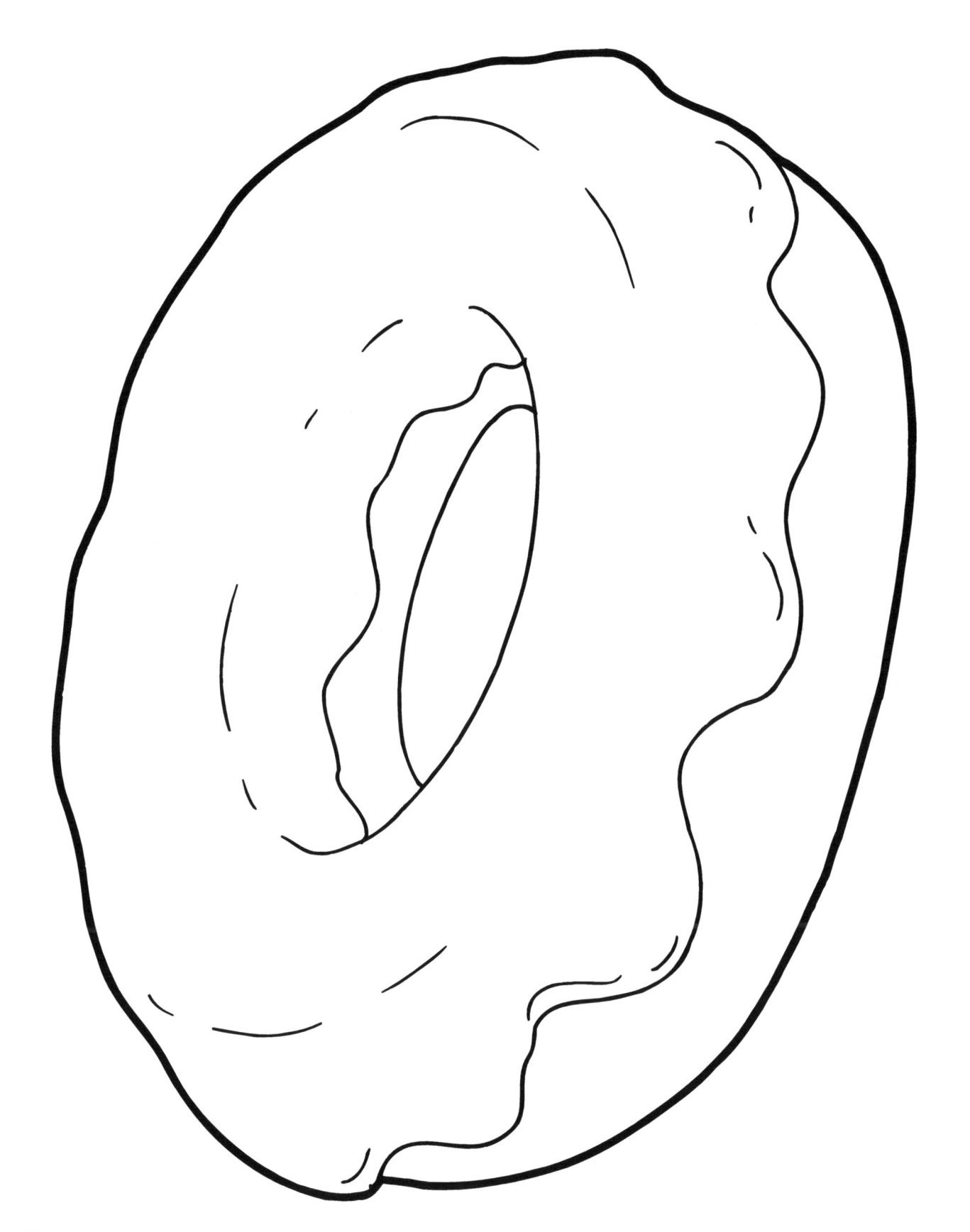

dove

dragon (animated)

dragon (Komodo)

dragonfly (animated)

dress

dresser

dreidel

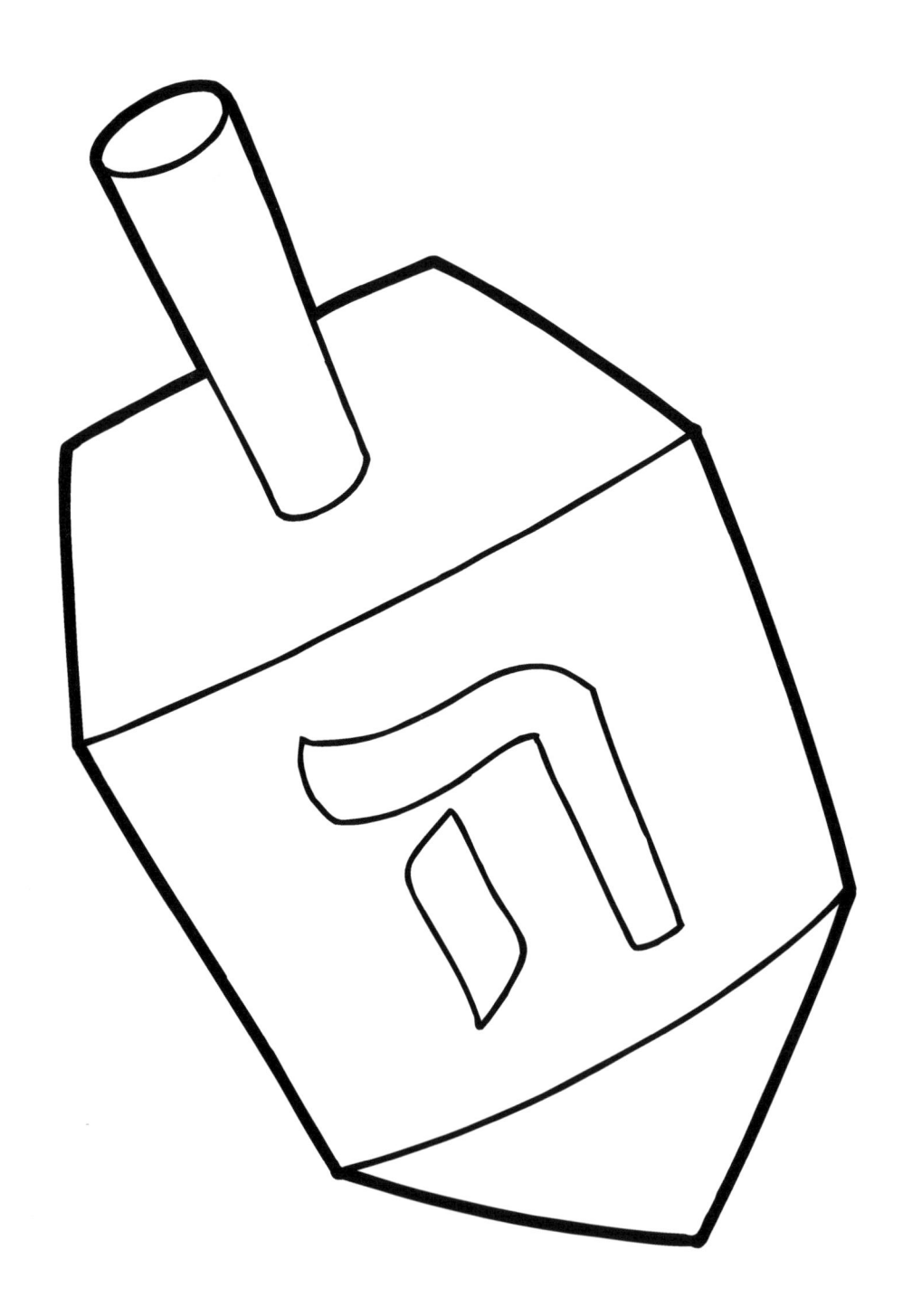

drill (power)

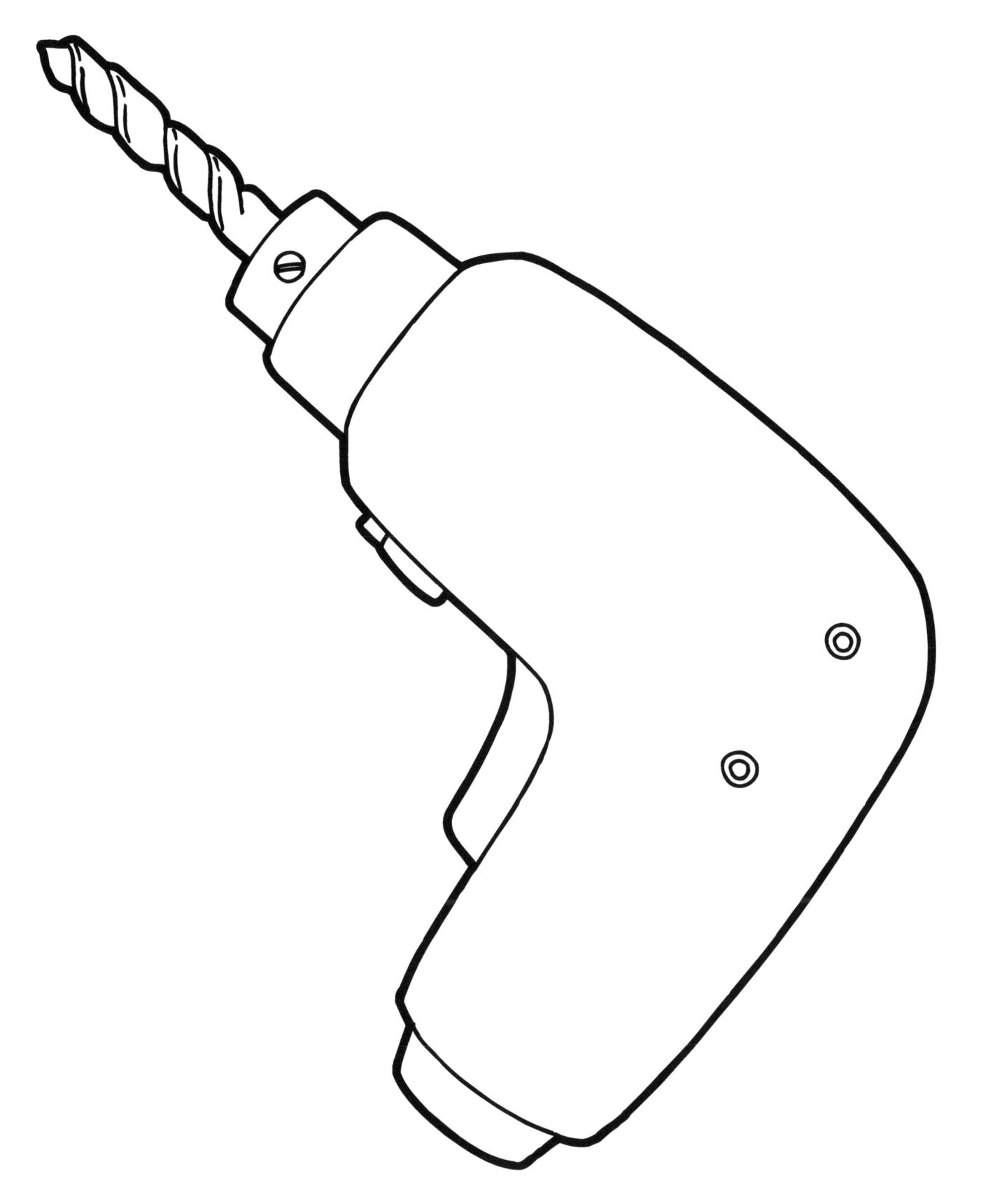

drum

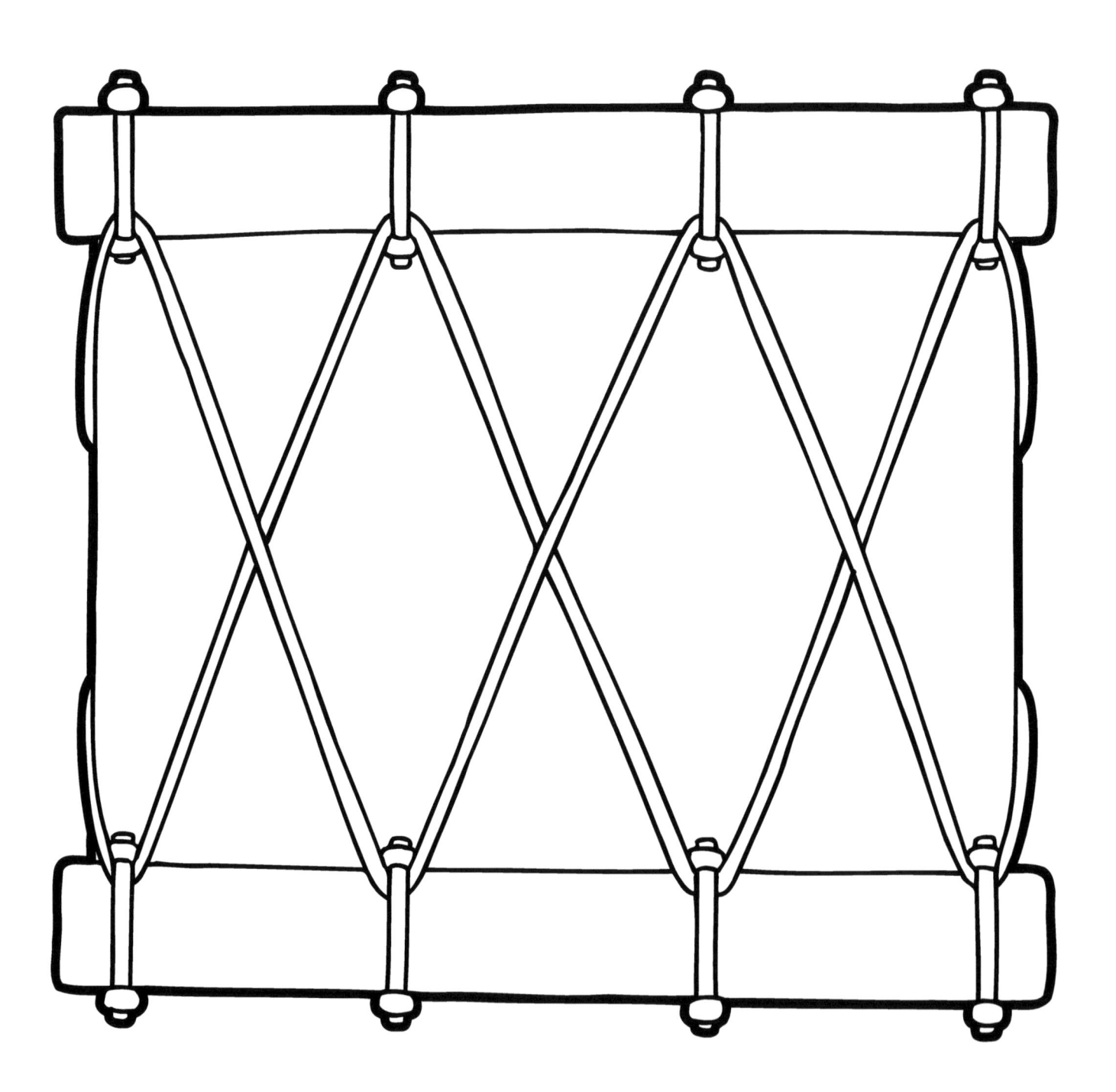

duck (animated)

duck

dugong

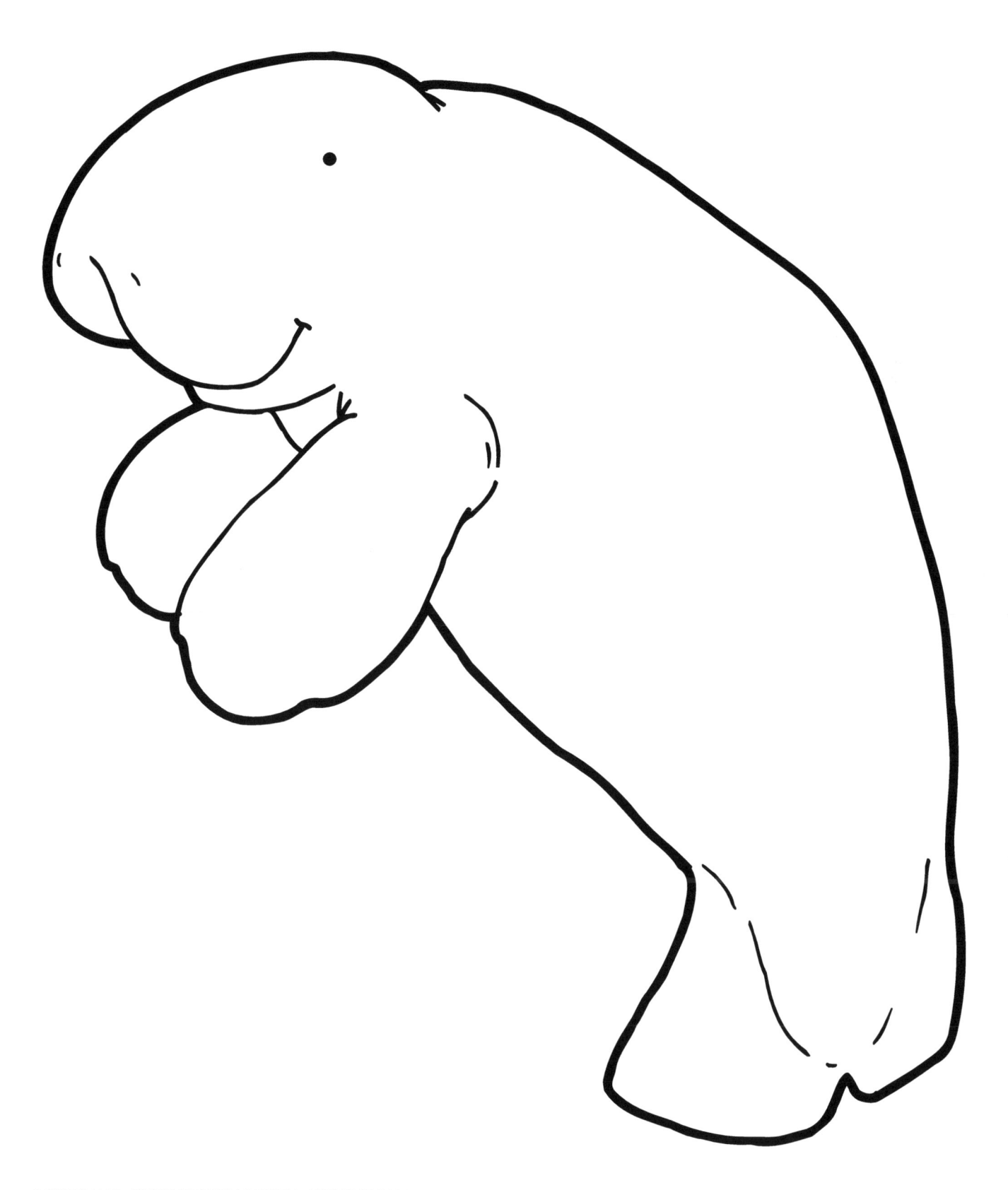

eagle (in flight)

earmuffs

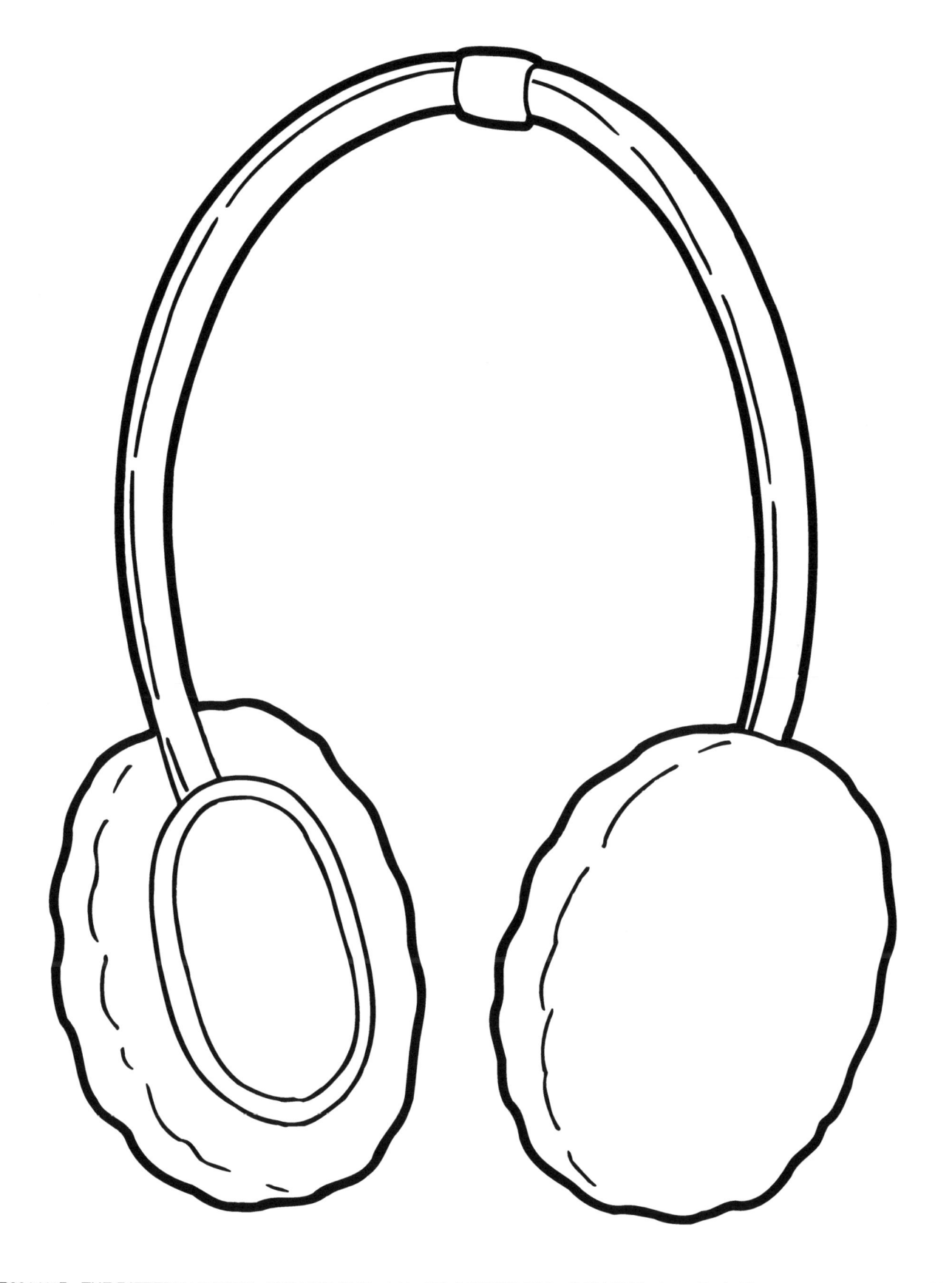

ears (bear & fox)

ears (elephant)

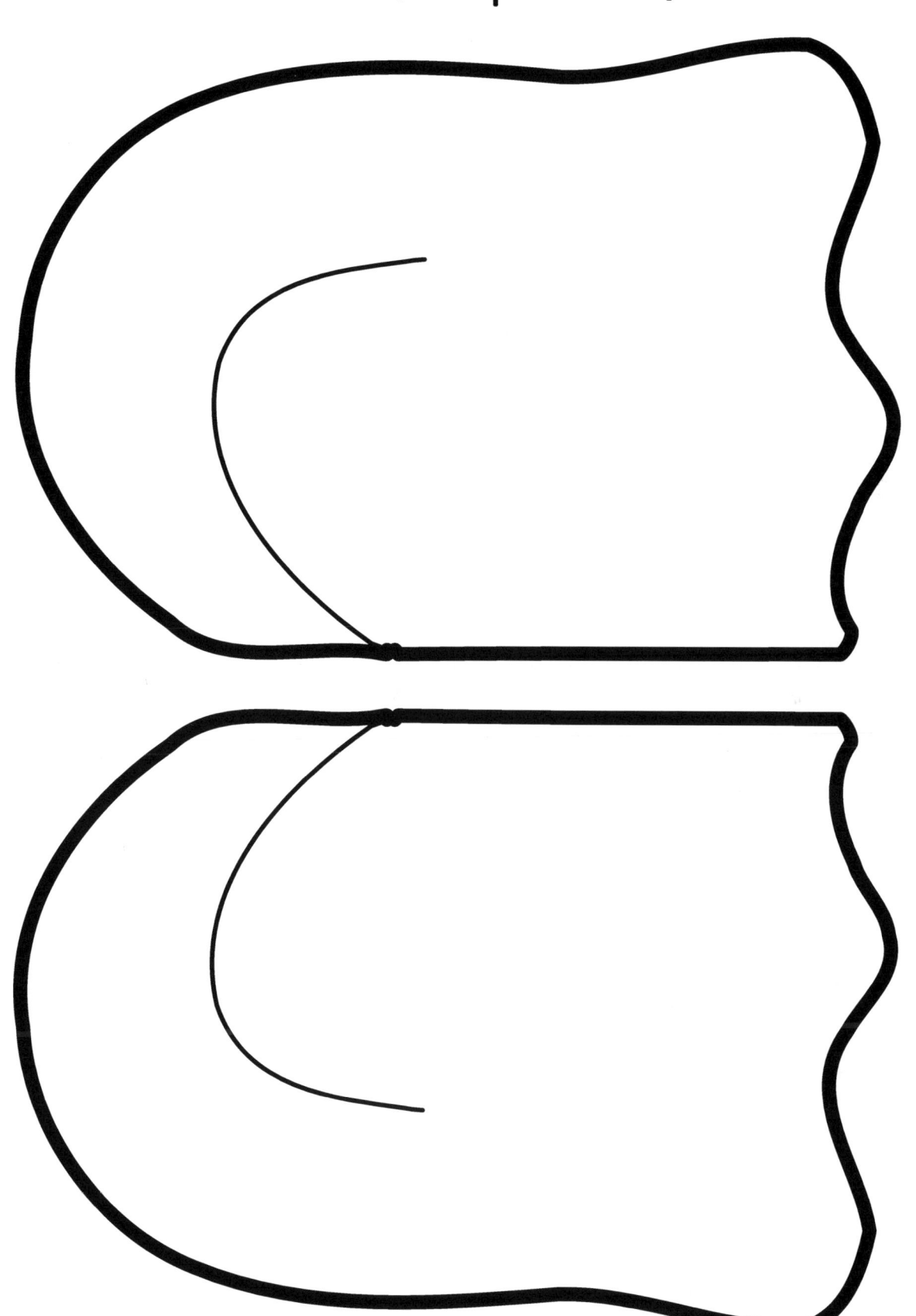

ears (human)

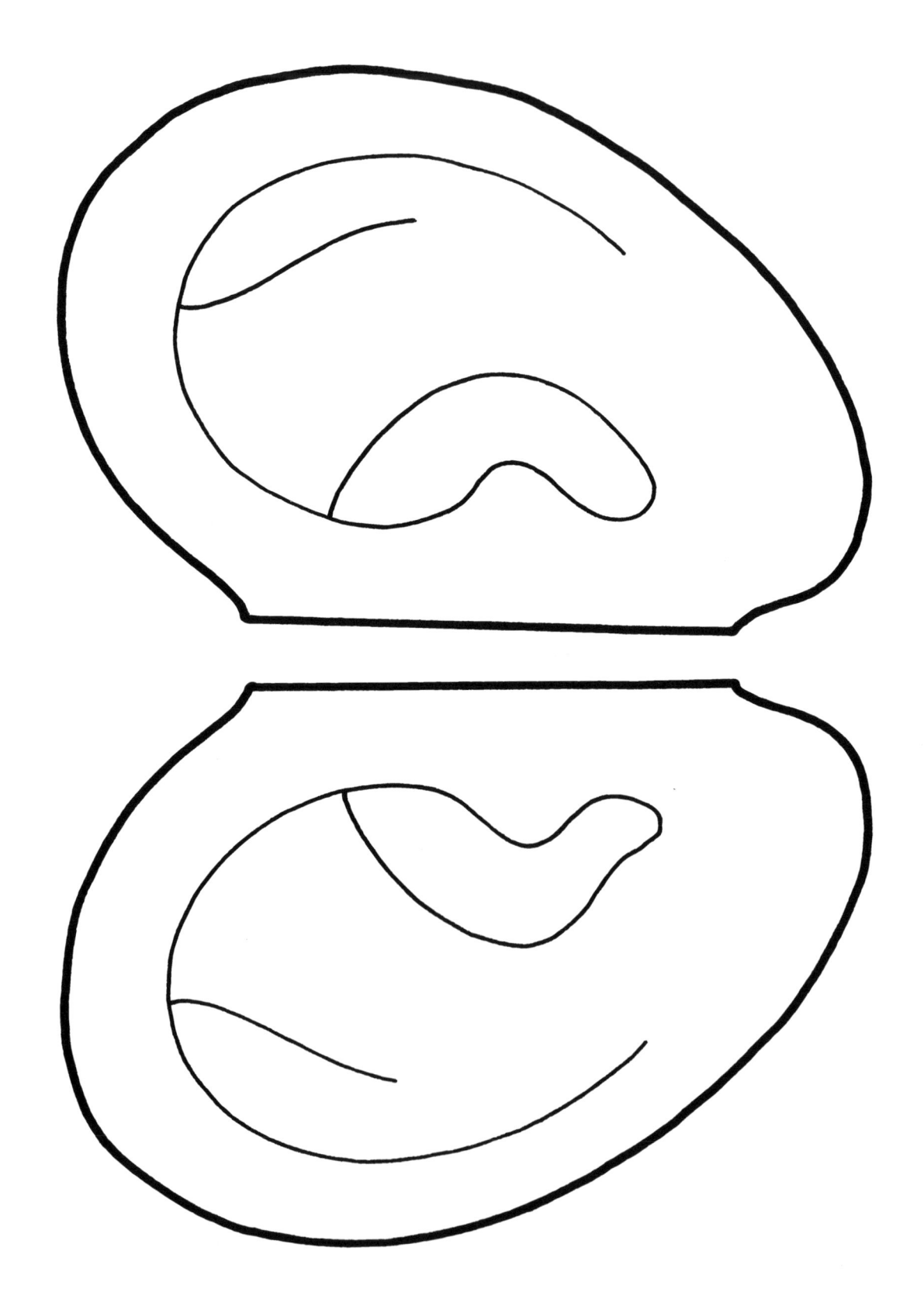

ears (wolf)

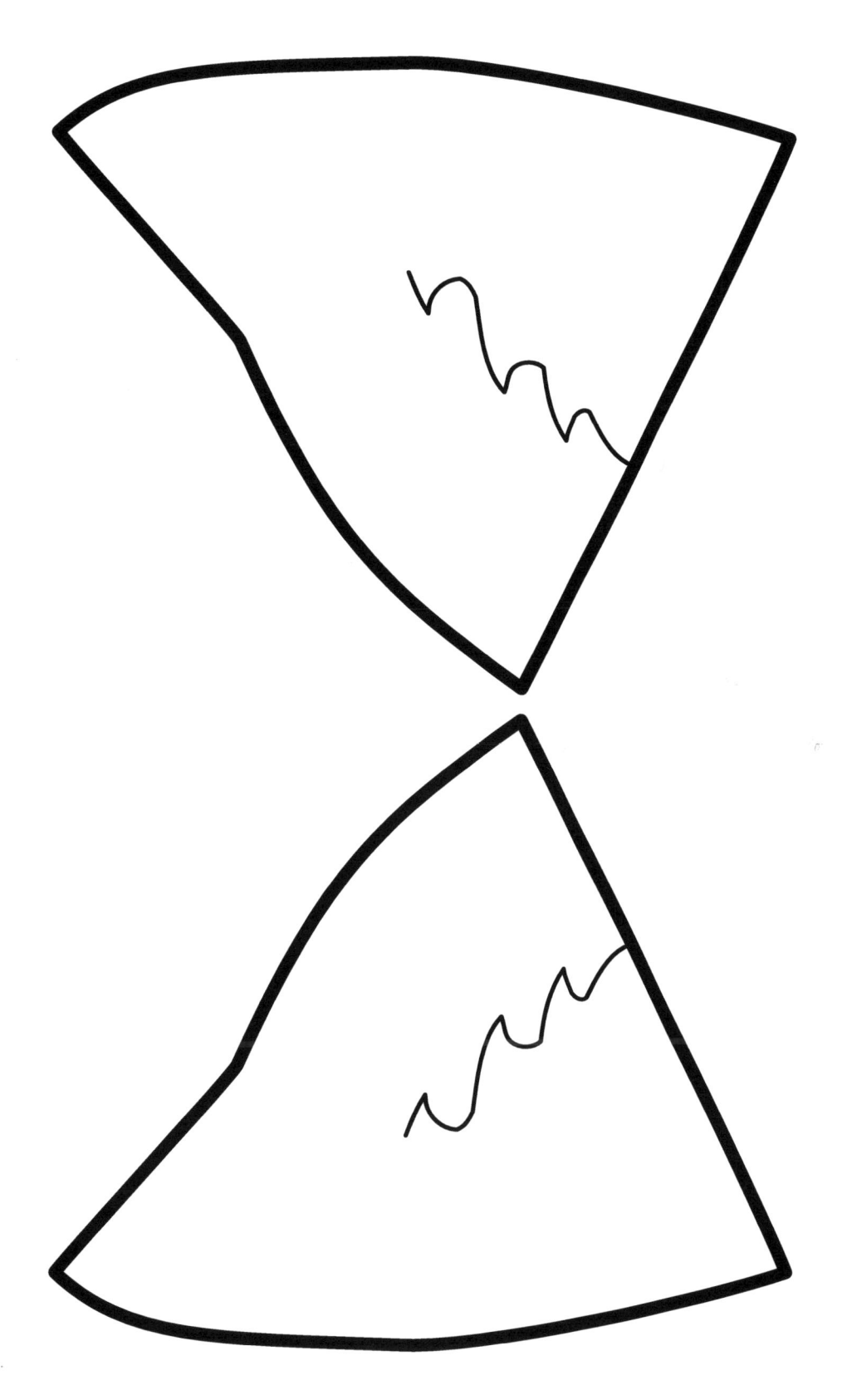

easel

echidna

eel

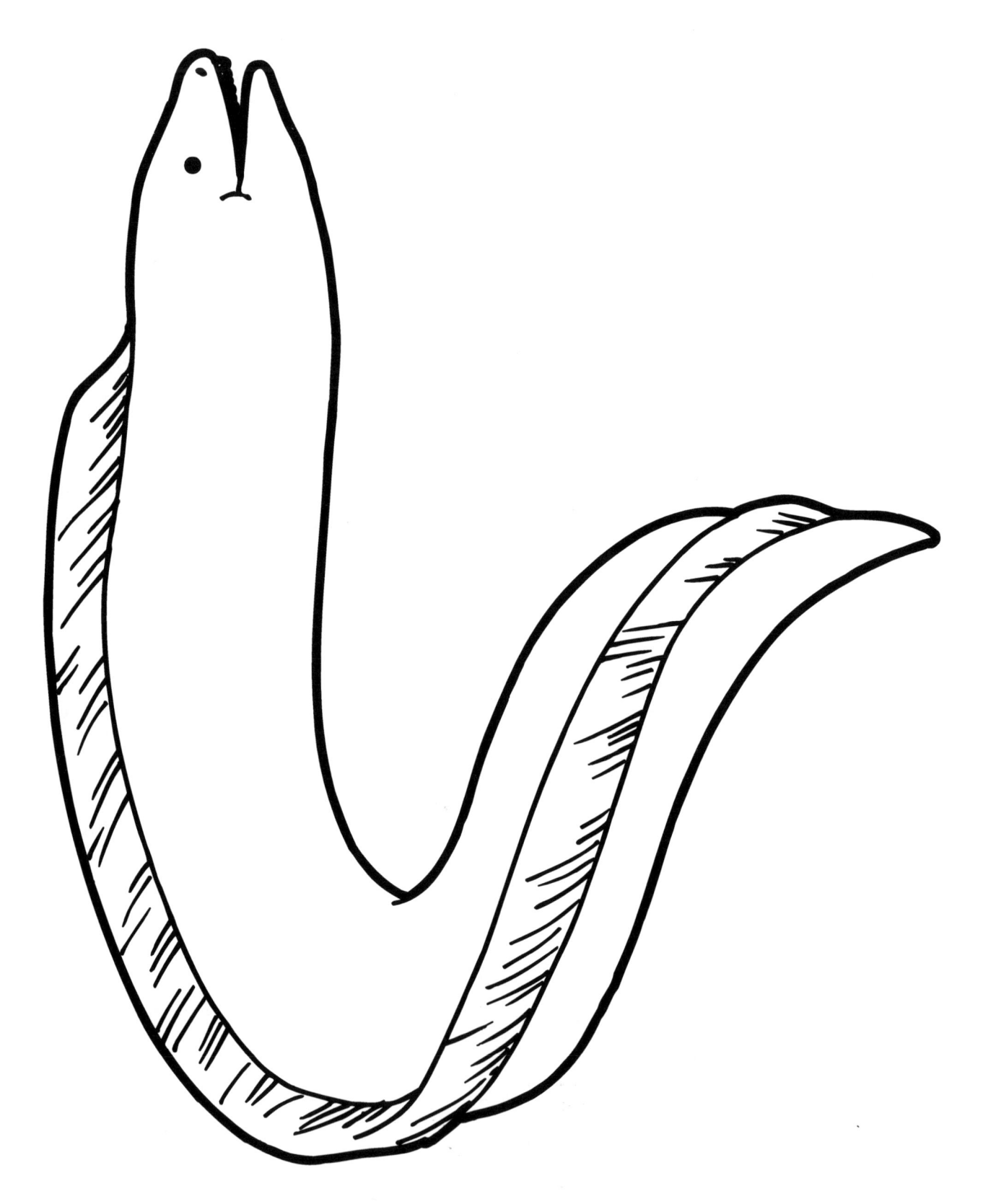

egg

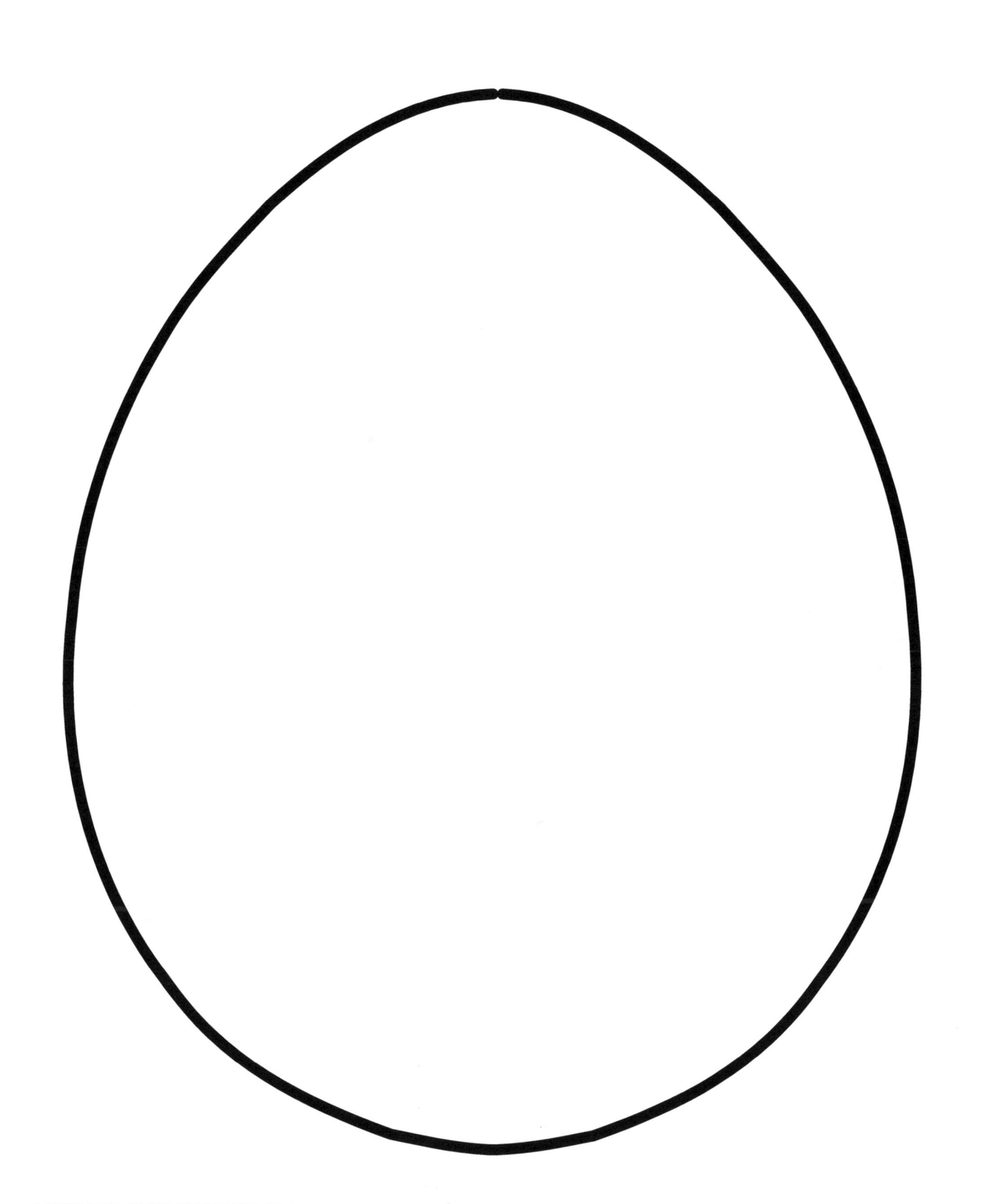

egg cup

egg (Easter)

eggplant

elasmasaurus

elephant (animated)

elephant (African)

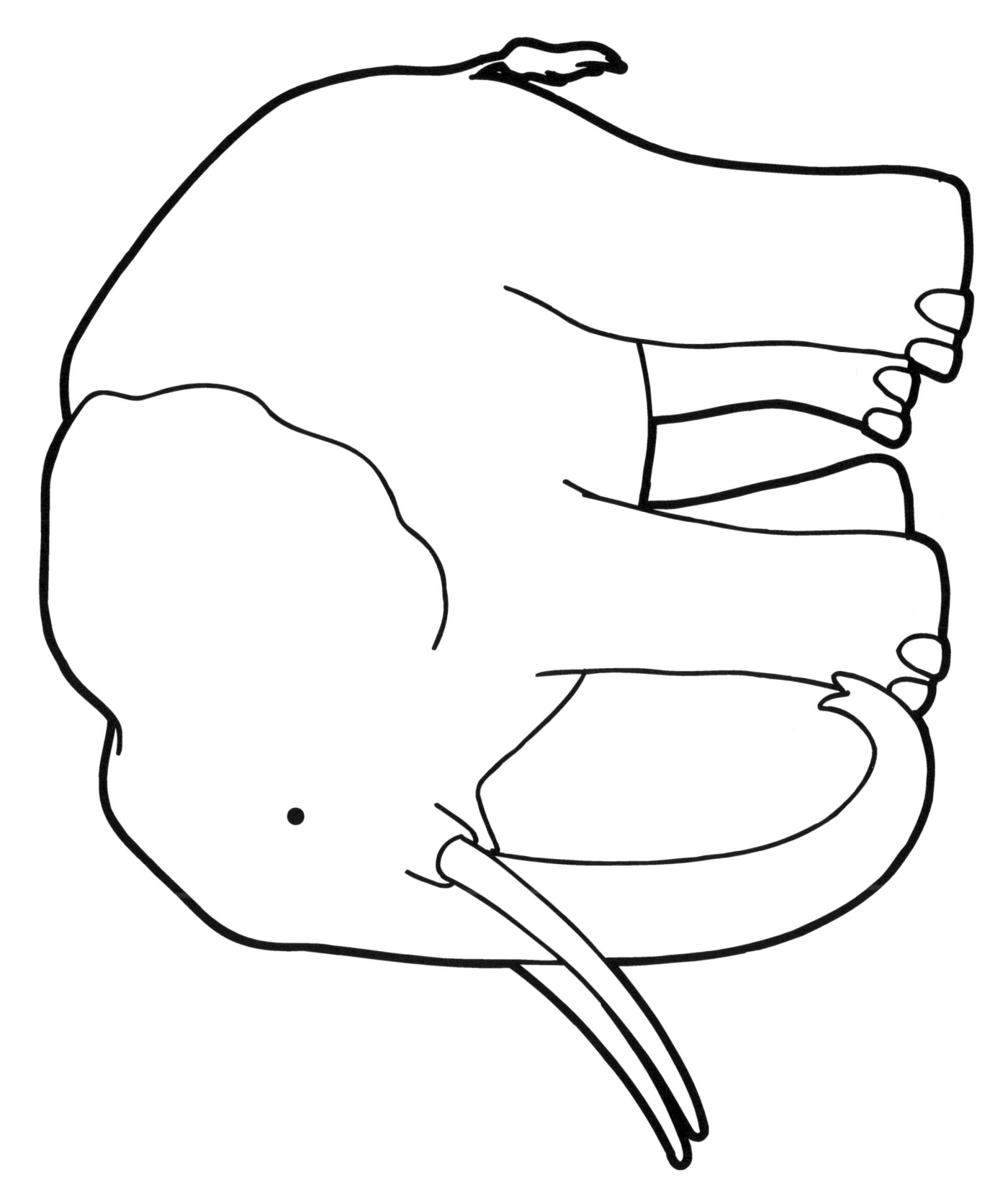

elephant (Indian)

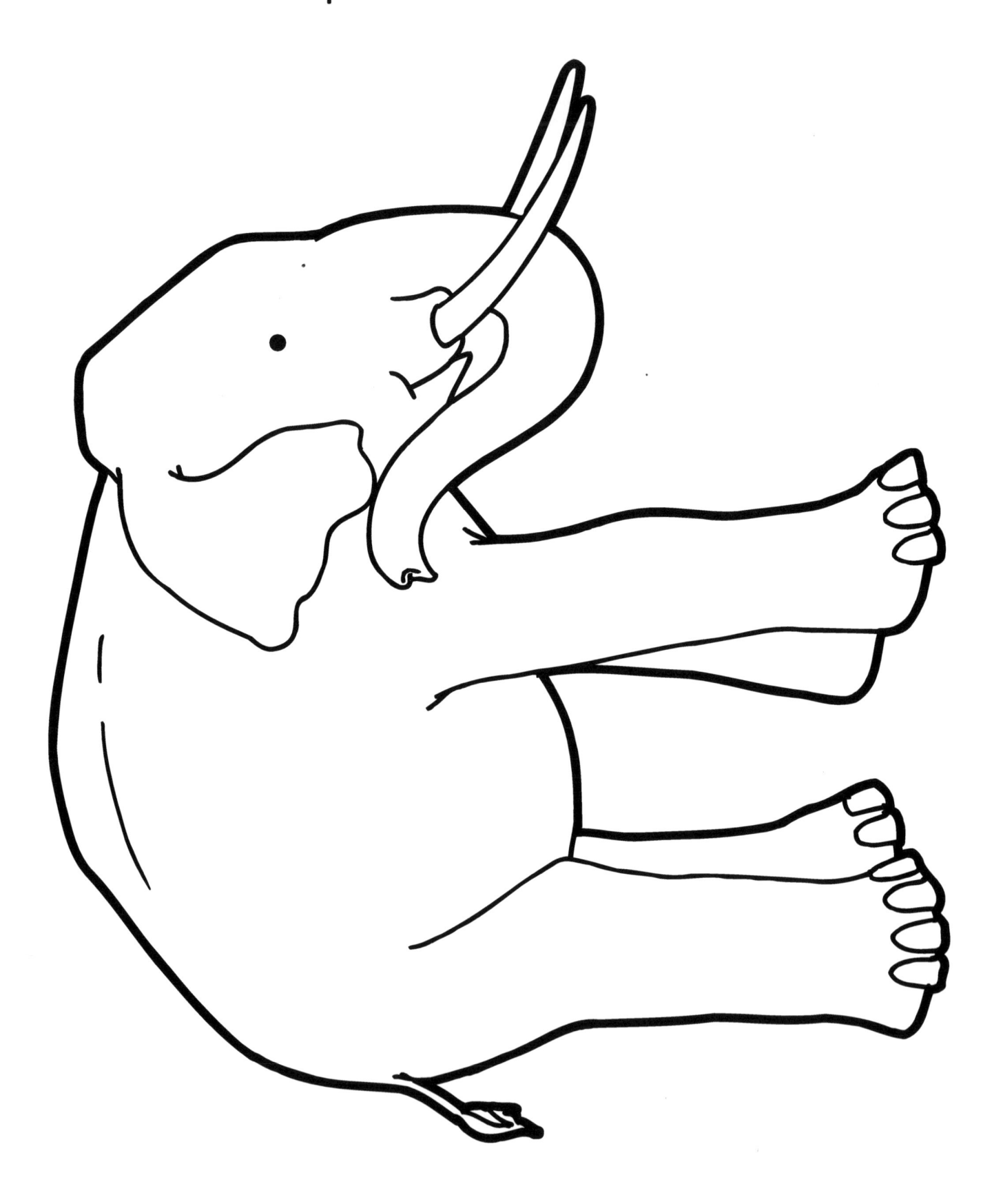

elephant (outline)

elf

elk

TPL

envelope (closed)

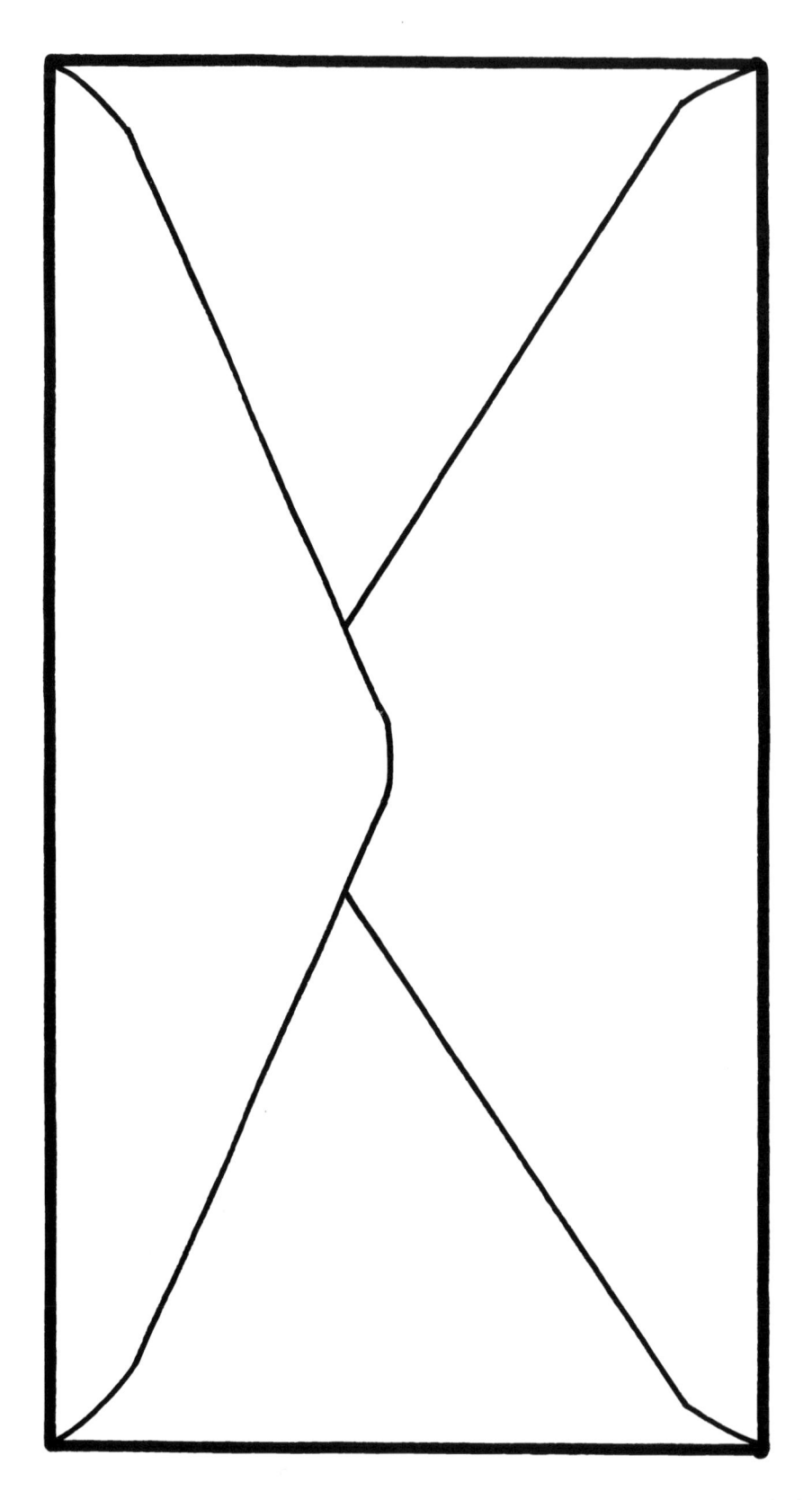

352 LAB201411P • THE PATTERN LIBRARY • VOLUME ONE • A-H • 978-1-937257-62-0 • © 2014 Little Acorn Books™

envelope (open)

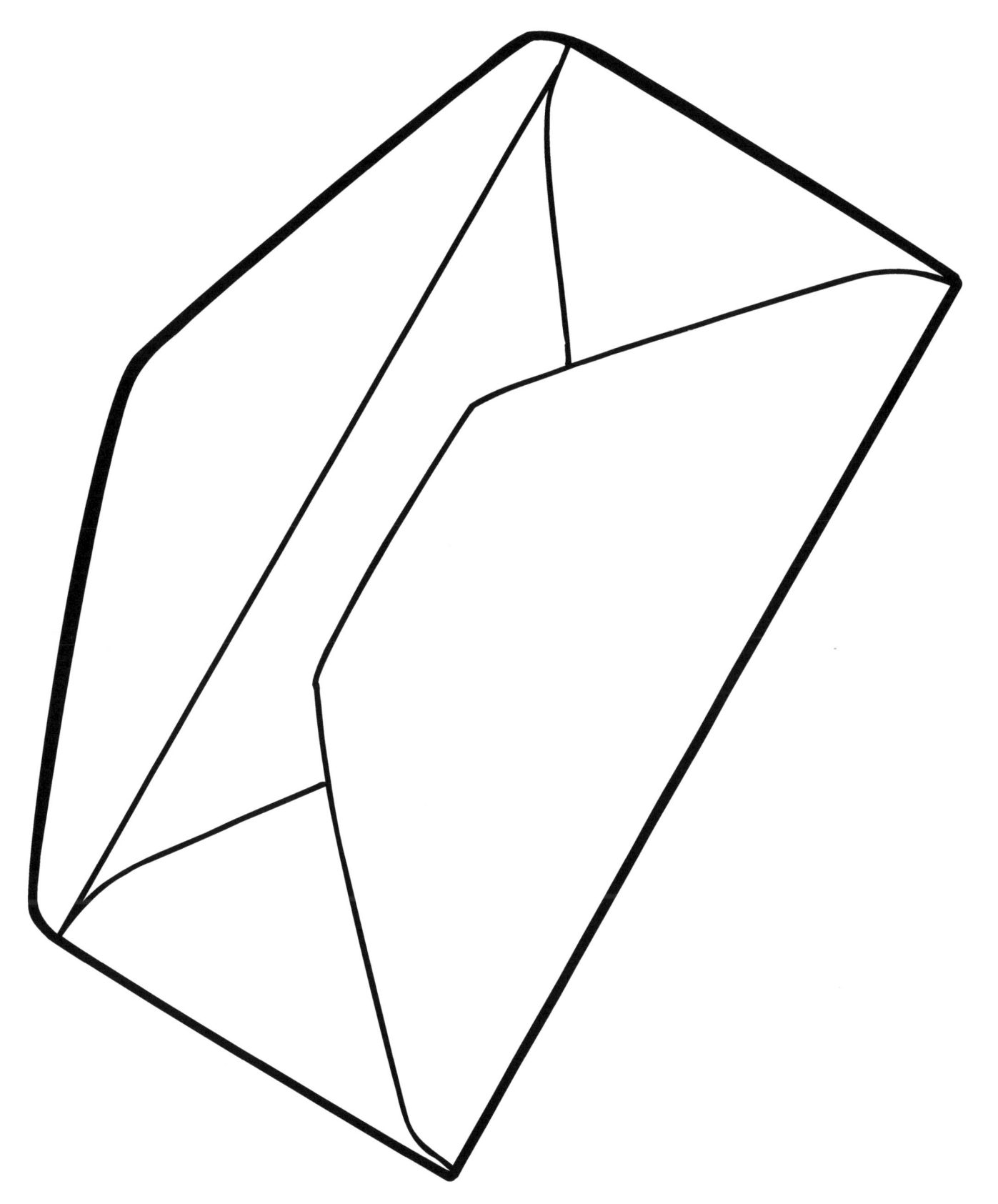

envelope (pattern)

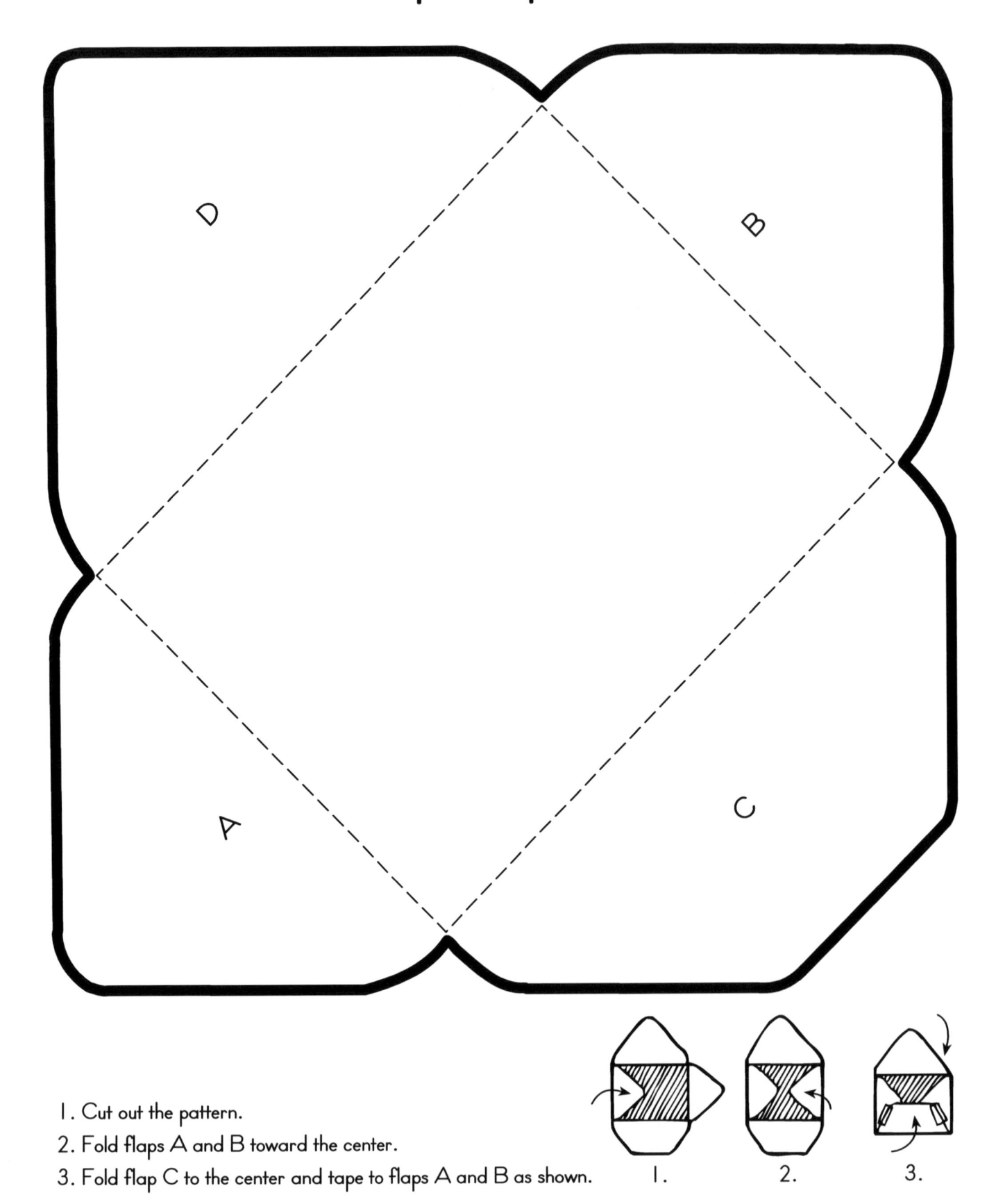

1. Cut out the pattern.
2. Fold flaps A and B toward the center.
3. Fold flap C to the center and tape to flaps A and B as shown.

1.   2.   3.

Europe

North
East
South
West

Maps are representations and boundaries are not exact.

eye

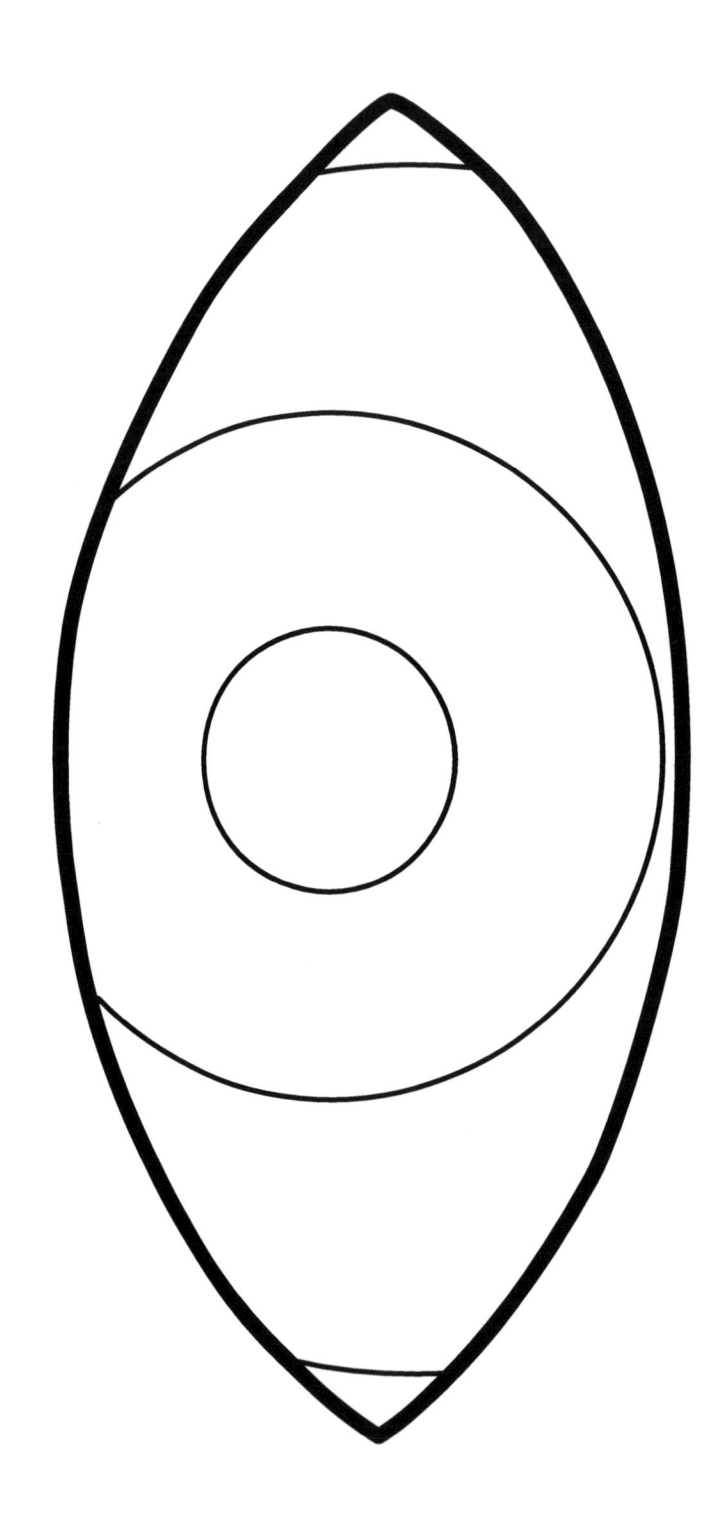

eyes (two pair)

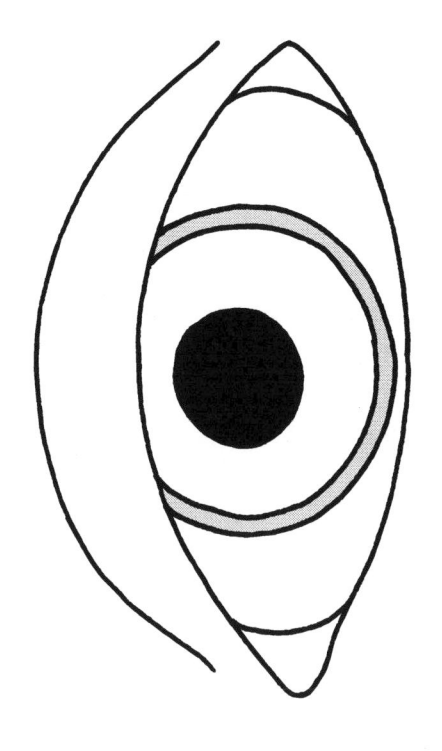

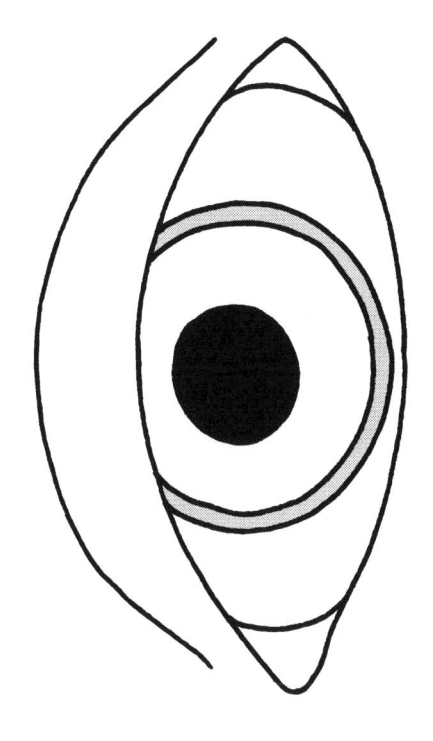

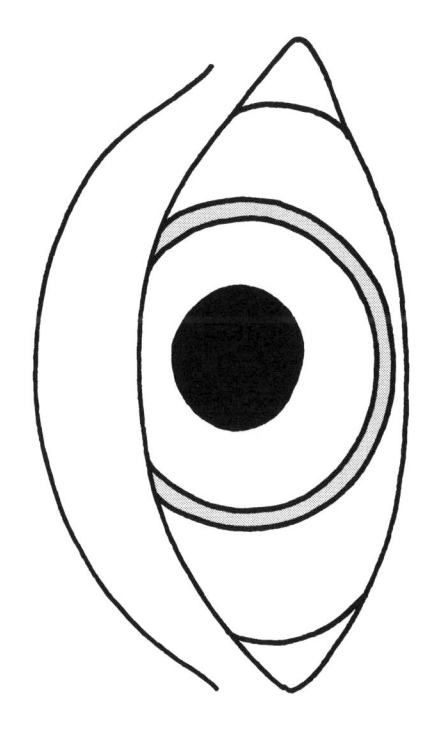

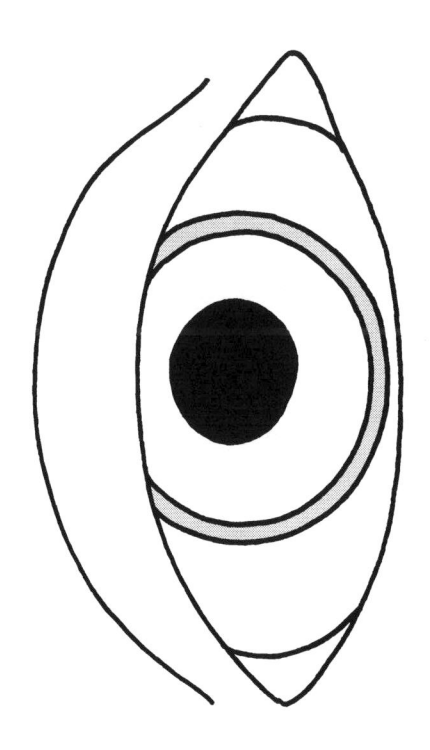

eyes (animated)

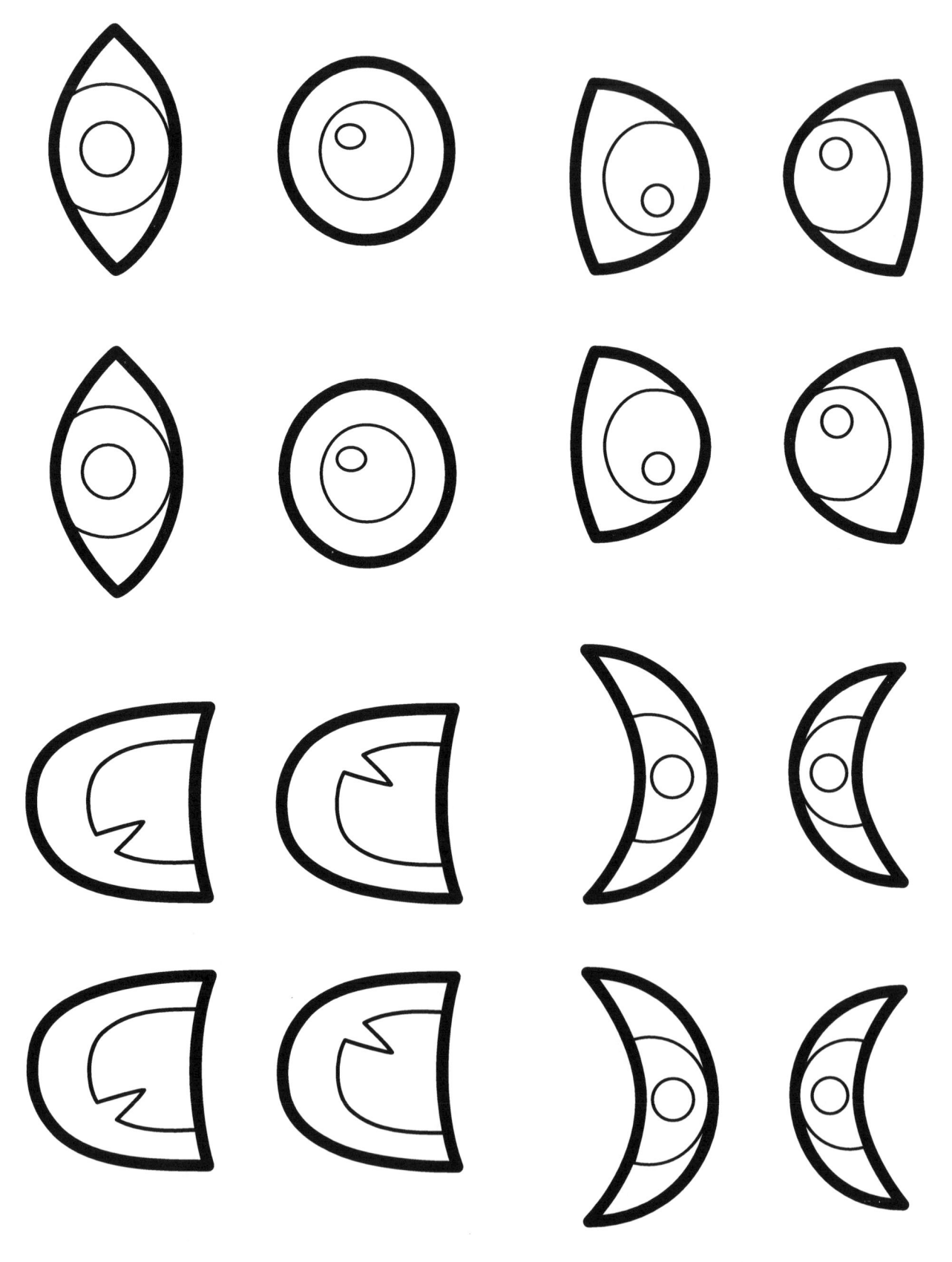

face (outline)

fairy

feather (broad)

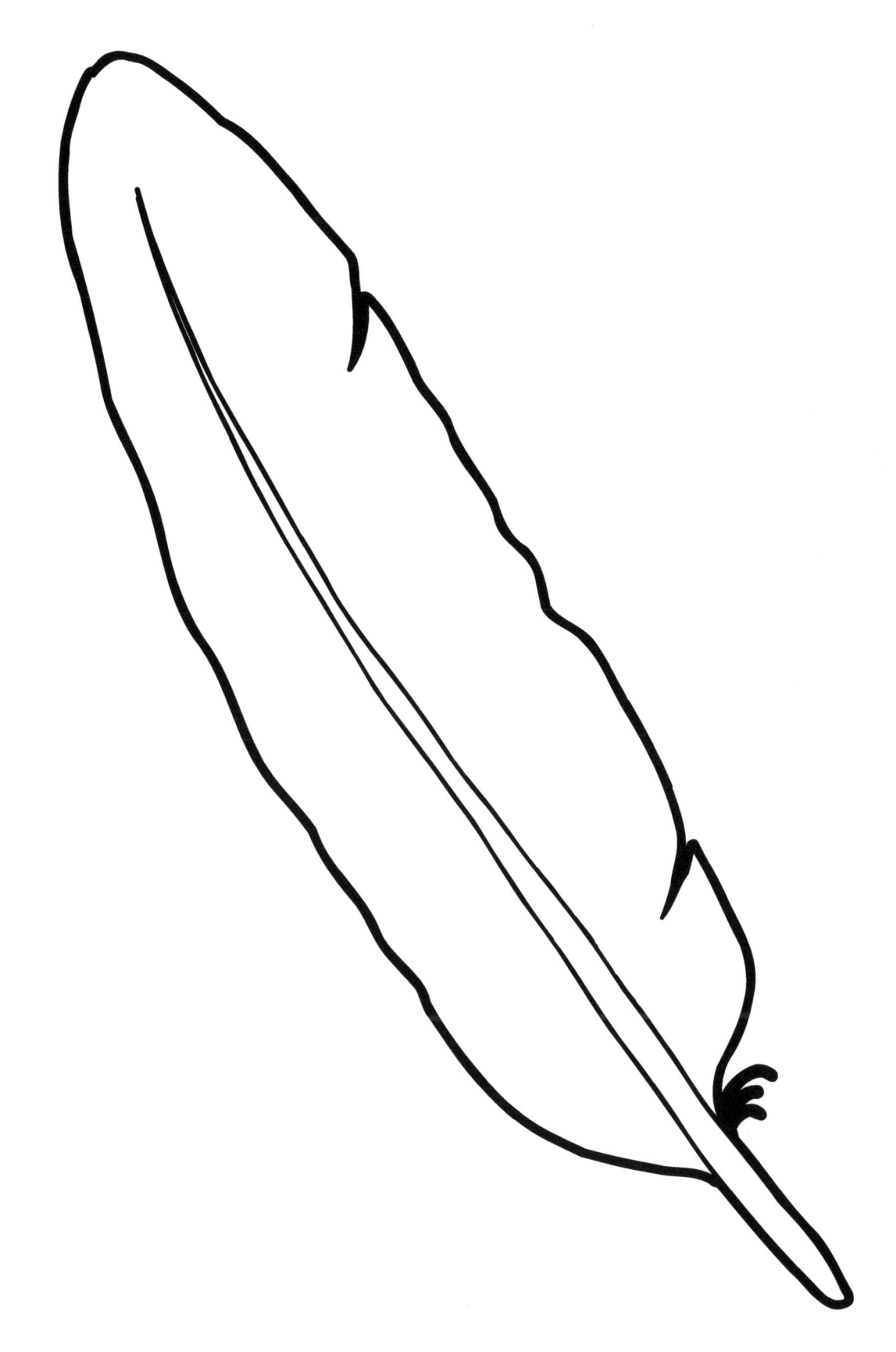

feather (pointed)

feathers

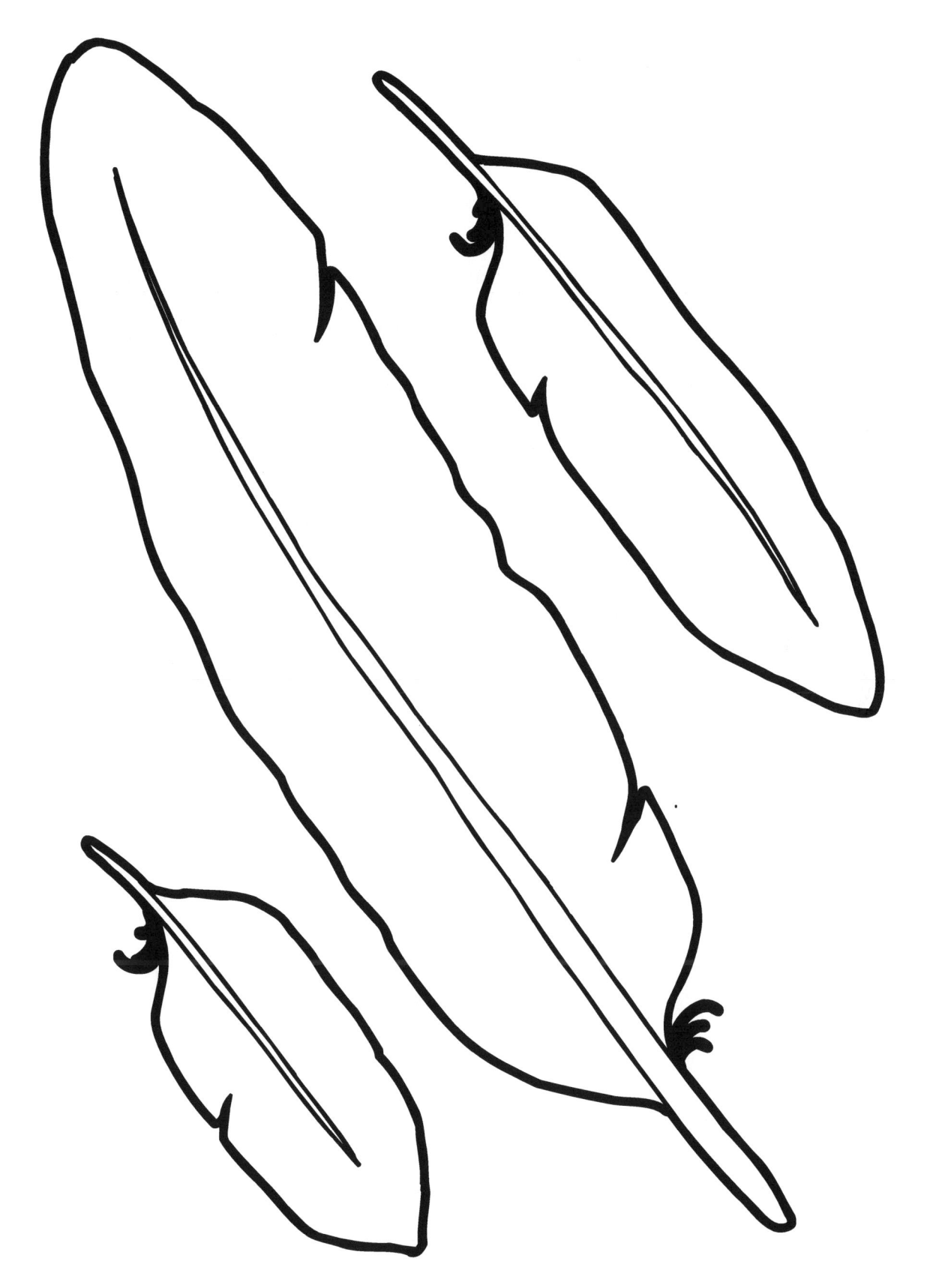

… fire hydrant (outline)

fire safety (poster)

fire truck

fire truck

fire truck

fireplace

fish bowl (empty)

fish bowl (with water)

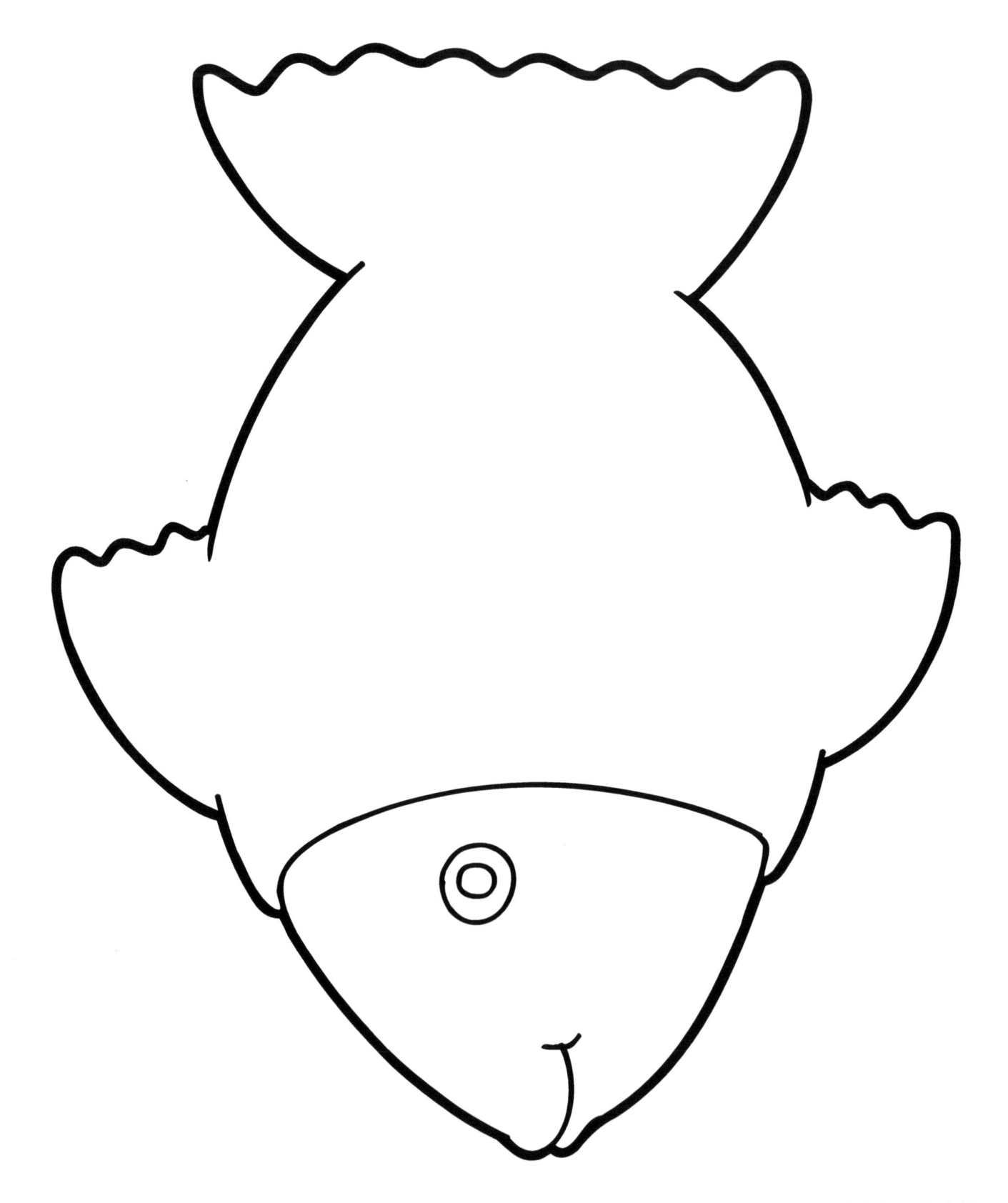

fish (animated-1)

fish (animated-2)

fish (Oscar)

flag

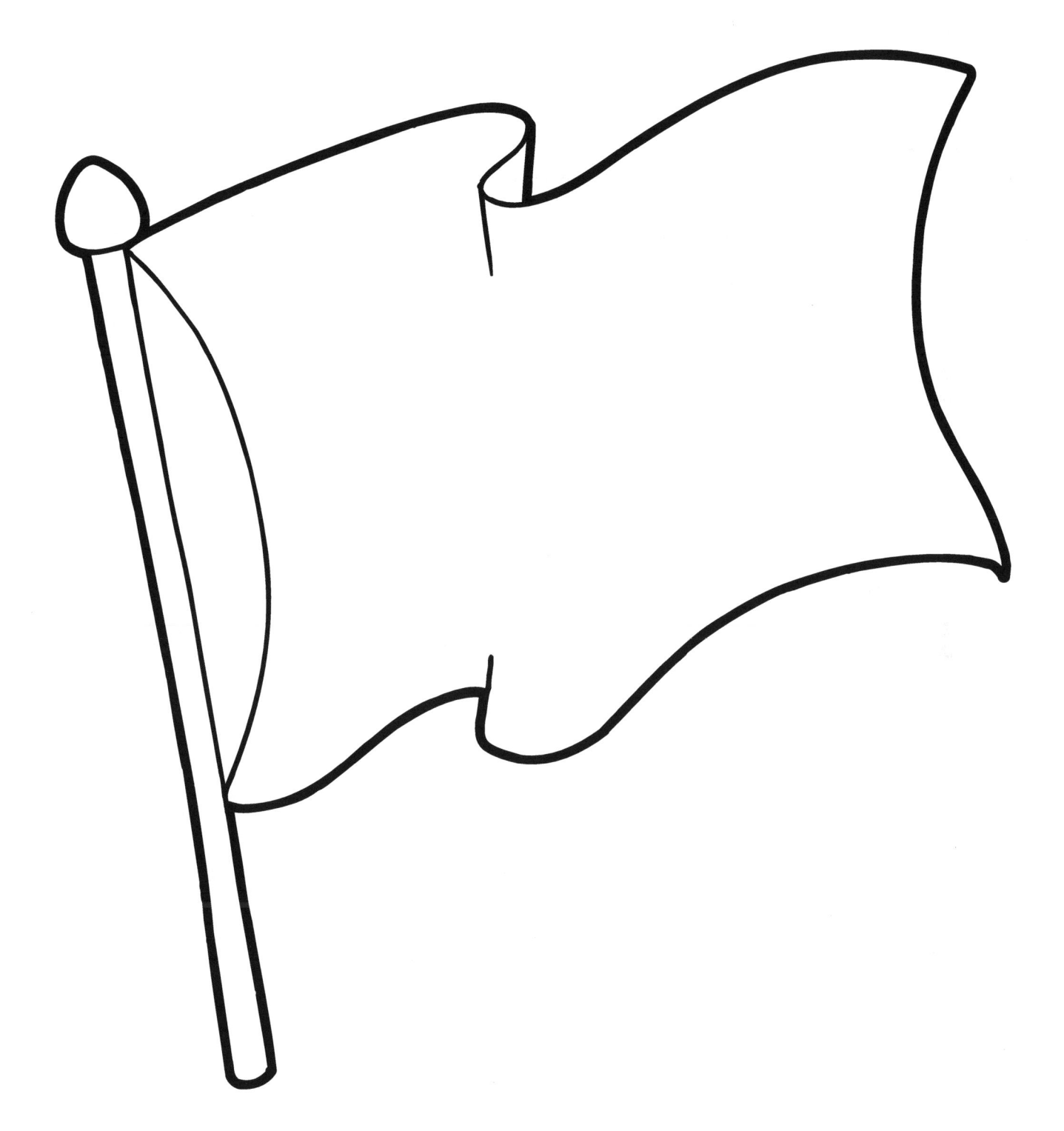

flashlight

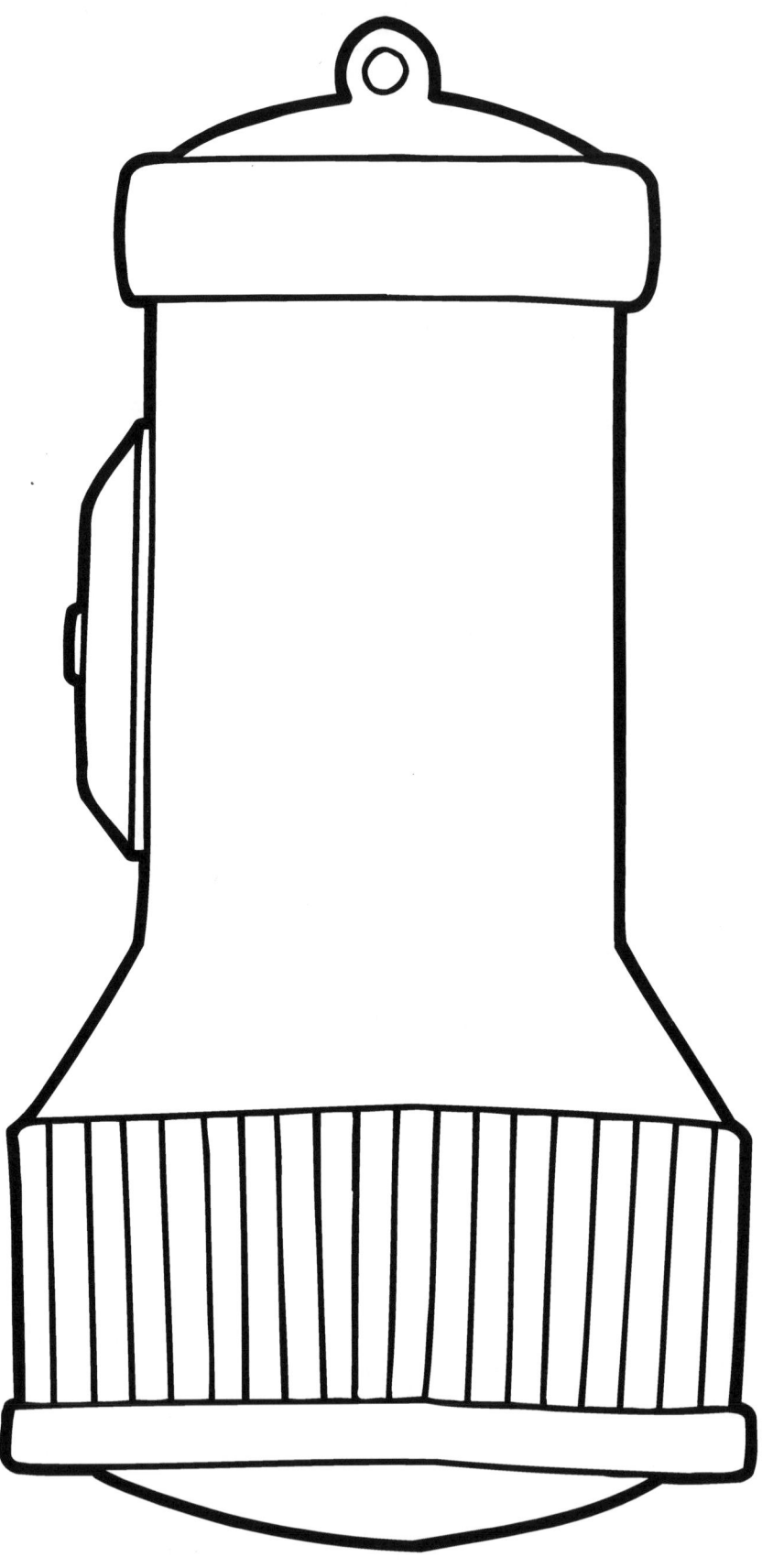

Florida, USA

flower pot

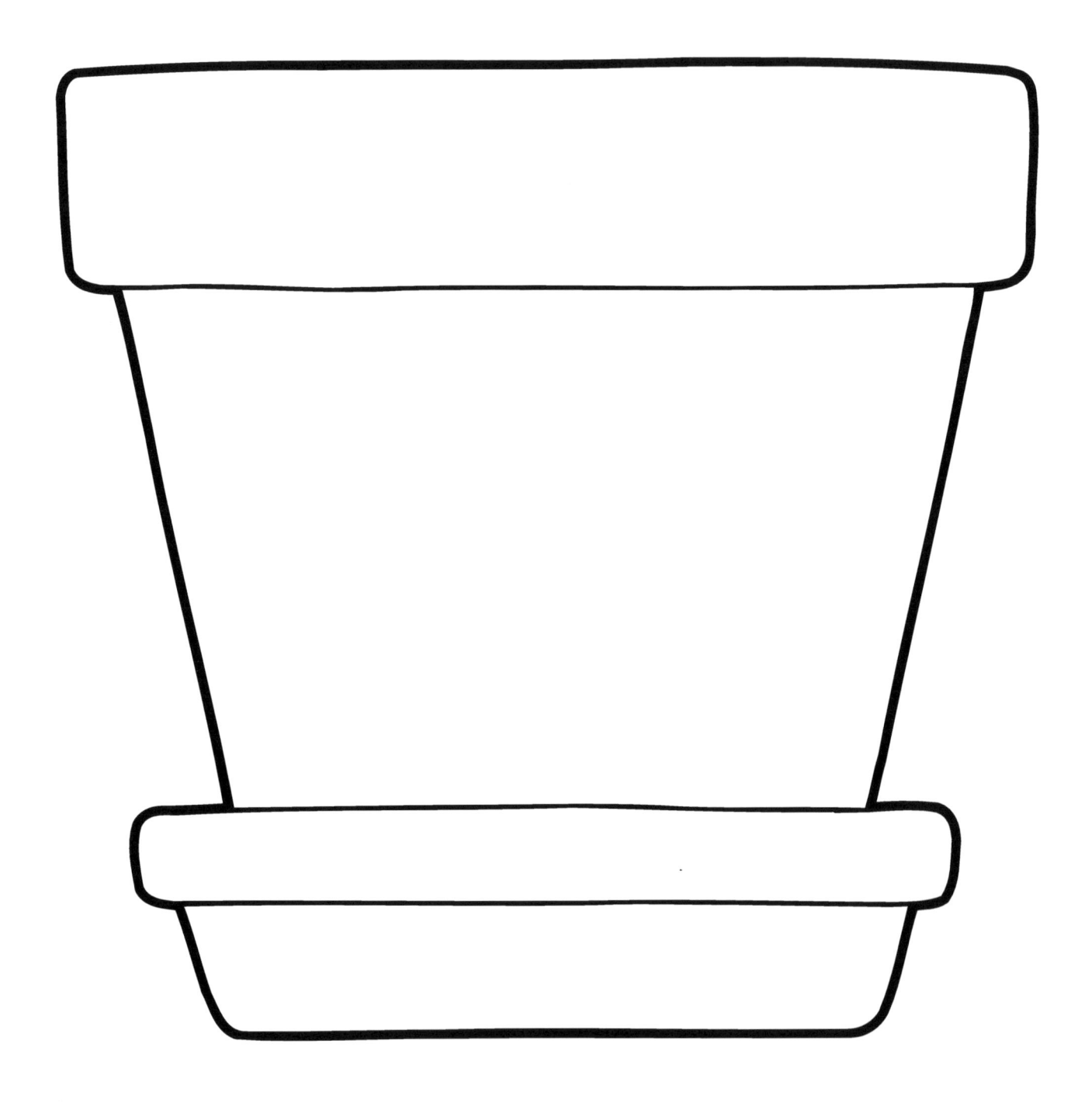

flower (multi-petal)

flower (tulip outline)

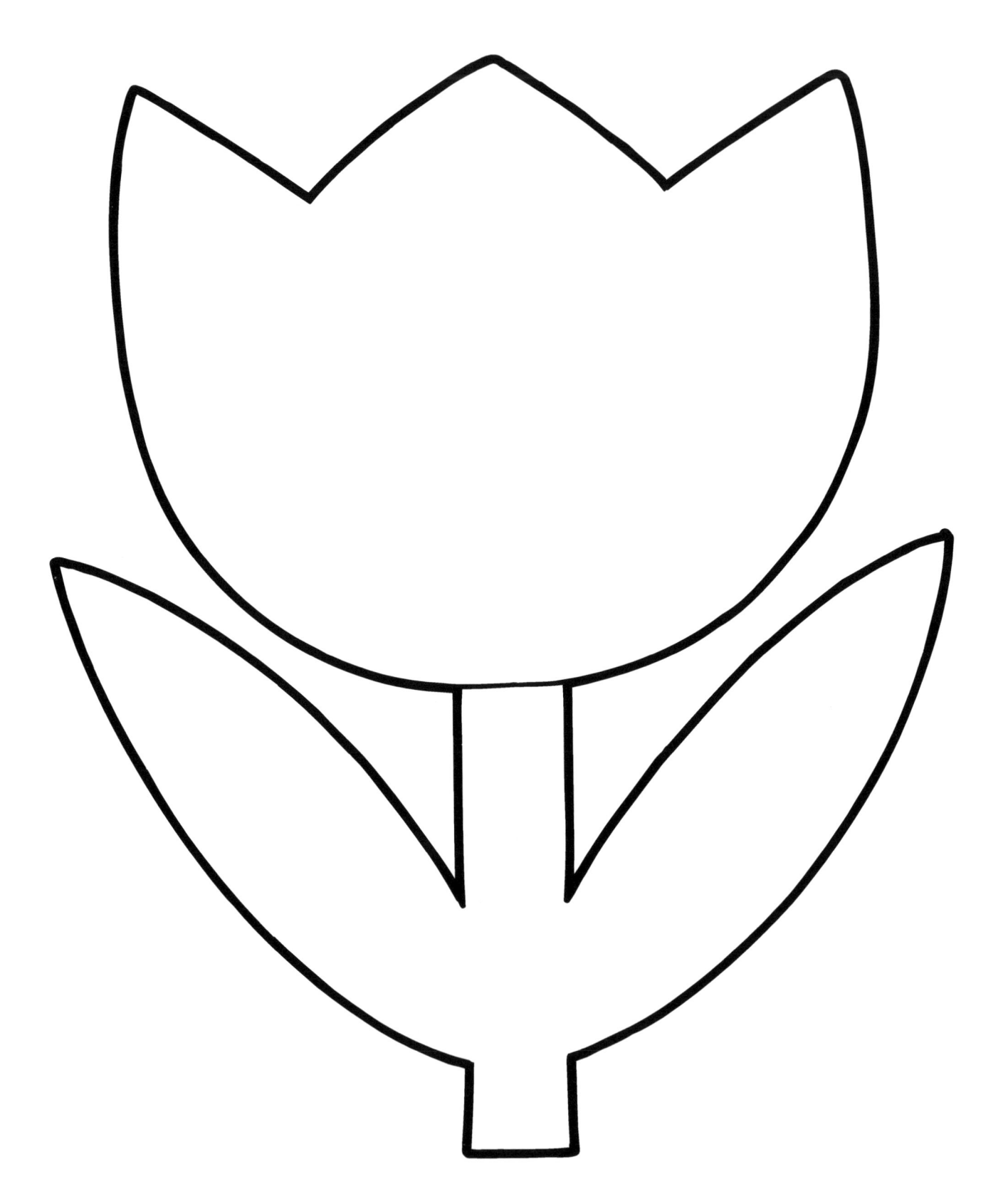

fly

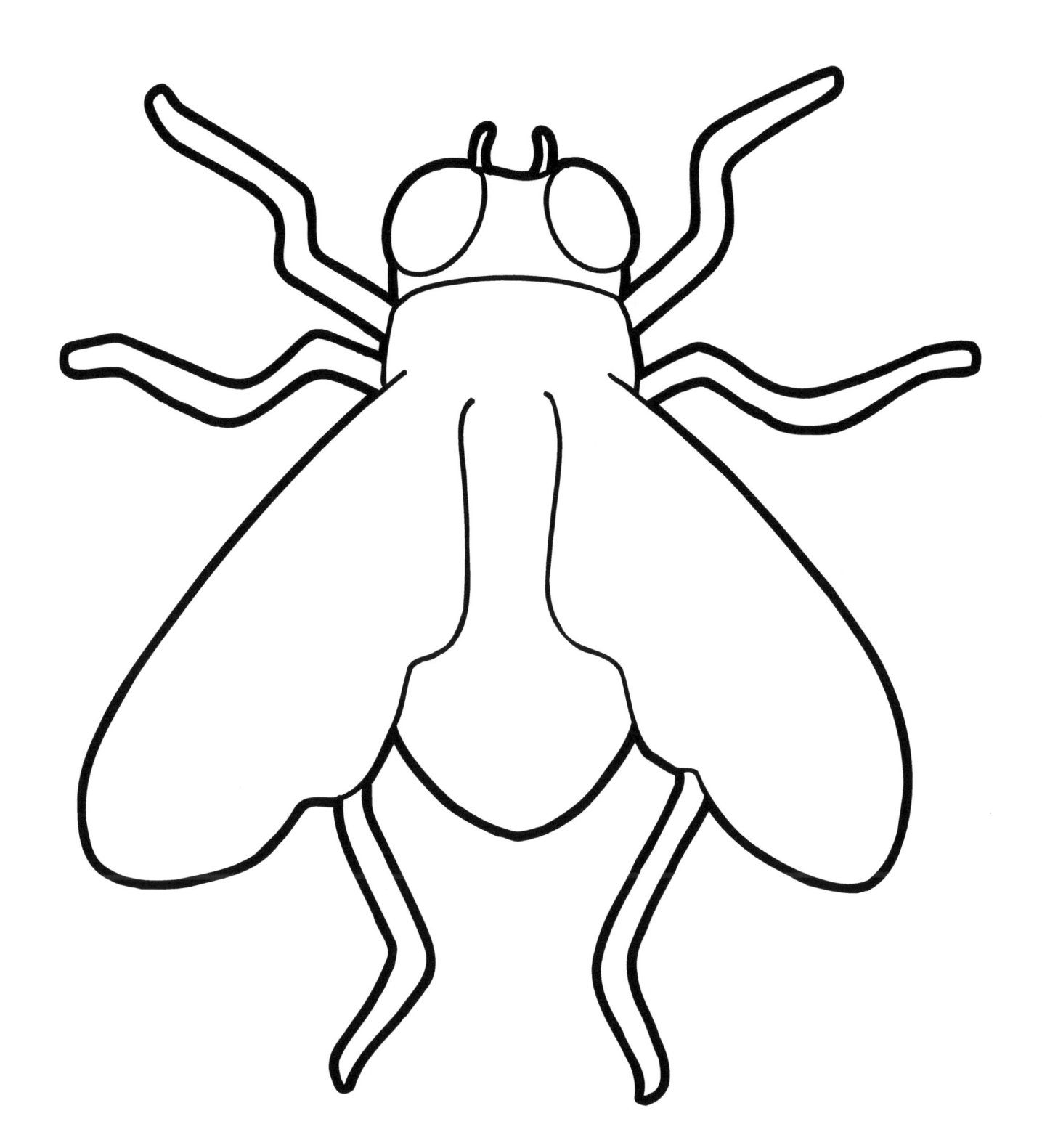

football

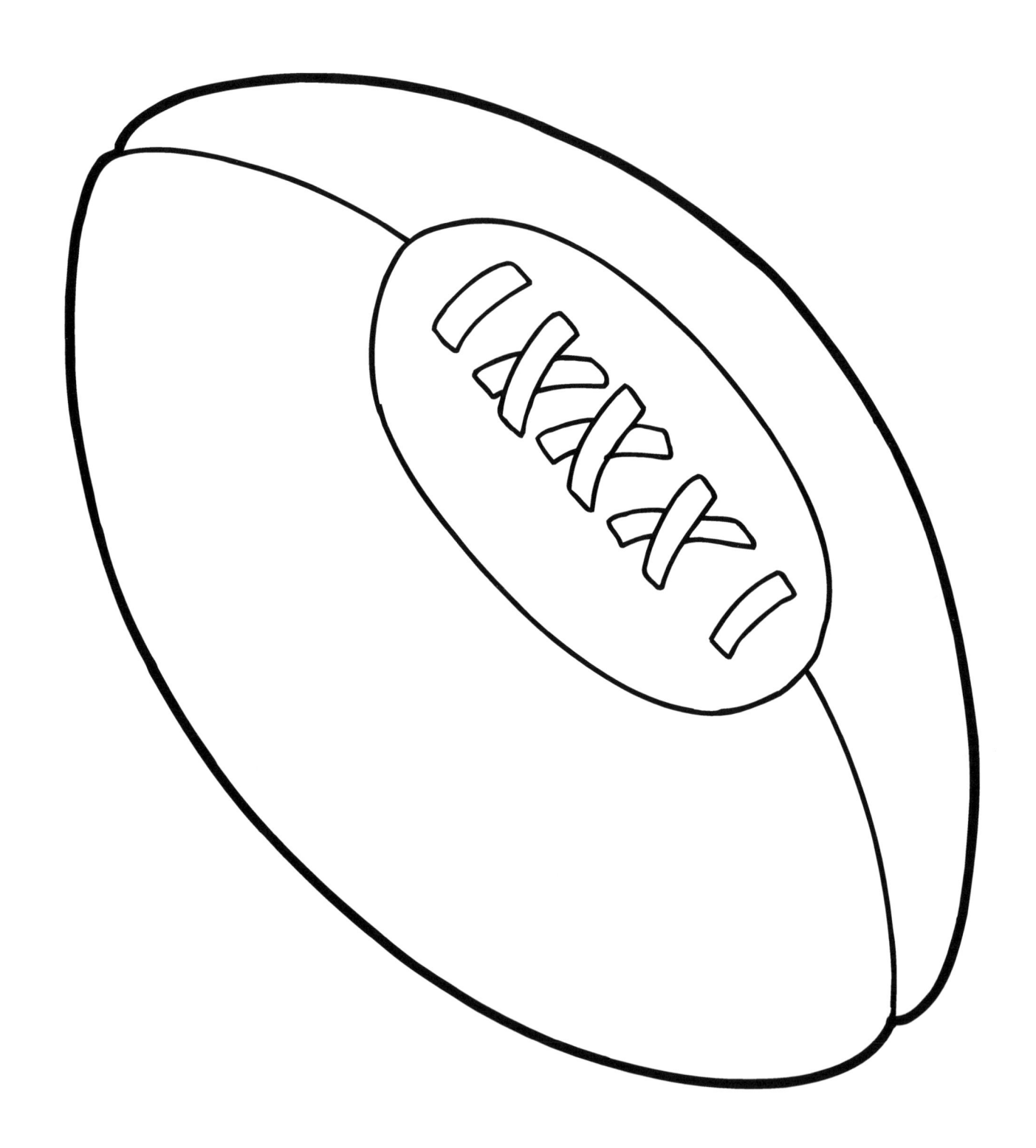

fork

fox (animated, sitting)

fox (animated, standing)

fox (stylized)

fraction pie (eighths)

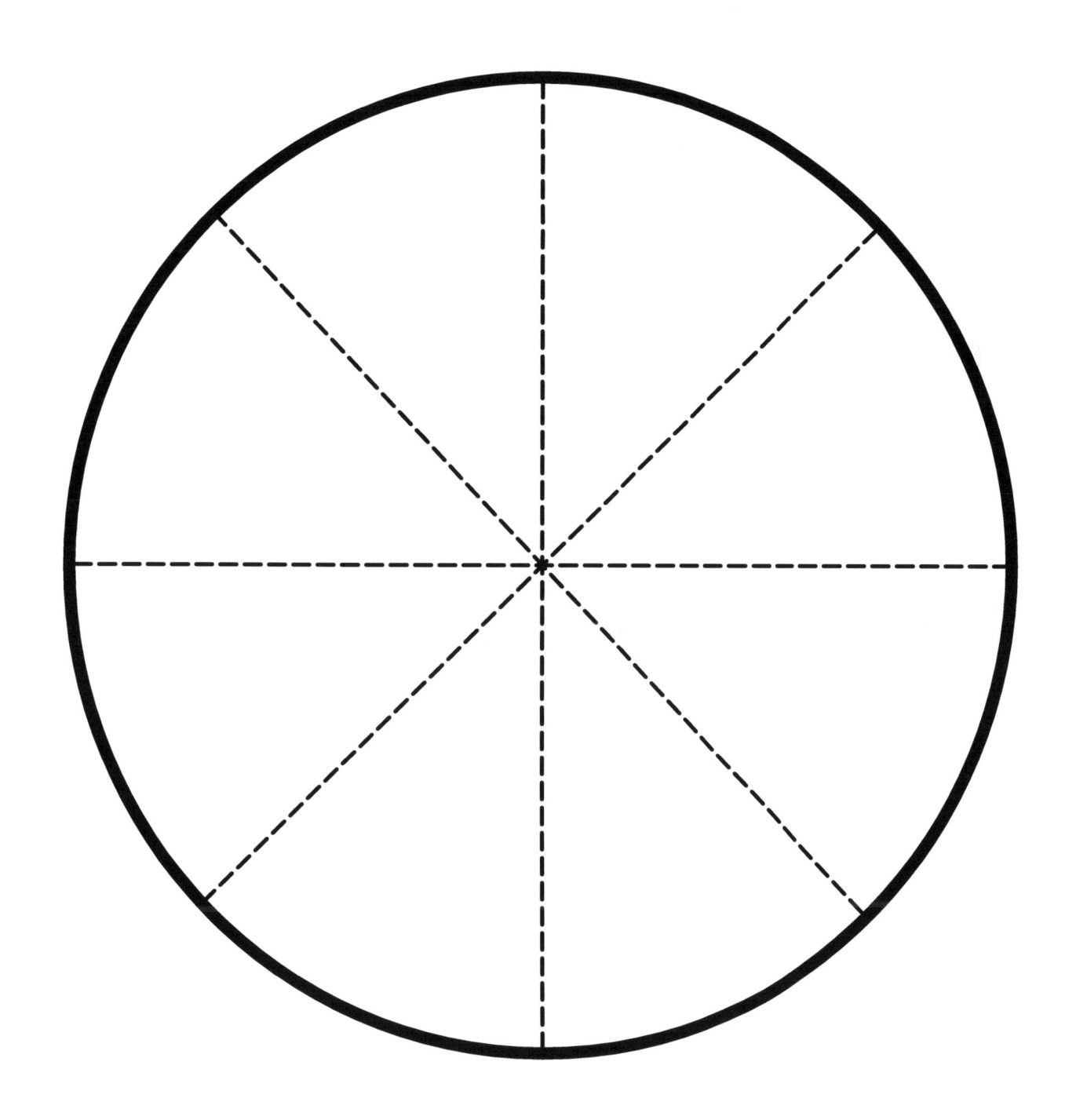

French fries

frigate

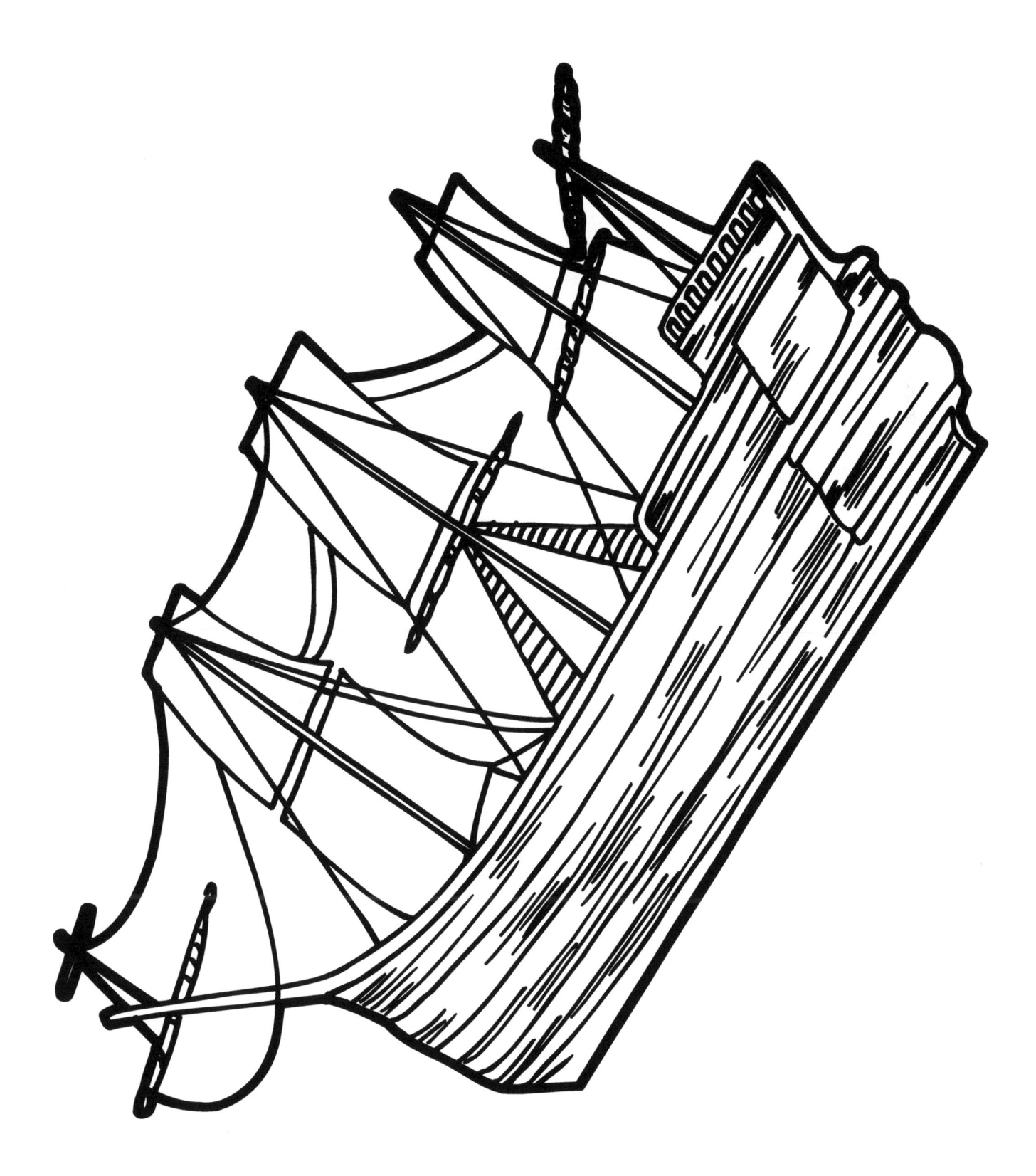

frisbee

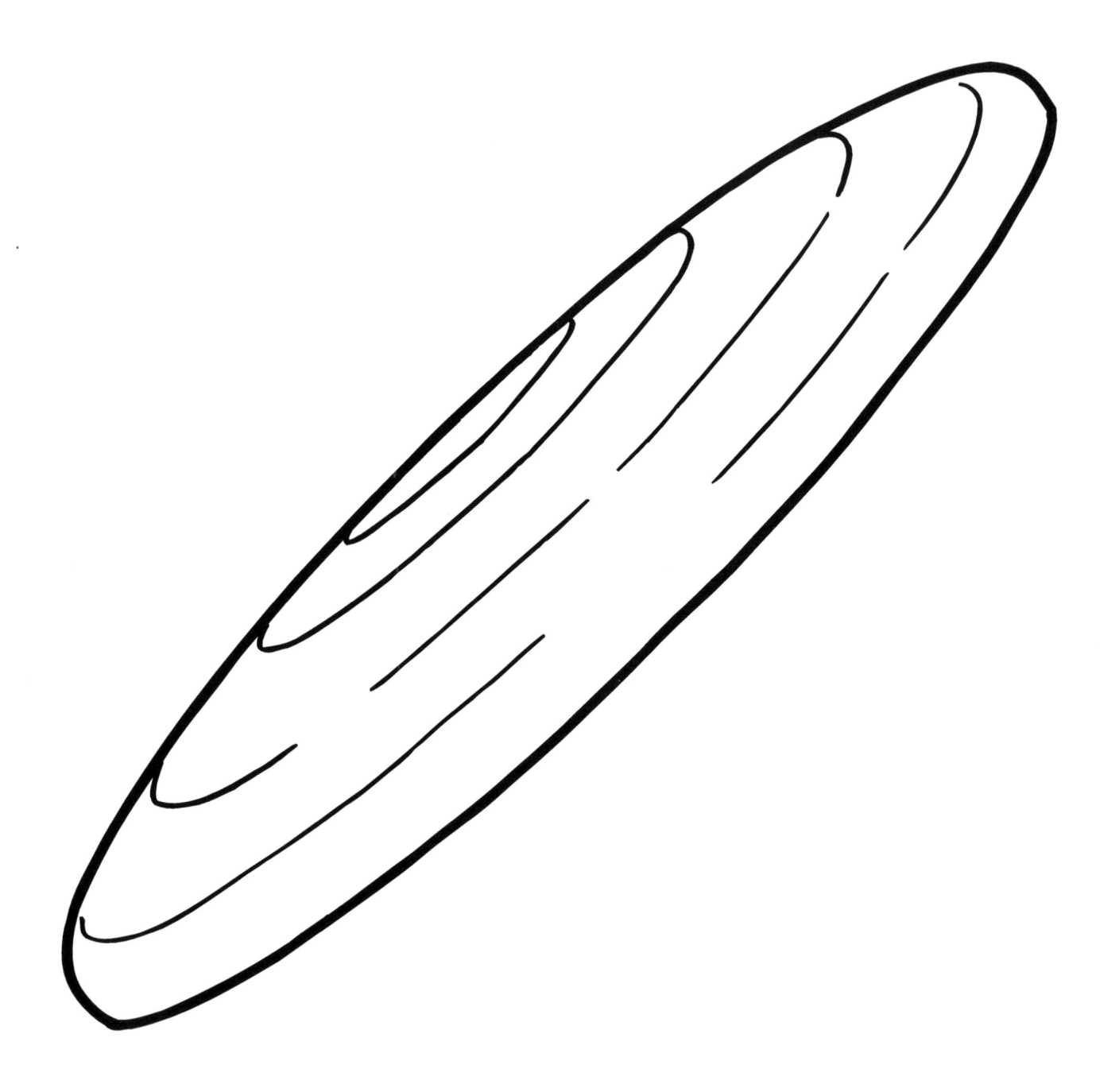

frog (animated, sitting)

frog (leaping)

frog (stylized)

funnel

gecko

Georgia, USA

North
West East
South

ghost

TPL

LAB201411P • THE PATTERN LIBRARY • VOLUME ONE • A-H • 978-1-937257-62-0 • © 2014 Little Acorn Books™   397

ghost (outline)

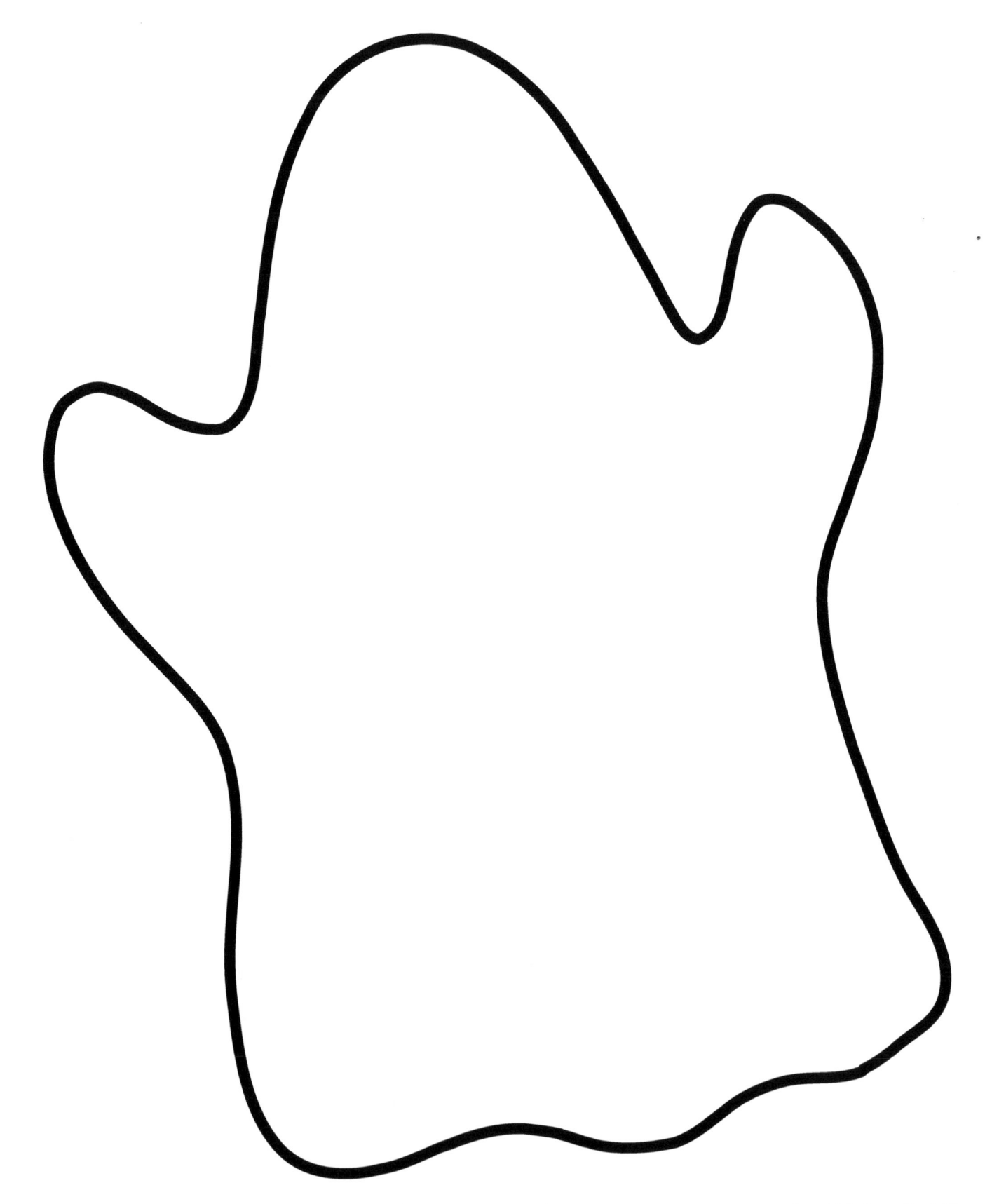

giant panda

gingerbread boy

ововgingerbread girl

giraffe

girl

girl

girl

girl

glass (drinking)

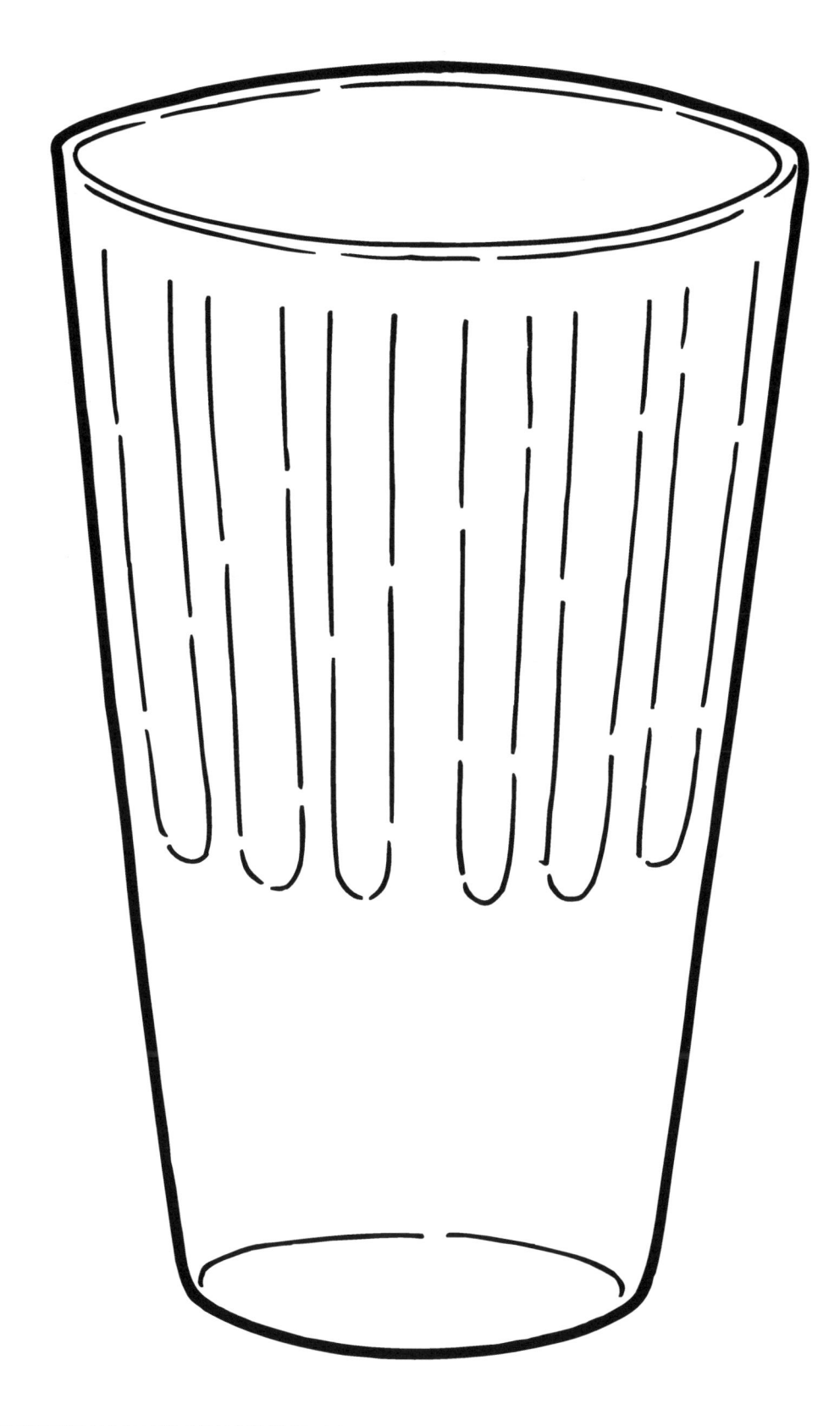

glasses

glove (left)

glove (right)

glue (bottle)

goat (frontal view)

goat (nanny)

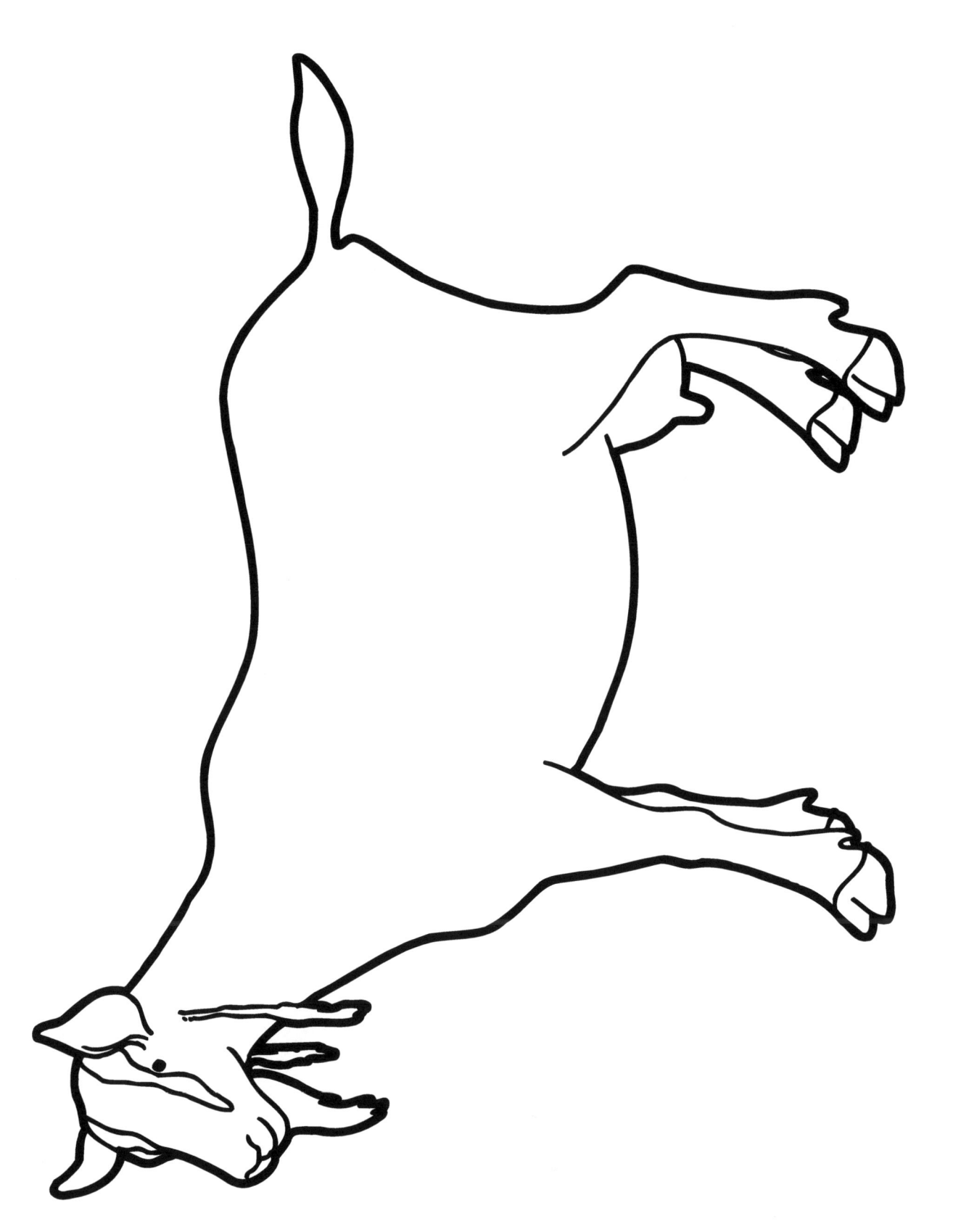

goat (mountain)

gold (crayon)

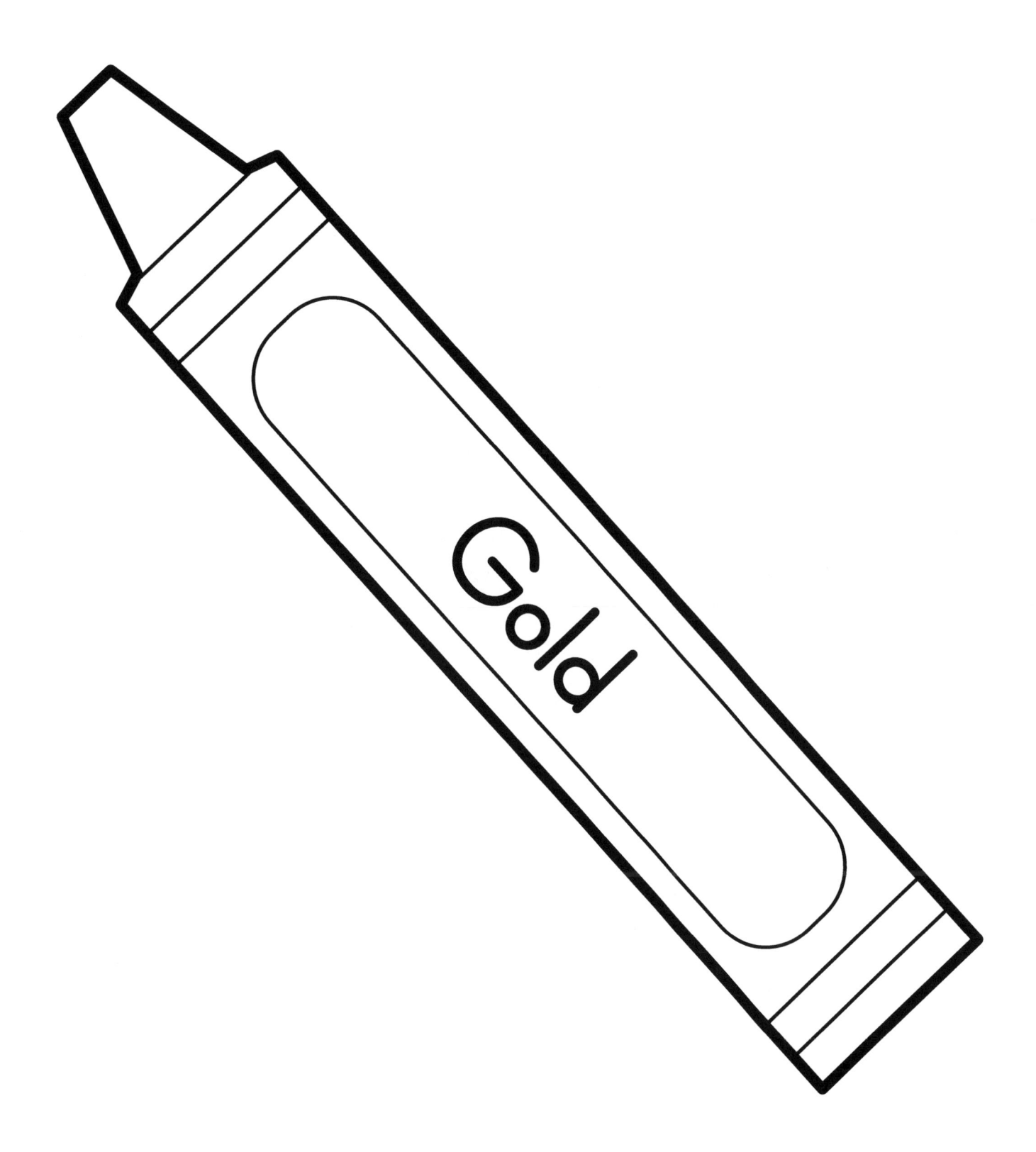

Gold

golf club and ball

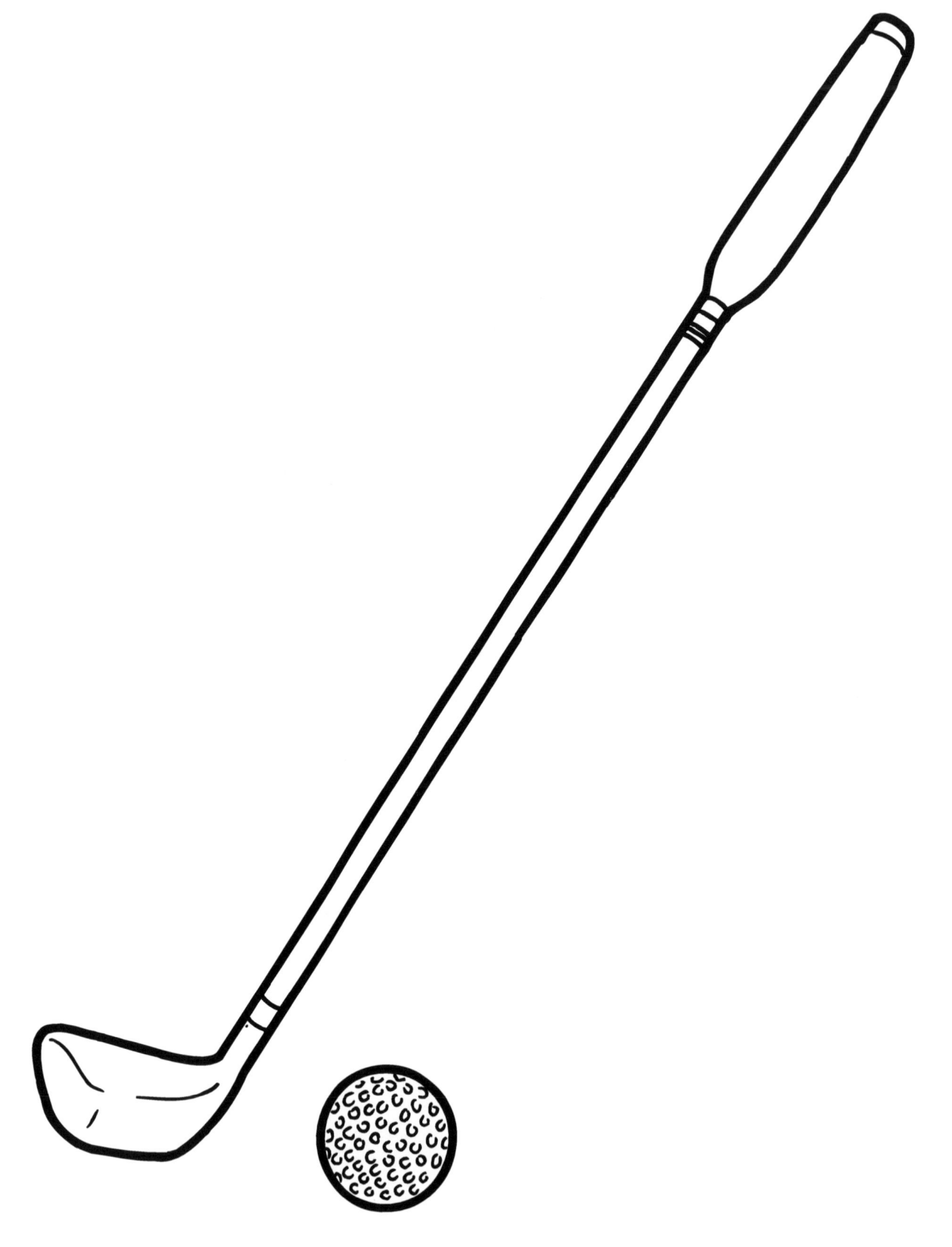

goose

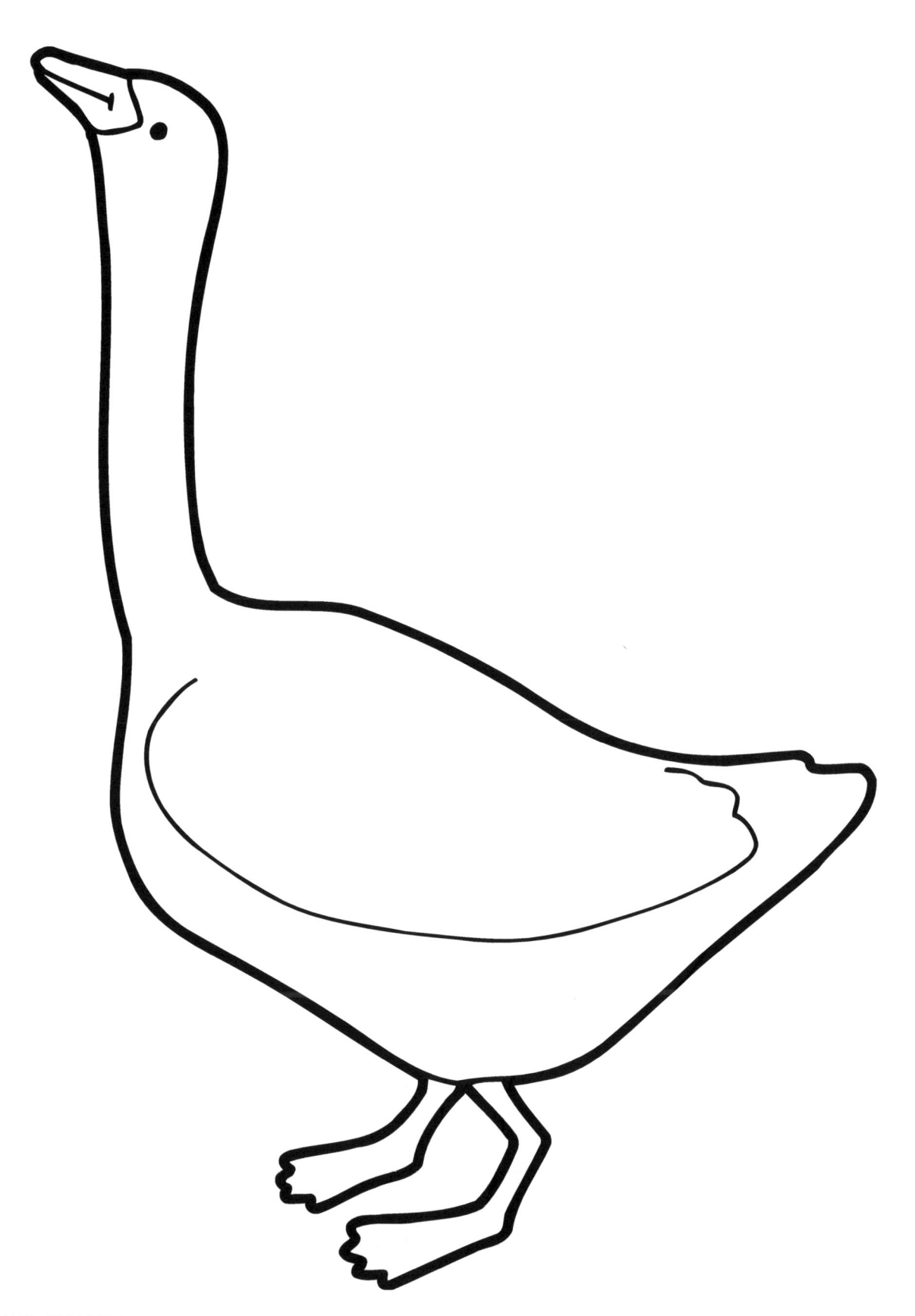

gorilla (frontal view)

gorilla (side view)

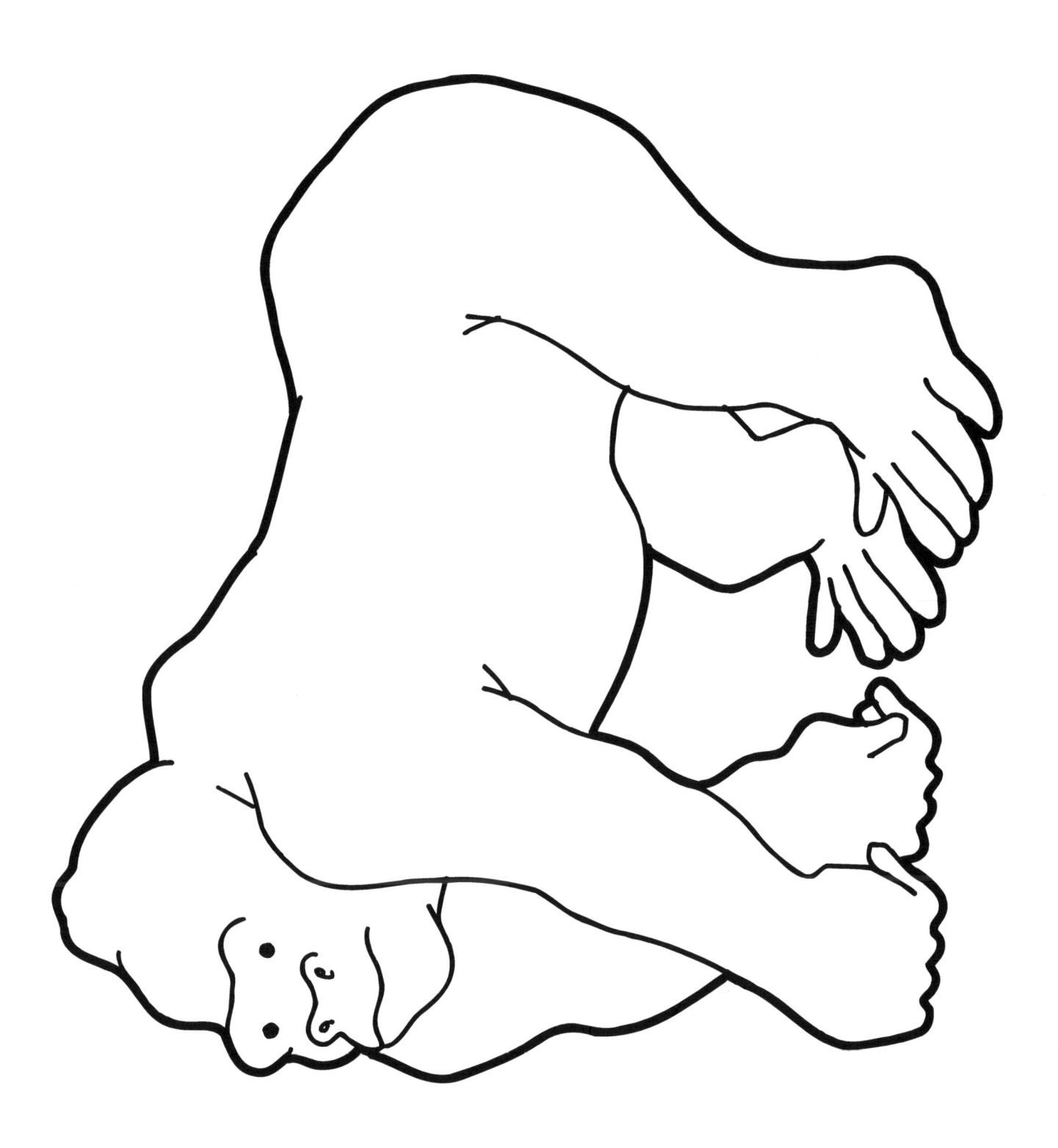

grapes

grasshopper

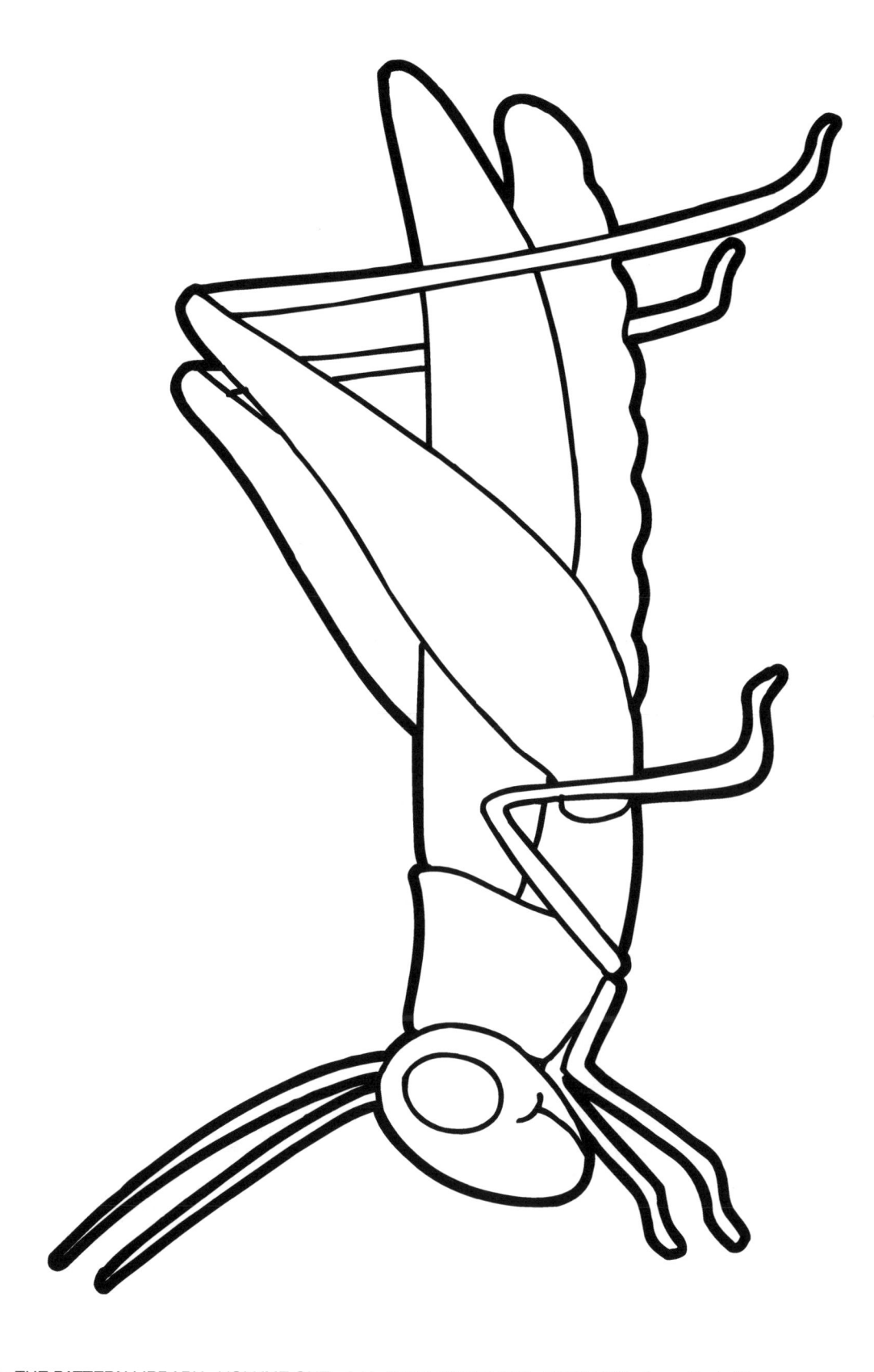

gray (crayon)

green (crayon)

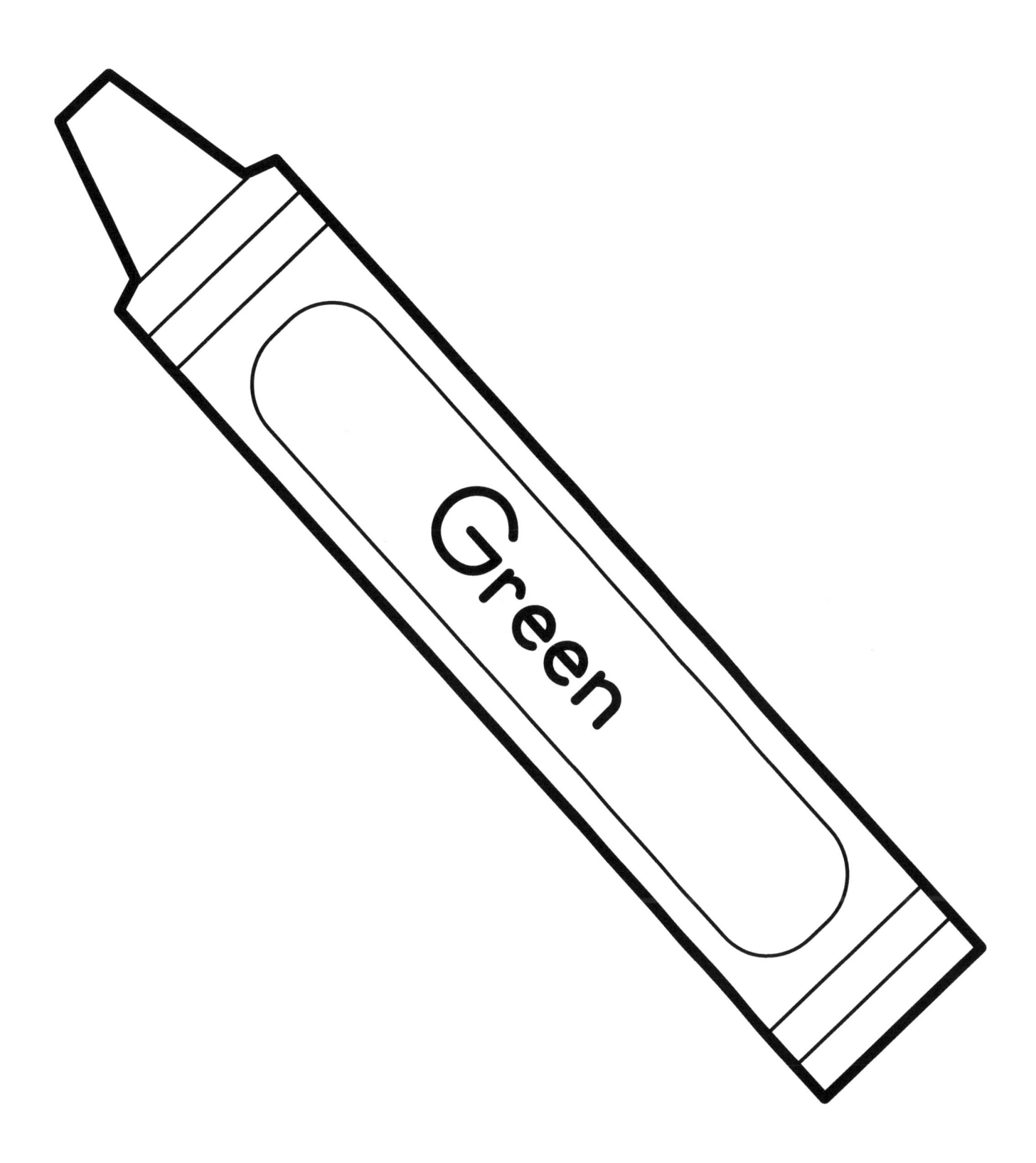

Guinea pig

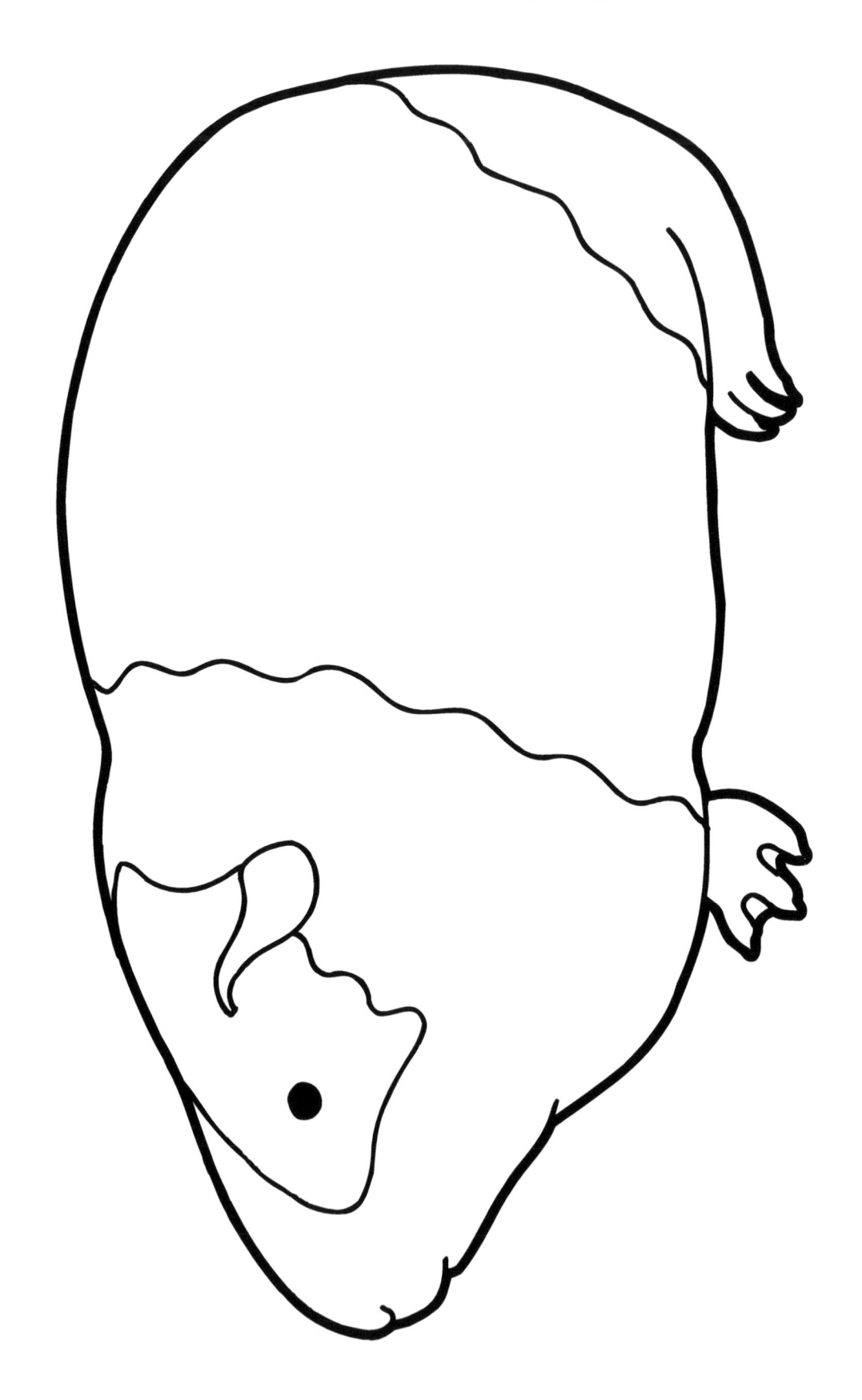

guitar

half-dollars

ham

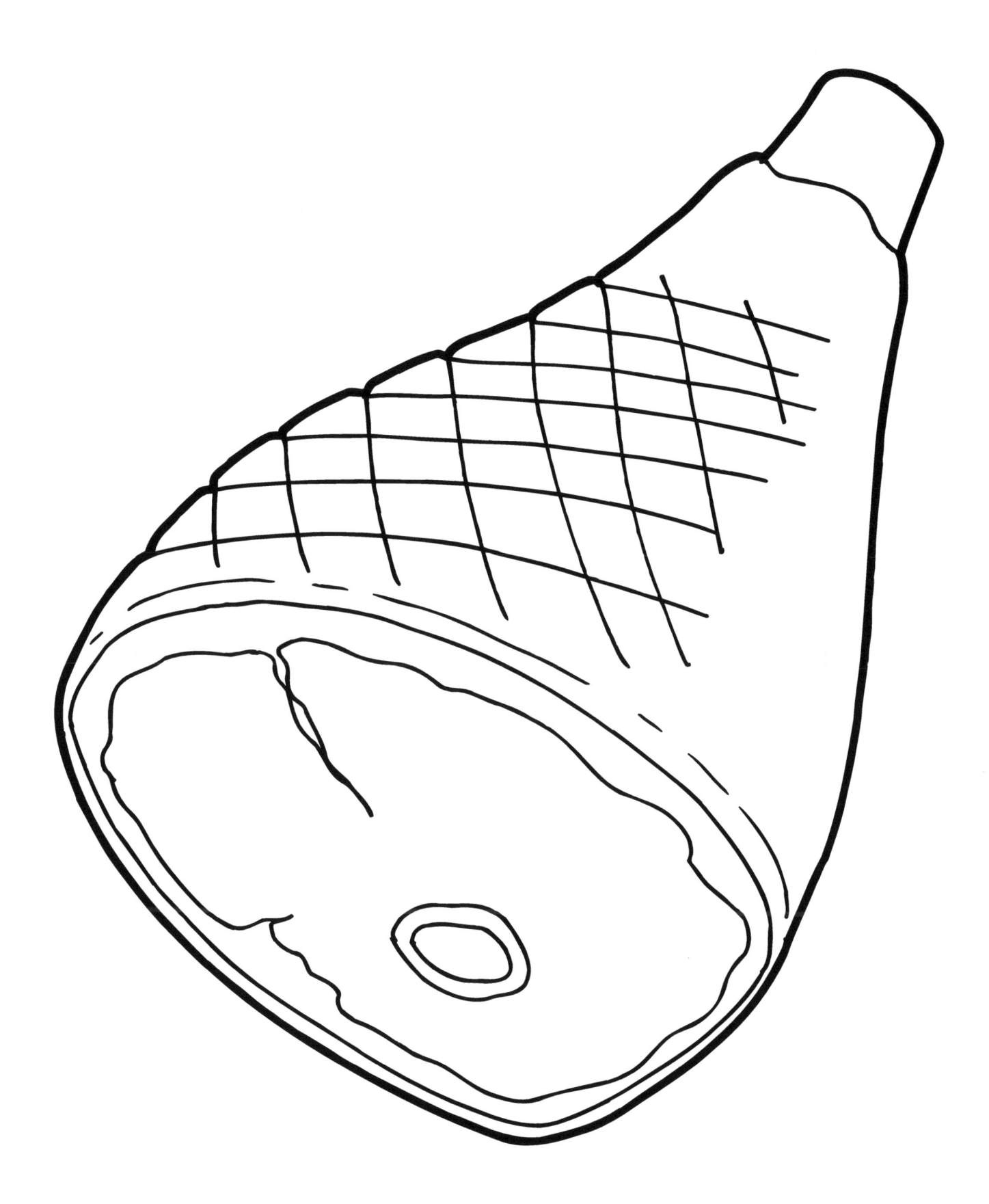

hamburger

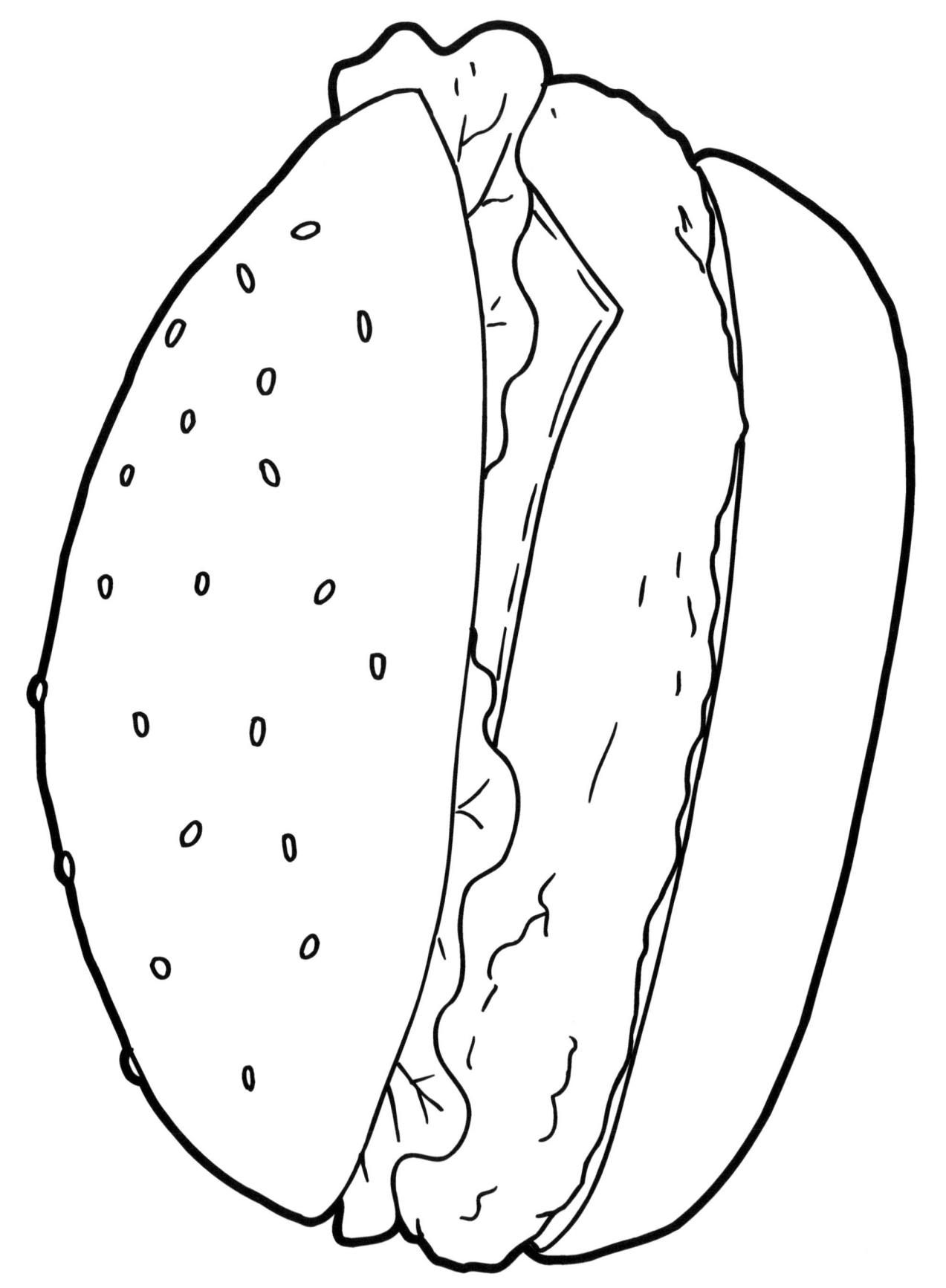

hammer

hamster

hands (outline)

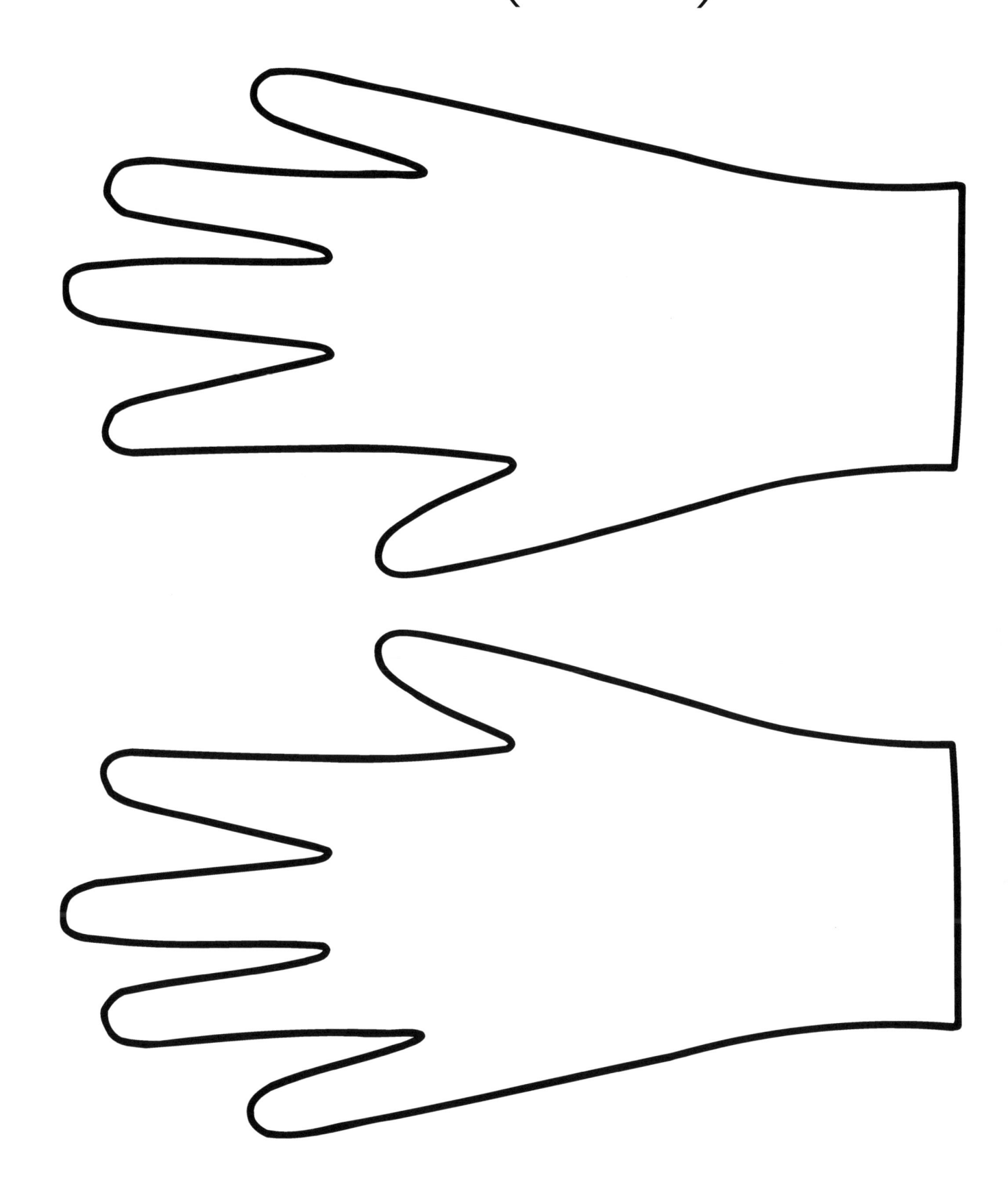

hanger

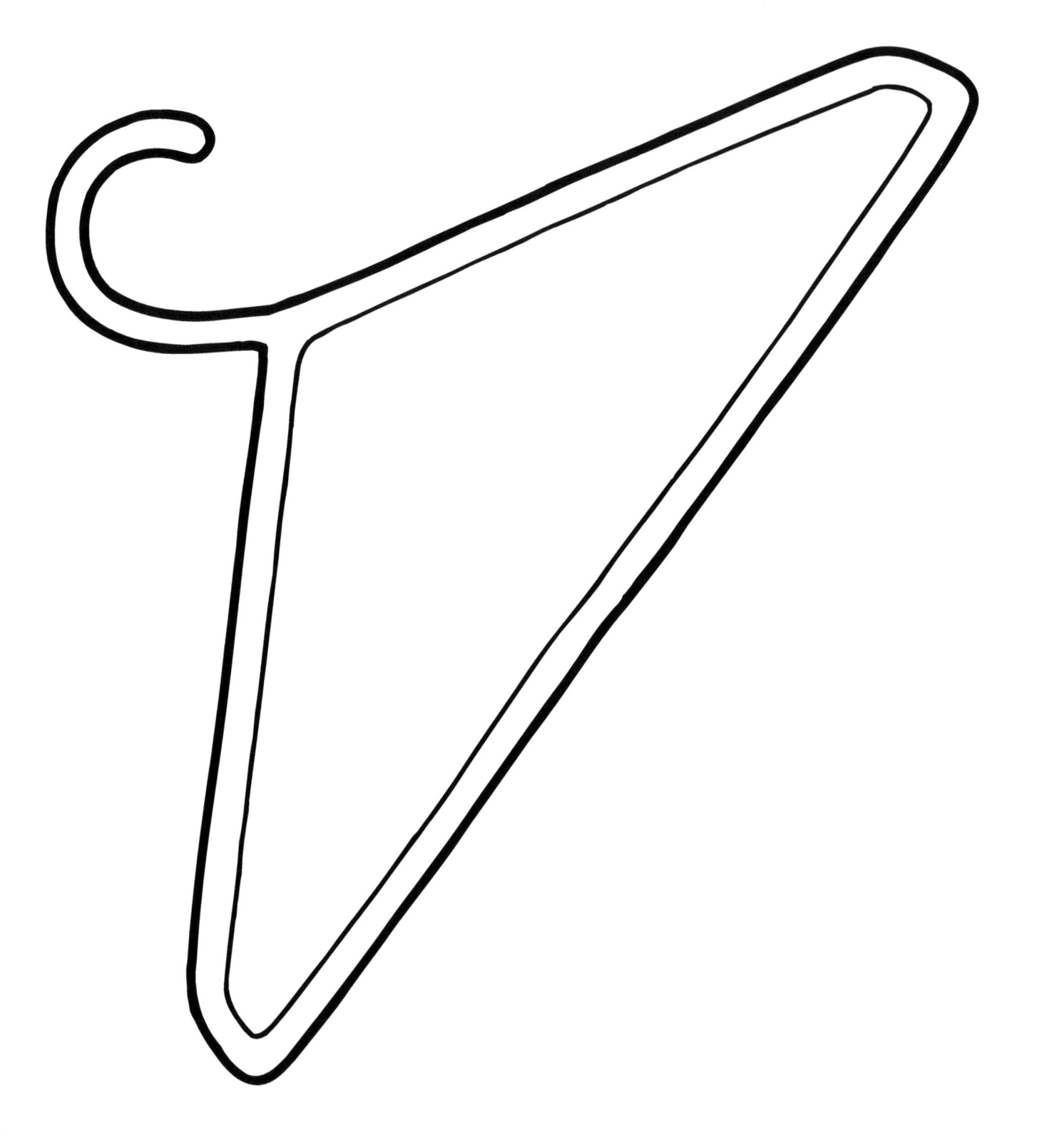

hat (cone)

hat (cowboy)

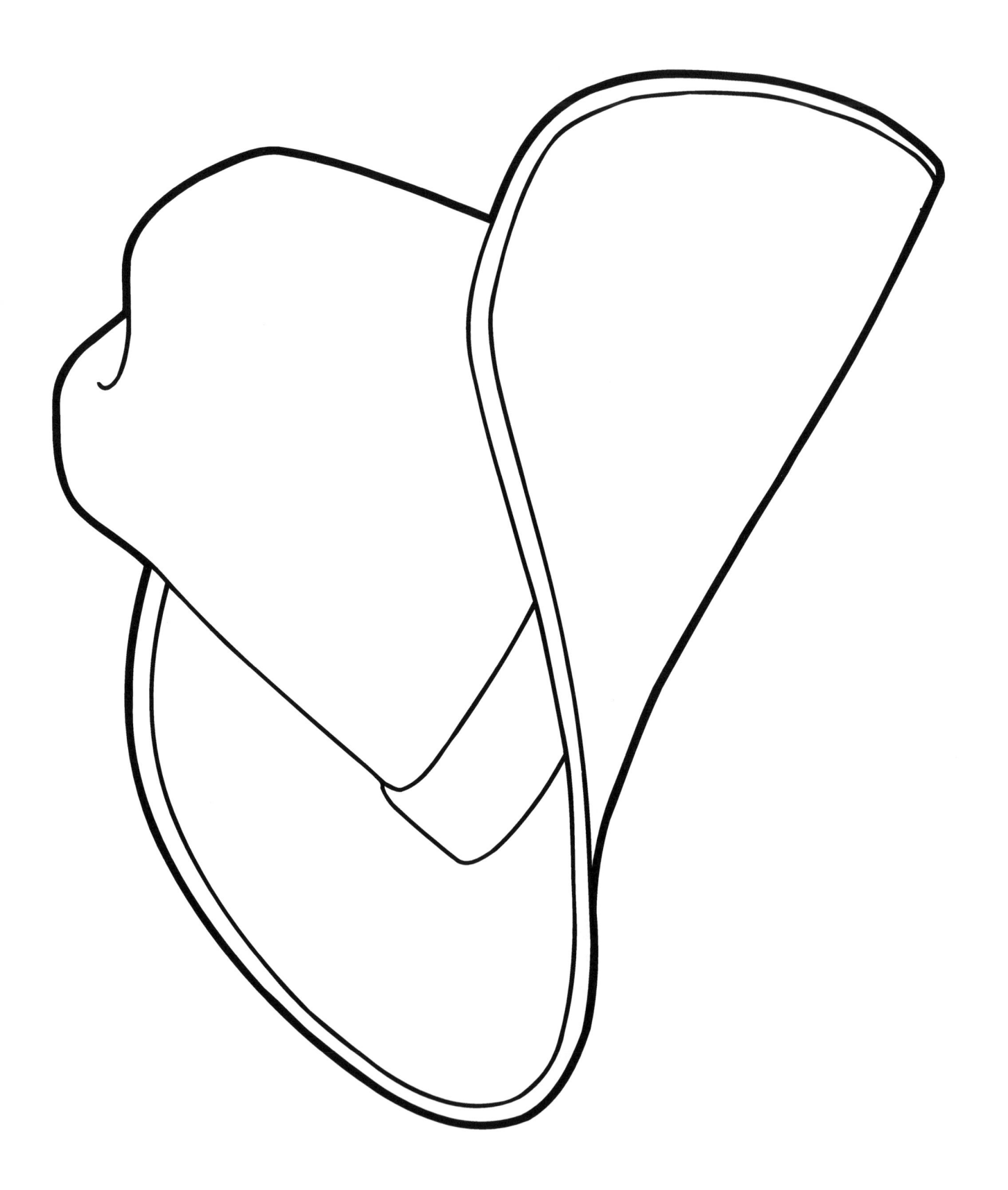

hat (derby)

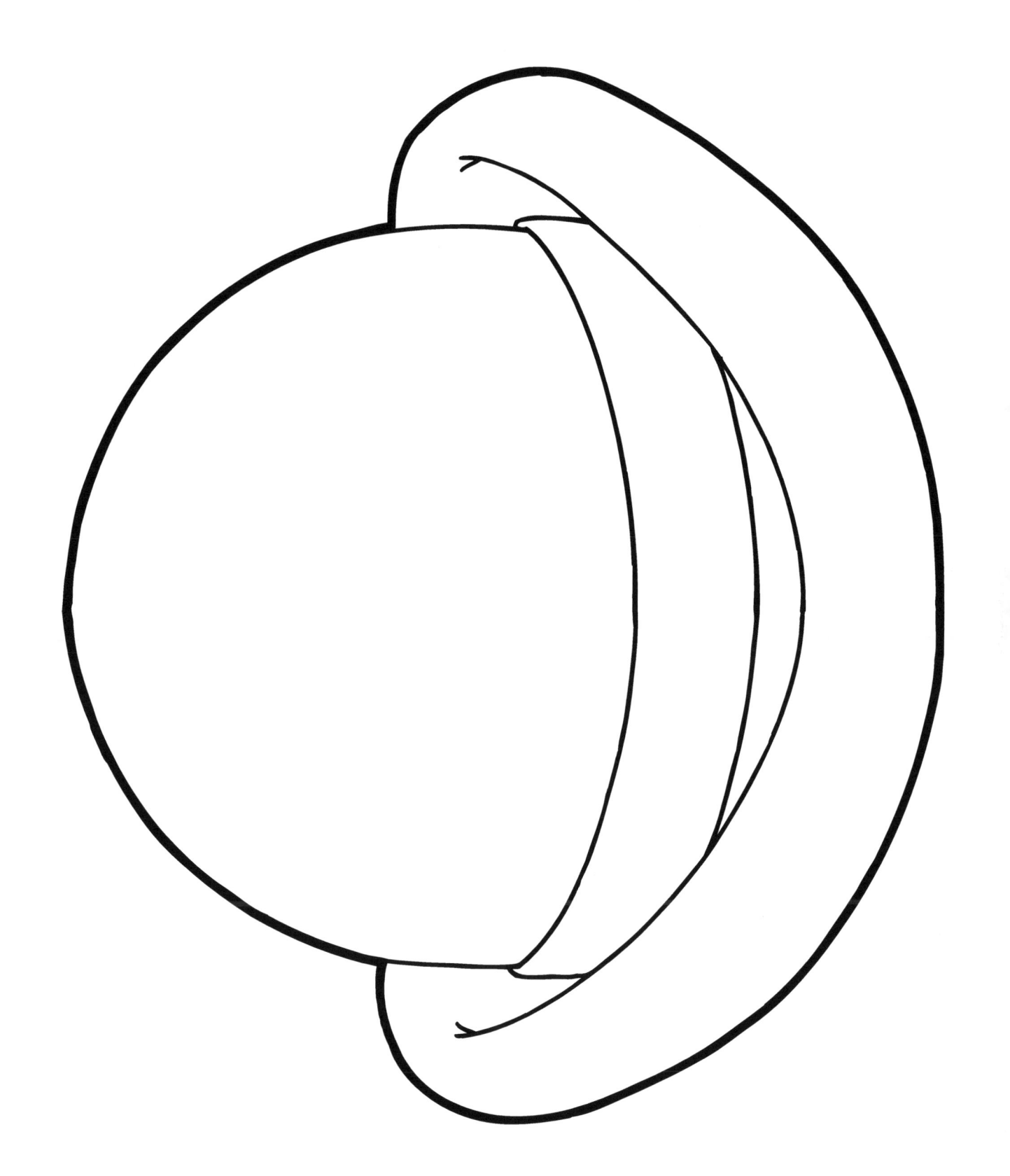

hat (fedora)

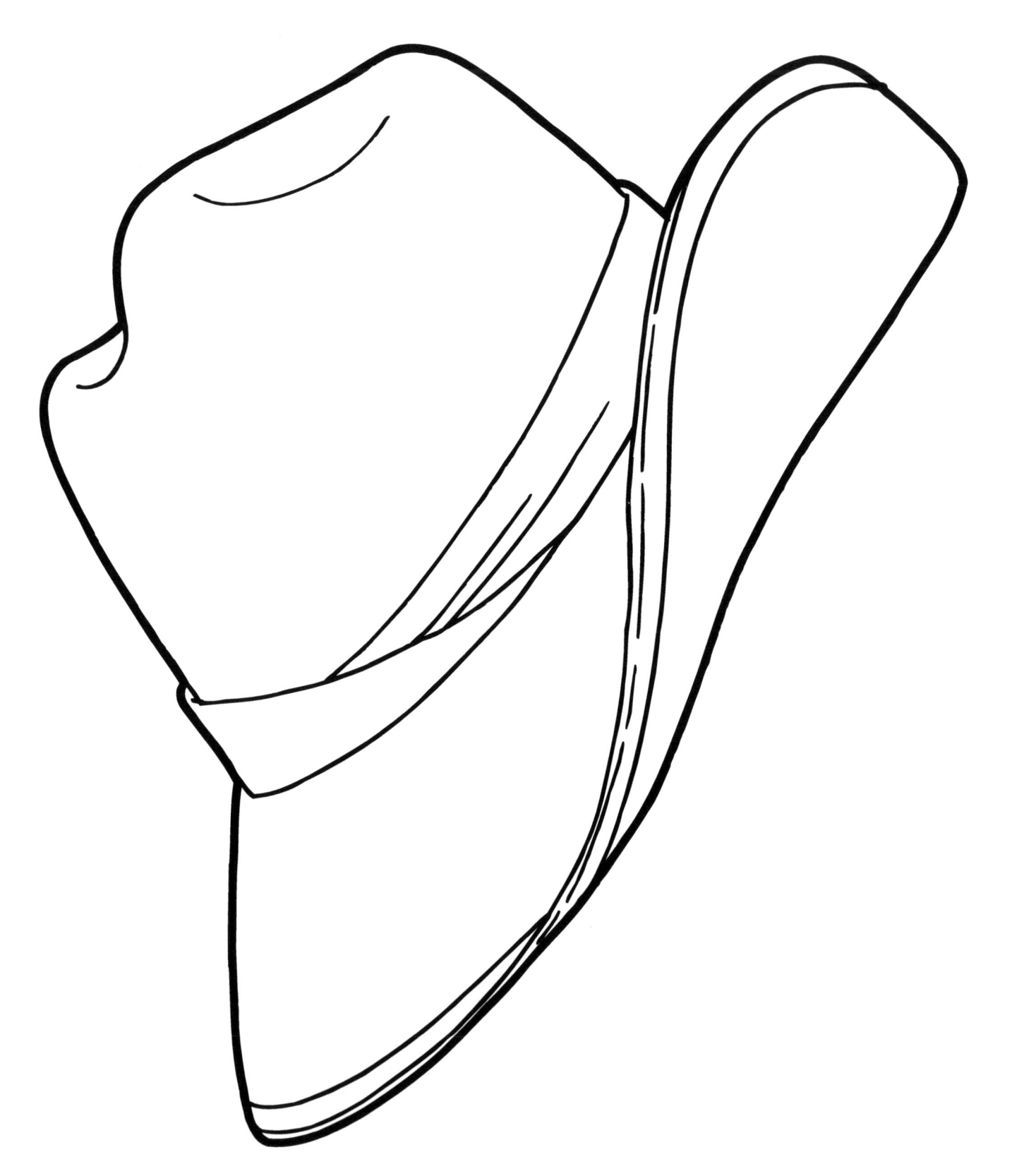

hat (firefighter's)

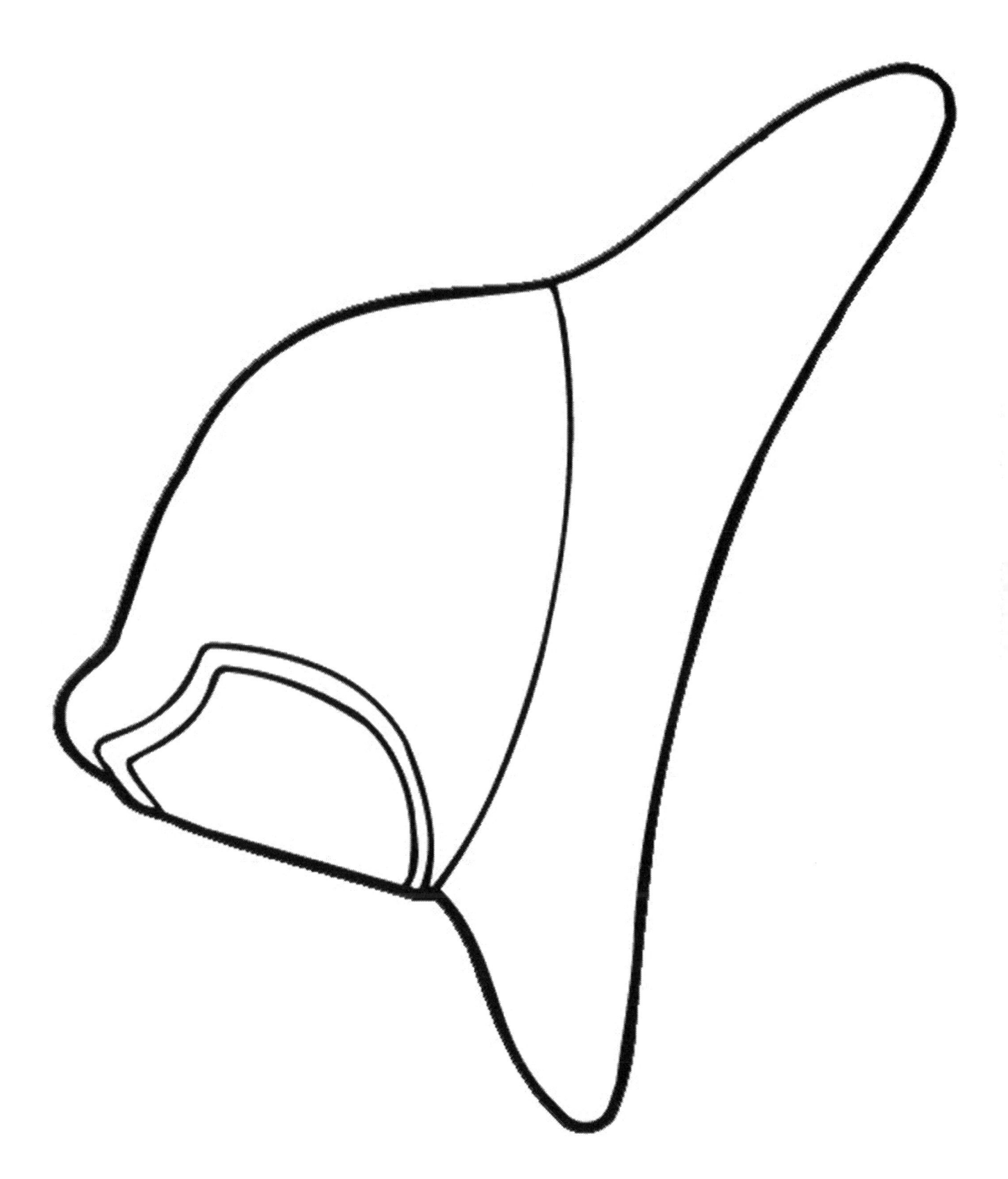

hat (lady's)

hat (mountie's)

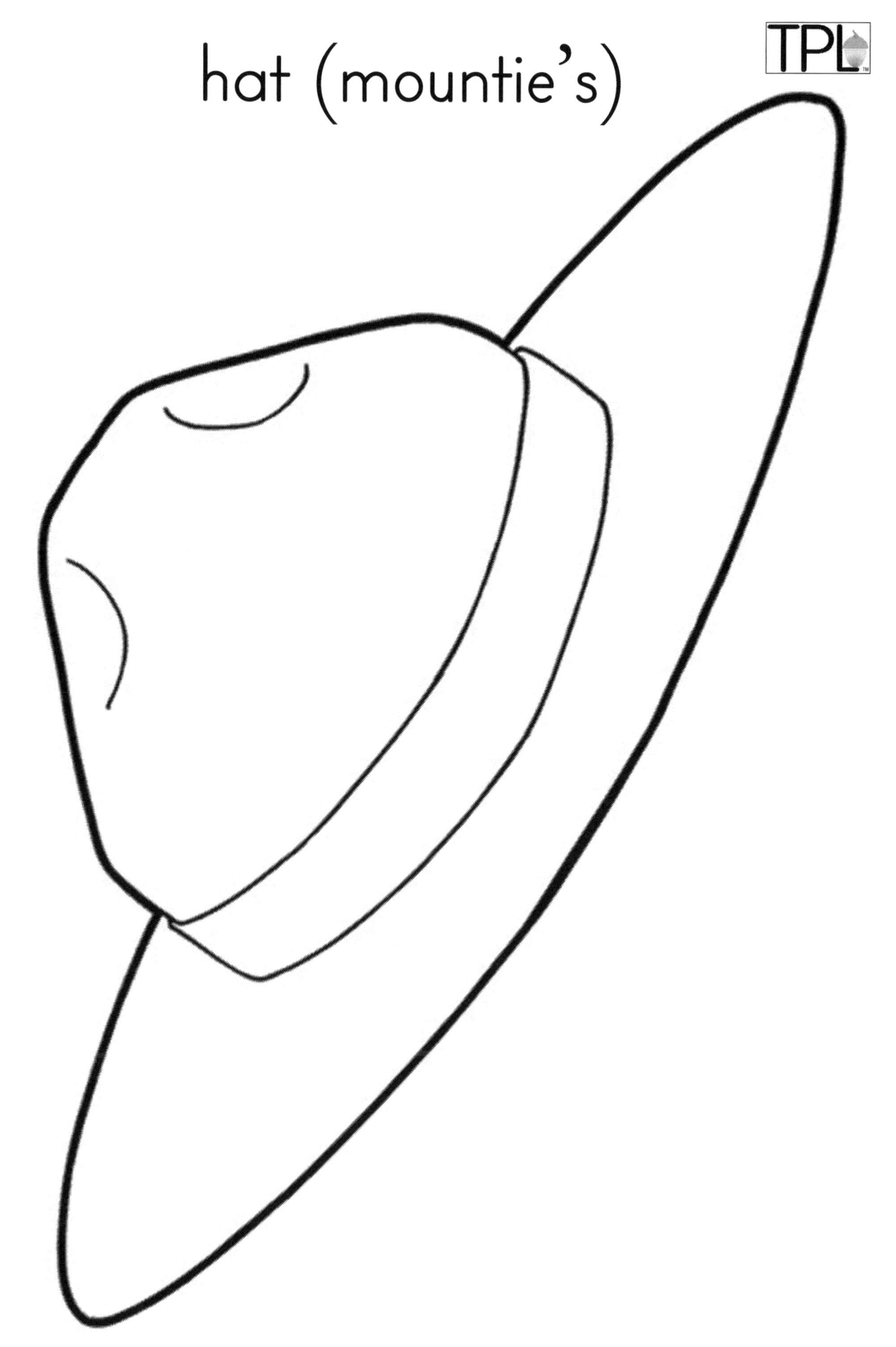

hat (pillbox)

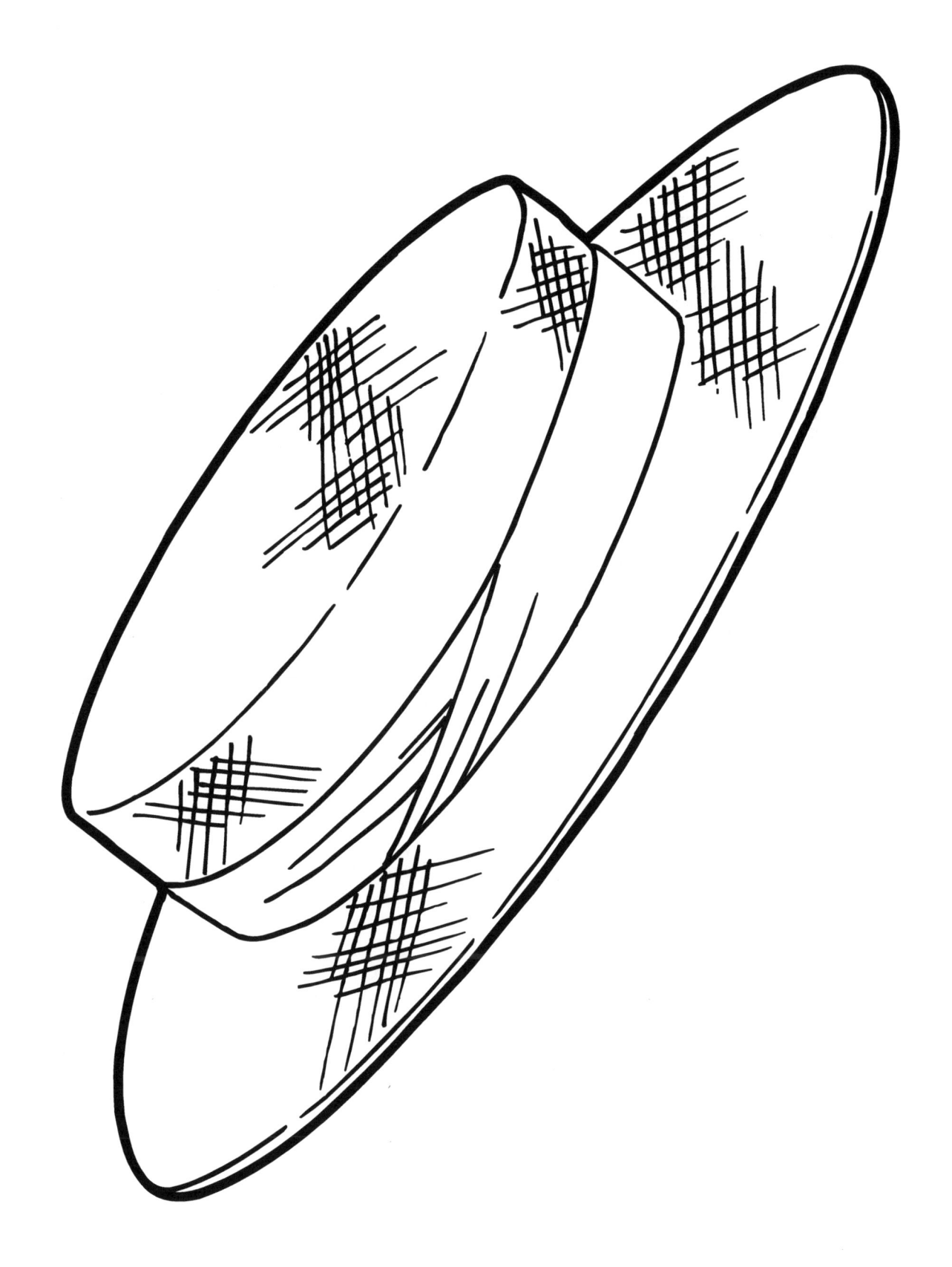

hat (straw)

hat (top hat)

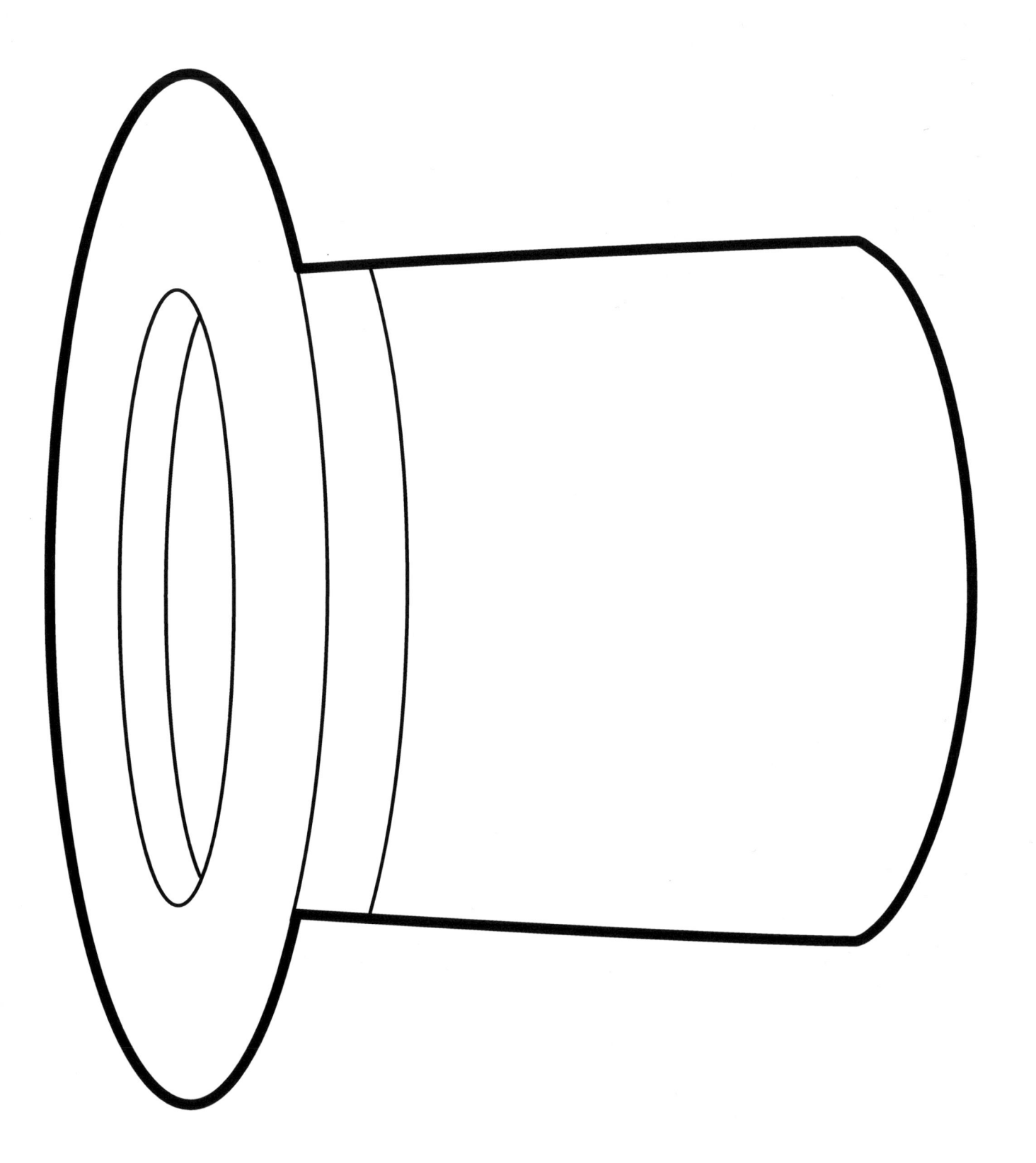

hat (top hat)

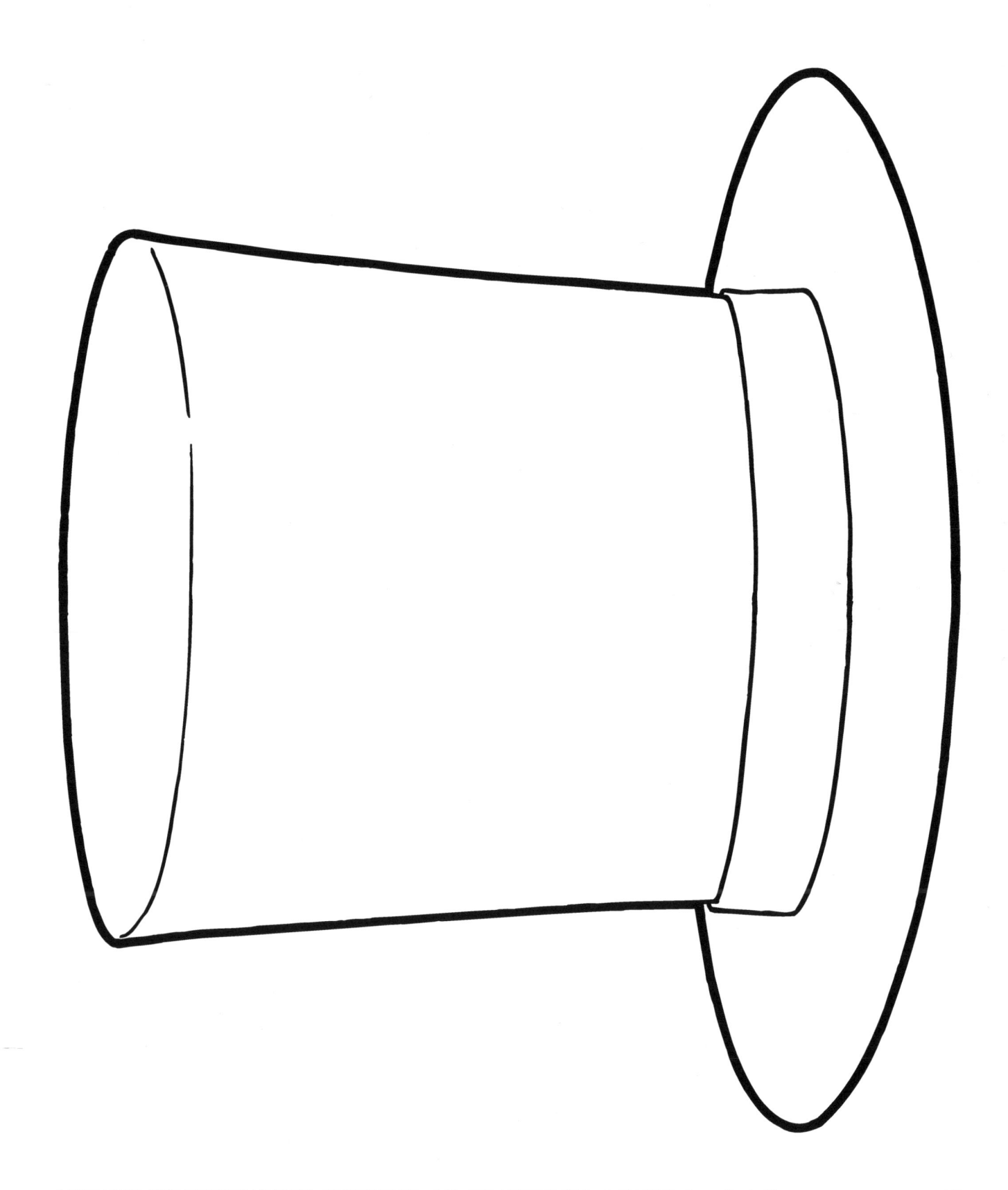

Hawaii, USA

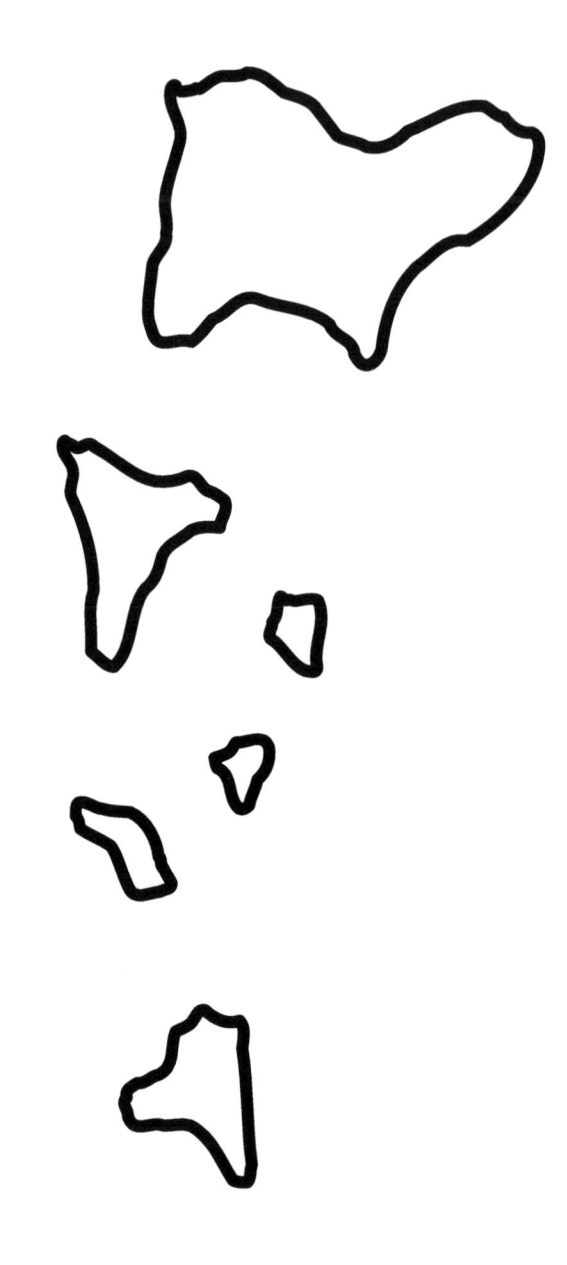

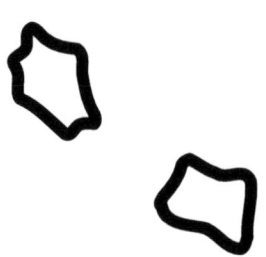

heart (shape)

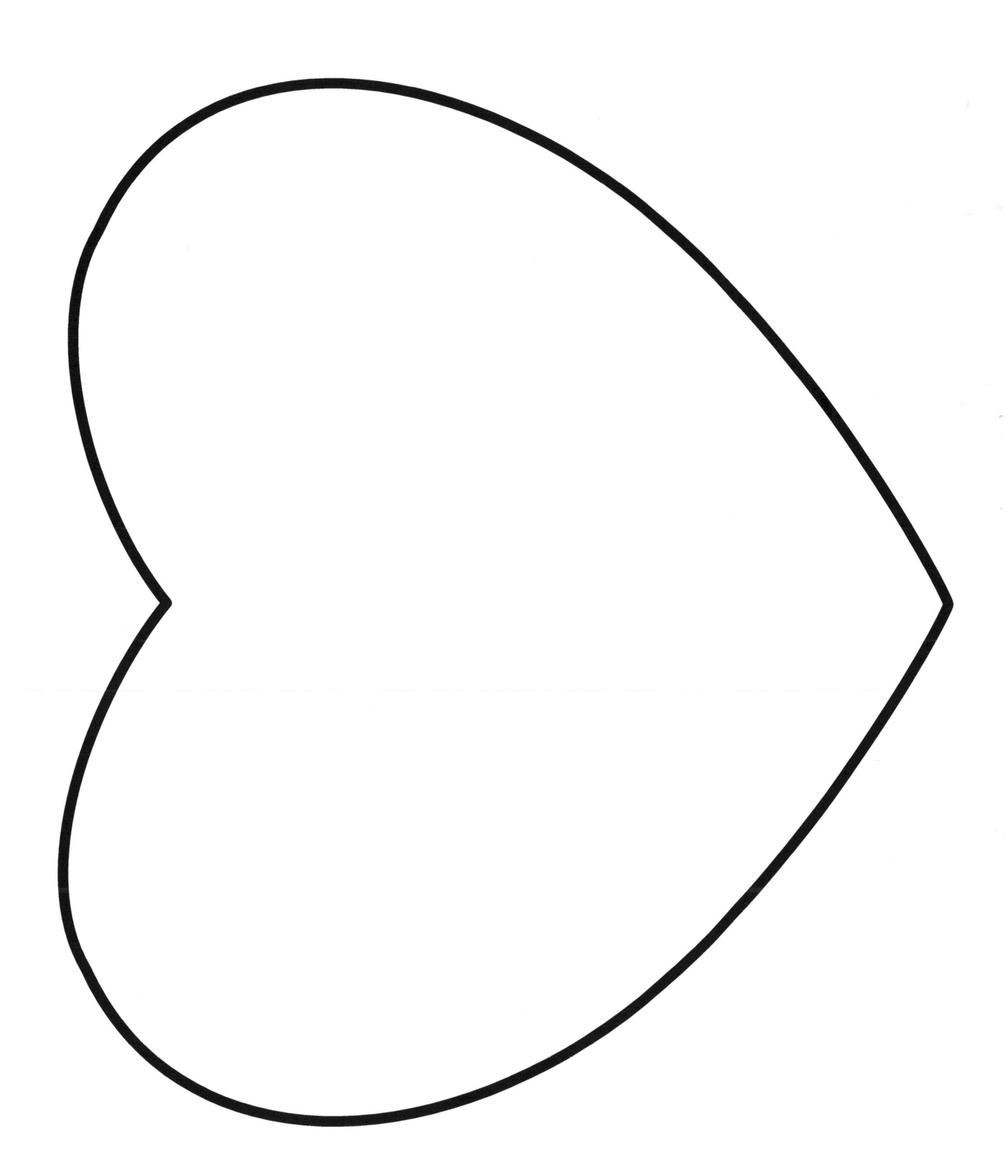

helicopter

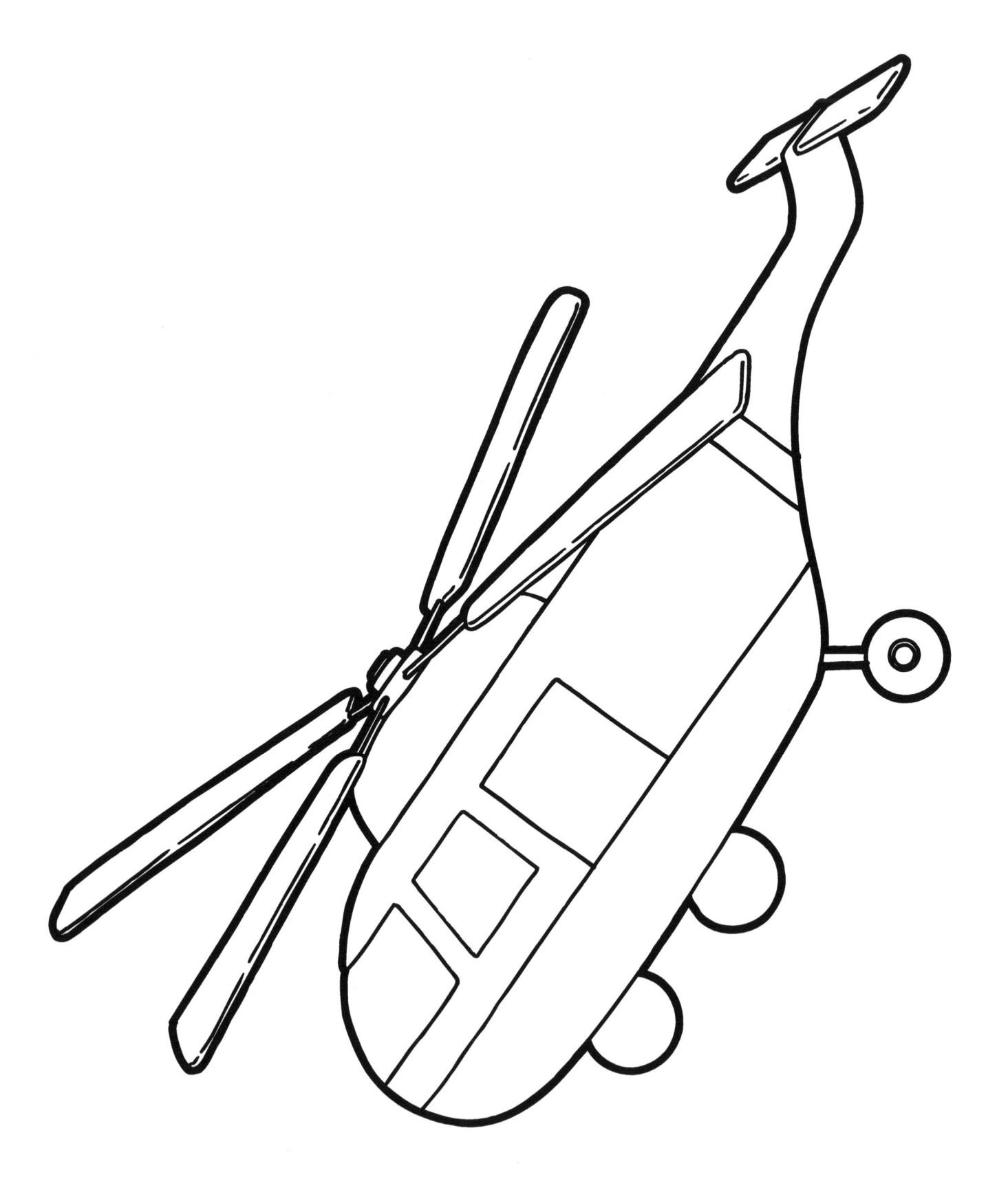

helmet (football-3D)

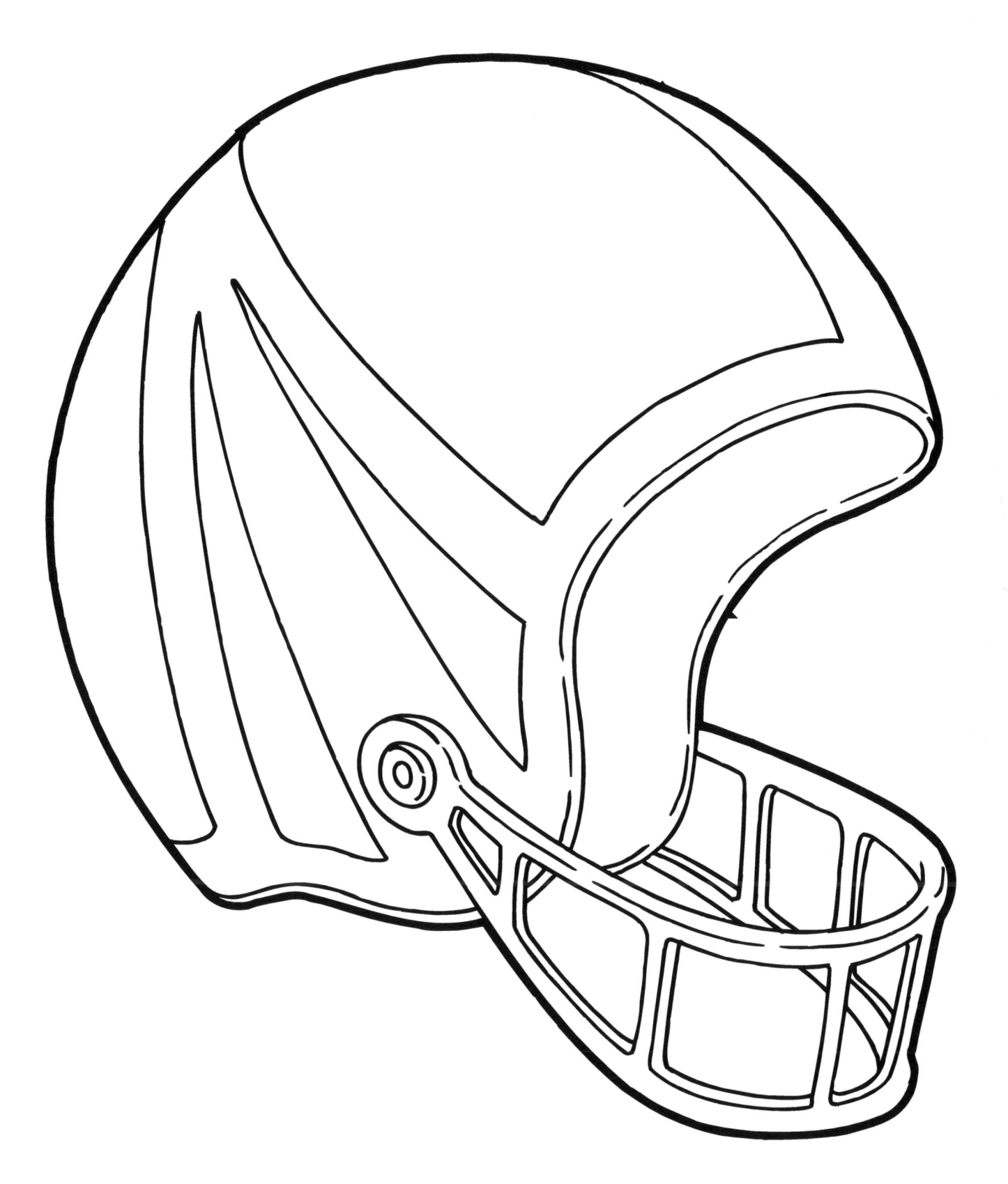

helmet (football-side view)

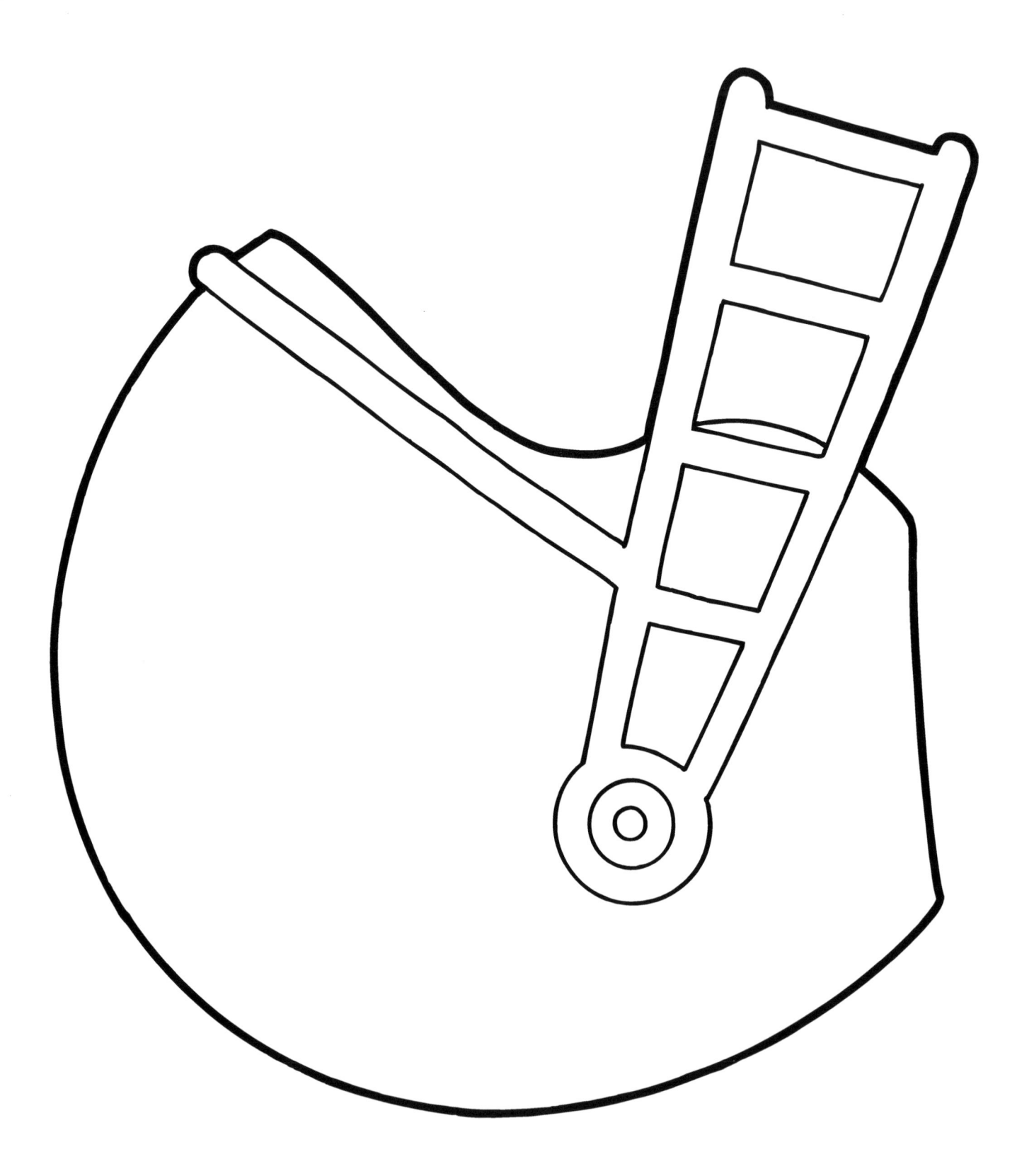

helmet (race car)

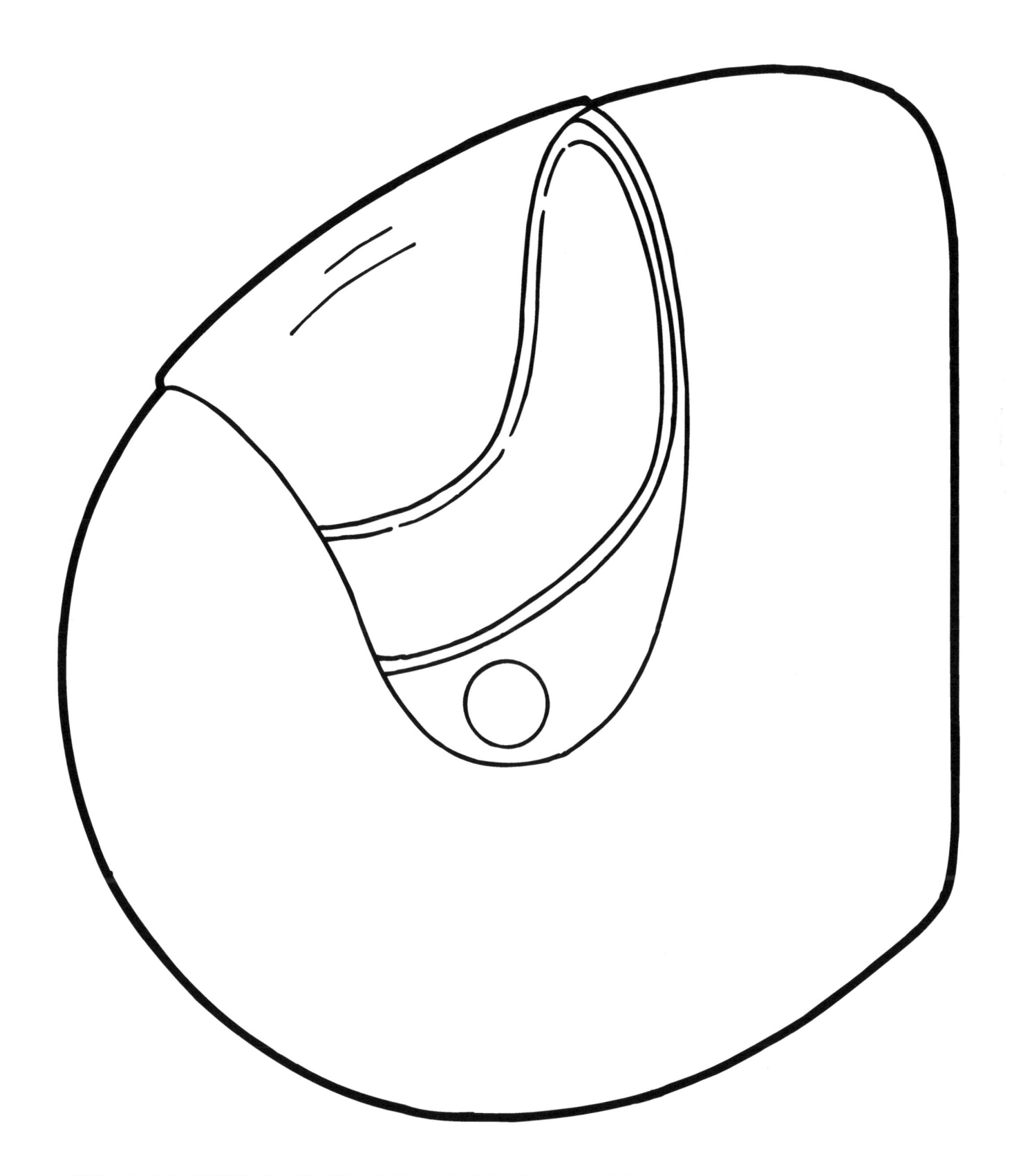

hemisphere (Eastern)

hemisphere (Western)

hen (animated)

hen (stylized)

hermit crab

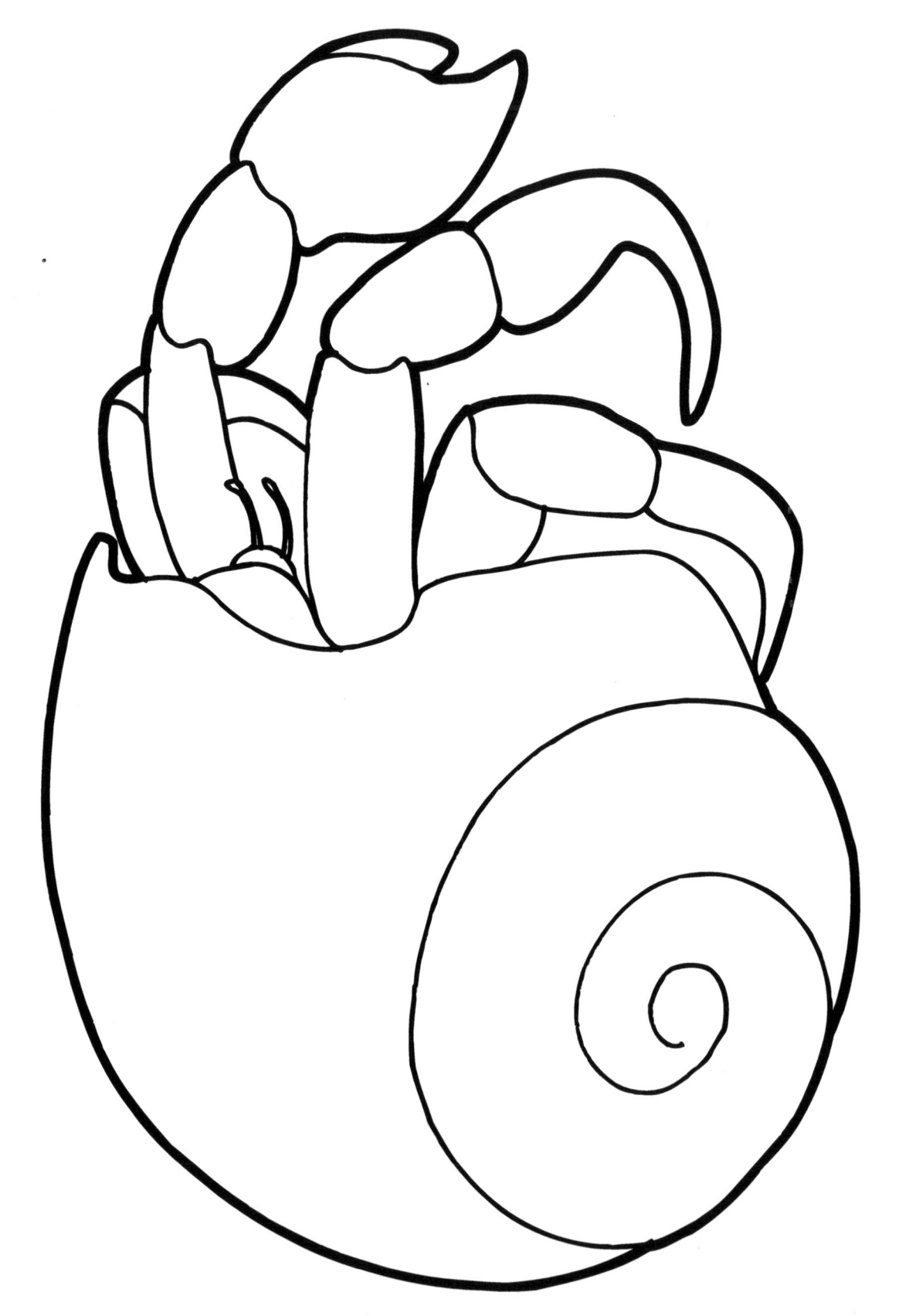

hexagon

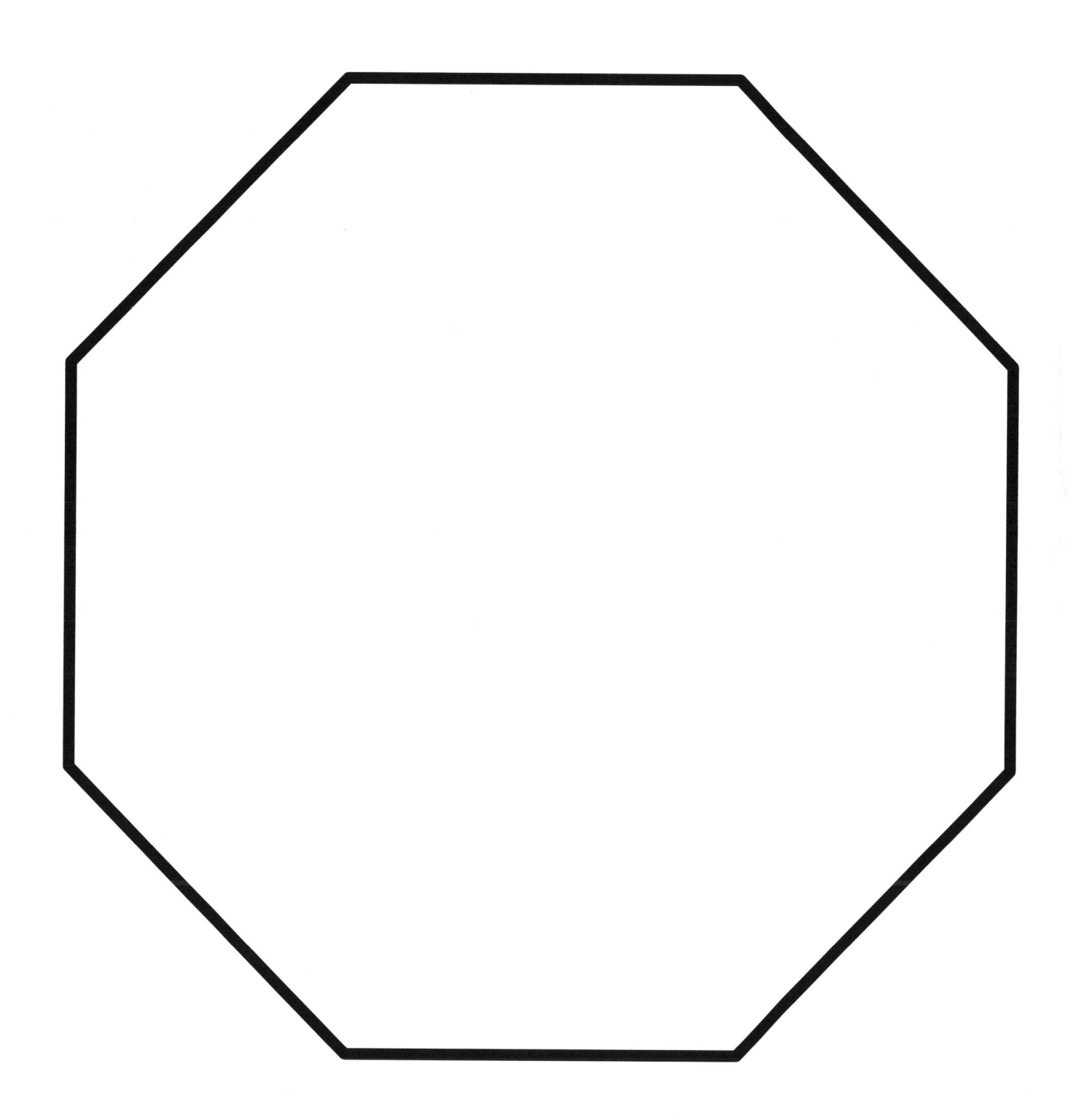

hippopotamus

hippopotamus (animated)

hippopotamus (outline)

holly (with veins)

holly (plain)

horse (animated)

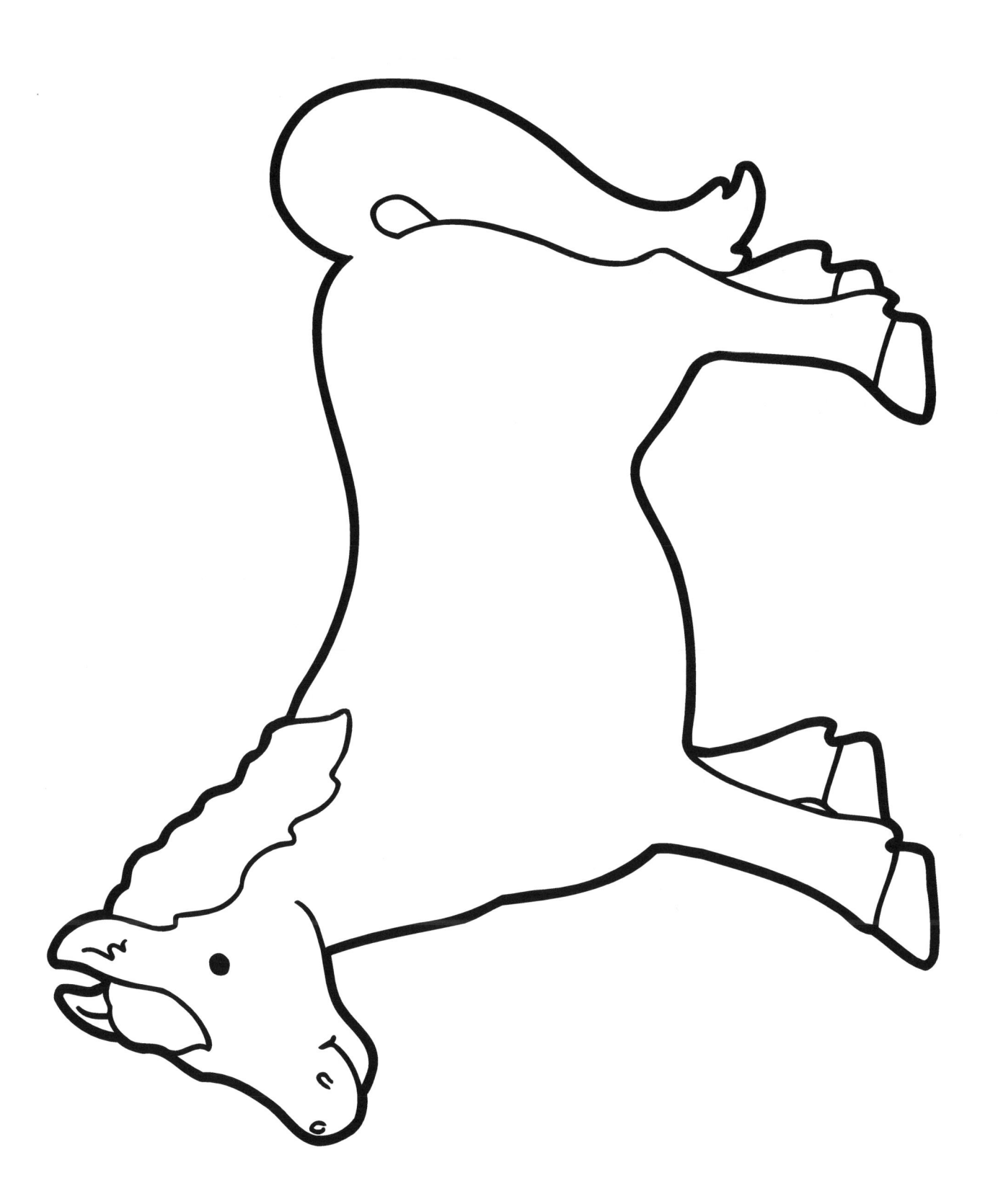

horse (stylized)

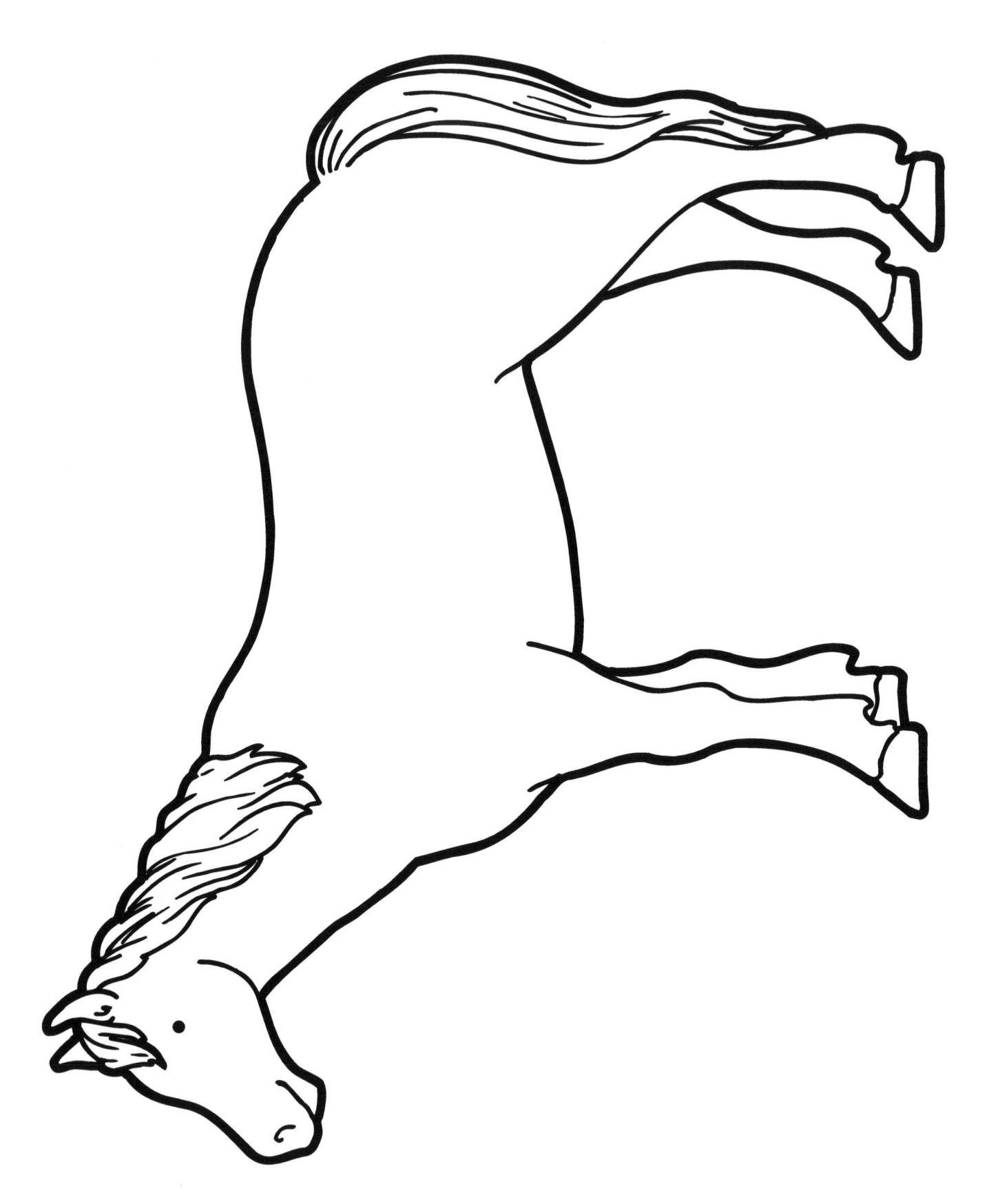

horseshoe

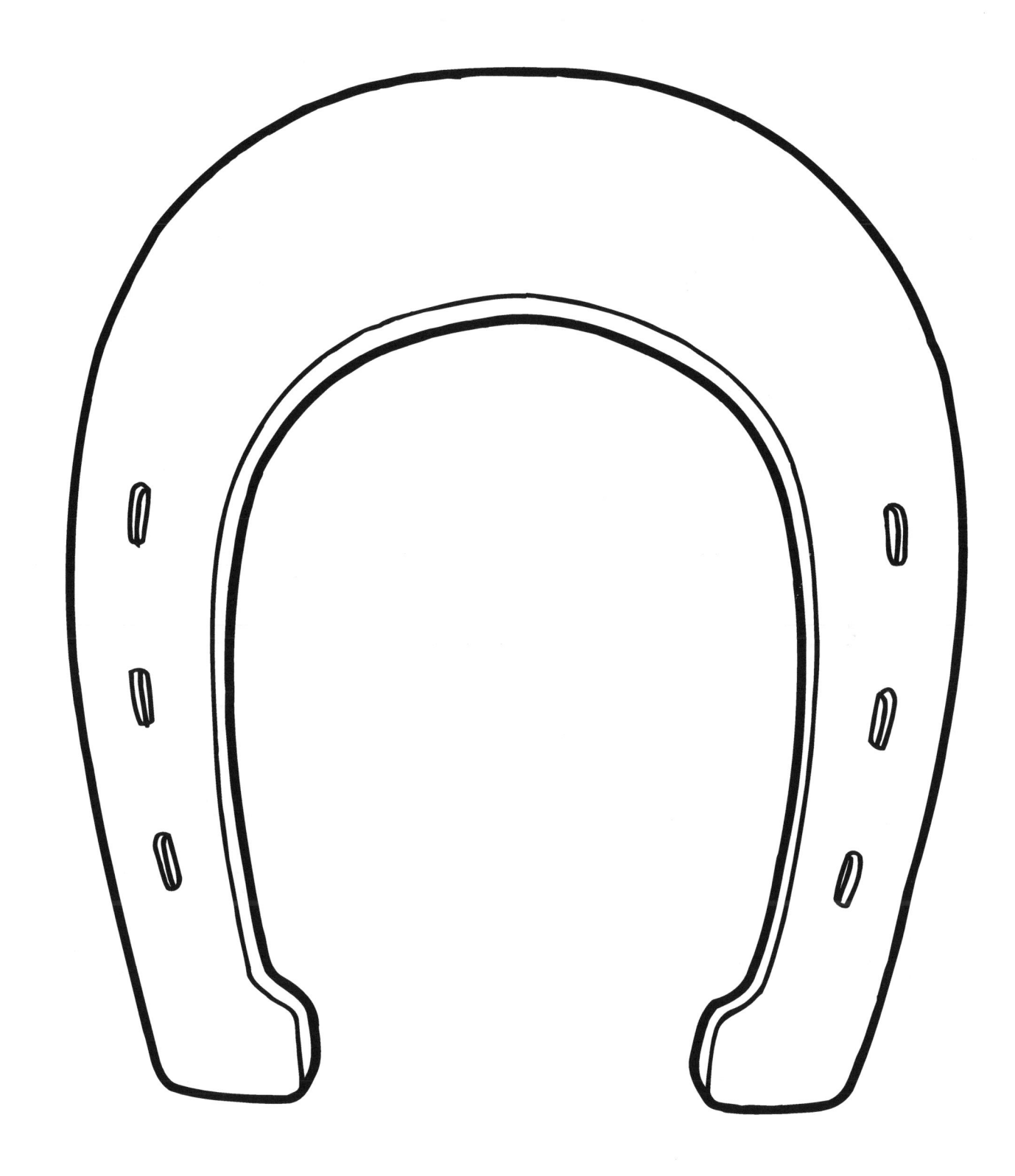

hot air balloon

hourglass

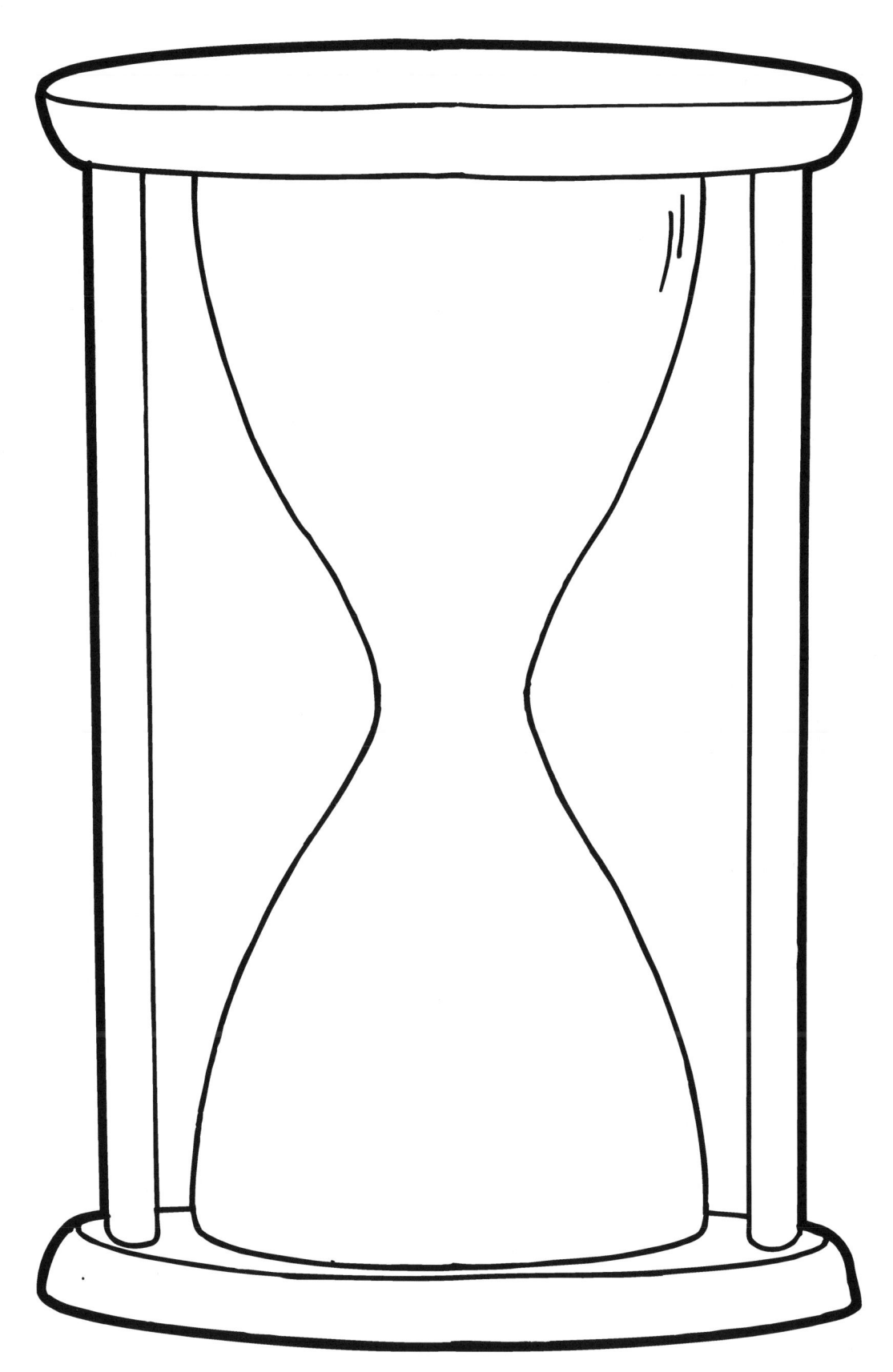

house

hummingbird

hummingbirds

Little Acorn Books™

Promoting Early Skills for a Lifetime™

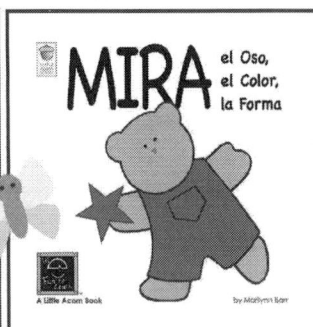

SEE the Bear, the Color, the Shape

MIRA el Oso, el Color, la Forma

CUENTA los Osos

COUNT the Bears

A Hands-on Picture Book Series • Infancy–Age 4

Using Crayons, Scissors, & Glue for Crafts
Preschool–Grade 1

Miss Pitty Pat & Friends
Preschool–Grade 1

Mookie's Christmas Tree
For All Ages and Not Just for Christmas

It's Fun to Learn

Little Acorn Books™
Visit our web site:
www.littleacornbooks.com

Made in the USA
Lexington, KY
11 June 2016